by Arina Tanemura

SAKURA HIME

The Legend of Princess Sakura

12

Characters

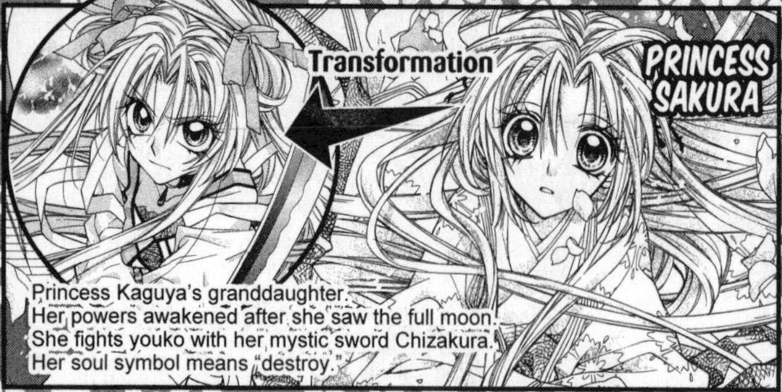
PRINCESS SAKURA
Transformation
Princess Kaguya's granddaughter. Her powers awakened after she saw the full moon. She fights youko with her mystic sword Chizakura. Her soul symbol means "destroy."

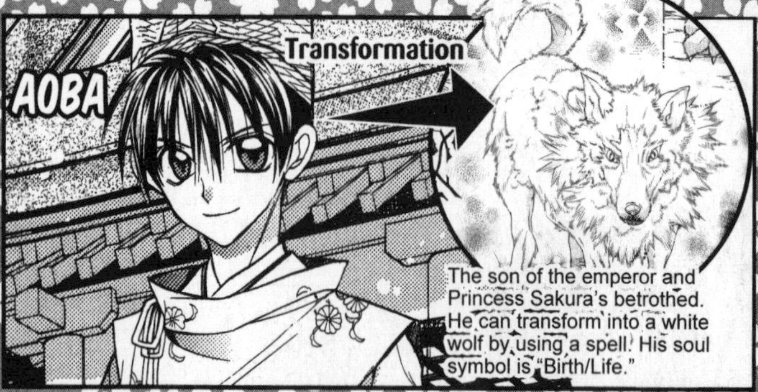
Transformation
AOBA
The son of the emperor and Princess Sakura's betrothed. He can transform into a white wolf by using a spell. His soul symbol is "Birth/Life."

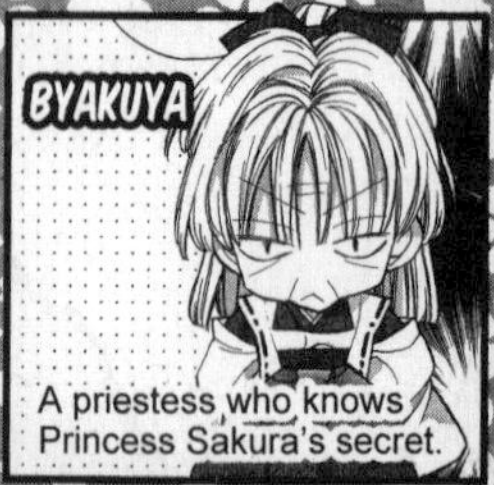
BYAKUYA
A priestess who knows Princess Sakura's secret.

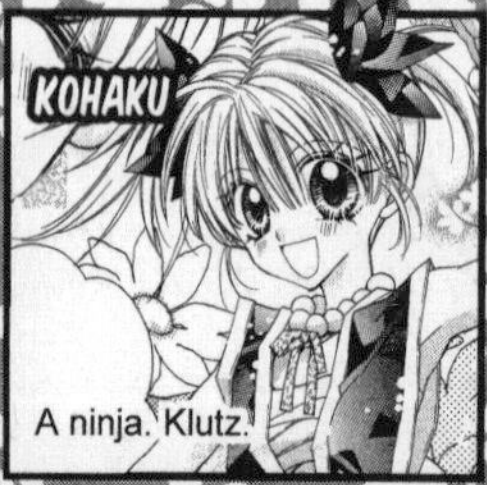
KOHAKU
A ninja. Klutz.

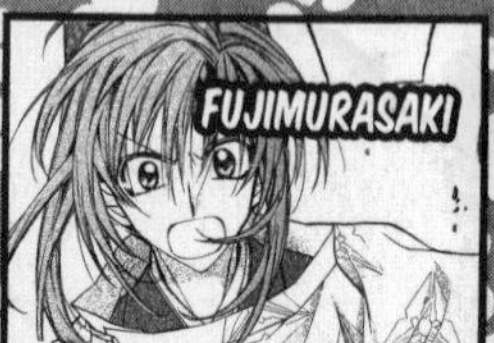
FUJIMURASAKI
The Togu (the next emperor). Aoba's uncle. His soul symbol is "greed."

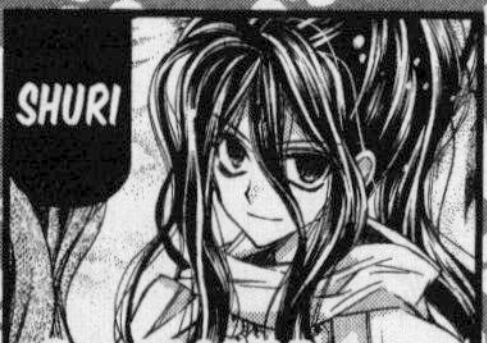
SHURI
One of Enju's followers. He betrayed the ninja village.

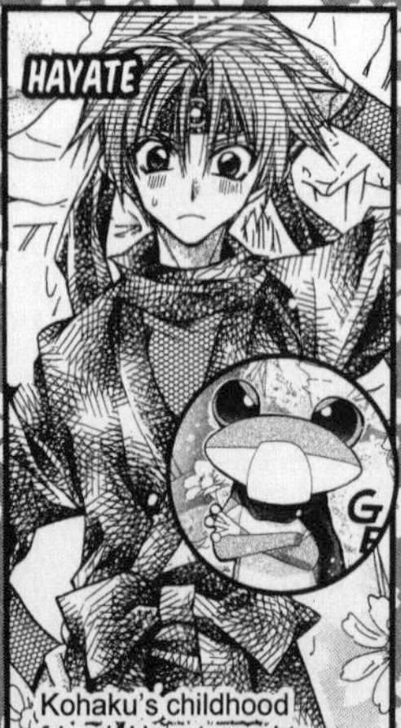
HAYATE
Kohaku's childhood friend. He returned to his human form with the help of Rurijo.

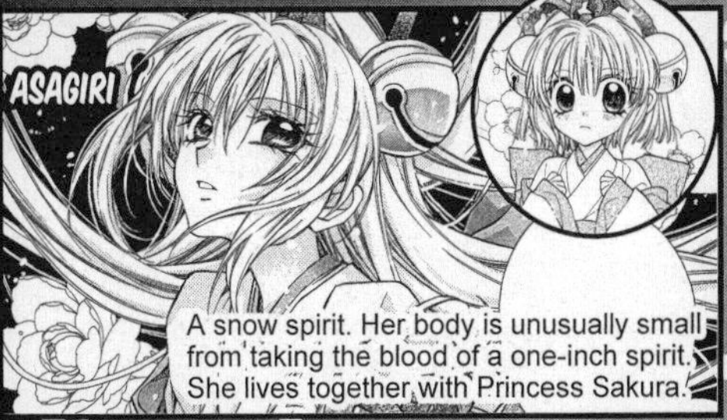
ASAGIRI
A snow spirit. Her body is unusually small from taking the blood of a one-inch spirit. She lives together with Princess Sakura.

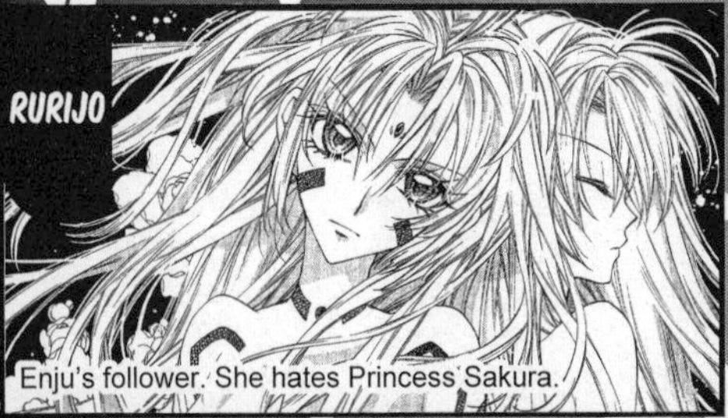
RURIJO
Enju's follower. She hates Princess Sakura.

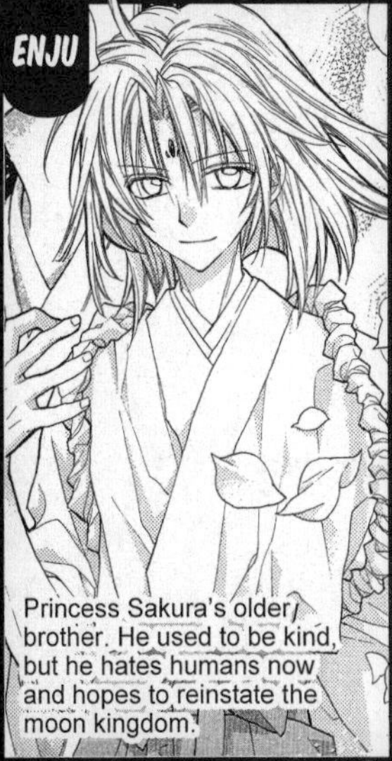
ENJU
Princess Sakura's older brother. He used to be kind, but he hates humans now and hopes to reinstate the moon kingdom.

SAKURA HIME
The Legend of Princess Sakura

Story Thus Far

Heian era. Princess Sakura, granddaughter to Princess Kaguya, has the power to wield the mystic sword Chizakura. Under orders from the Emperor, she must hunt down youko with Aoba, her betrothed.

Enju, whom she thought dead, kidnaps her and takes her to Shura Yugenden. While under Enju's control, Sakura kills Ukyo with her sword Chizakura. Sakura also learns of Enju's plans to resurrect Princess Kaguya and decides to part ways with him. She escapes Shura Yugenden with the help of Aoba, Fujimurasaki, and her other allies who came to save her.

Sakura and Aoba return to their daily lives, but Sakura discovers that Aoba will have a life cut short, just like Asagiri. Sakura is determined to take responsibility for his fate and begins her search for Enju once again.

The Emperor is murdered, and Enju kidnaps Asagiri to use her power to revive Princess Kaguya. Sakura disguises herself as Rurijo to meet Enju and save Asagiri. But Asagiri had been turned into a youko, and Sakura accidentally impales Asagiri without recognizing her!

SAKURA HIME
The Legend of Princess Sakura

CONTENTS

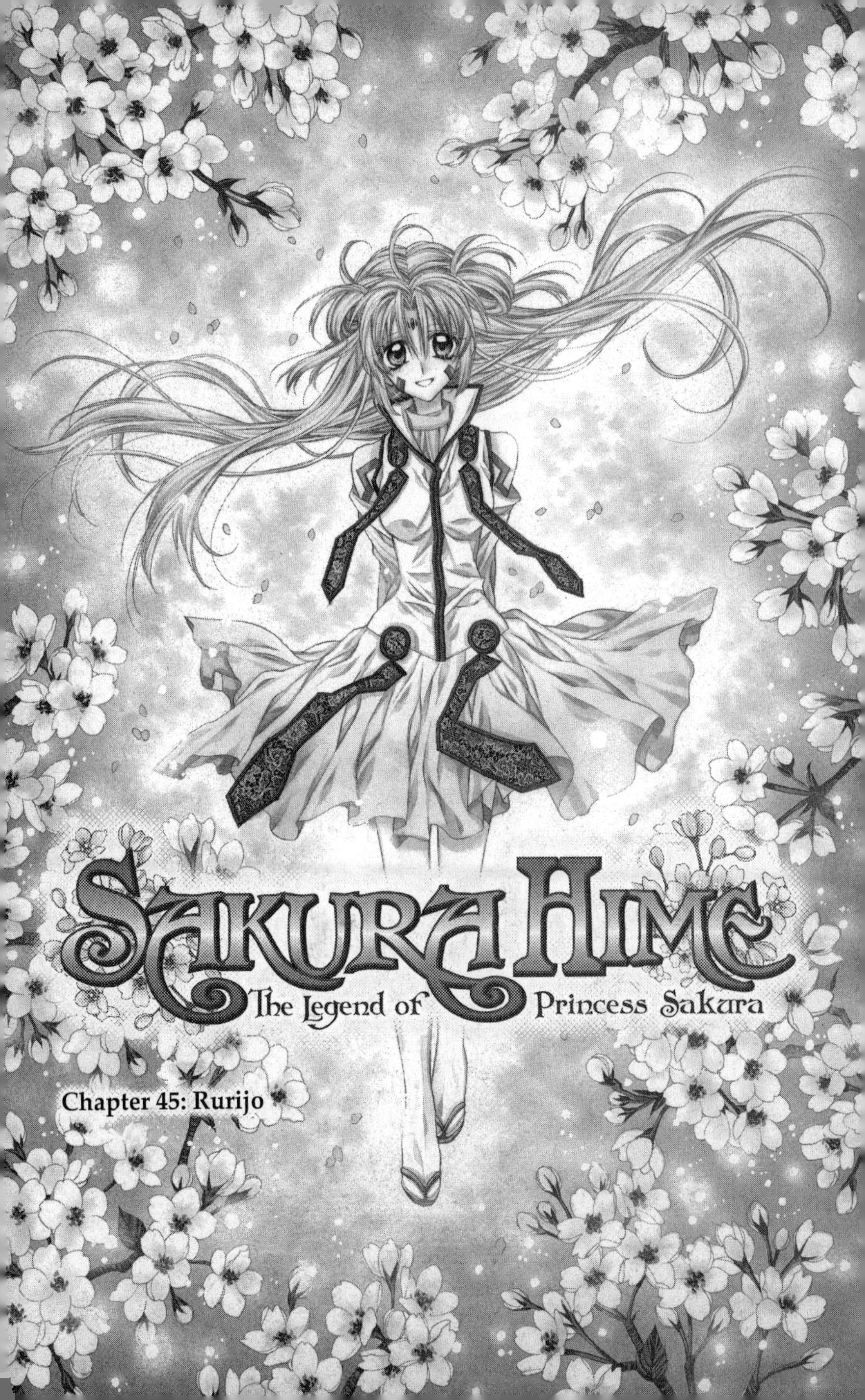
Sakura Hime
The Legend of Princess Sakura
Chapter 45: Rurijo

Sakura Hime
The Legend of Princess Sakura

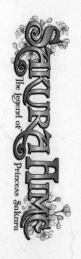

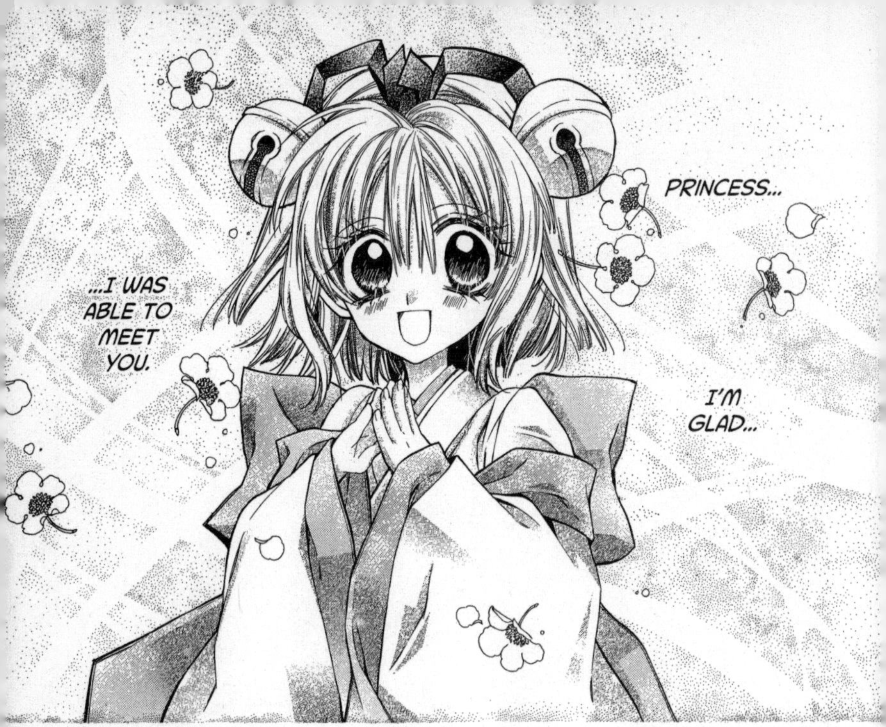
PRINCESS...
I'M GLAD...
...I WAS ABLE TO MEET YOU.

Chapter 45: Rurijo ※I'm giving away the story.

This is a chapter about Rurijo. Rurijo may be the character who has grown the most during this series.

But the one thing that remained constant was her love for Enju. She likes Hayate too, but he's more of a friend to her. I wanted to continue seeing Rurijo and Sakura getting along like twin sisters, but the story wouldn't allow it... I have some regrets about that. I had come up with the last scene a long time ago. Ever since I made the decision that those who were killed by Chizakura would turn into cherry blossom petals (or to be exact, their souls are absorbed by Chizakura and their bodies turn into cherry blossom petals), I thought this was the perfect way for Rurijo to go.

Even though she could never become Sakura, Rurijo had great things about her. But all Enju could think of was Sakura, so it had to end this way. I feel sorry for her... As for the letter to Hayate, the only people who found out what was written in it were the readers(!), so I feel sorry for him too...

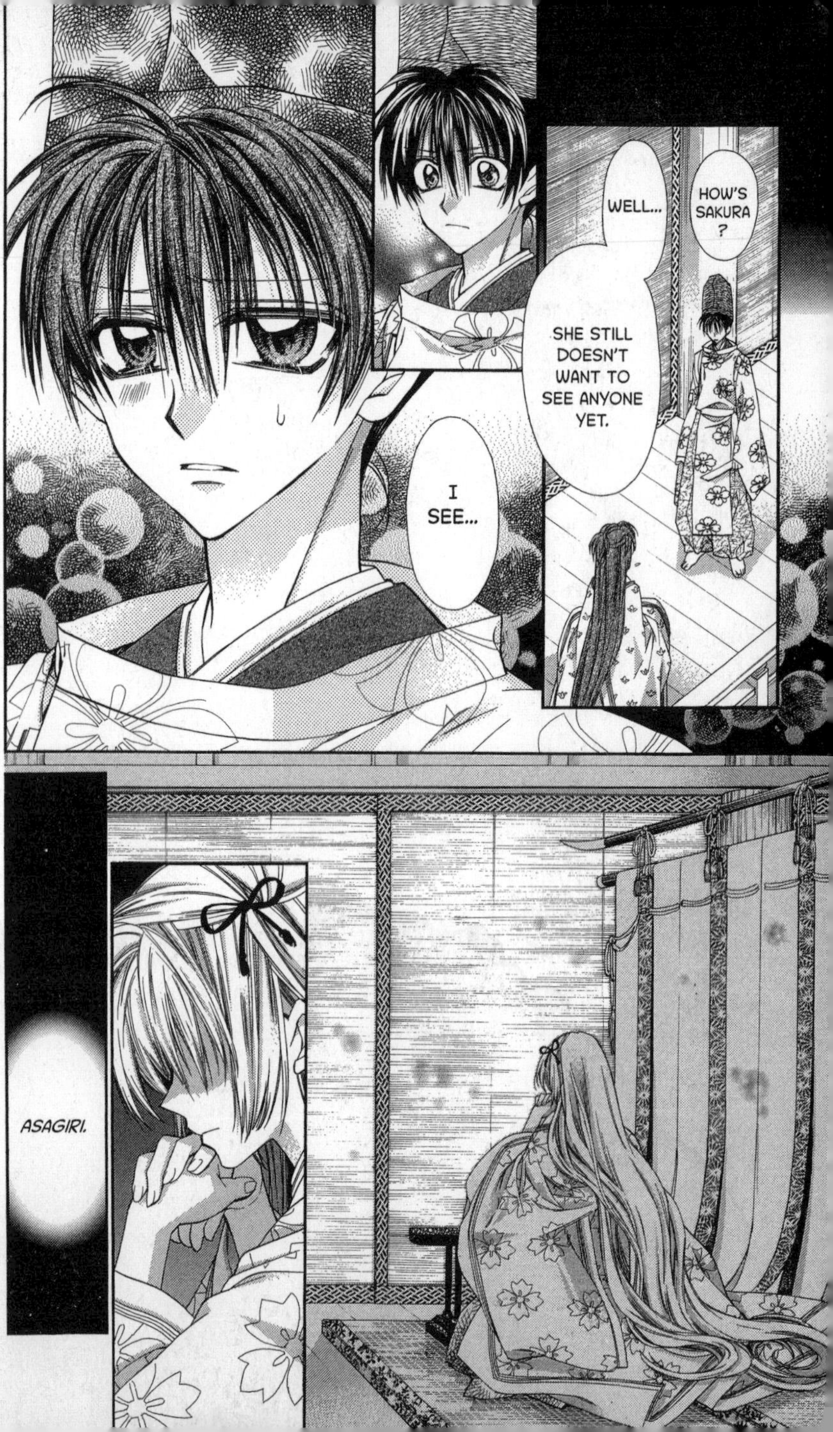
HOW'S SAKURA ?
WELL...
SHE STILL DOESN'T WANT TO SEE ANYONE YET.
I SEE...
ASAGIRI.

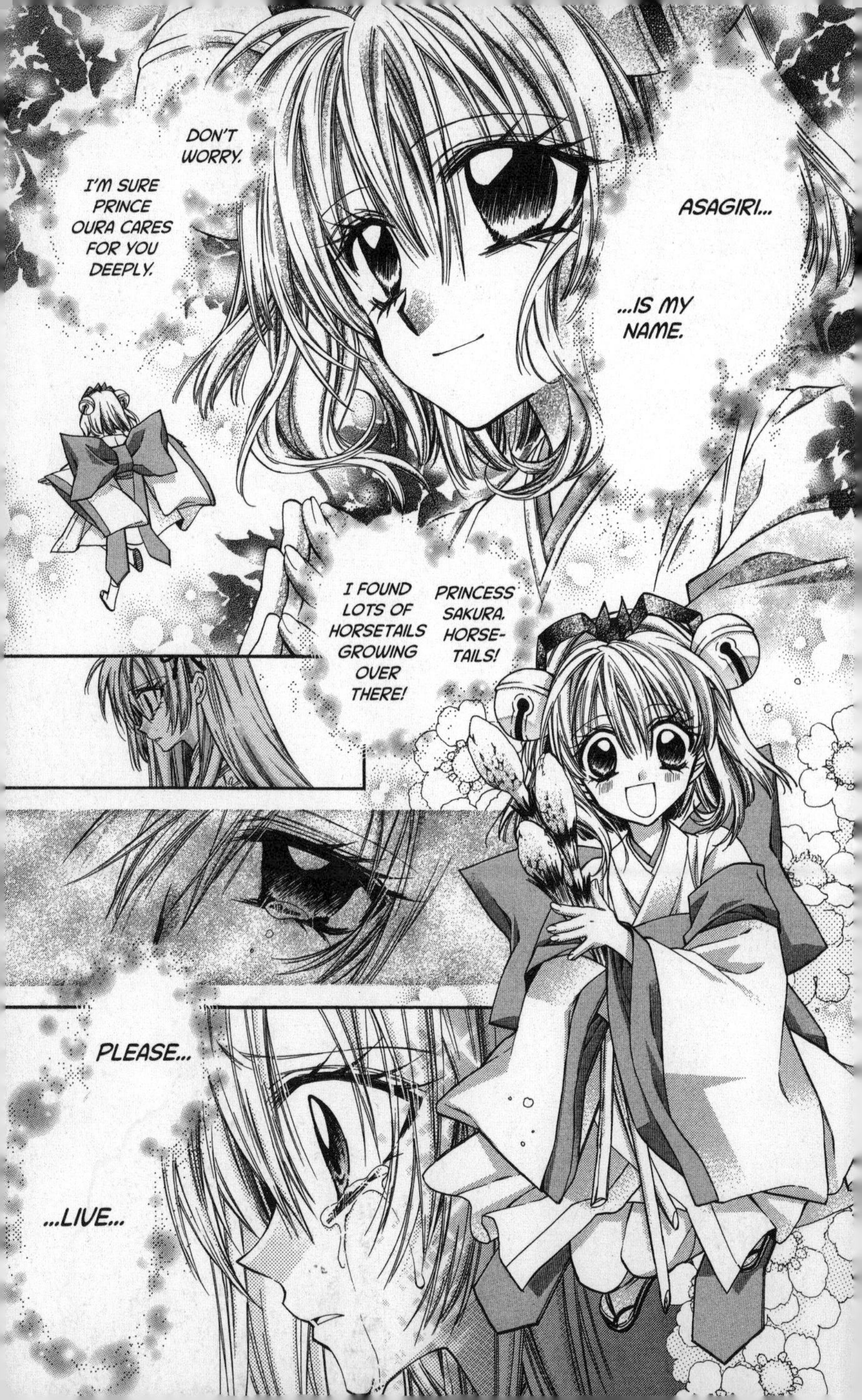
ASAGIRI...
...IS MY NAME.
DON'T WORRY.
I'M SURE PRINCE OURA CARES FOR YOU DEEPLY.
PRINCESS SAKURA. HORSE-TAILS!
I FOUND LOTS OF HORSETAILS GROWING OVER THERE!
PLEASE...
...LIVE...

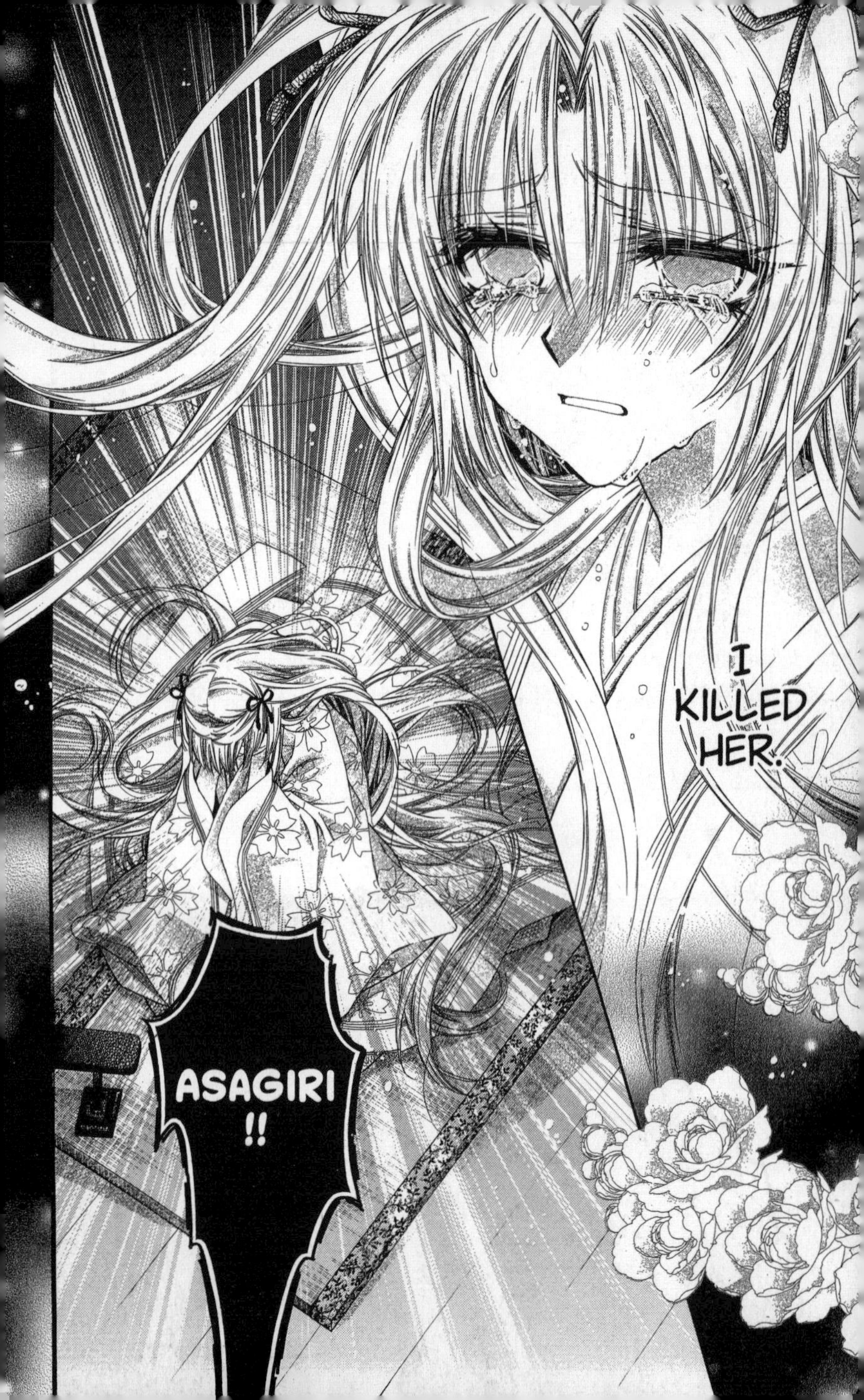
I KILLED HER.
ASAGIRI !!

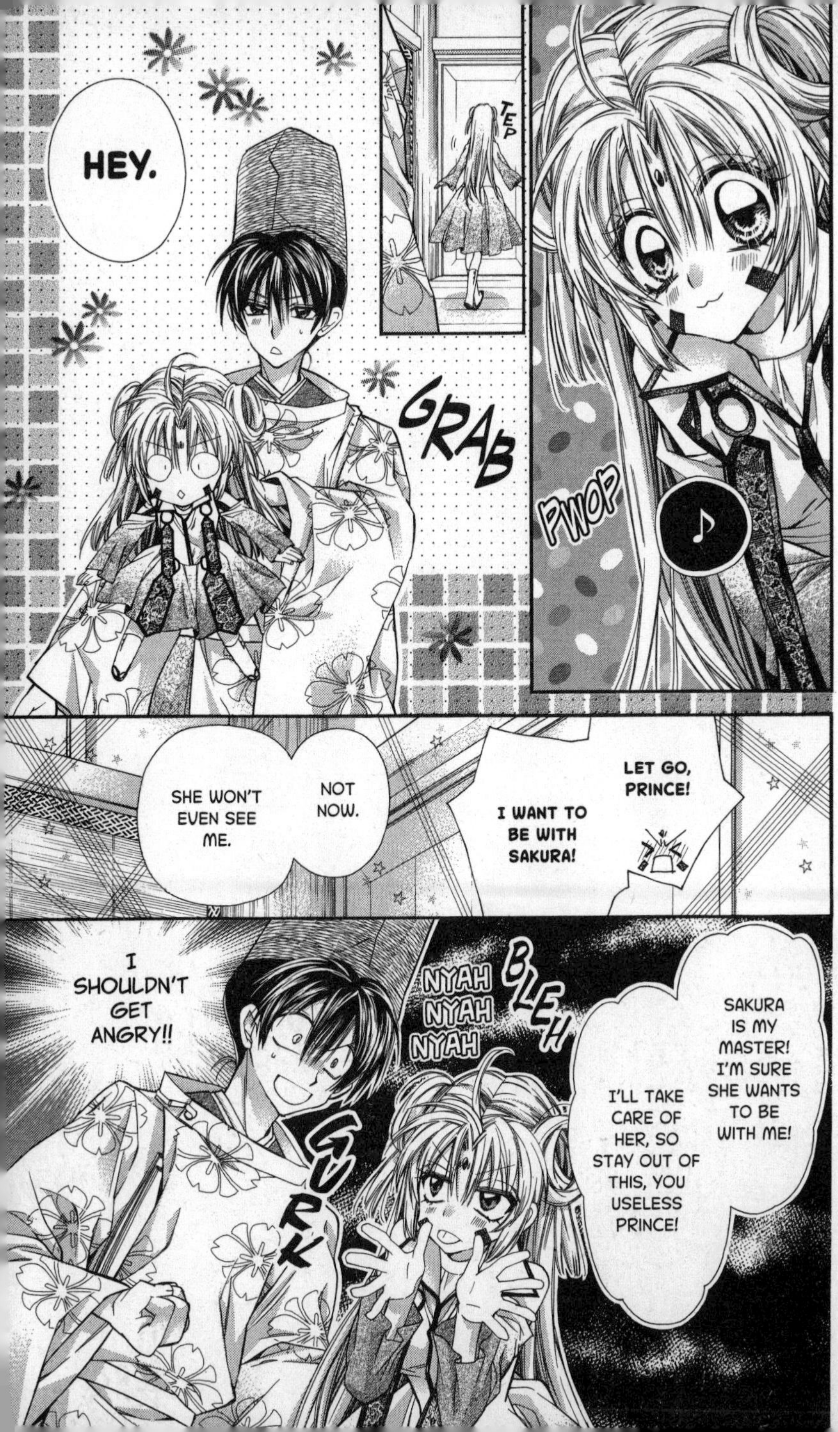

PWOP
♪
TEP
HEY.
GRAB
LET GO, PRINCE!
I WANT TO BE WITH SAKURA!
NOT NOW.
SHE WON'T EVEN SEE ME.
SAKURA IS MY MASTER! I'M SURE SHE WANTS TO BE WITH ME!
I'LL TAKE CARE OF HER, SO STAY OUT OF THIS, YOU USELESS PRINCE!
BLEH
NYAH NYAH NYAH
GURK
I SHOULDN'T GET ANGRY!!

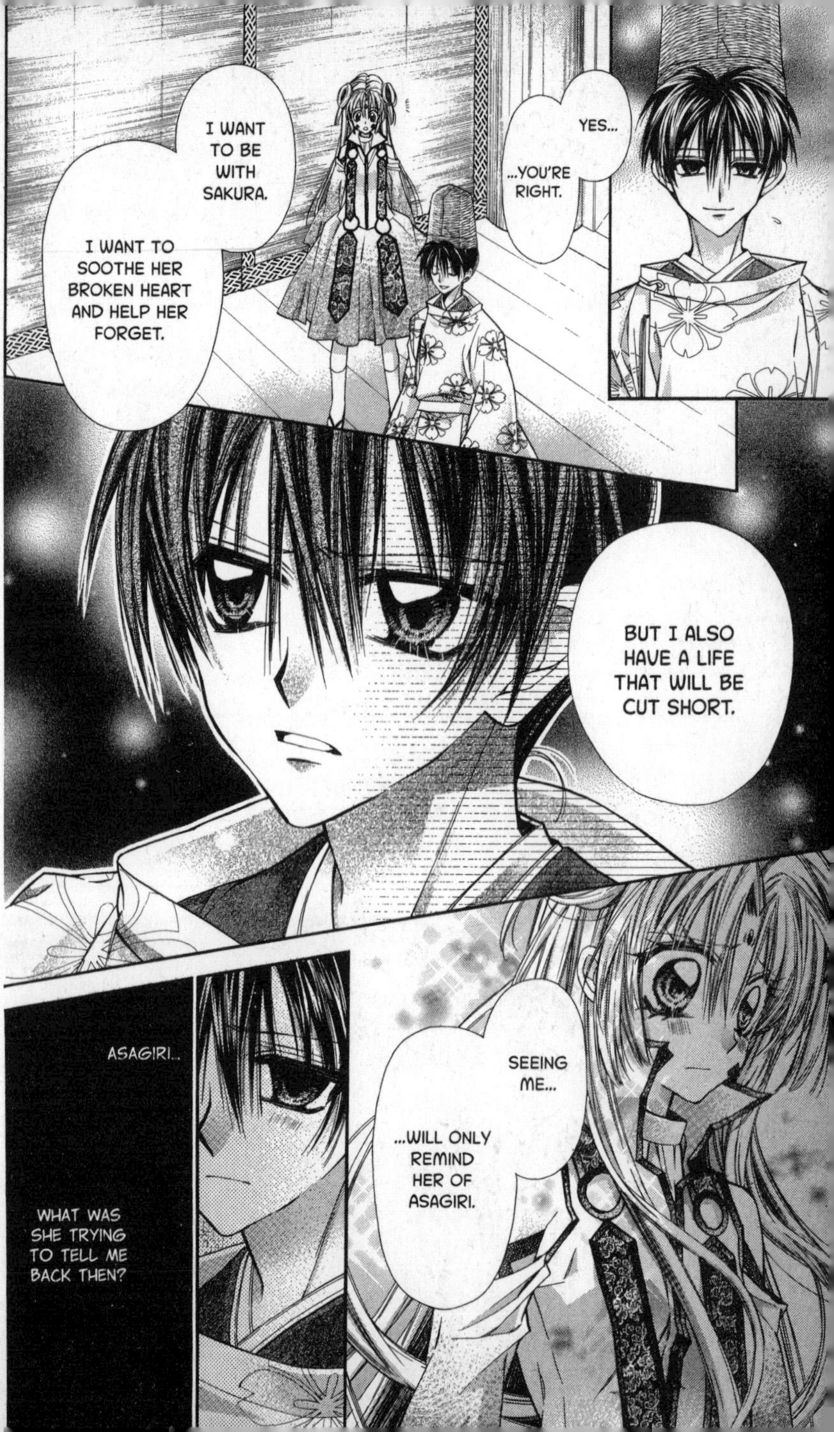
YES...
...YOU'RE RIGHT.
I WANT TO BE WITH SAKURA.
I WANT TO SOOTHE HER BROKEN HEART AND HELP HER FORGET.
BUT I ALSO HAVE A LIFE THAT WILL BE CUT SHORT.
SEEING ME...
...WILL ONLY REMIND HER OF ASAGIRI.
ASAGIRI...
WHAT WAS SHE TRYING TO TELL ME BACK THEN?

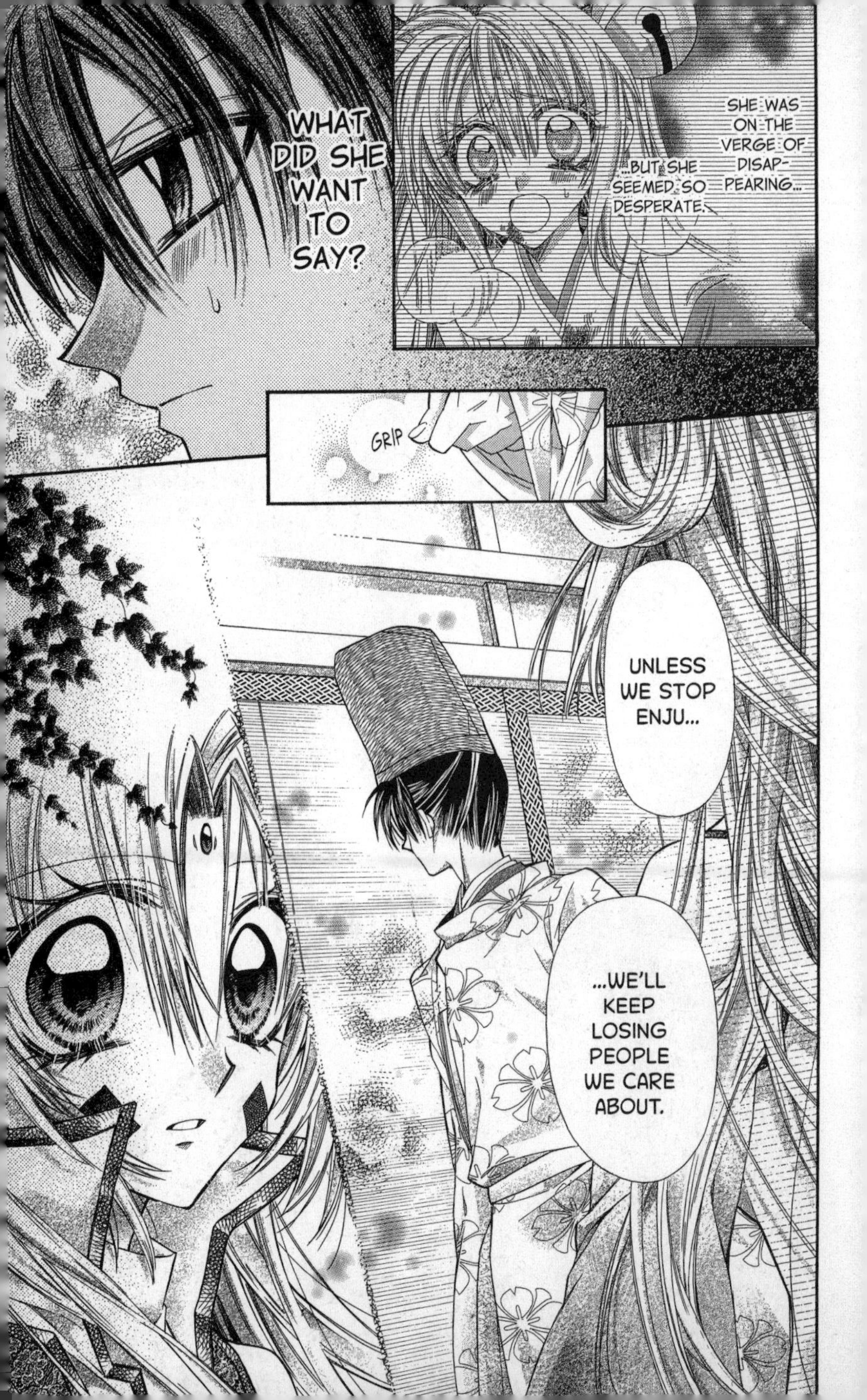
SHE WAS ON THE VERGE OF DISAPPEARING...
...BUT SHE SEEMED SO DESPERATE.
WHAT DID SHE WANT TO SAY?
GRIP
UNLESS WE STOP ENJU...
...WE'LL KEEP LOSING PEOPLE WE CARE ABOUT.

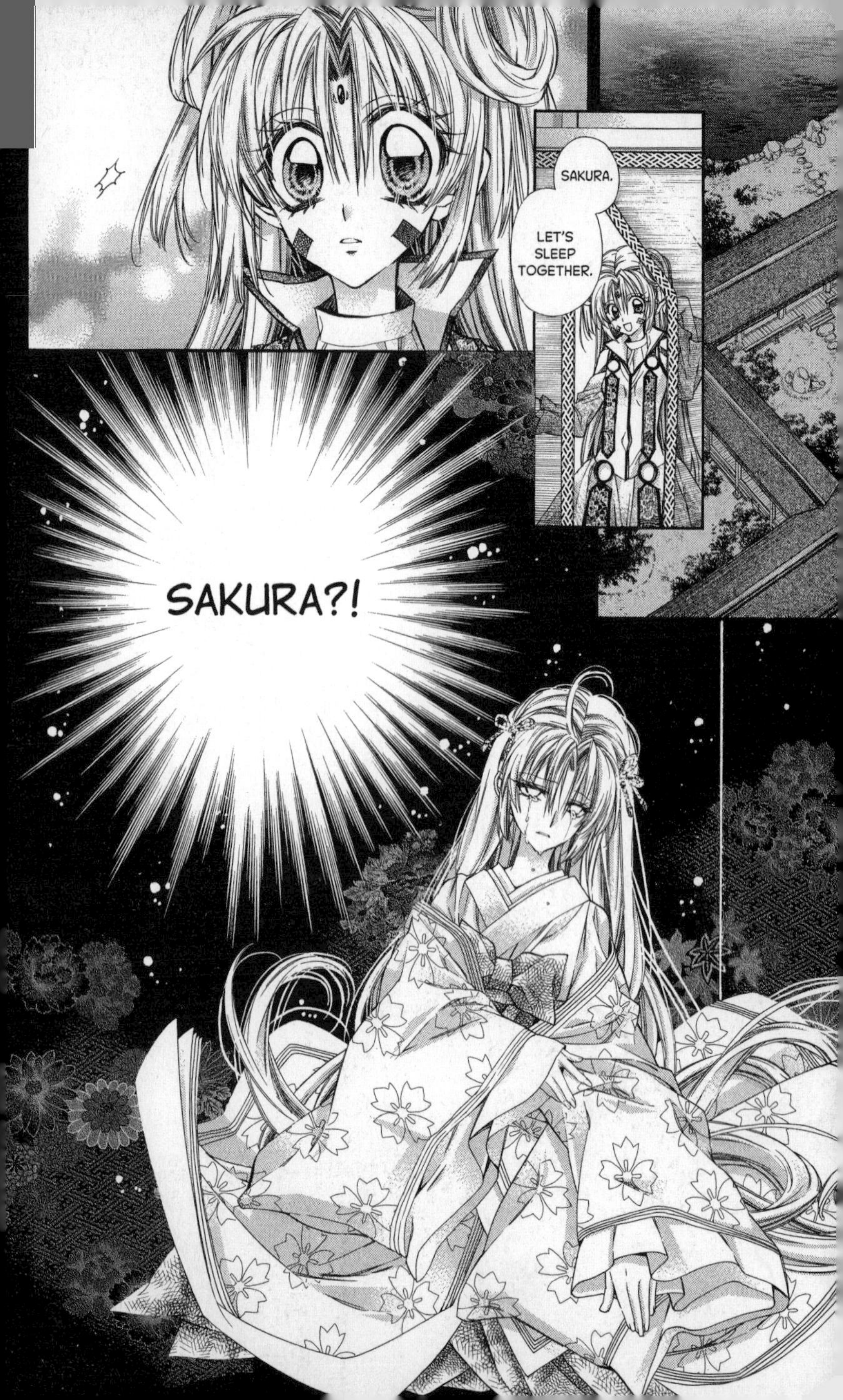
SAKURA.
LET'S SLEEP TOGETHER.
SAKURA?!

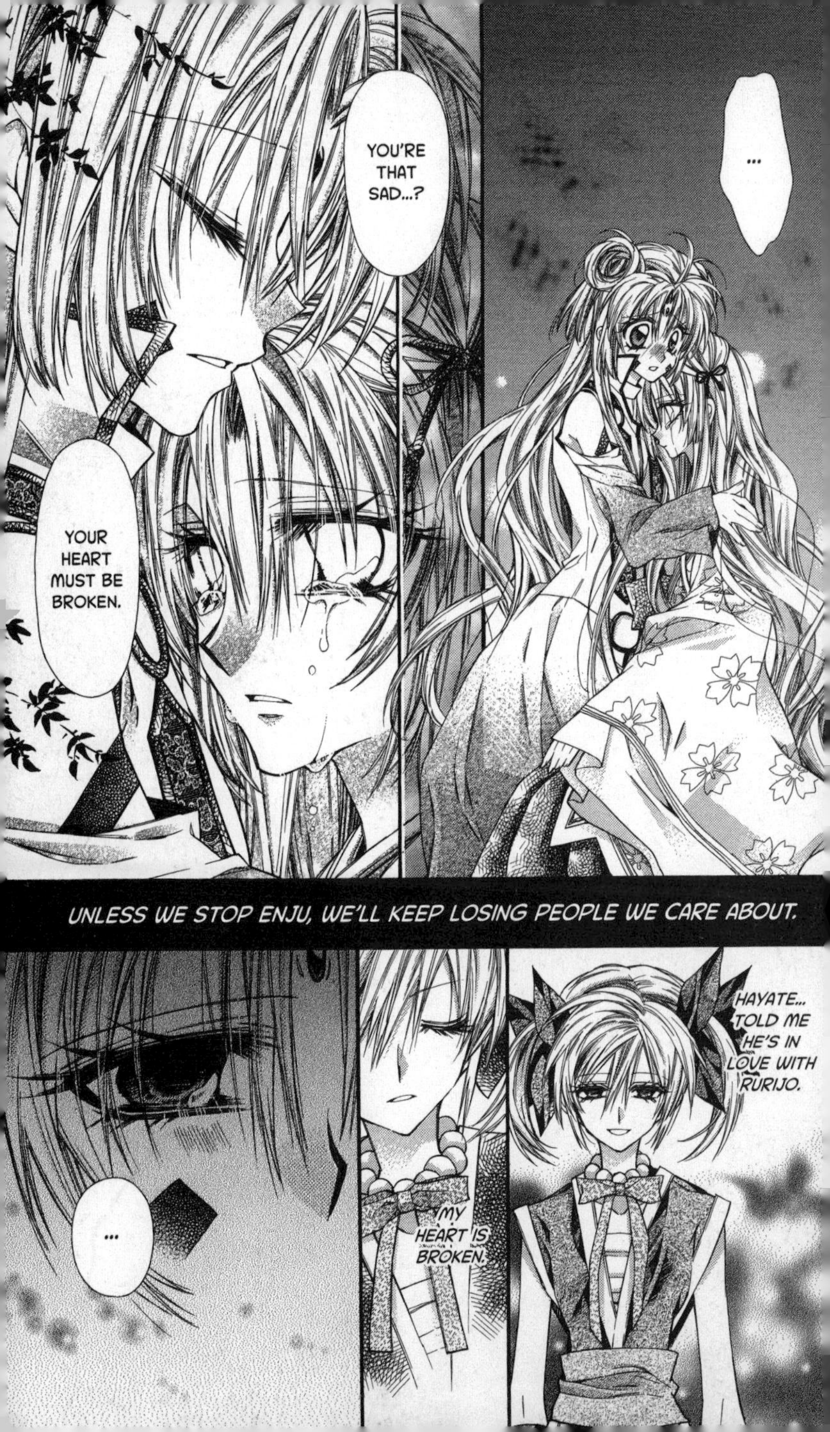
...
YOU'RE THAT SAD...?
YOUR HEART MUST BE BROKEN.
UNLESS WE STOP ENJU, WE'LL KEEP LOSING PEOPLE WE CARE ABOUT.
HAYATE... TOLD ME HE'S IN LOVE WITH RURIJO.
MY HEART IS BROKEN.
...

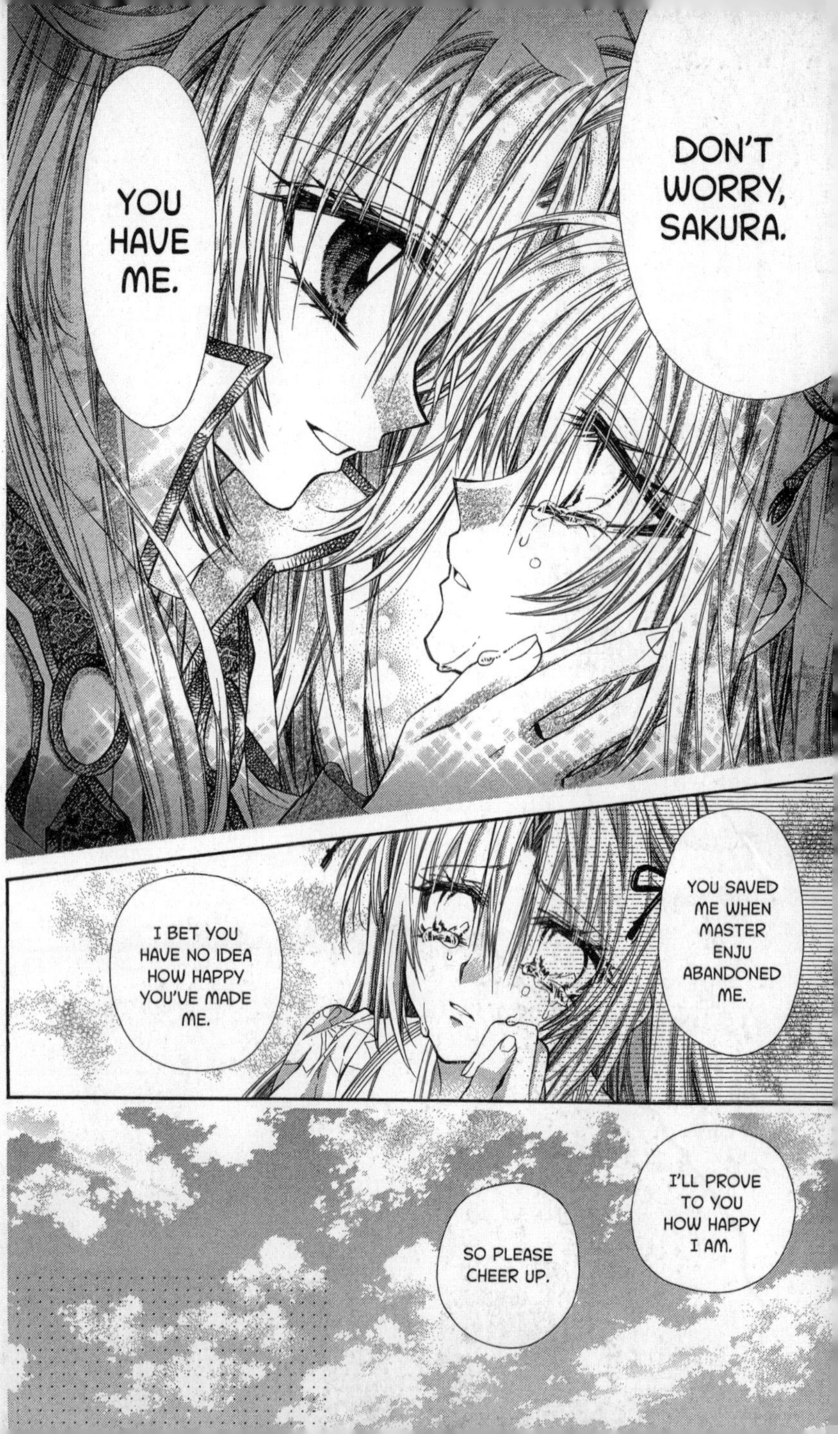
DON'T WORRY, SAKURA.
YOU HAVE ME.
YOU SAVED ME WHEN MASTER ENJU ABANDONED ME.
I BET YOU HAVE NO IDEA HOW HAPPY YOU'VE MADE ME.
I'LL PROVE TO YOU HOW HAPPY I AM.
SO PLEASE CHEER UP.

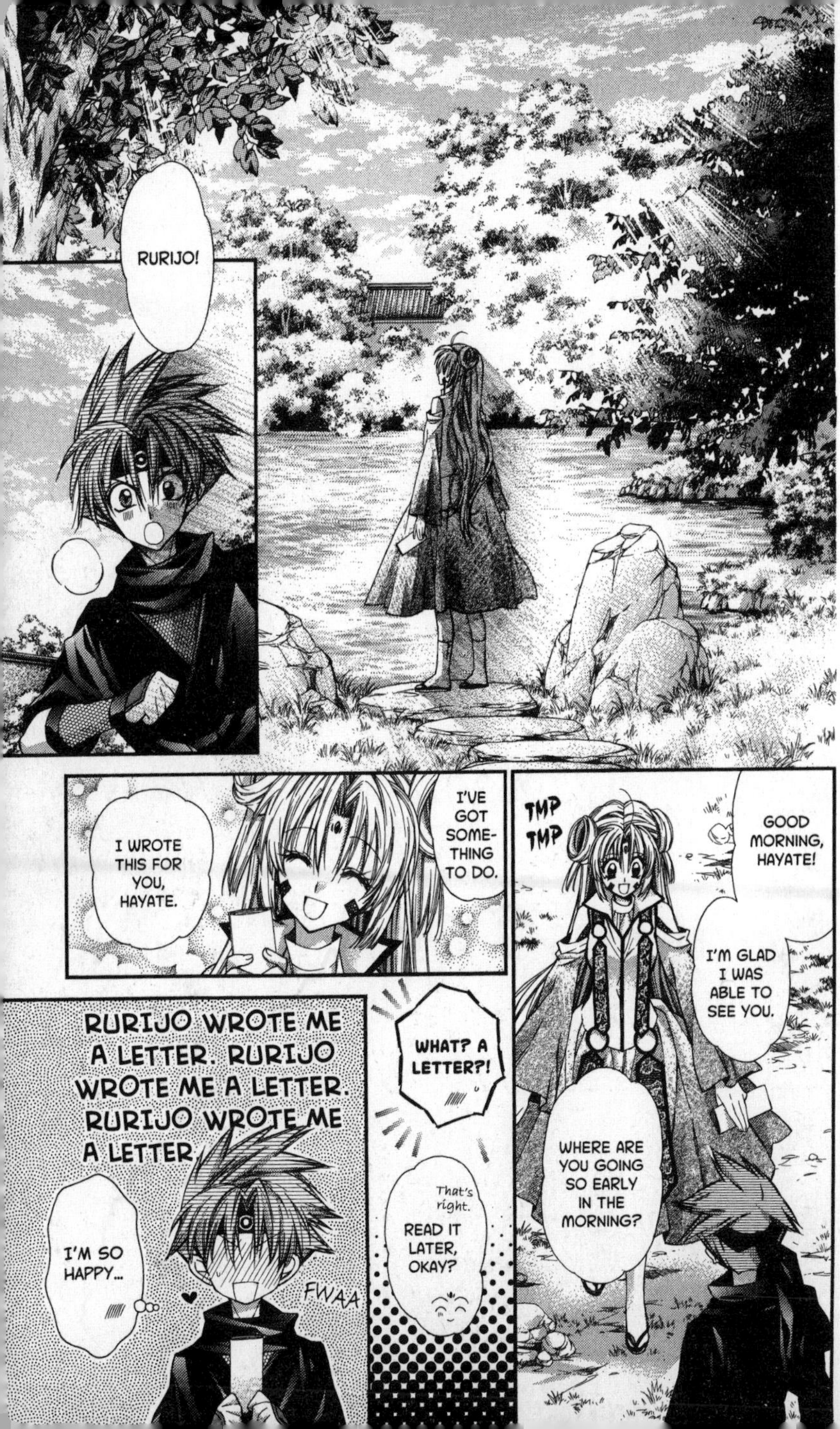
RURIJO!
TMP TMP
GOOD MORNING, HAYATE!
I'M GLAD I WAS ABLE TO SEE YOU.
WHERE ARE YOU GOING SO EARLY IN THE MORNING?
I'VE GOT SOMETHING TO DO.
I WROTE THIS FOR YOU, HAYATE.
WHAT? A LETTER?!
That's right.
READ IT LATER, OKAY?
RURIJO WROTE ME A LETTER. RURIJO WROTE ME A LETTER. RURIJO WROTE ME A LETTER.
I'M SO HAPPY...
FWAA

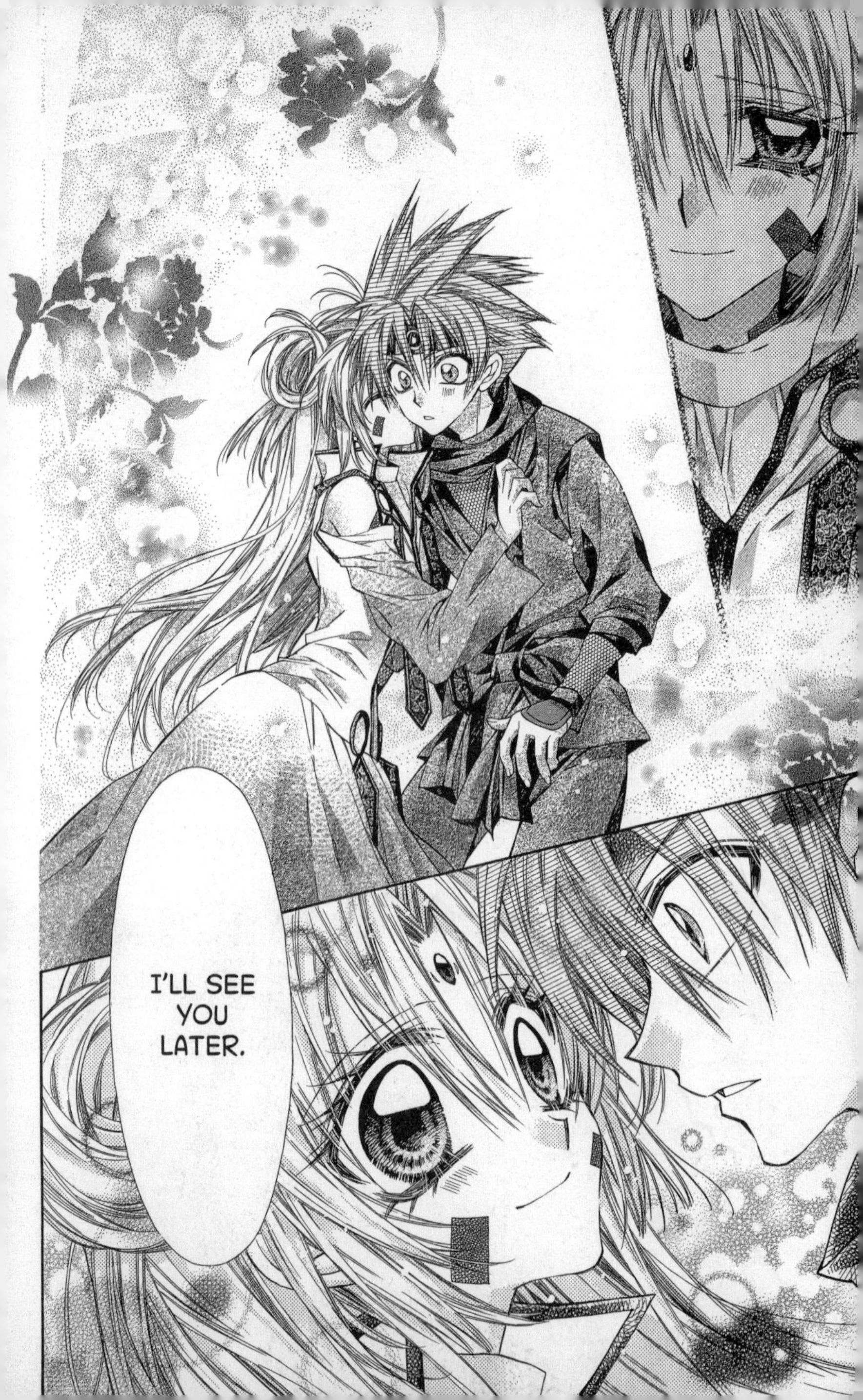
I'LL SEE YOU LATER.

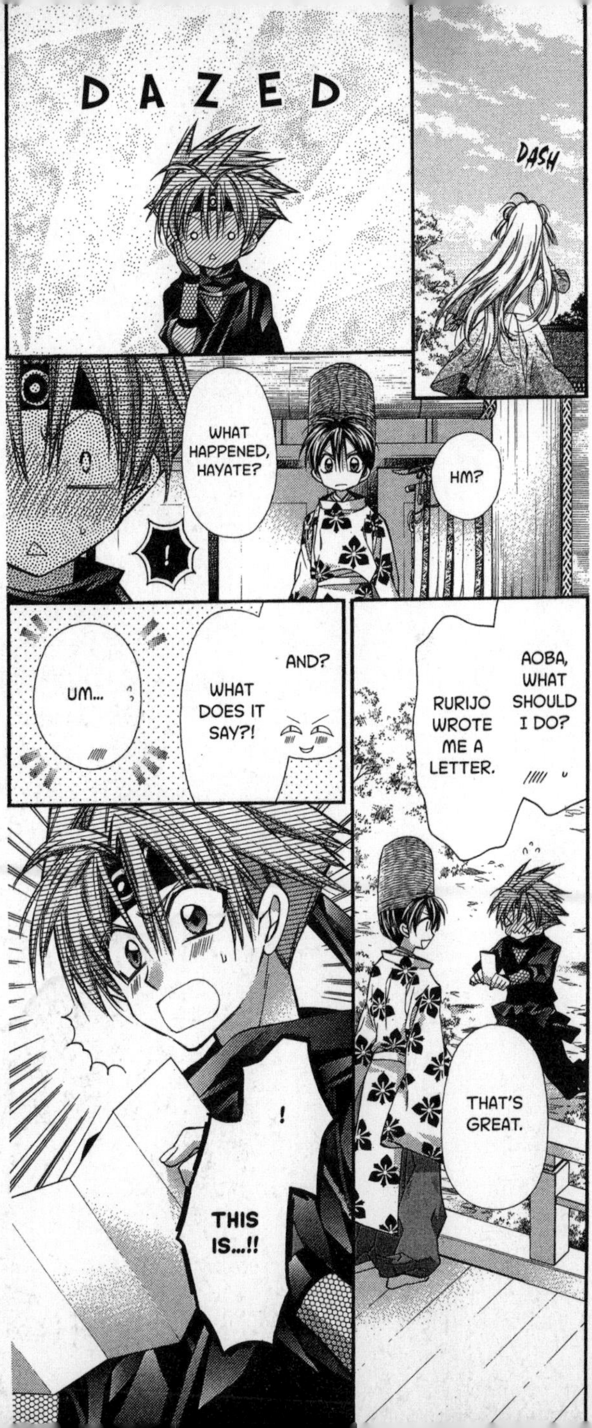
DASH
DAZED
HM?
WHAT HAPPENED, HAYATE?
!
AOBA, WHAT SHOULD I DO?
RURIJO WROTE ME A LETTER.
THAT'S GREAT.
AND? WHAT DOES IT SAY?!
UM...
!
THIS IS...!!

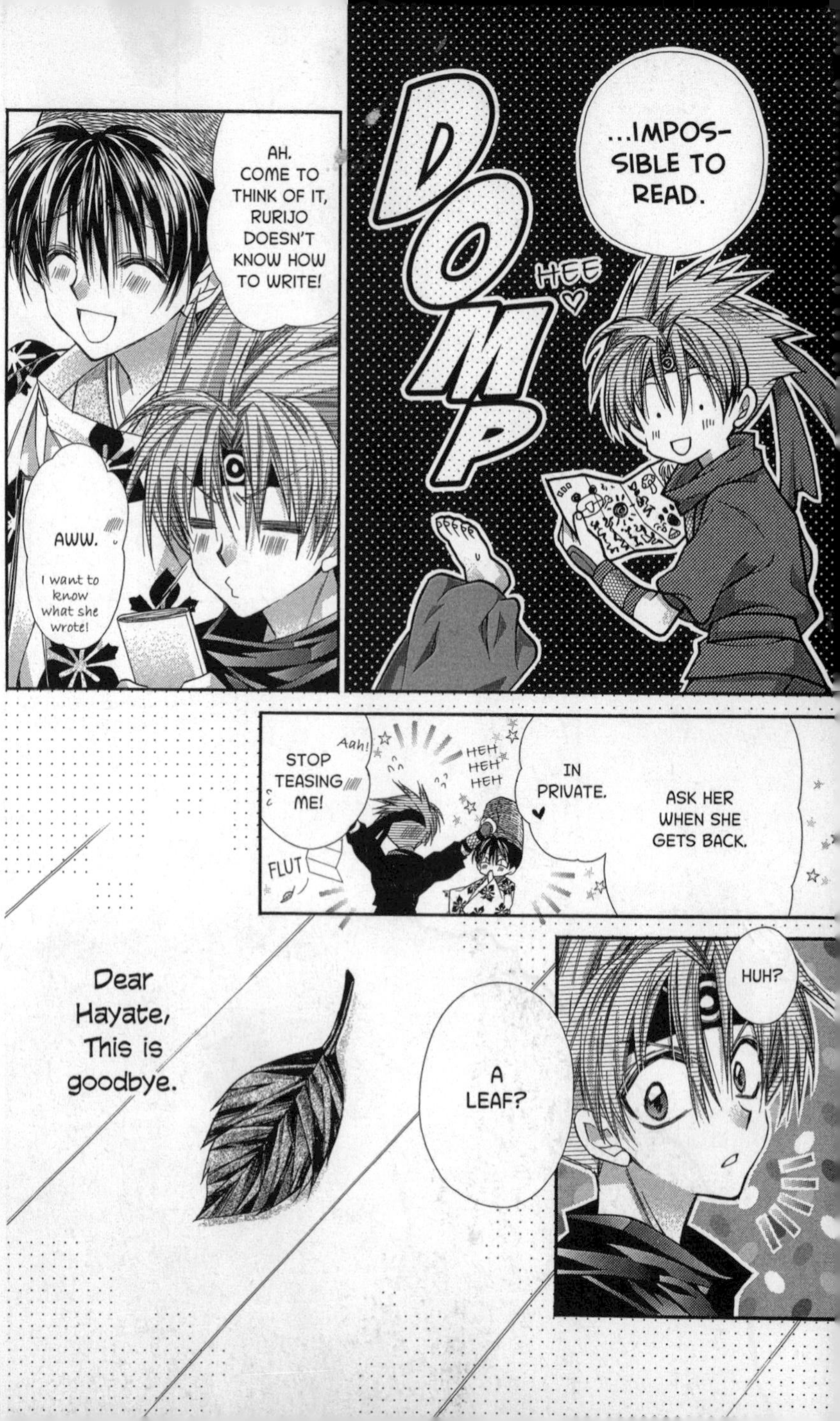
...IMPOS-SIBLE TO READ.
DOMP
HEE
AH. COME TO THINK OF IT, RURIJO DOESN'T KNOW HOW TO WRITE!
AWW.
I want to know what she wrote!
ASK HER WHEN SHE GETS BACK.
IN PRIVATE.
HEH HEH HEH
STOP TEASING ME!
Aah!
FLUT
HUH?
A LEAF?
Dear Hayate, This is goodbye.

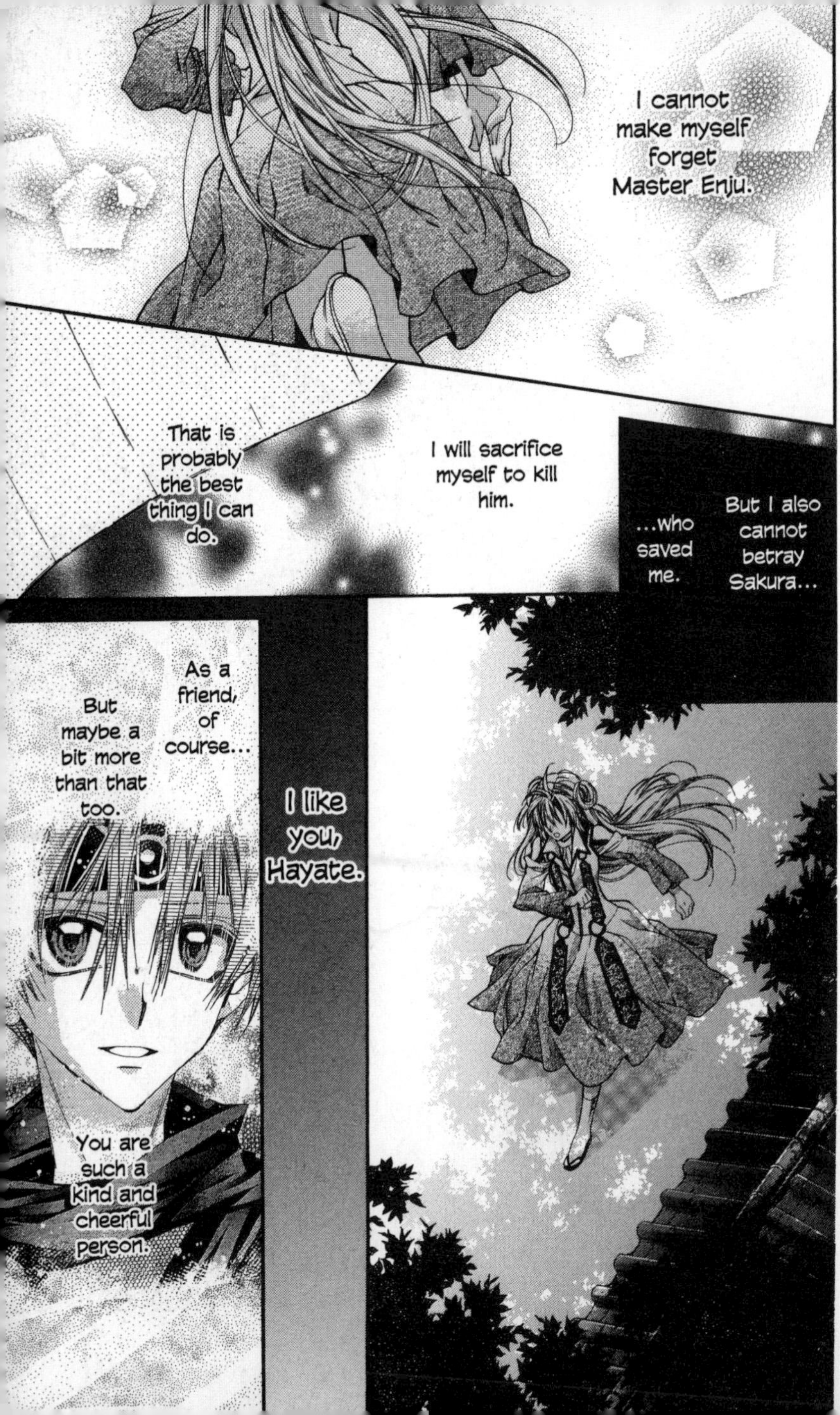
I cannot make myself forget Master Enju.
But I also cannot betray Sakura...
...who saved me.
I will sacrifice myself to kill him.
That is probably the best thing I can do.
I like you, Hayate.
As a friend, of course...
But maybe a bit more than that too.
You are such a kind and cheerful person.

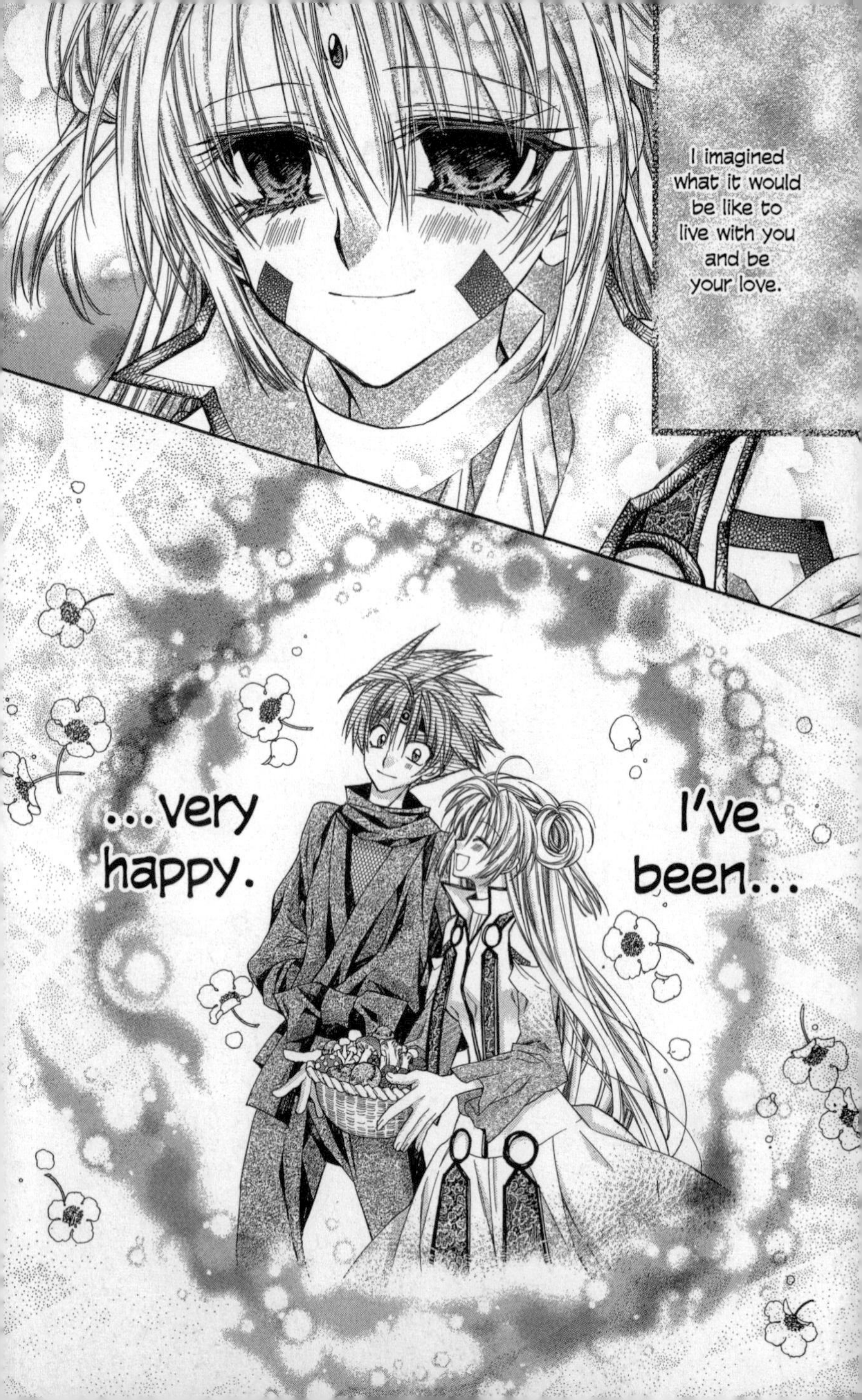
I imagined what it would be like to live with you and be your love.
I've been...
...very happy.

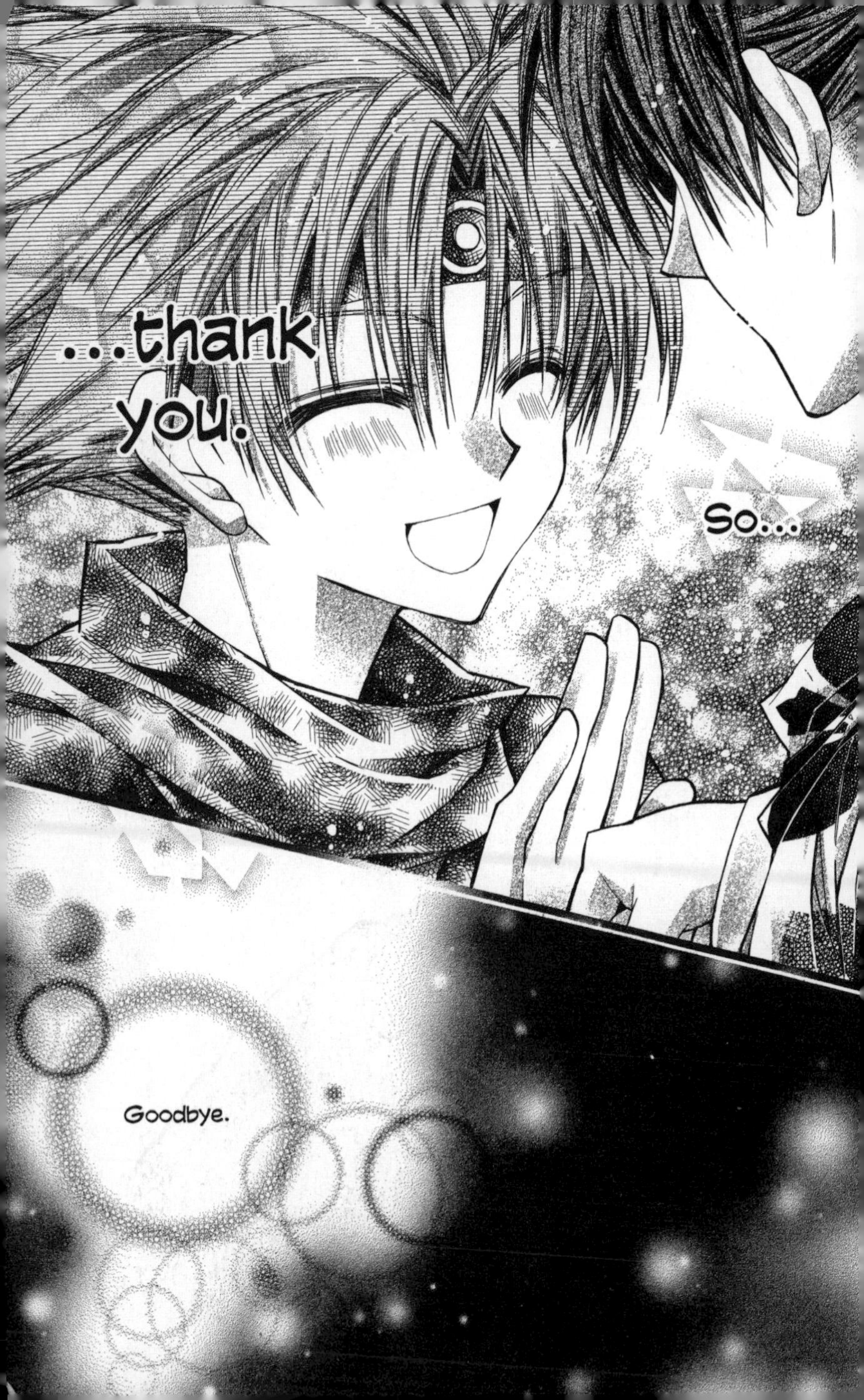
So...
...thank you.
Goodbye.

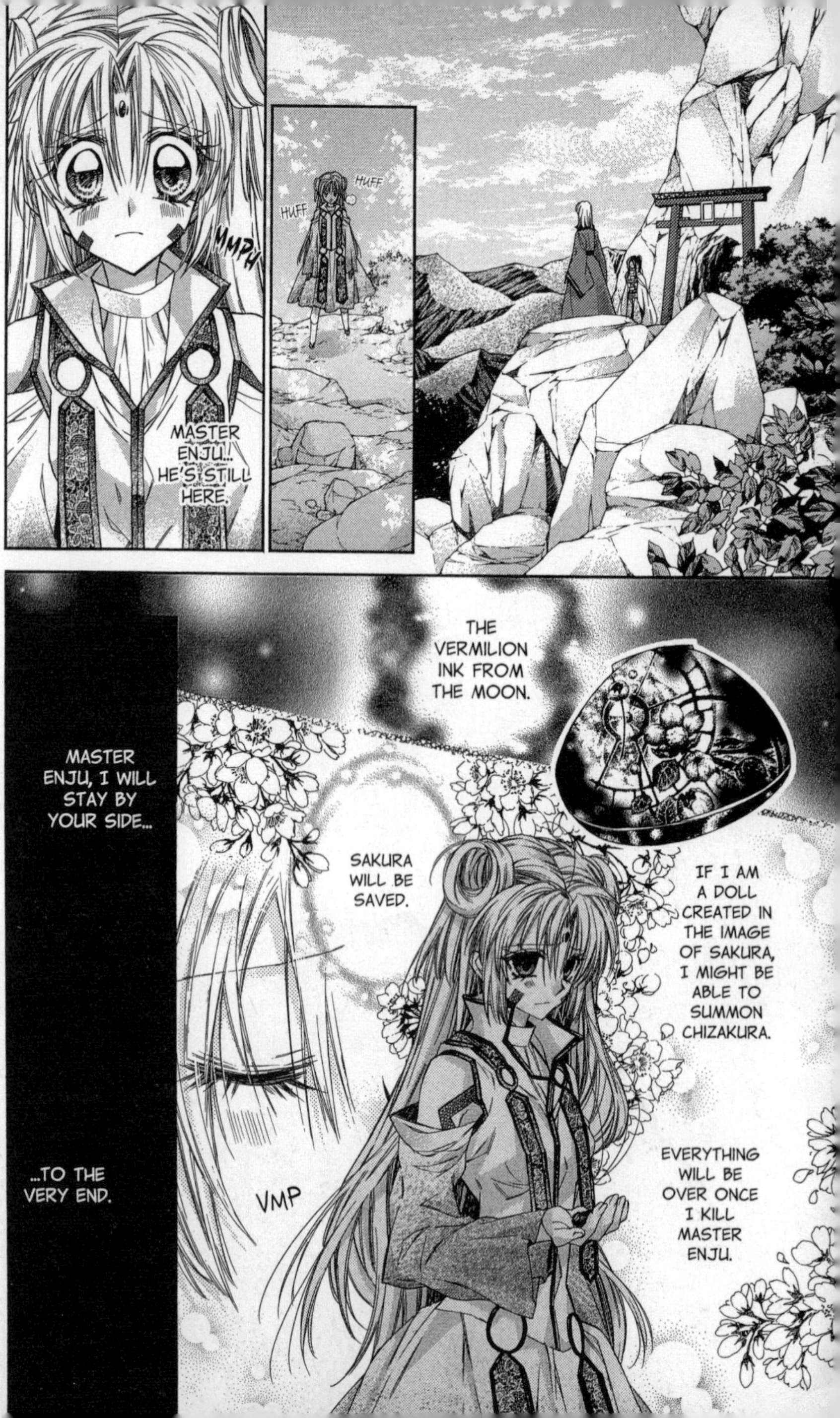
HUFF
HUFF
MMPH
MASTER ENJU... HE'S STILL HERE.
THE VERMILION INK FROM THE MOON.
IF I AM A DOLL CREATED IN THE IMAGE OF SAKURA, I MIGHT BE ABLE TO SUMMON CHIZAKURA.
SAKURA WILL BE SAVED.
EVERYTHING WILL BE OVER ONCE I KILL MASTER ENJU.
MASTER ENJU, I WILL STAY BY YOUR SIDE...
VMP
...TO THE VERY END.

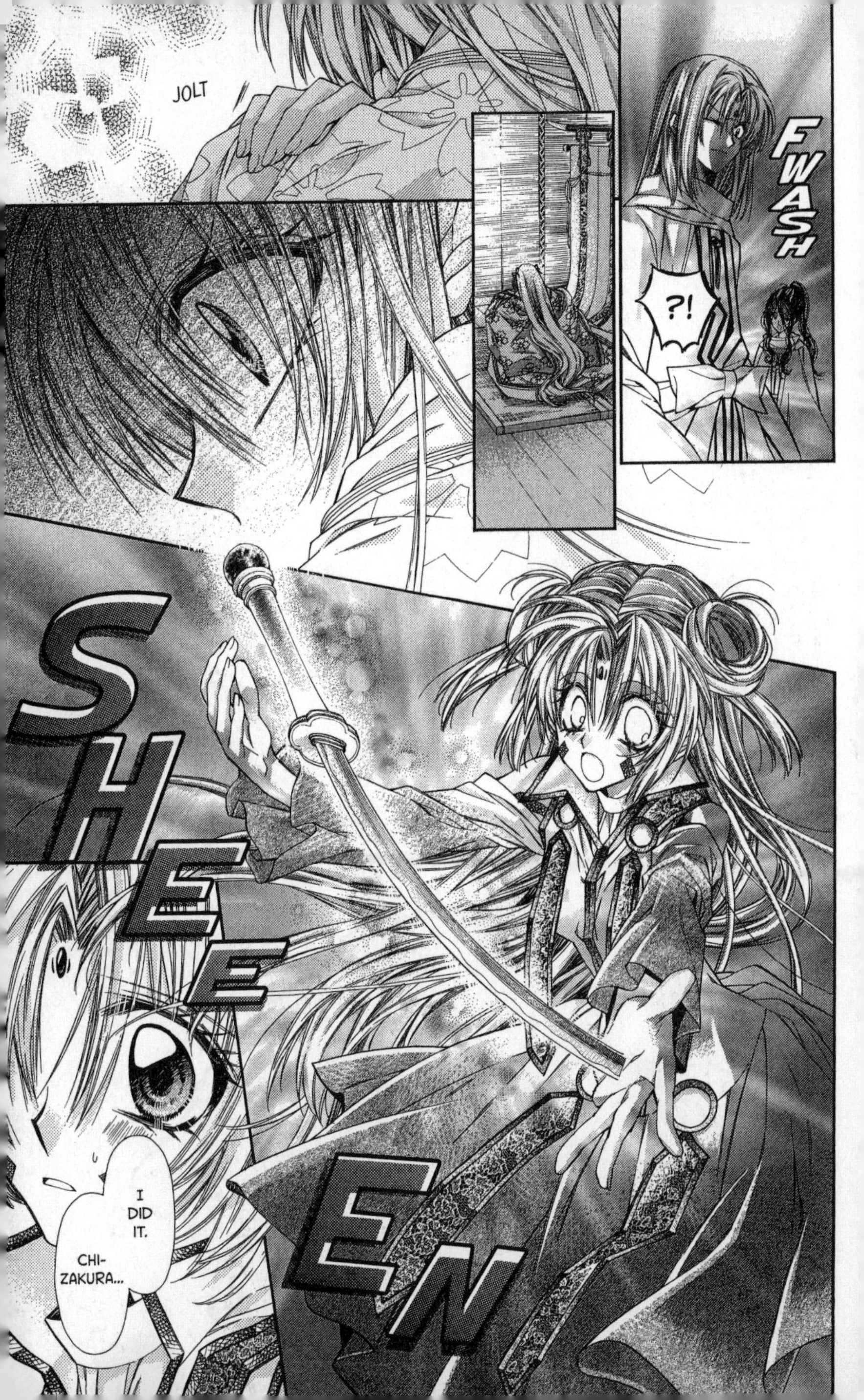
FWASH
?!
JOLT
SHEEEEN
I DID IT.
CHI-ZAKURA...

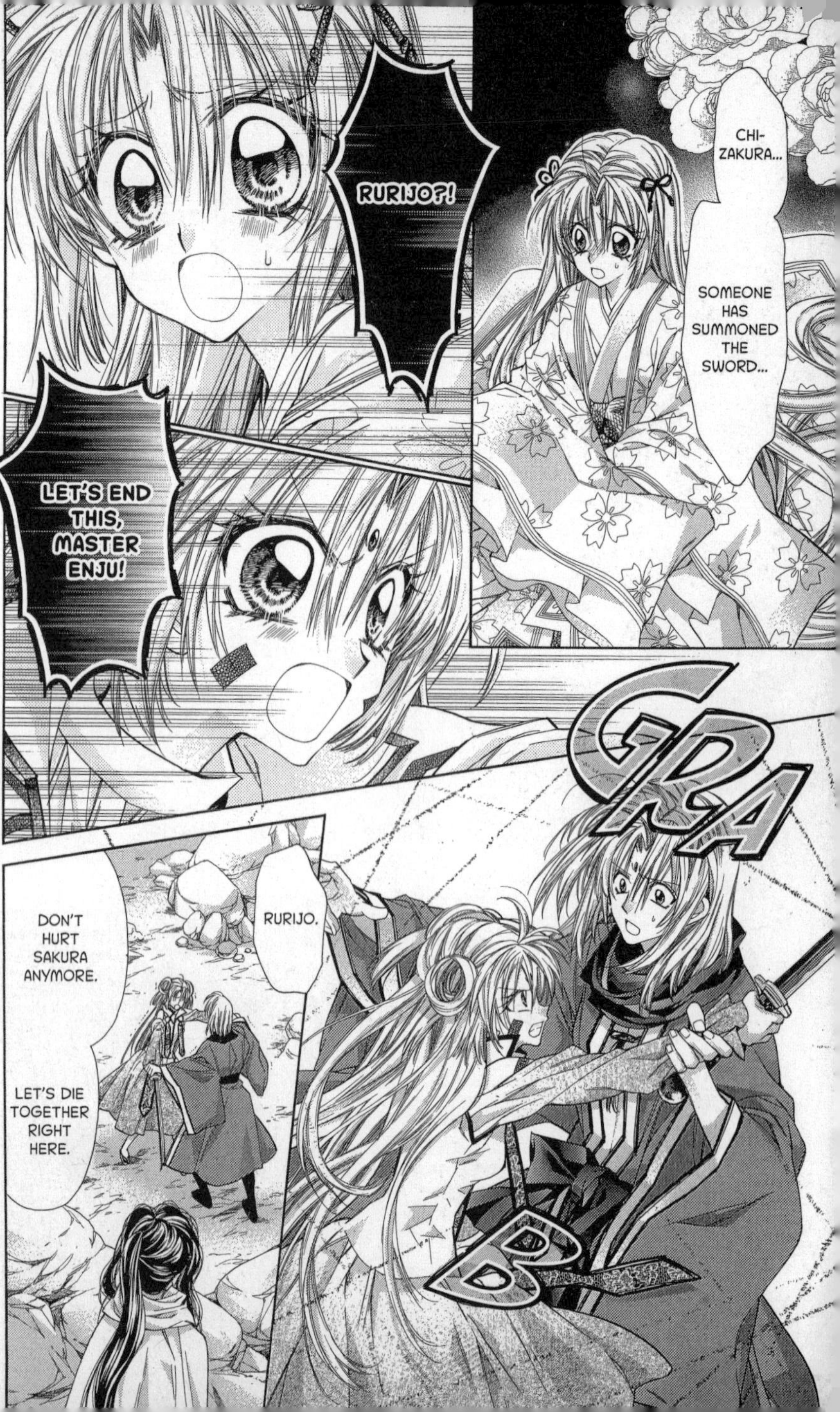
CHI-ZAKURA...
SOMEONE HAS SUMMONED THE SWORD...
RURIJO?!
LET'S END THIS, MASTER ENJU!
GRA
B
RURIJO.
DON'T HURT SAKURA ANYMORE.
LET'S DIE TOGETHER RIGHT HERE.

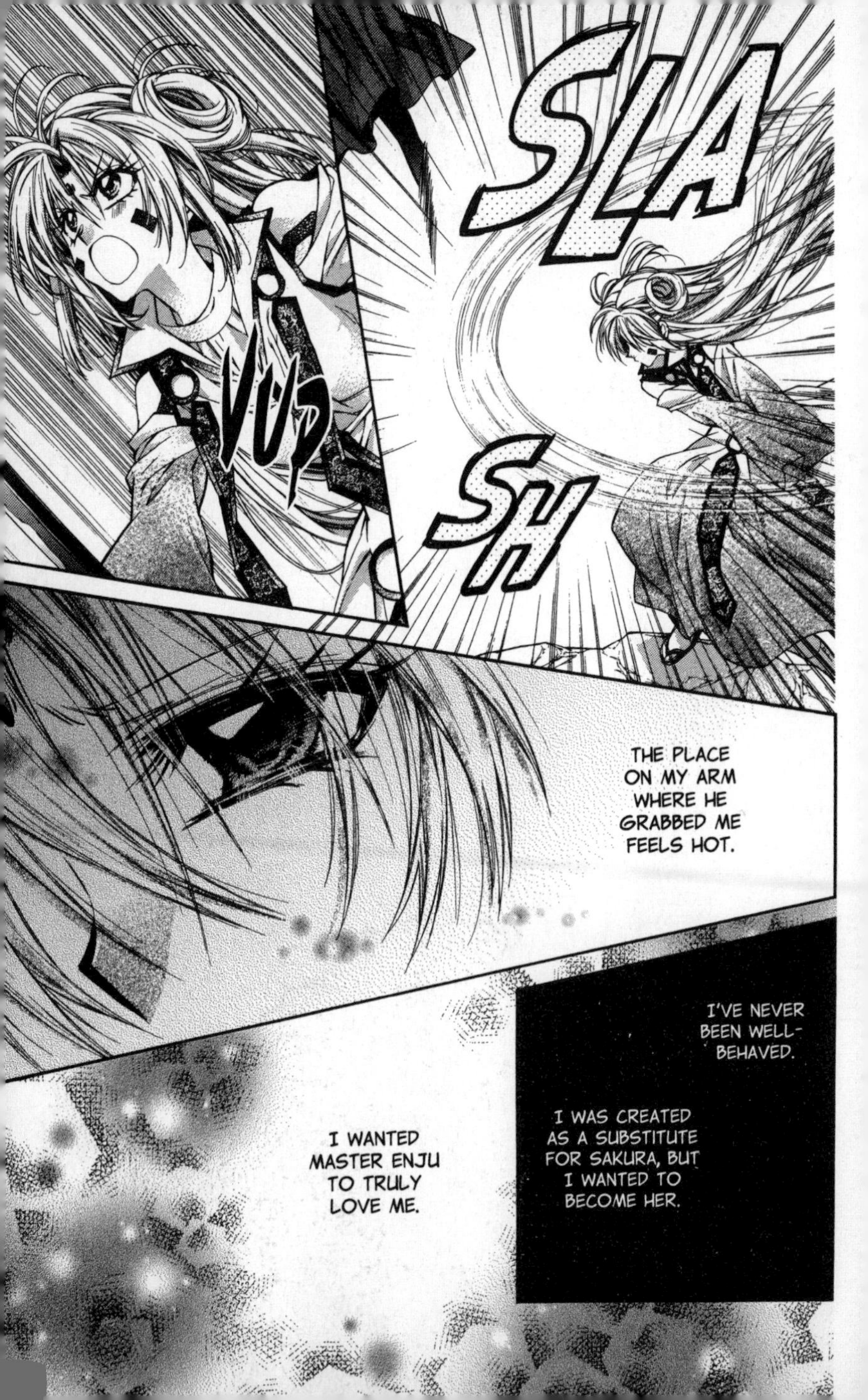
SLA
SH
VUD
THE PLACE ON MY ARM WHERE HE GRABBED ME FEELS HOT.
I'VE NEVER BEEN WELL-BEHAVED.
I WAS CREATED AS A SUBSTITUTE FOR SAKURA, BUT I WANTED TO BECOME HER.
I WANTED MASTER ENJU TO TRULY LOVE ME.

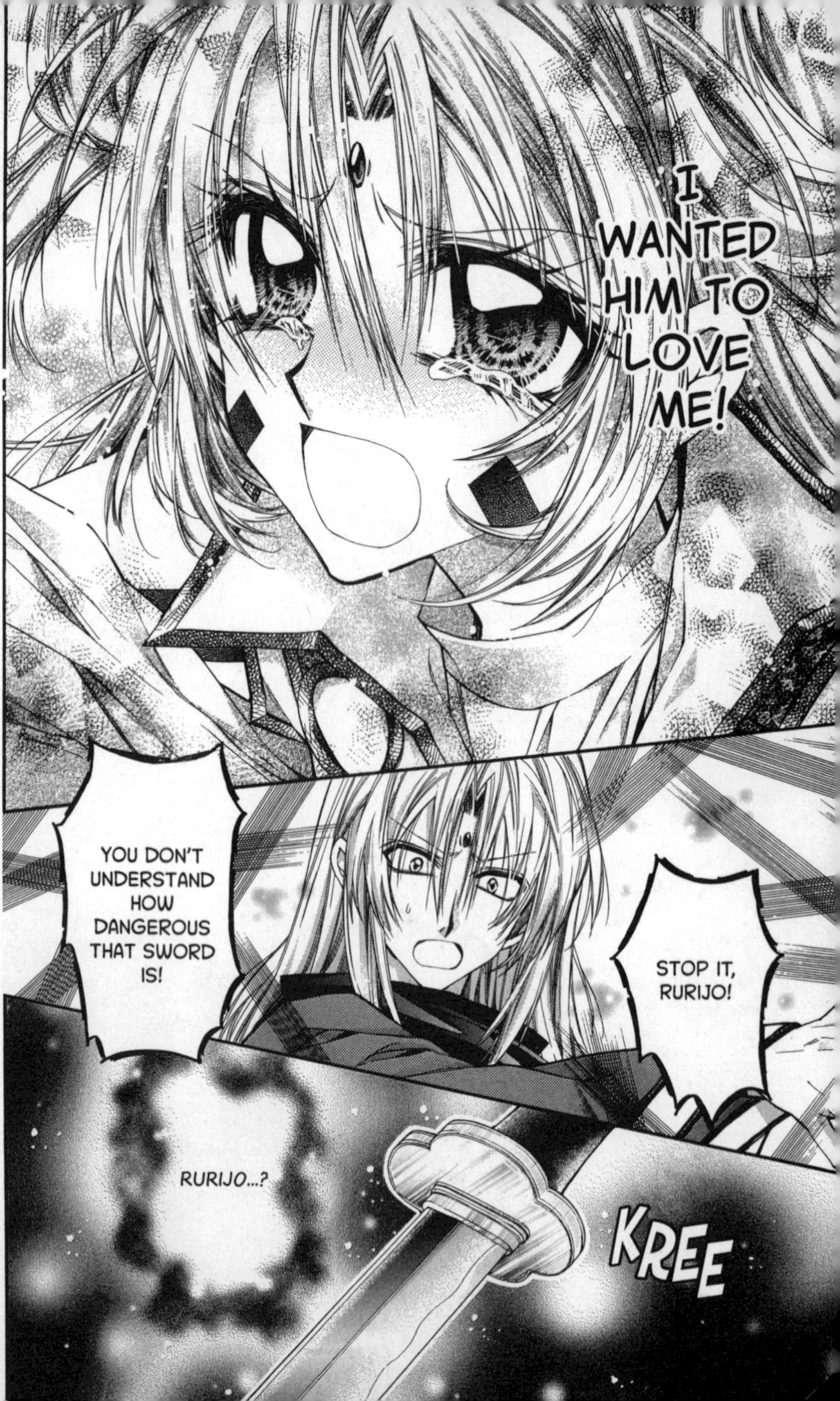
I WANTED HIM TO LOVE ME!
STOP IT, RURIJO!
YOU DON'T UNDERSTAND HOW DANGEROUS THAT SWORD IS!
KREE
RURIJO...?

Greetings

Hello, I'm Arina Tanemura. I bring to you the final volume of *Sakura Hime: The Legend of Princess Sakura*.

And as of volume 12 of this series, I will be leaving *Ribon* magazine. I already wrote about this in my blog about a year ago. I announced it on Twitter recently, and I received so many responses, it made me both happy and surprised.

Long ago I wrote in a manga that I would stay with *Ribon* all my life! My feelings have not changed. I would have wanted to stay with *Ribon* for the rest of my life if possible. But both *Ribon* and I have gradually begun to change, and I have not been able to feel the same way. That's why I decided to leave.

So, I'm truly graduating from *Ribon*.

But I am still filled with love for *Ribon*, and I will continue to support it.

I will always be indebted to that magazine for raising me as their mangaka. I would like to thank everyone in the Editorial Department and all the readers for supporting me.

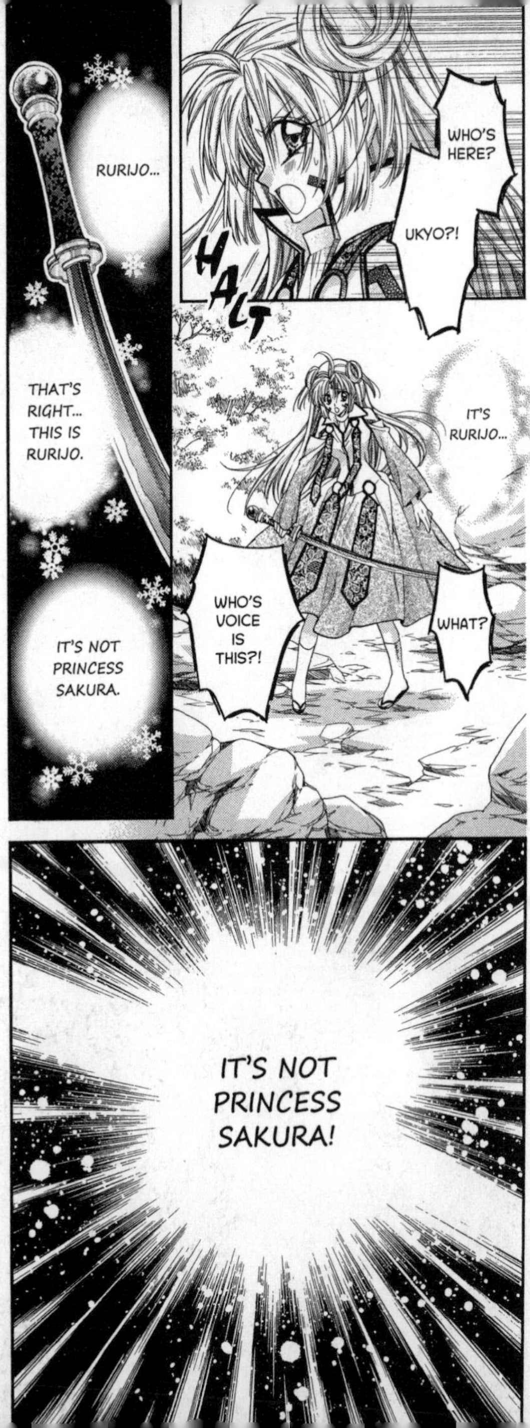
WHO'S HERE?
UKYO?!
HALT
IT'S RURIJO...
WHAT?
WHO'S VOICE IS THIS?!
RURIJO...
THAT'S RIGHT... THIS IS RURIJO.
IT'S NOT PRINCESS SAKURA.
IT'S NOT PRINCESS SAKURA!

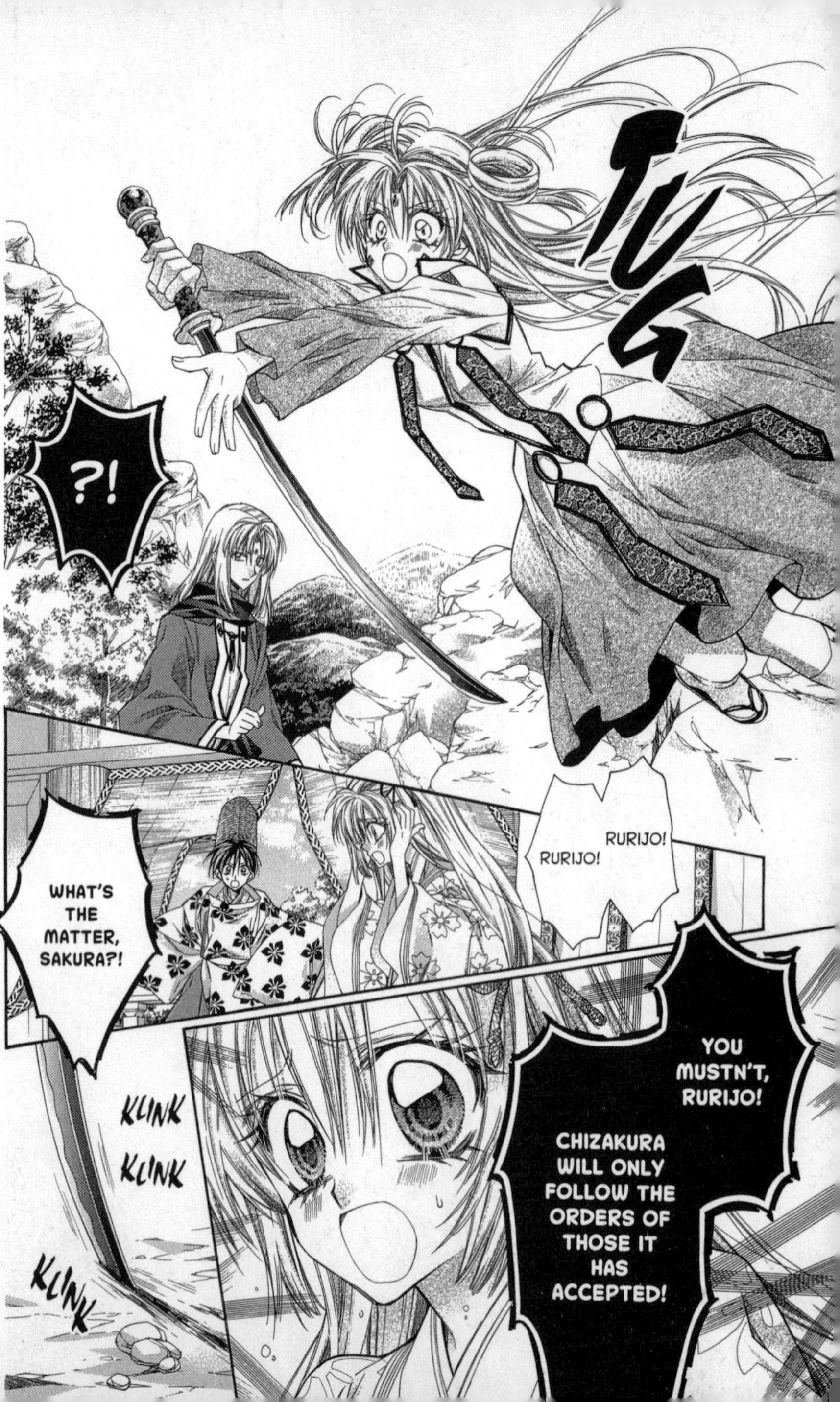
TUG
?!
RURIJO!
RURIJO!
WHAT'S THE MATTER, SAKURA?!
YOU MUSTN'T, RURIJO!
CHIZAKURA WILL ONLY FOLLOW THE ORDERS OF THOSE IT HAS ACCEPTED!
KLINK
KLINK
KLINK

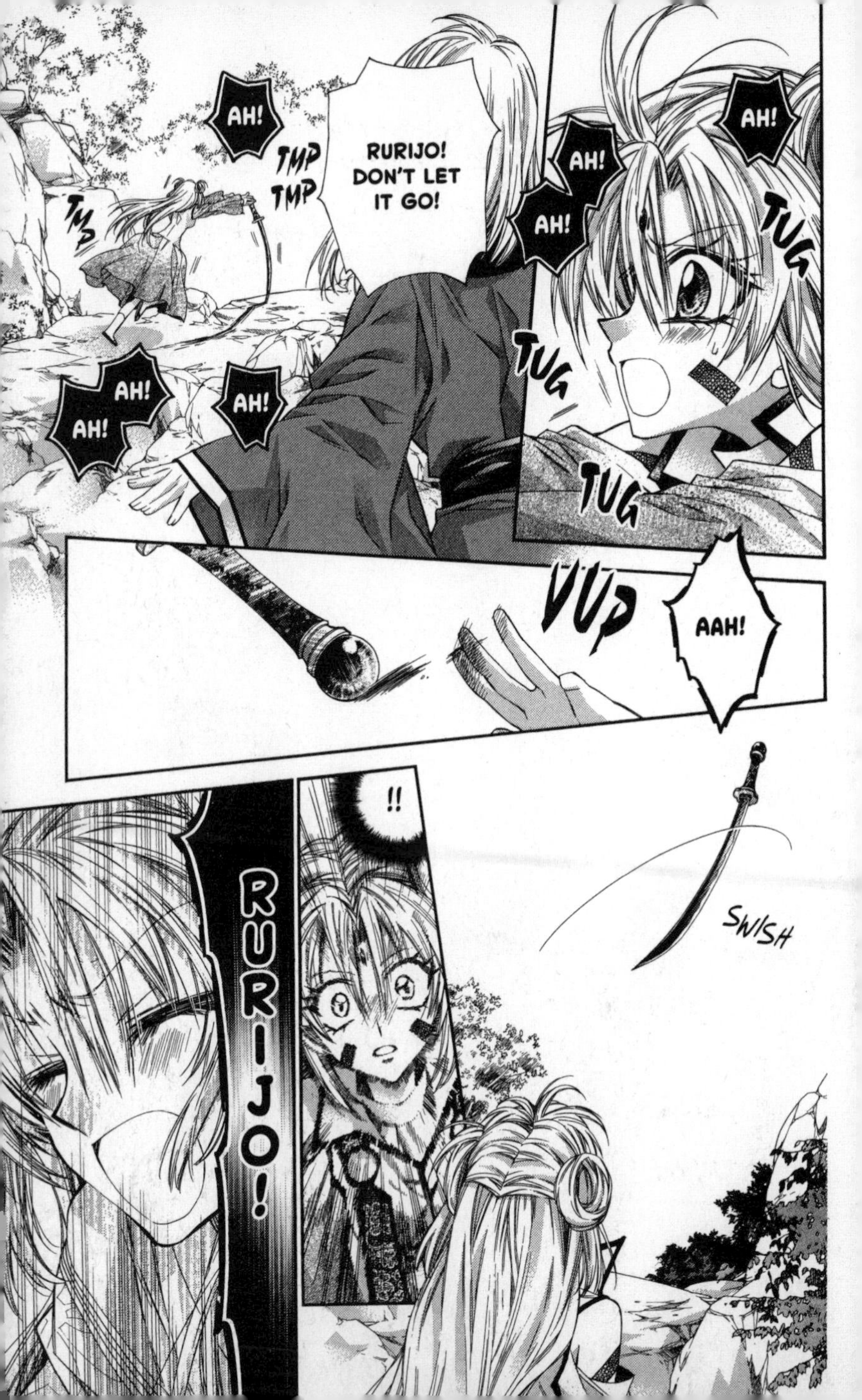
AH!
AH!
AH!
TUG
TUG
TUG
RURIJO! DON'T LET IT GO!
AH!
TMP TMP
TMP
AH!
AH! AH!
AAH!
VUP
SWISH
!!
RURIJO!

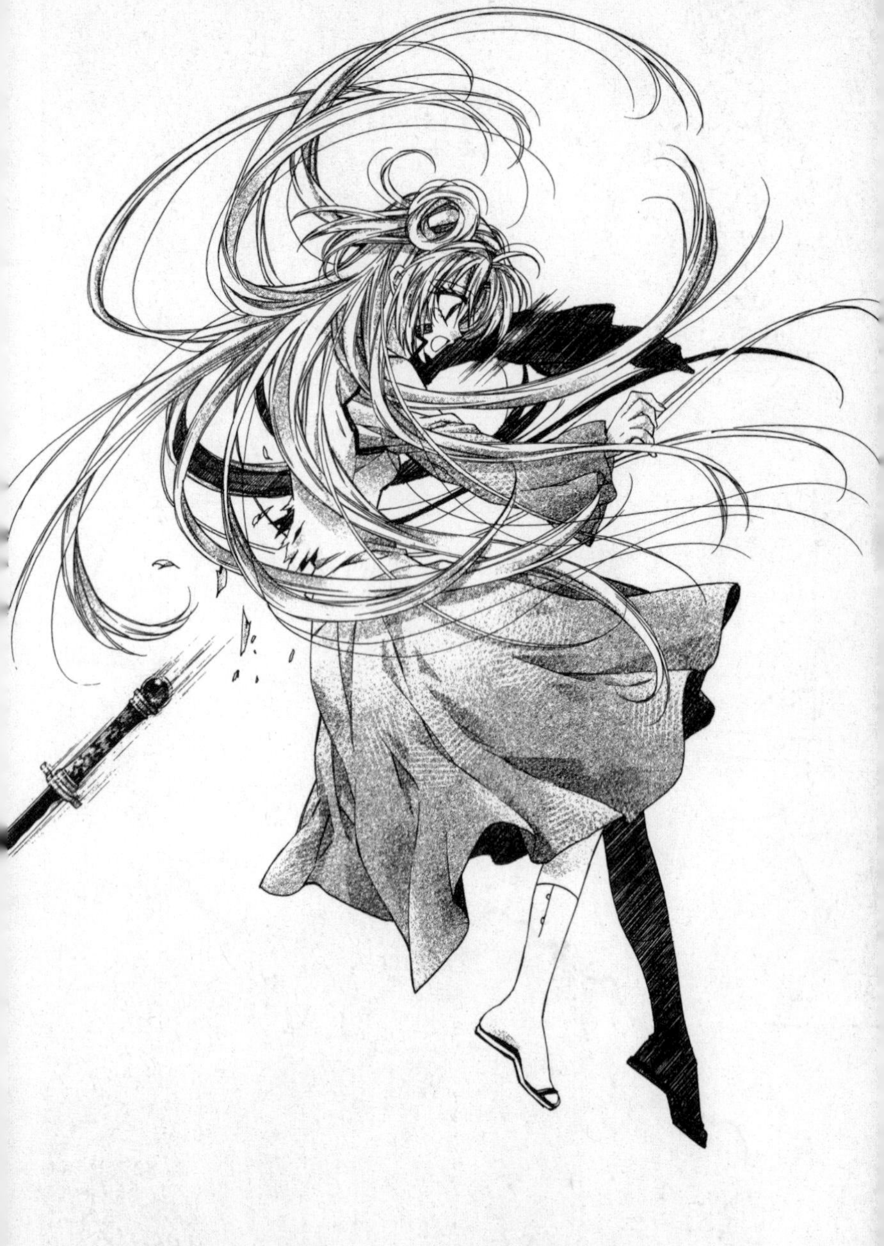

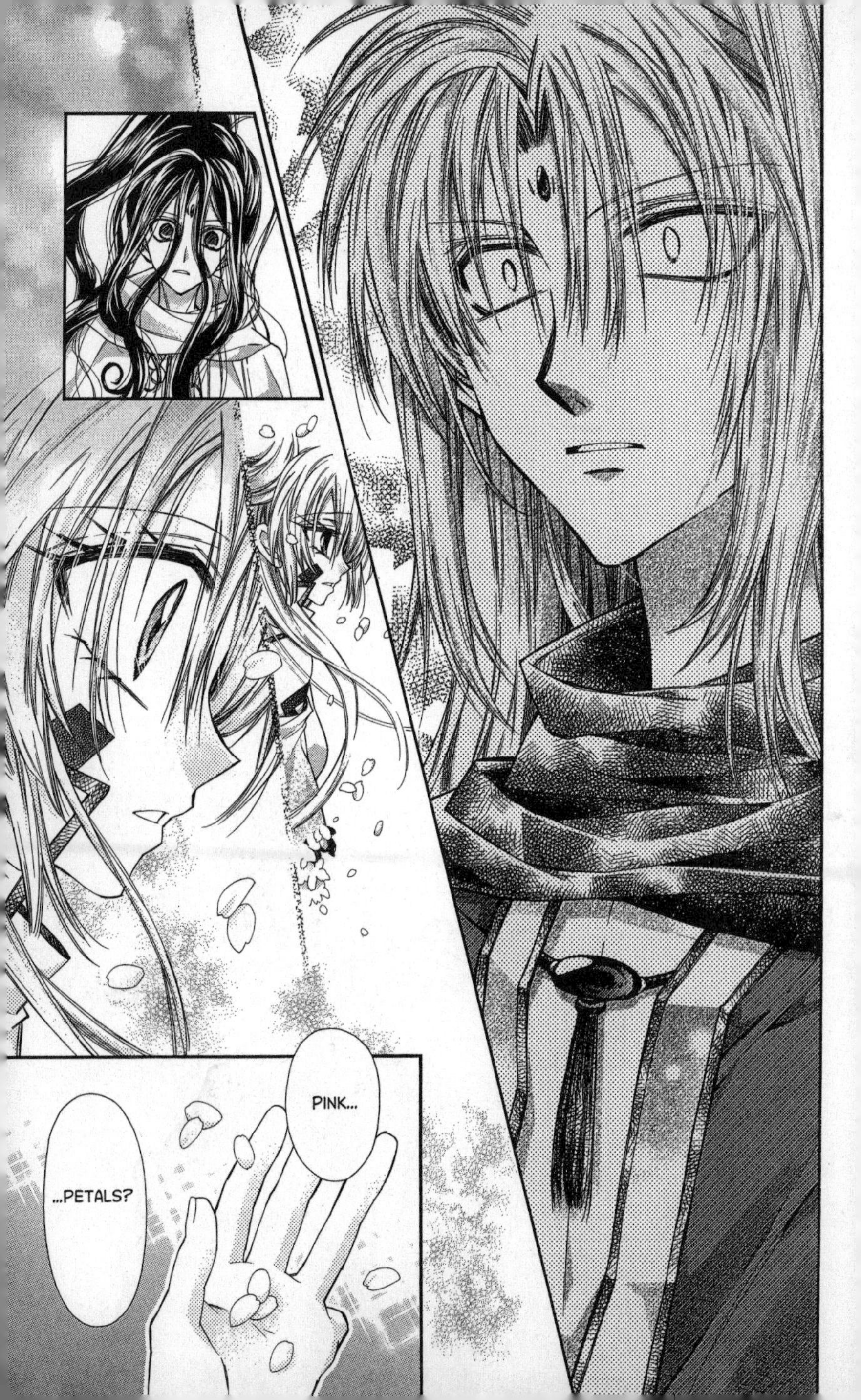
PINK...
...PETALS?

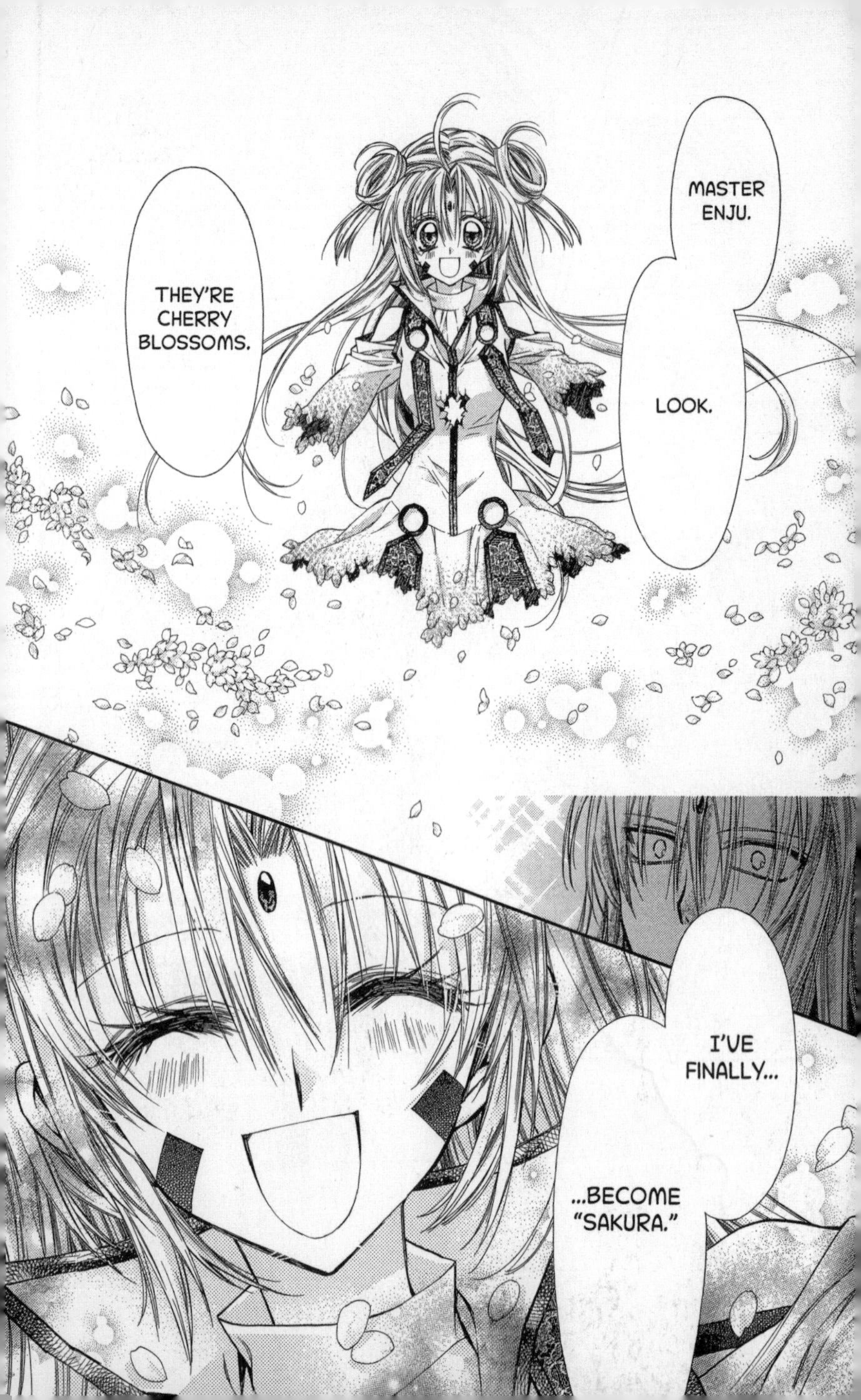
MASTER ENJU.
LOOK.
THEY'RE CHERRY BLOSSOMS.
I'VE FINALLY...
...BECOME "SAKURA."

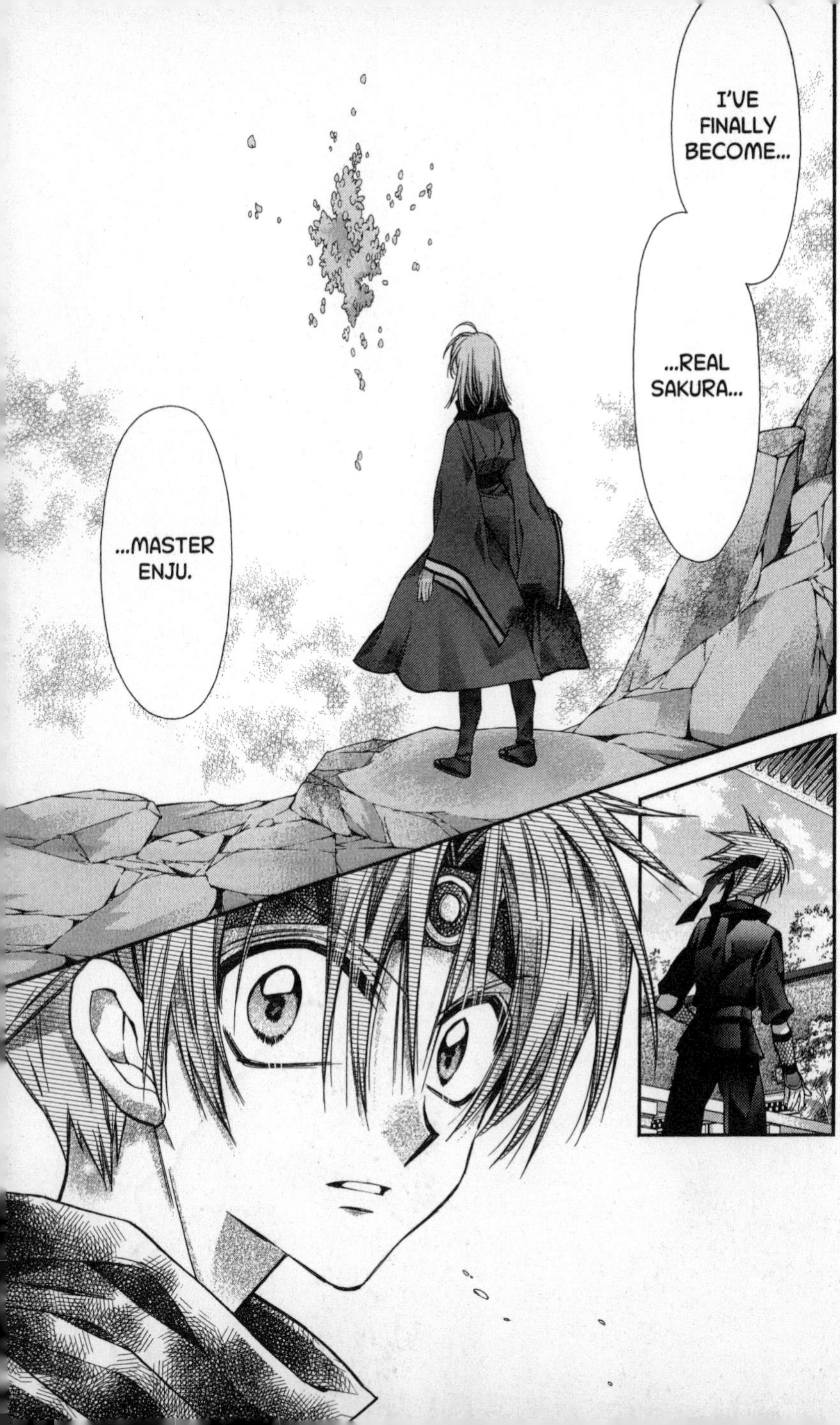
I'VE FINALLY BECOME...
...REAL SAKURA...
...MASTER ENJU.

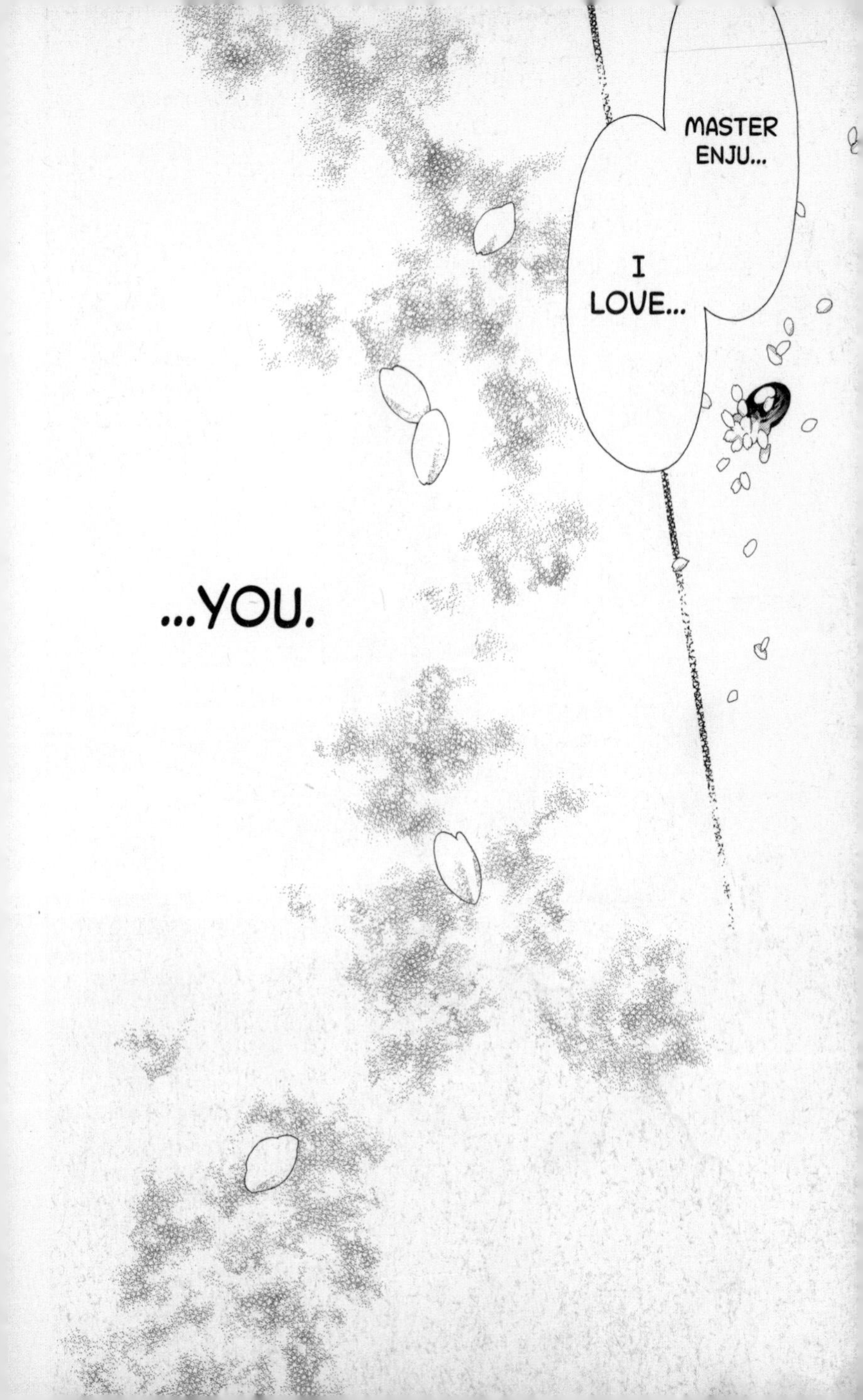
MASTER ENJU...
I LOVE...
...YOU.

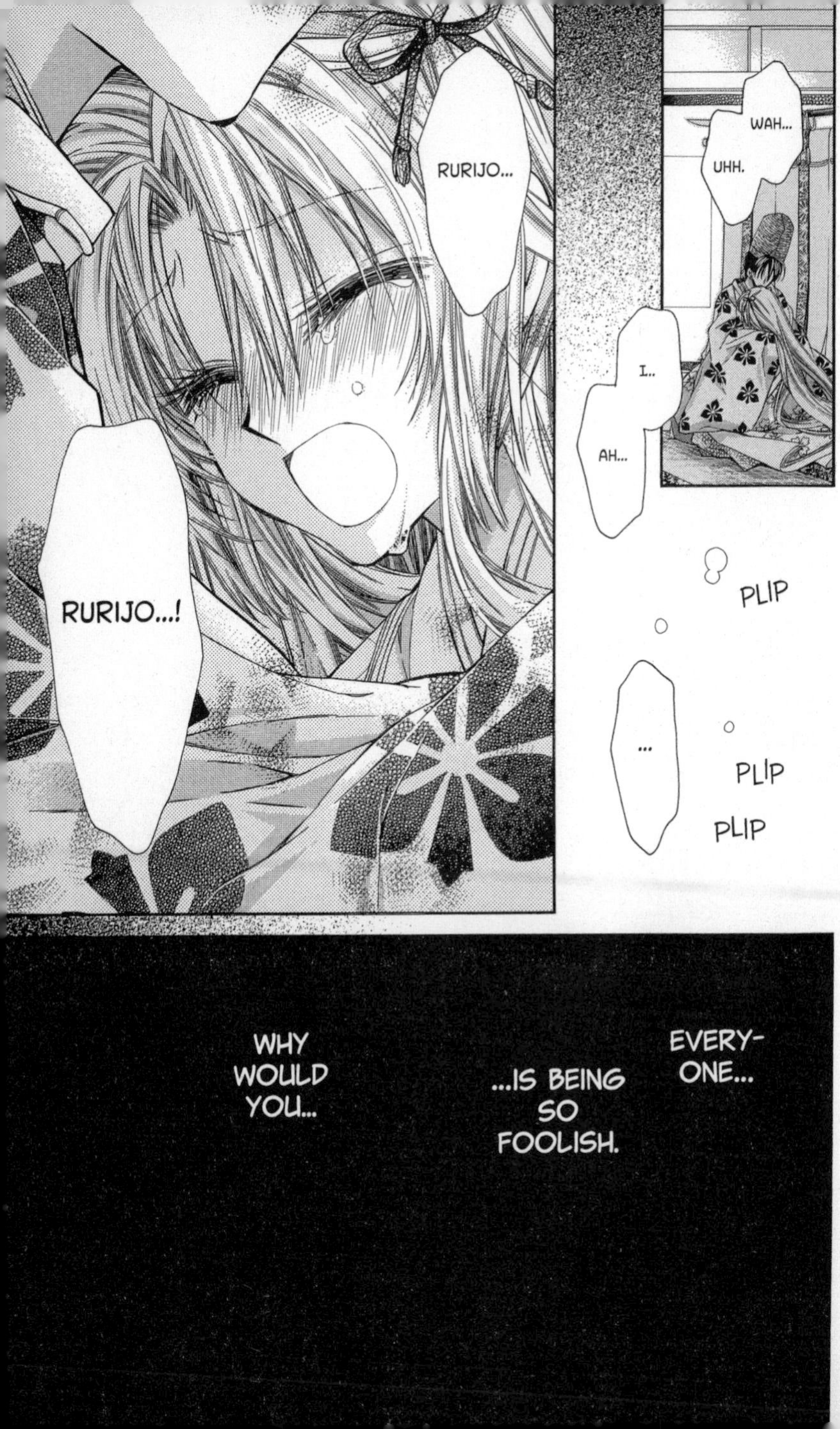
WAH...
UHH.
I..
AH...
PLIP
...
PLIP
PLIP
RURIJO...
RURIJO...!
EVERY-ONE...
...IS BEING SO FOOLISH.
WHY WOULD YOU...

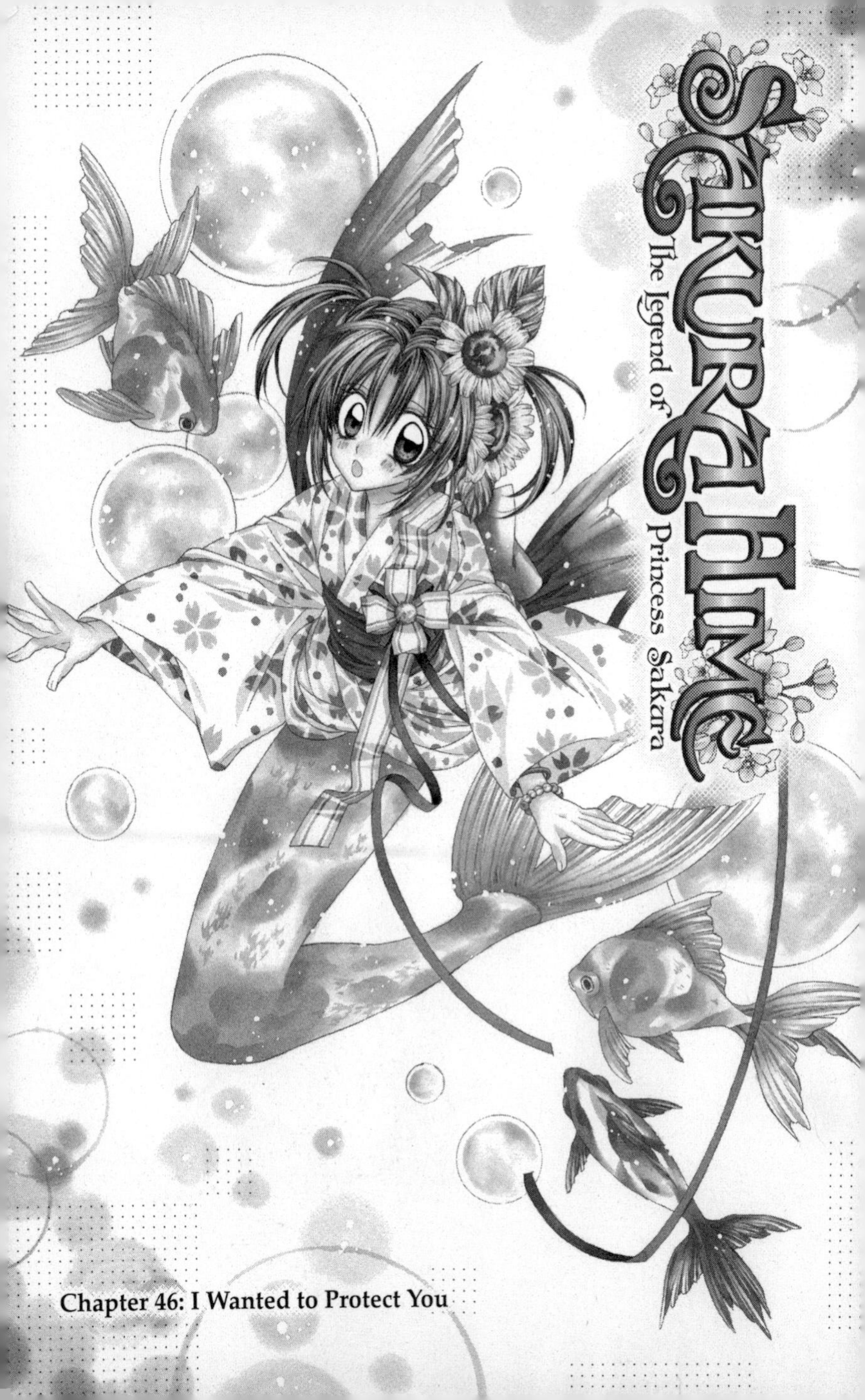
SAKURA HIME
The Legend of Princess Sakura

Chapter 46: I Wanted to Protect You

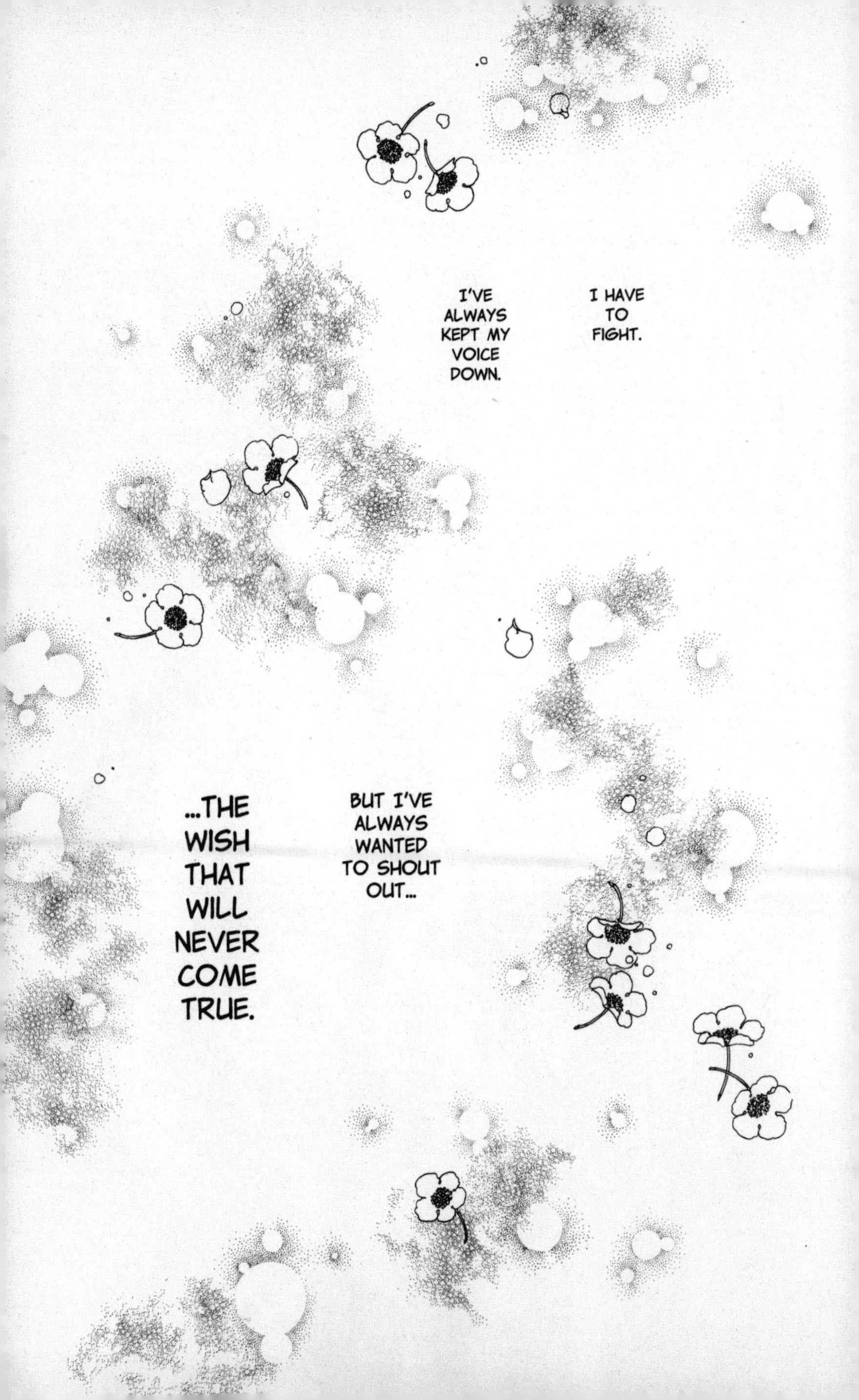
I HAVE TO FIGHT.
I'VE ALWAYS KEPT MY VOICE DOWN.
BUT I'VE ALWAYS WANTED TO SHOUT OUT...
...THE WISH THAT WILL NEVER COME TRUE.

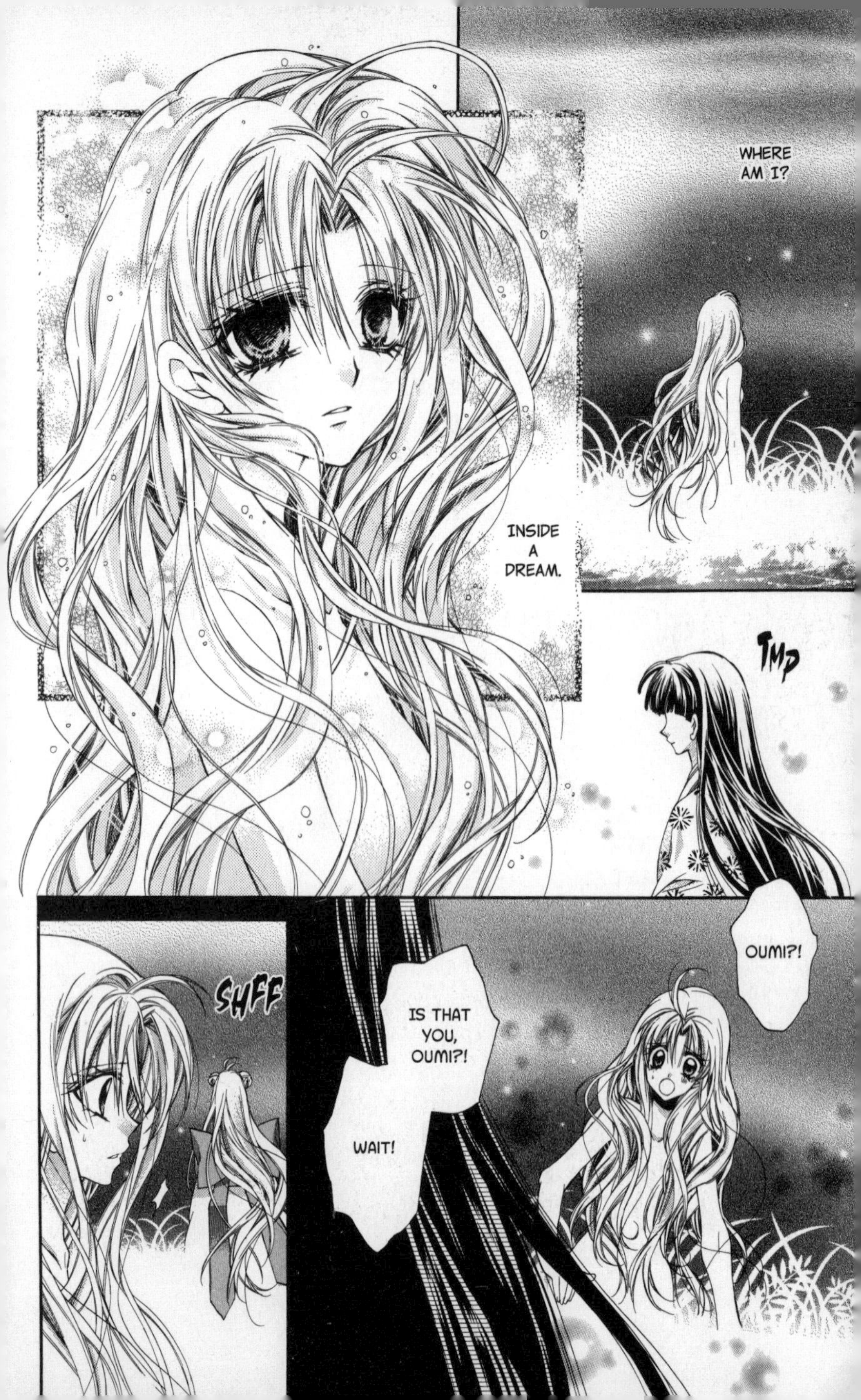
WHERE AM I?
TMP
INSIDE A DREAM.
OUMI?!
IS THAT YOU, OUMI?!
WAIT!
SHFF

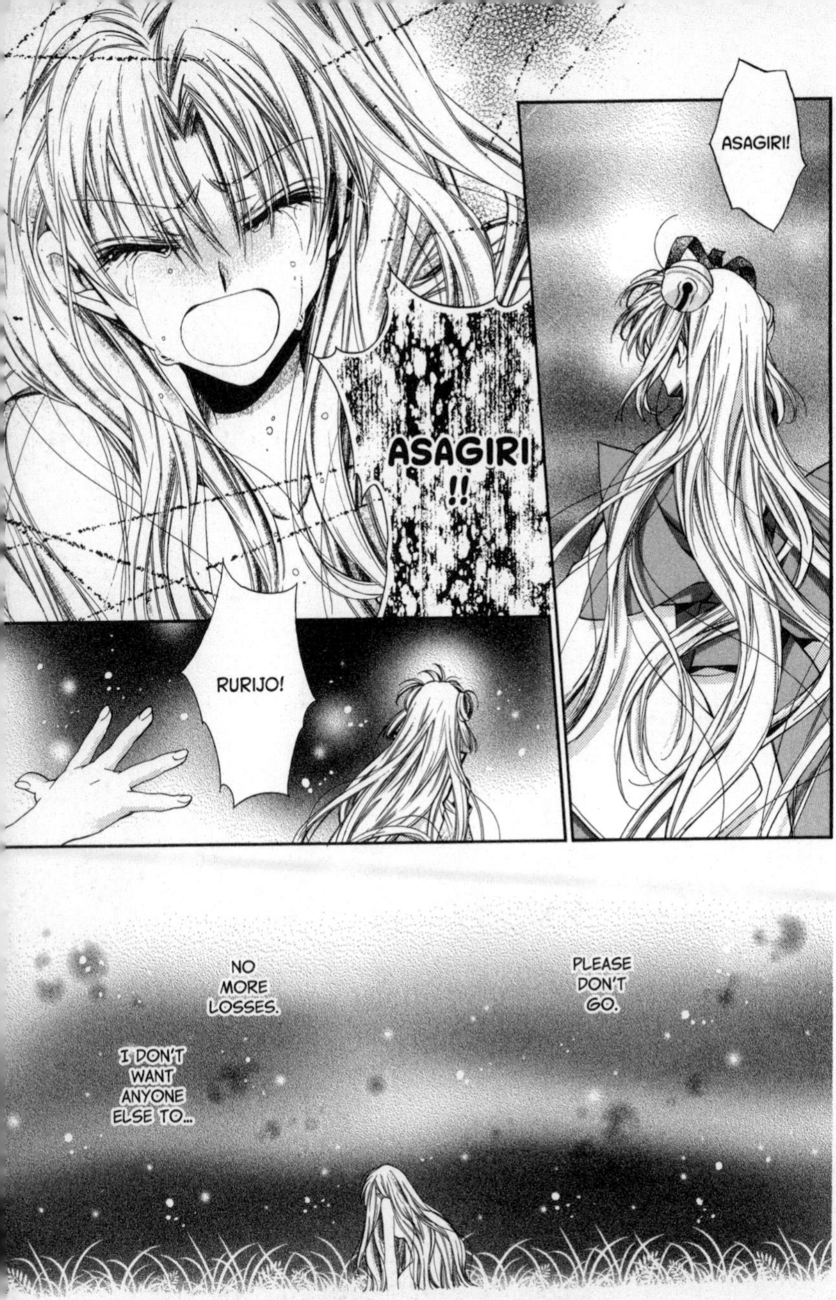
ASAGIRI!
ASAGIRI !!
RURIJO!
PLEASE DON'T GO.
NO MORE LOSSES.
I DON'T WANT ANYONE ELSE TO...

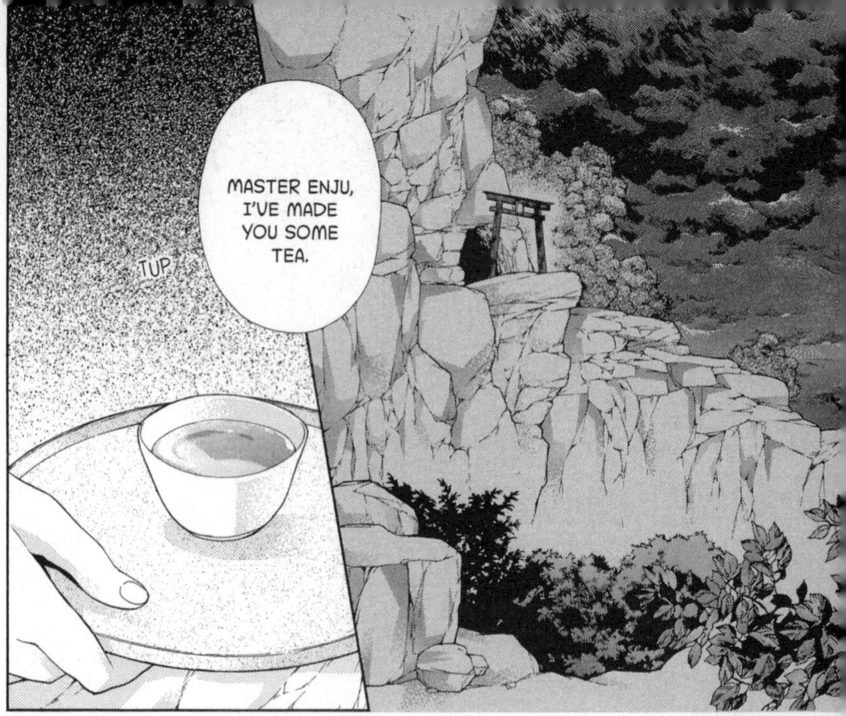
MASTER ENJU, I'VE MADE YOU SOME TEA.
TUP

Chapter 46: I Wanted to Protect You

※ I'm giving away the story.
Aoba is probably one of my more low-key heroes, but he can be reliable in times like these. This series really starts to corner its characters at the end, doesn't it? I was working on this series so desperately that I never realized it was this tough. (Sorry.) It was around this chapter that the story went out of my control, and it changed drastically from what I had first intended it to be. I thought, "So this is how it is" when I was working on the scene in which Sakura pours out her feelings. I felt like her parent.

Although Aoba asks Sakura to elope, she knows it's impossible and that Aoba understands how she feels. He asked that out of kindness. But I thought I was able to show their bond better here, which I had not been able to draw a lot. I was extremely surprised at the impact the end of this chapter had on the readers. I'm very sorry. Yeah, but um, didn't you see it coming...? Sorry.

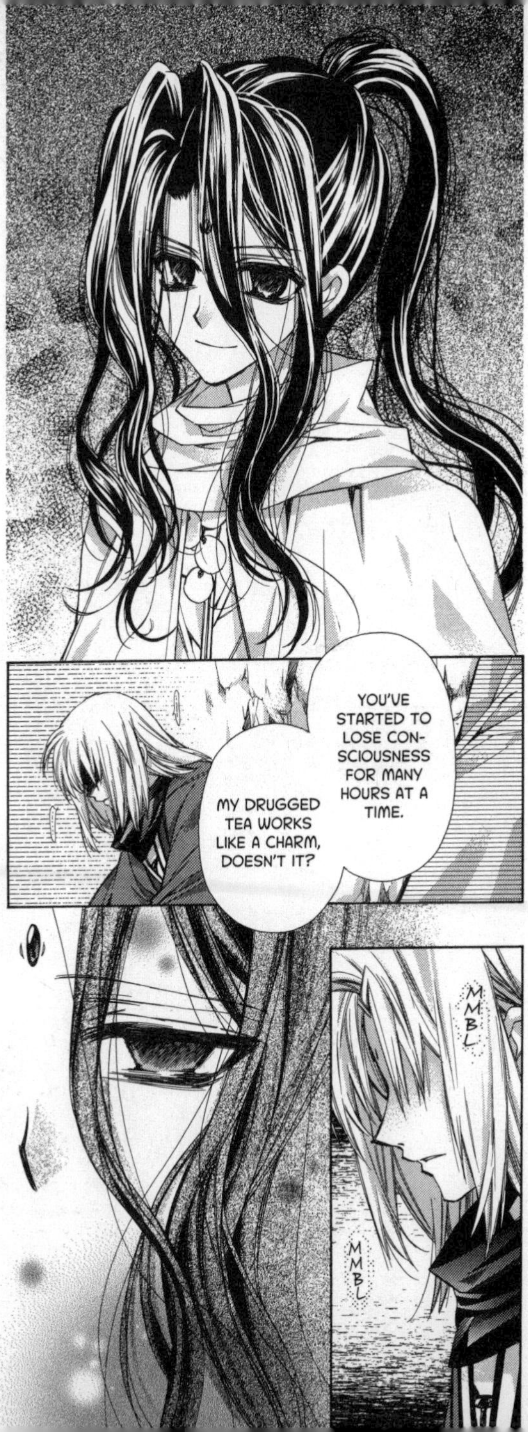
YOU'VE STARTED TO LOSE CONSCIOUSNESS FOR MANY HOURS AT A TIME.
MY DRUGGED TEA WORKS LIKE A CHARM, DOESN'T IT?
MMBL
MMBL

The Cat's and My Friday

My next new series will start in *Margaret* from Shueisha, the same publisher of *Ribon*. Chapter 1 will be in Issue 5 that comes out February 5, 2013.
The title is *The Cat's and My Friday*. It's a super-girly?! romantic comedy about Nekota and Ai. When I wrote about it on my blog, many asked whether it is a fantasy story. I was surprised how many people were interested in knowing that. Well, I had mainly been creating fantasy manga in *Ribon* since it fit their style, so maybe it can't be helped that people see me as a mangaka who writes fantasy. But when I was still sending my work in as a rookie, I hardly ever drew fantasy manga, so my work after I made my debut is less like me.
(But I've pretty much been creating fantasy manga for 16 years now, so maybe it's become a part of me?)
I got sidetracked, but *The Cat's and My Friday* is not fantasy. The story setting is a bit unusual, but it is an ordinary romance about a female high school student. I have wanted to work on this series for about five years now (?), so I hope you are looking forward to it. Thank you very much.

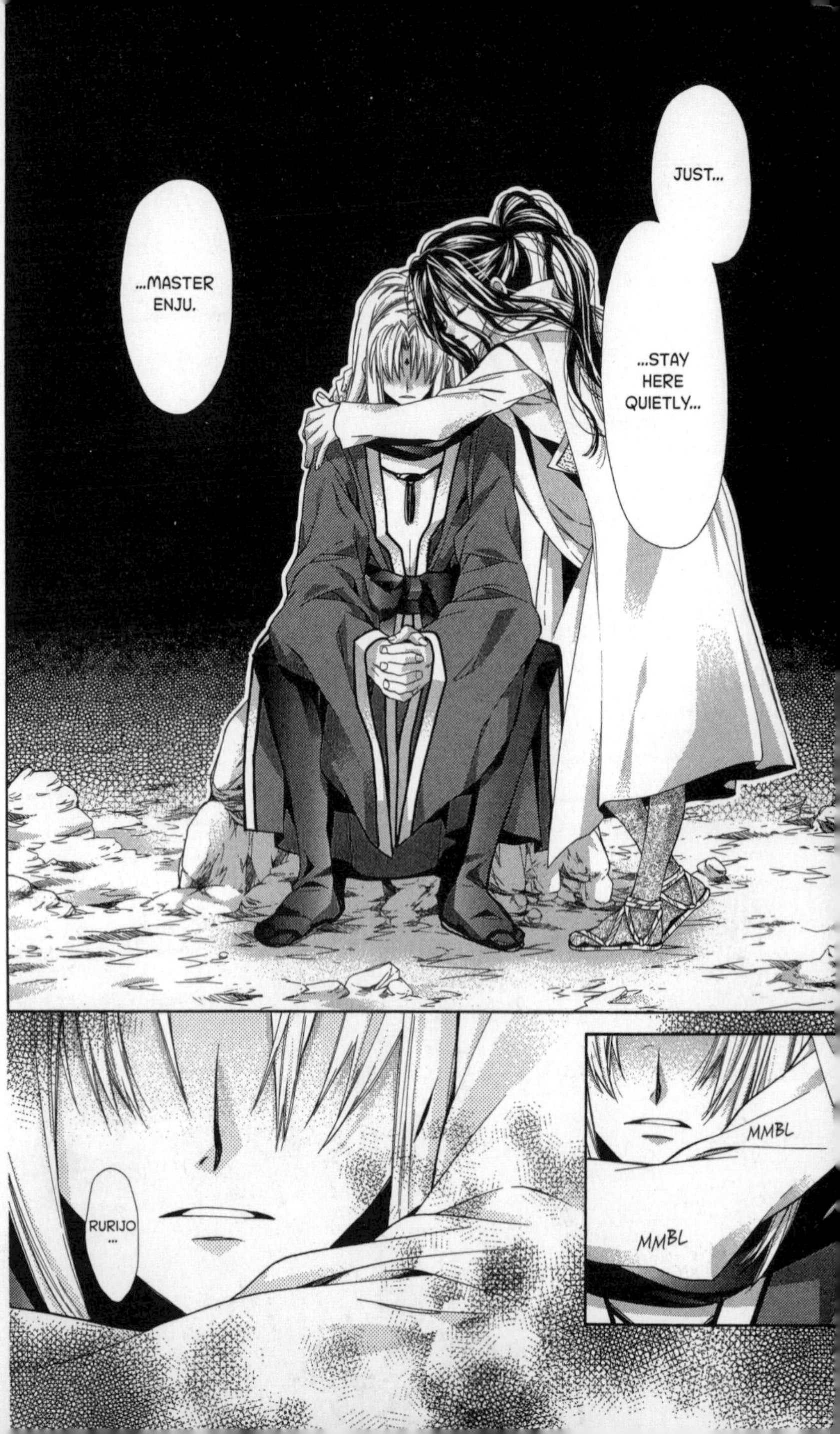
JUST...
...STAY HERE QUIETLY...
...MASTER ENJU.
MMBL
MMBL
RURIJO...

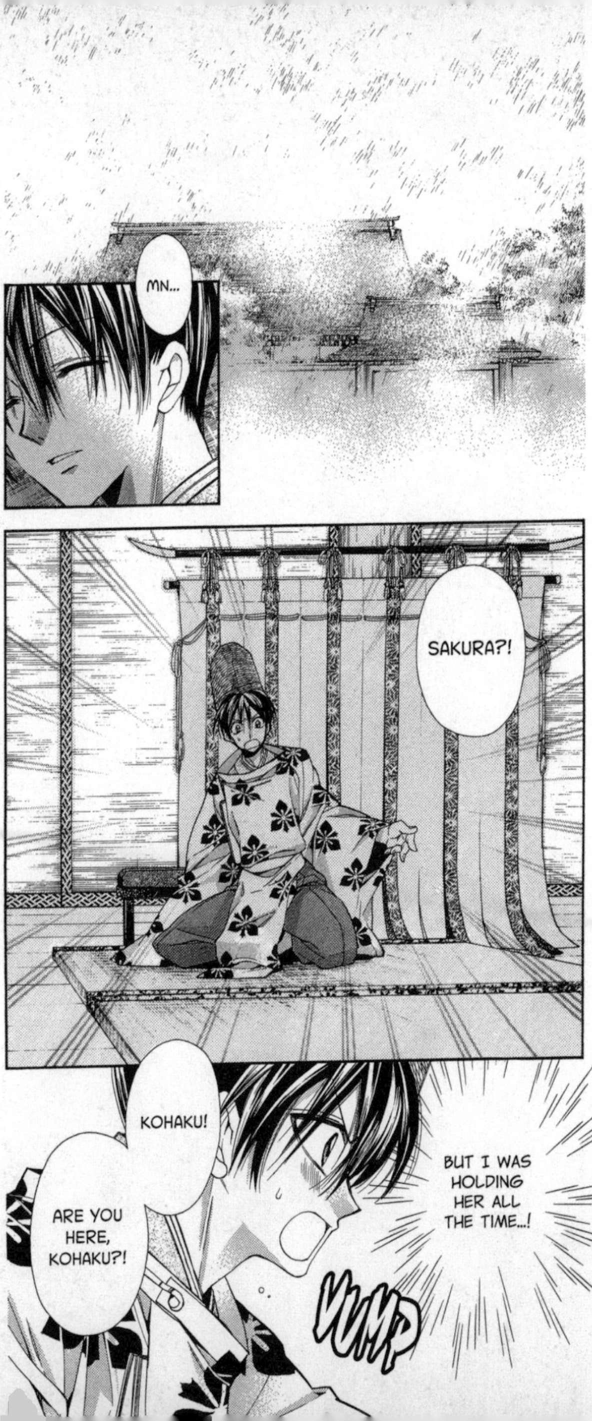
MN...
SAKURA?!
BUT I WAS HOLDING HER ALL THE TIME...!
KOHAKU!
ARE YOU HERE, KOHAKU?!
VUMP

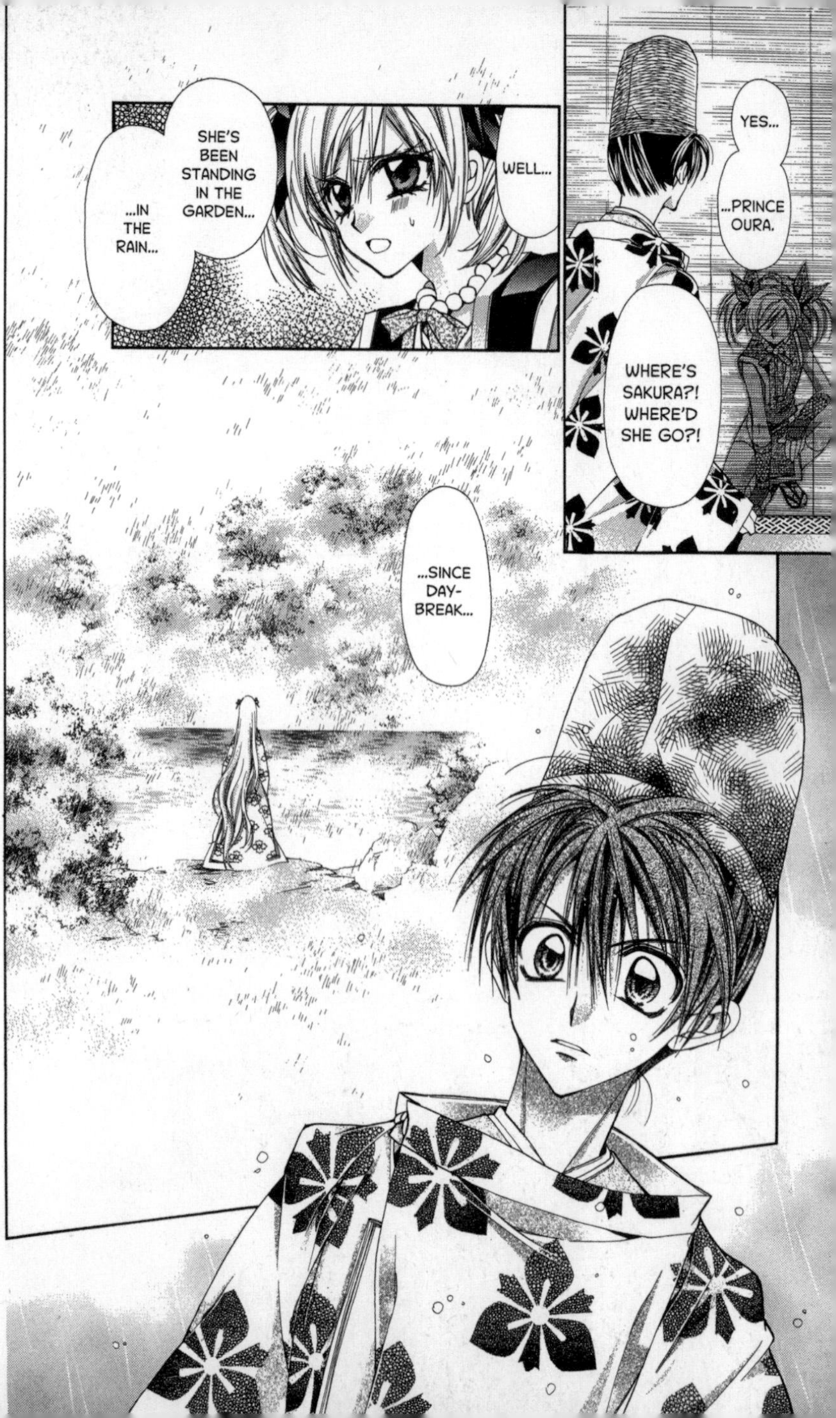
YES...
...PRINCE OURA.
WHERE'S SAKURA?! WHERE'D SHE GO?!
WELL...
SHE'S BEEN STANDING IN THE GARDEN...
...IN THE RAIN...
...SINCE DAY-BREAK...

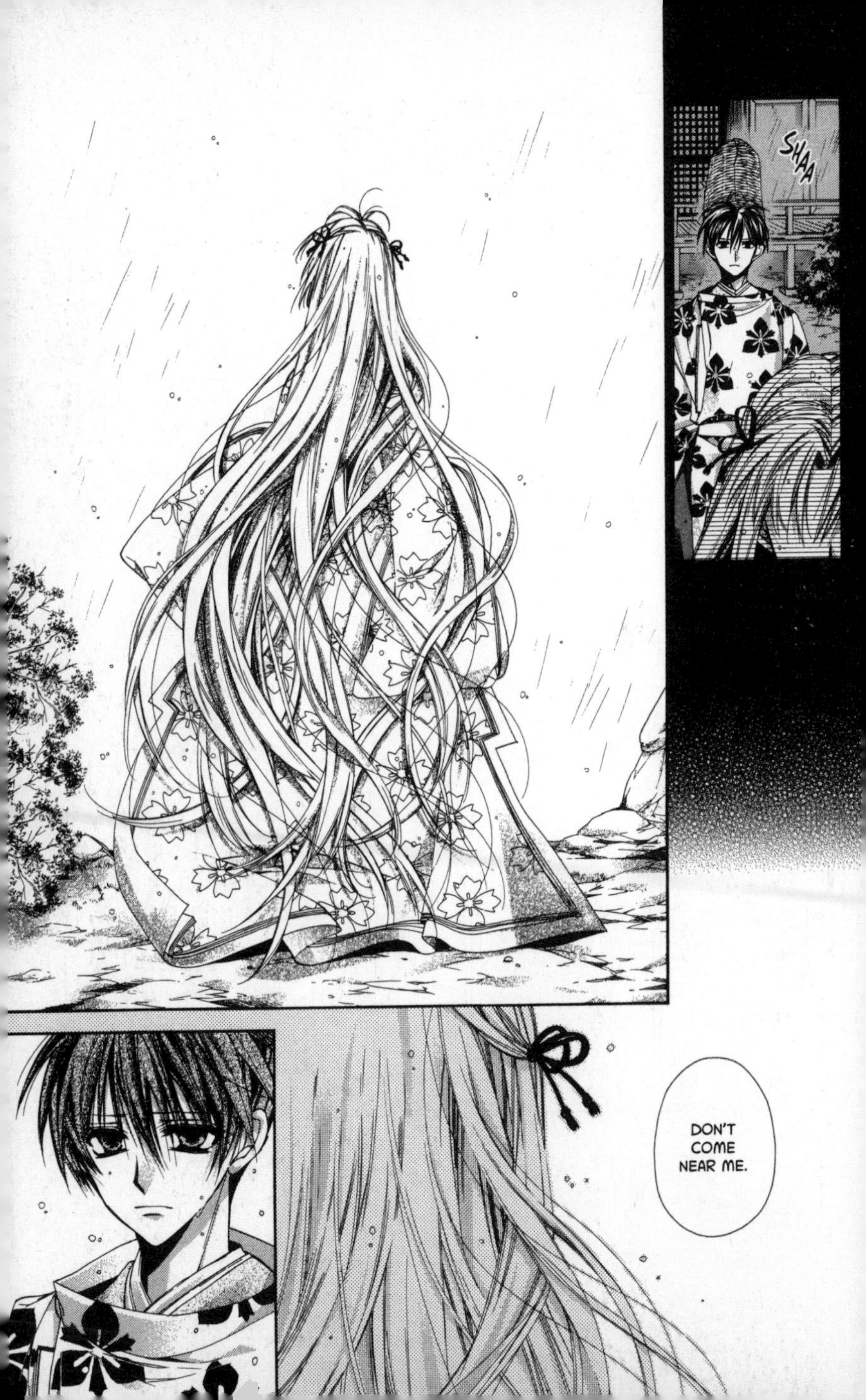
SHAA
DON'T COME NEAR ME.

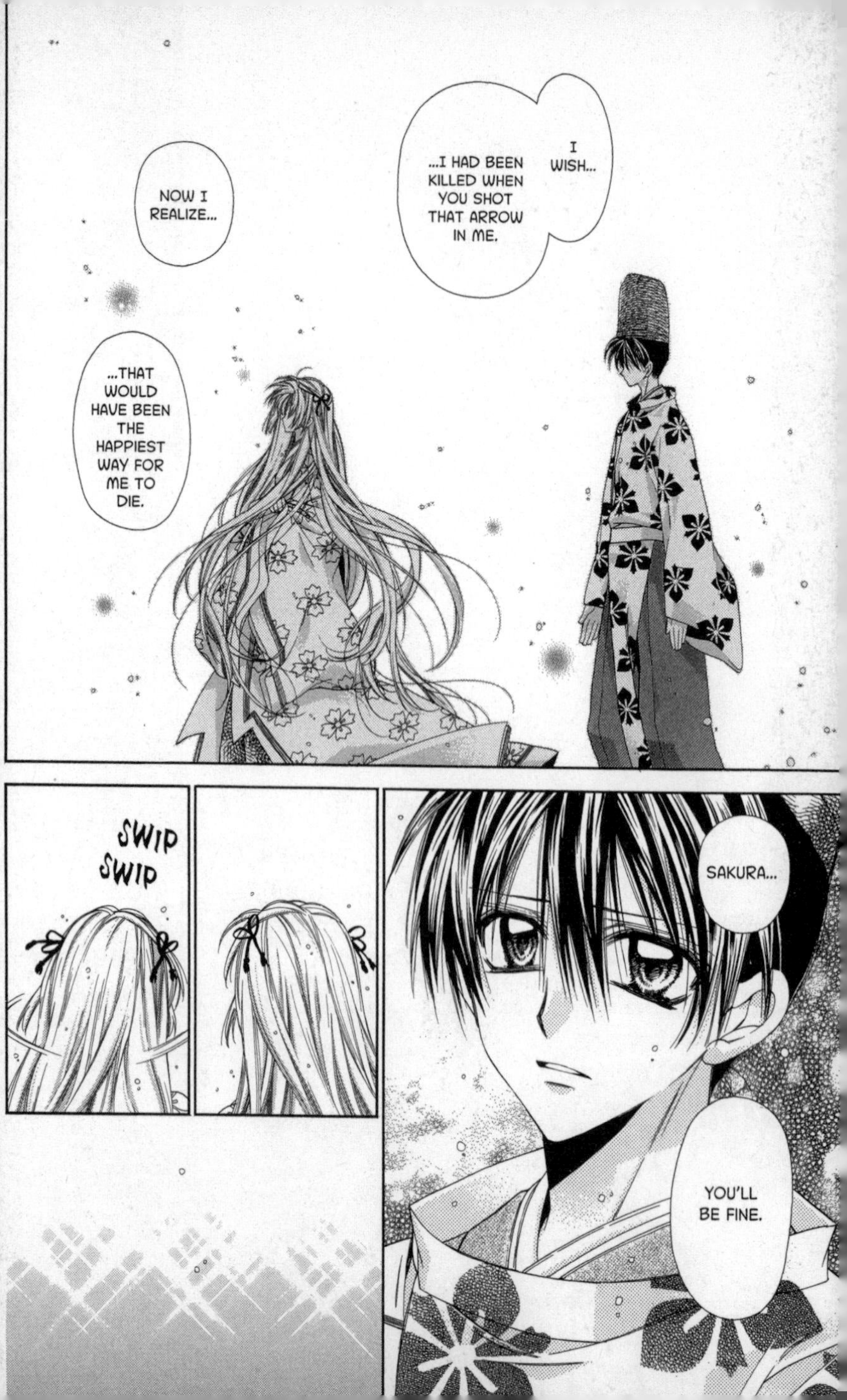
I WISH...
...I HAD BEEN KILLED WHEN YOU SHOT THAT ARROW IN ME.
NOW I REALIZE...
...THAT WOULD HAVE BEEN THE HAPPIEST WAY FOR ME TO DIE.
SAKURA...
YOU'LL BE FINE.
SWIP SWIP

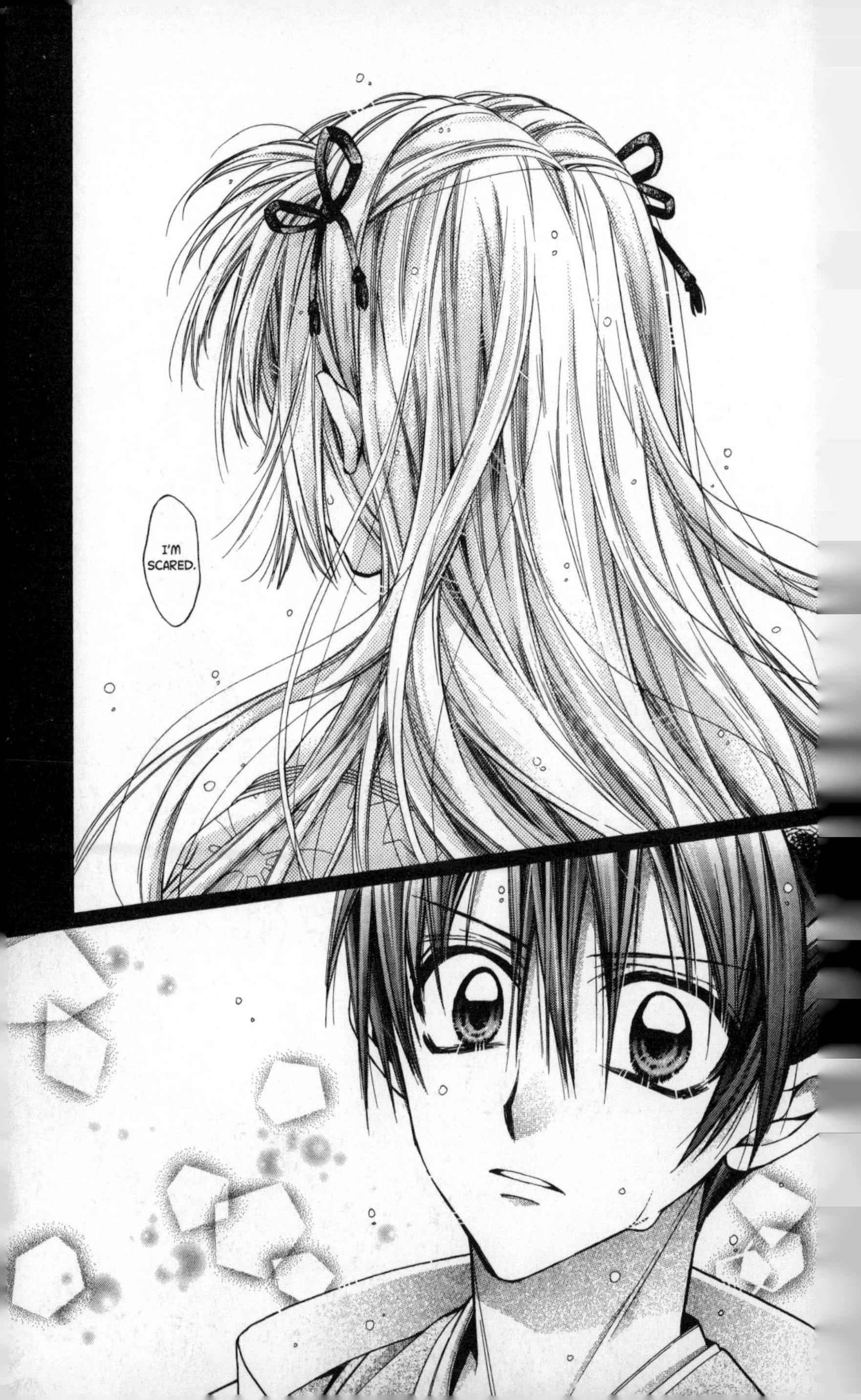
I'M SCARED.

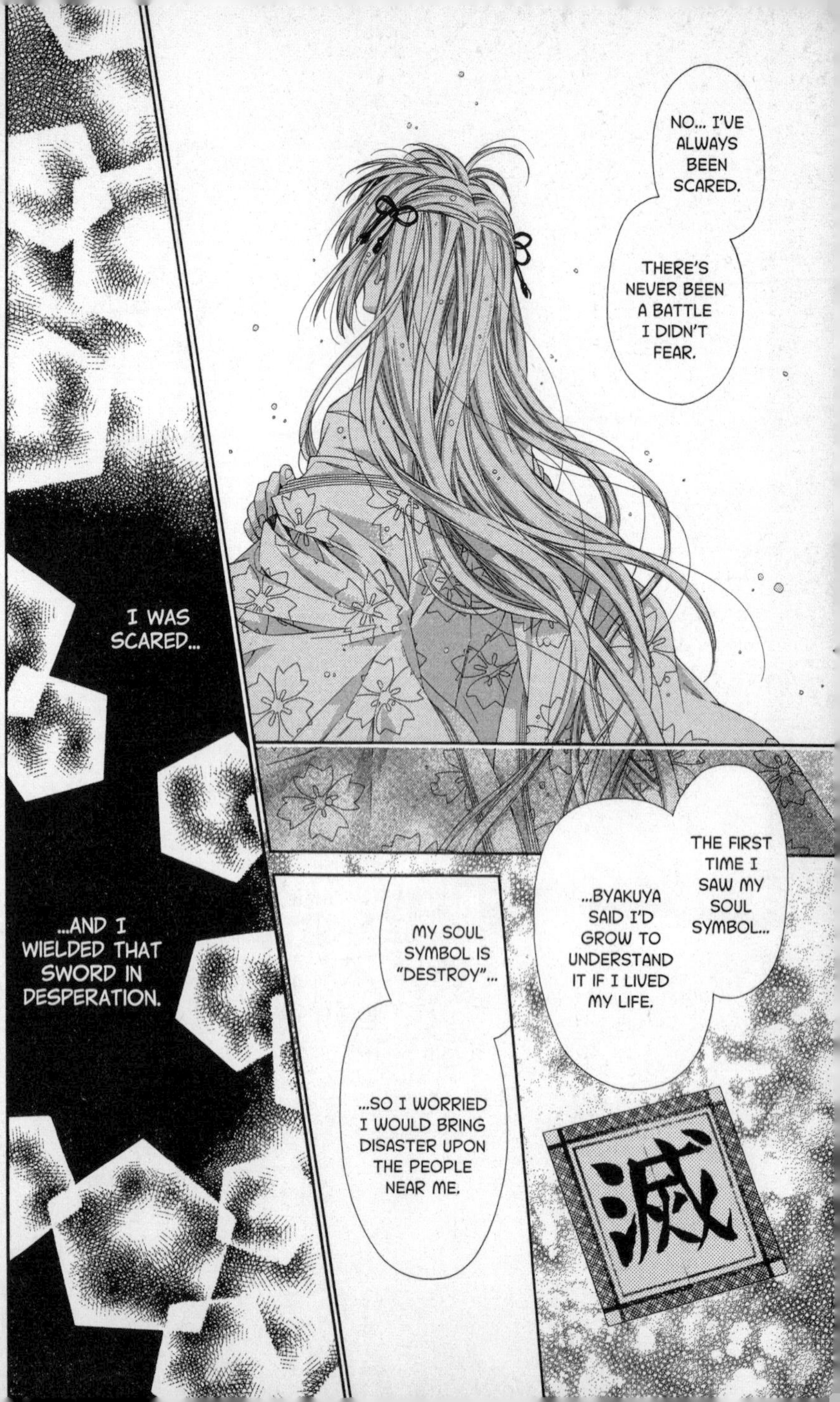
NO... I'VE ALWAYS BEEN SCARED.
THERE'S NEVER BEEN A BATTLE I DIDN'T FEAR.
THE FIRST TIME I SAW MY SOUL SYMBOL...
...BYAKUYA SAID I'D GROW TO UNDERSTAND IT IF I LIVED MY LIFE.
MY SOUL SYMBOL IS "DESTROY"...
...SO I WORRIED I WOULD BRING DISASTER UPON THE PEOPLE NEAR ME.
滅
I WAS SCARED...
...AND I WIELDED THAT SWORD IN DESPERATION.

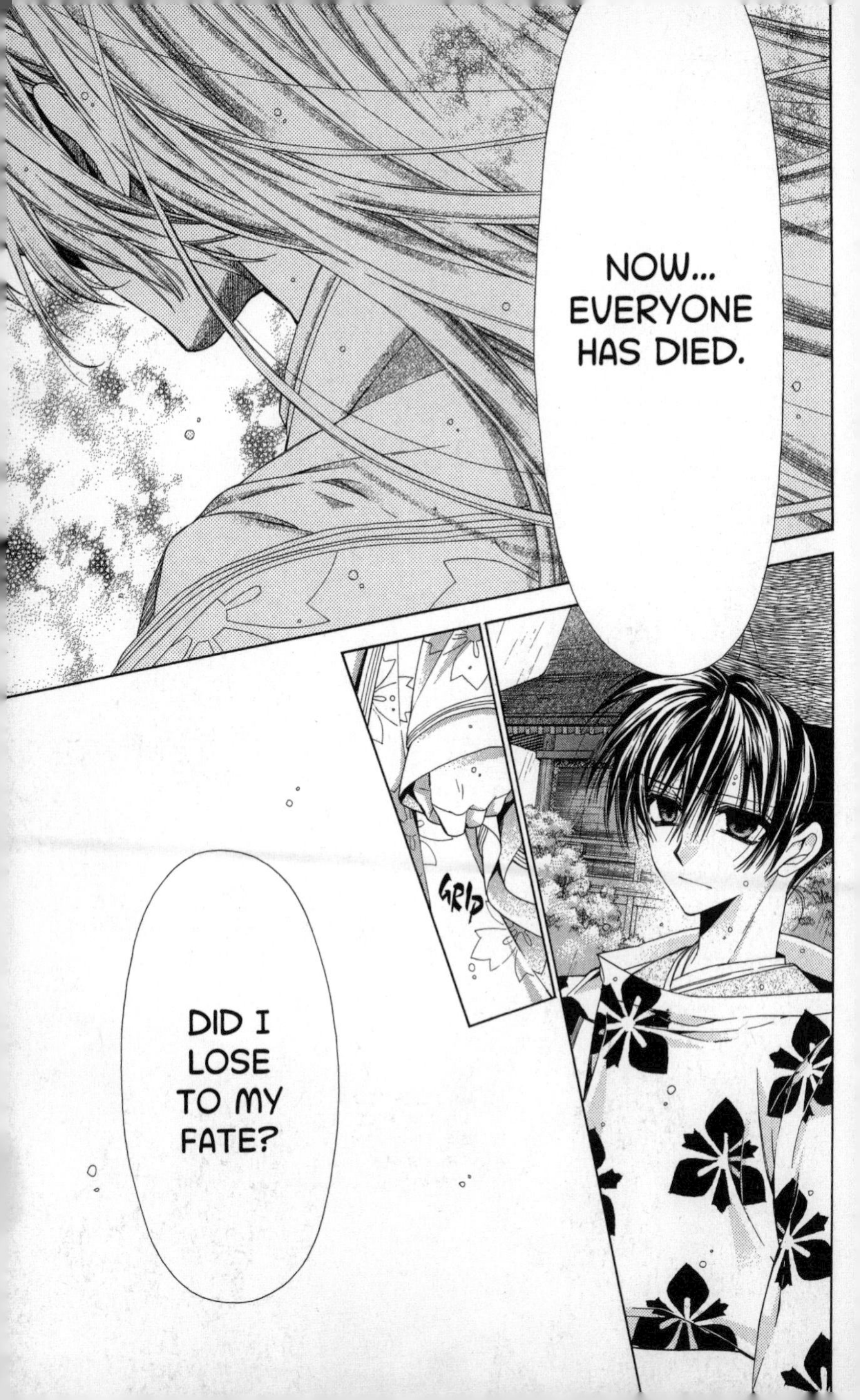
NOW... EVERYONE HAS DIED.
GRIP
DID I LOSE TO MY FATE?

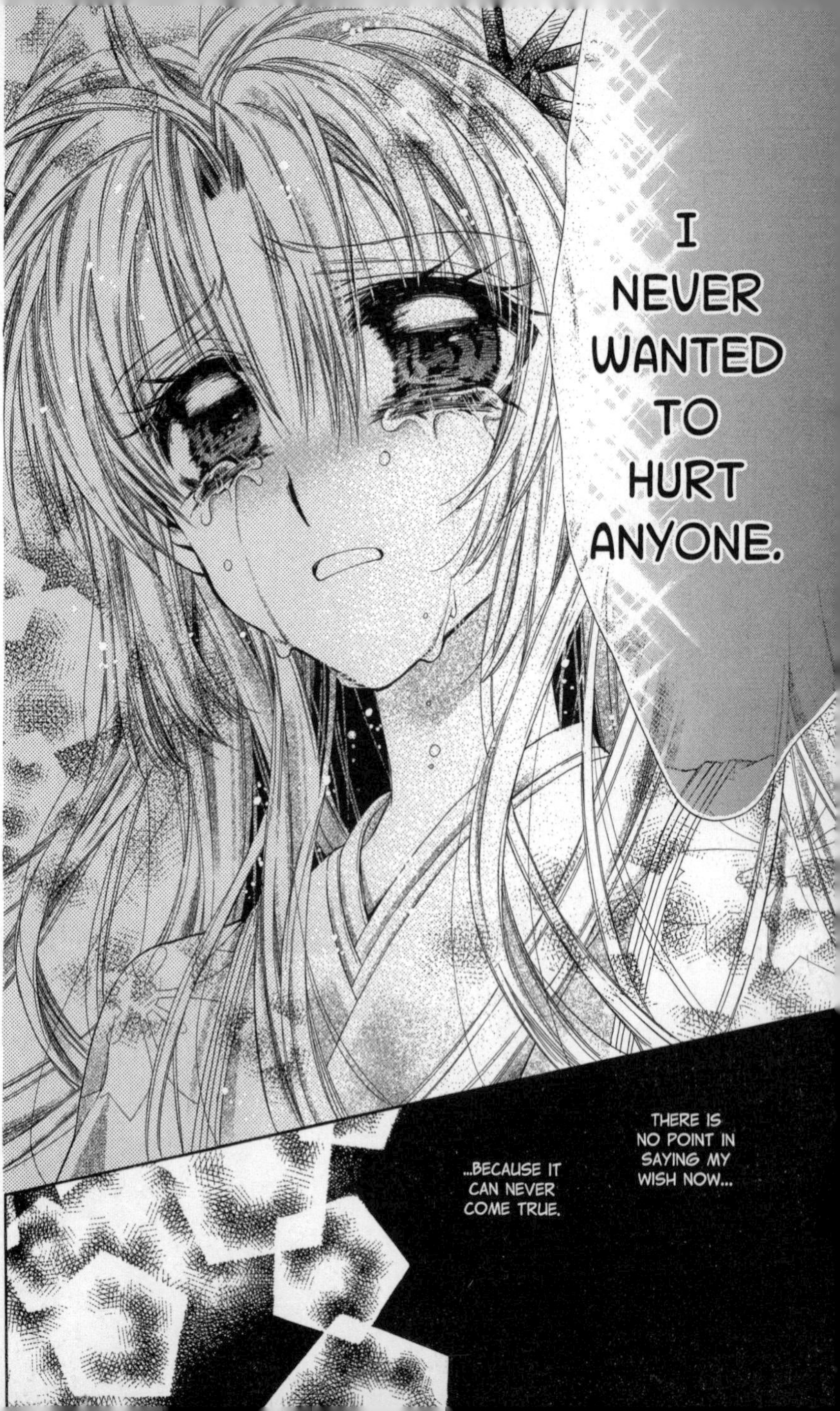
I NEVER WANTED TO HURT ANYONE.
THERE IS NO POINT IN SAYING MY WISH NOW...
...BECAUSE IT CAN NEVER COME TRUE.

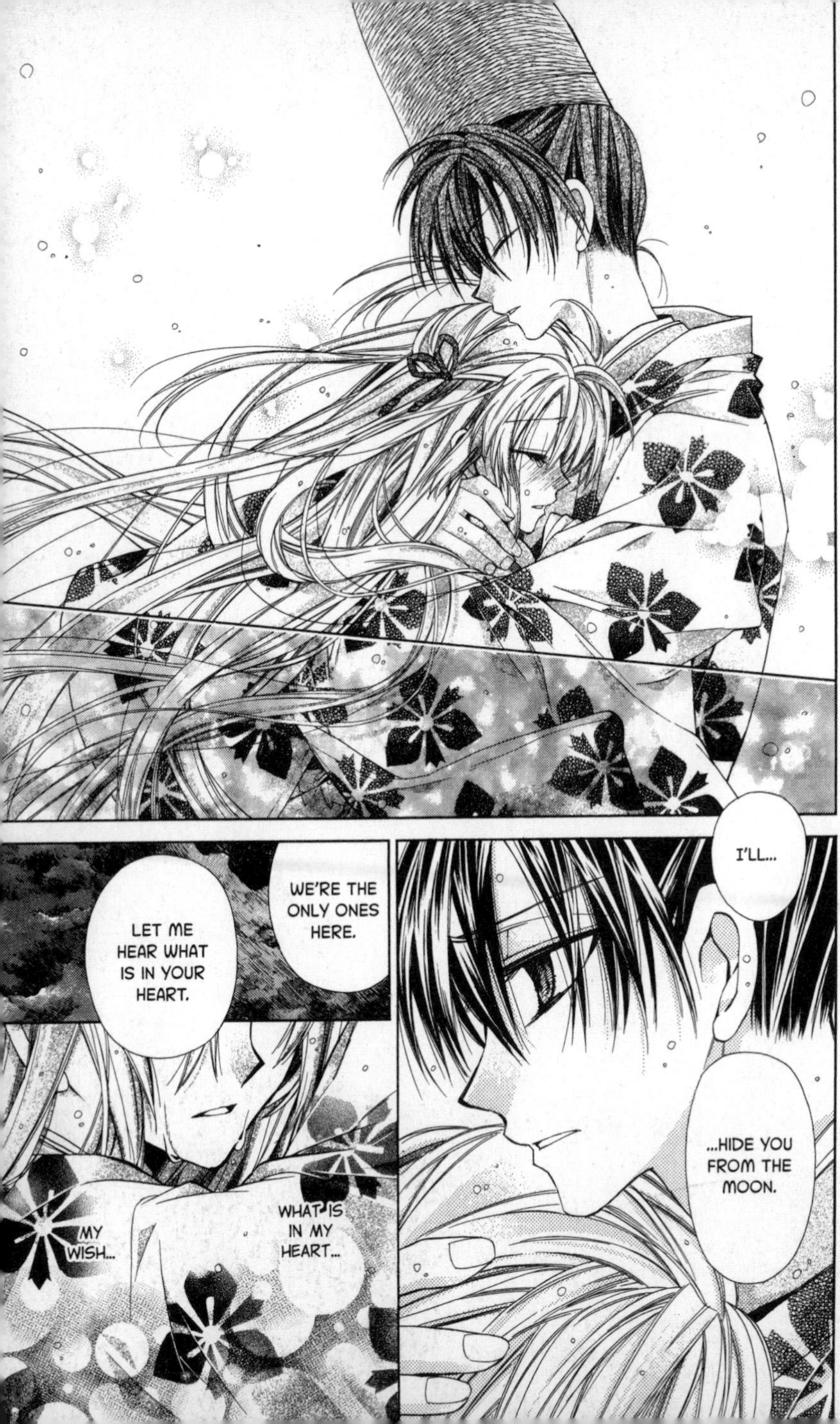
I'LL...
...HIDE YOU FROM THE MOON.
WE'RE THE ONLY ONES HERE.
LET ME HEAR WHAT IS IN YOUR HEART.
WHAT IS IN MY HEART...
MY WISH...

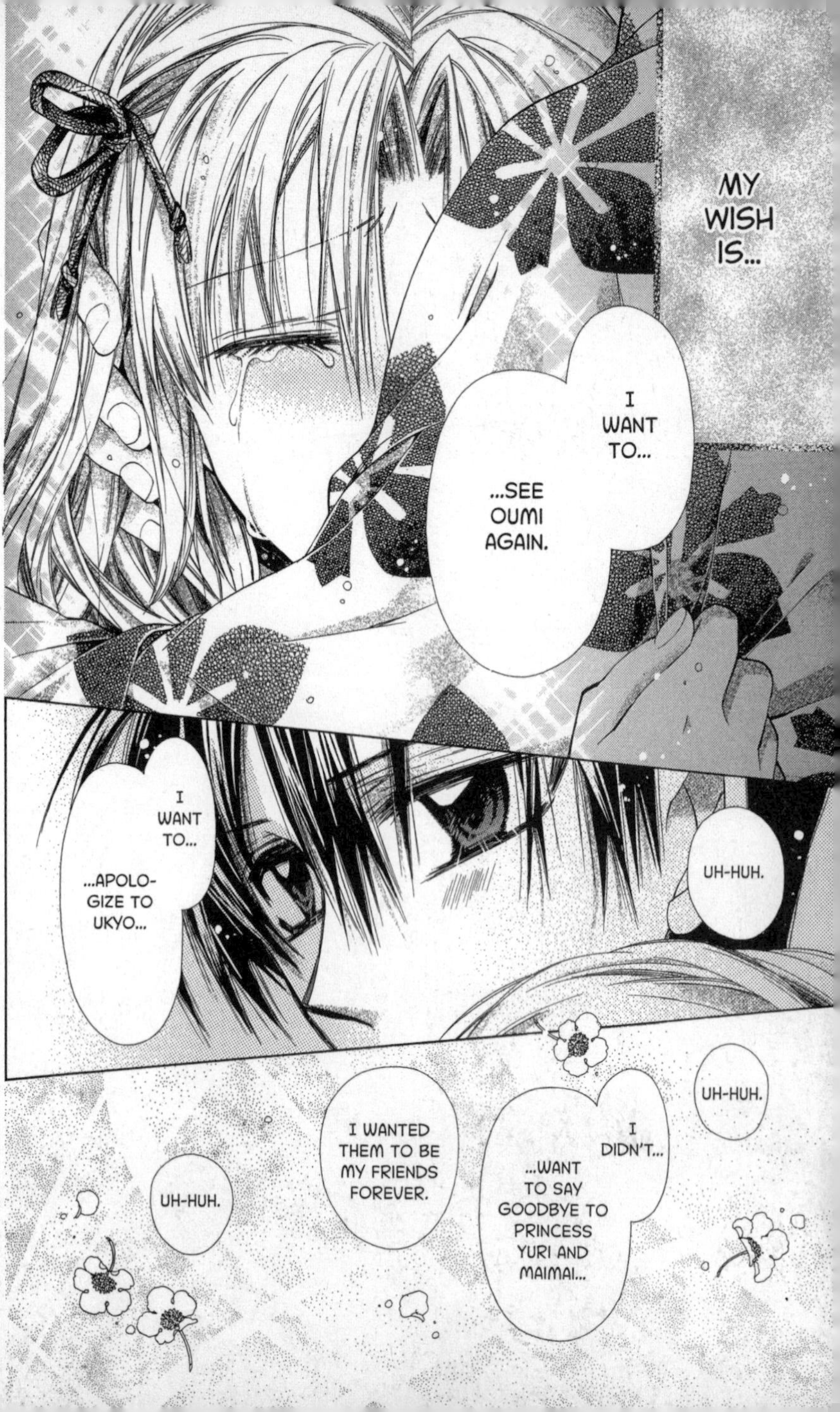
MY WISH IS...
I WANT TO... ...SEE OUMI AGAIN.
UH-HUH.
I WANT TO... ...APOLOGIZE TO UKYO...
UH-HUH.
I DIDN'T... ...WANT TO SAY GOODBYE TO PRINCESS YURI AND MAIMAI...
I WANTED THEM TO BE MY FRIENDS FOREVER.
UH-HUH.

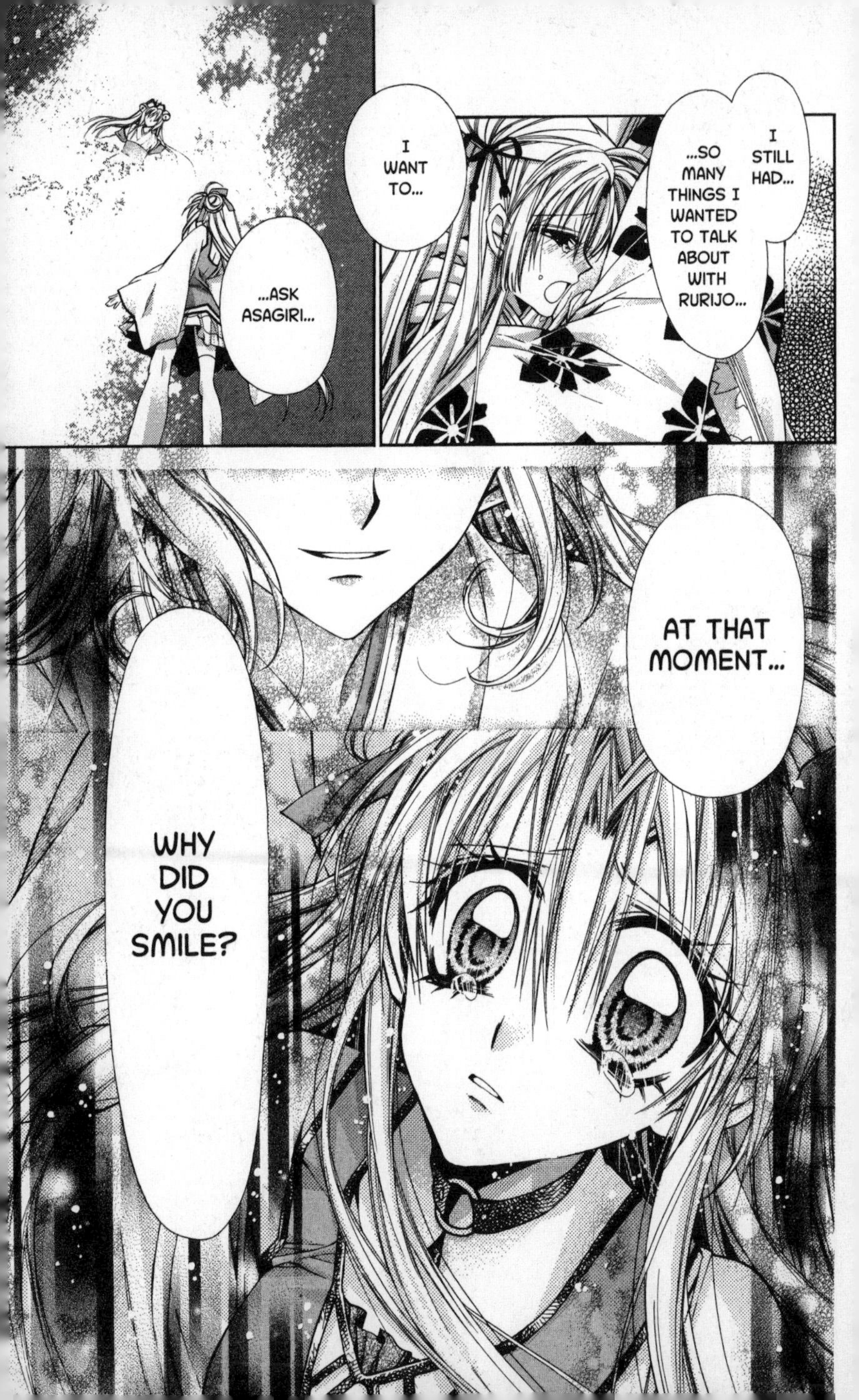
I STILL HAD...
...SO MANY THINGS I WANTED TO TALK ABOUT WITH RURIJO...
I WANT TO...
...ASK ASAGIRI...
AT THAT MOMENT...
WHY DID YOU SMILE?

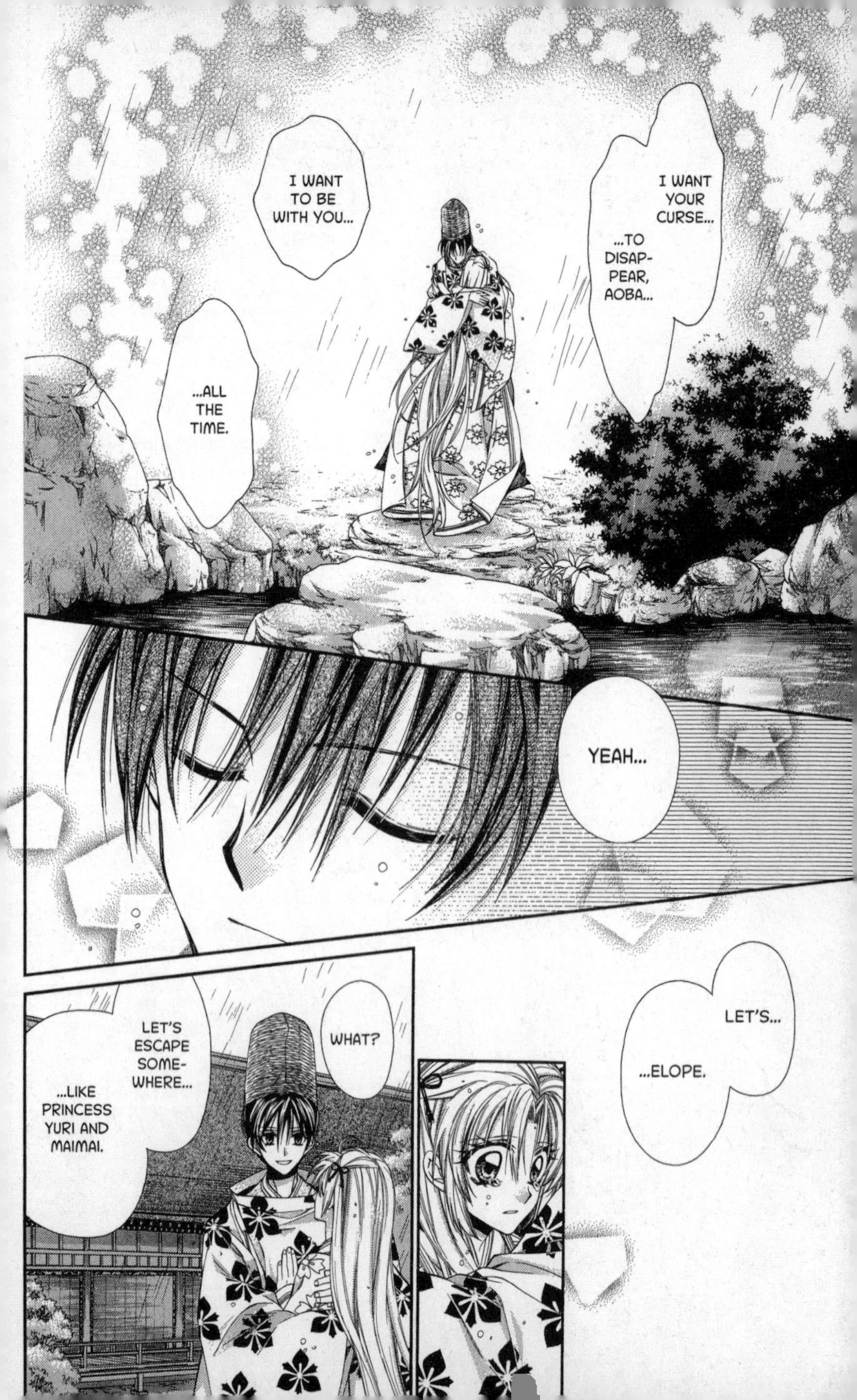
I WANT YOUR CURSE...
...TO DISAPPEAR, AOBA...
I WANT TO BE WITH YOU...
...ALL THE TIME.
YEAH...
LET'S...
...ELOPE.
WHAT?
LET'S ESCAPE SOMEWHERE...
...LIKE PRINCESS YURI AND MAIMAI.

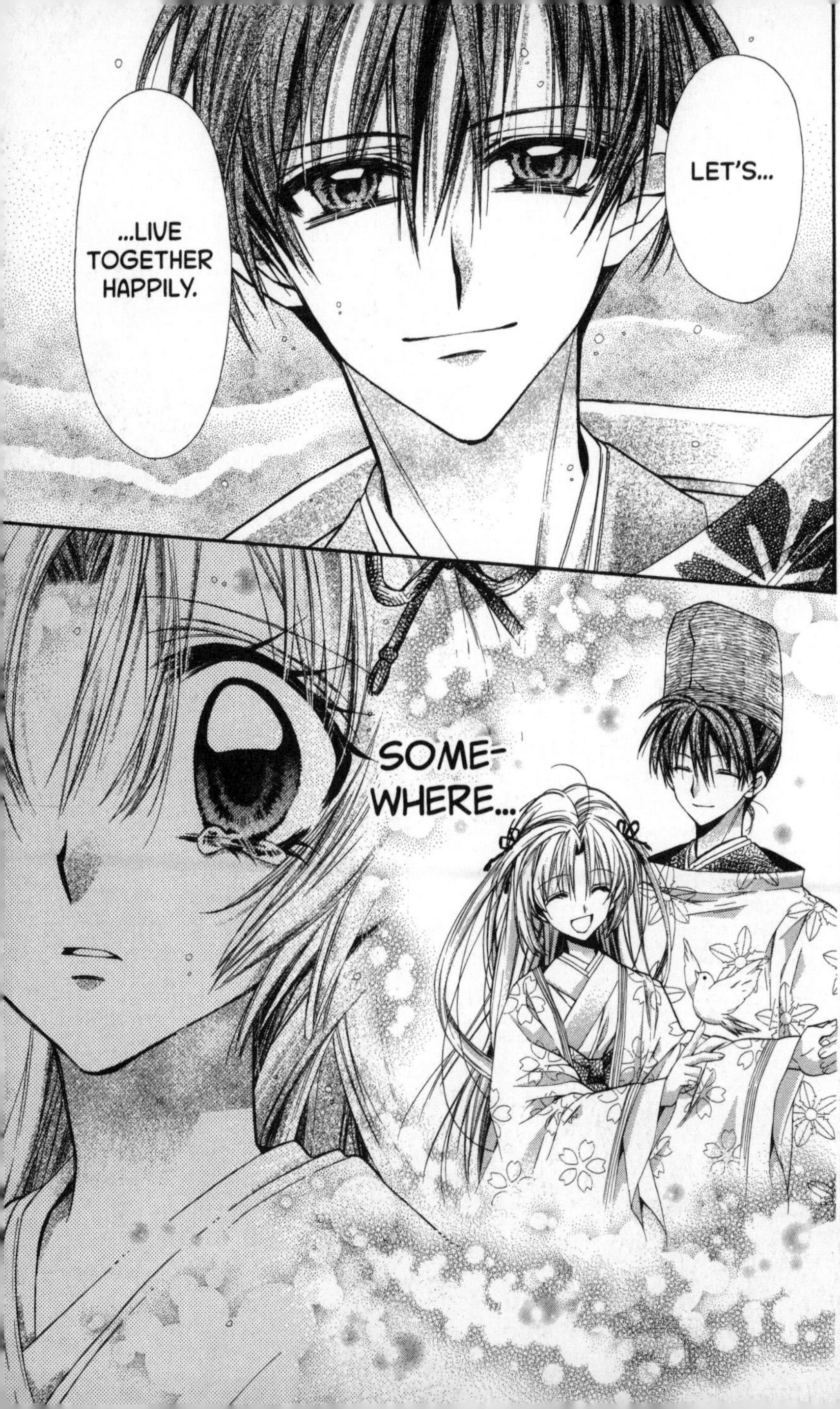
LET'S...
...LIVE TOGETHER HAPPILY.
SOME-WHERE...

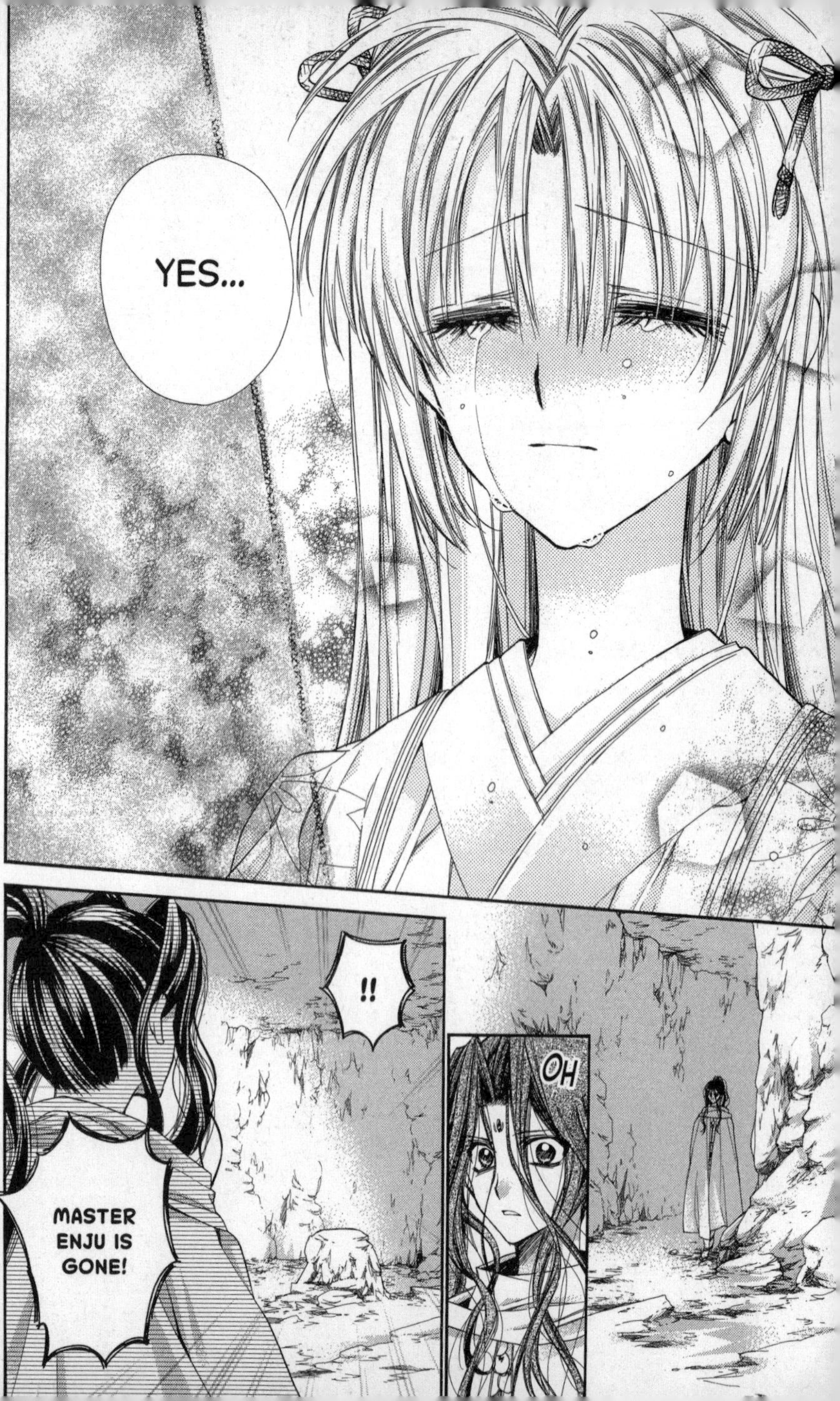
YES...
OH
!!
MASTER ENJU IS GONE!

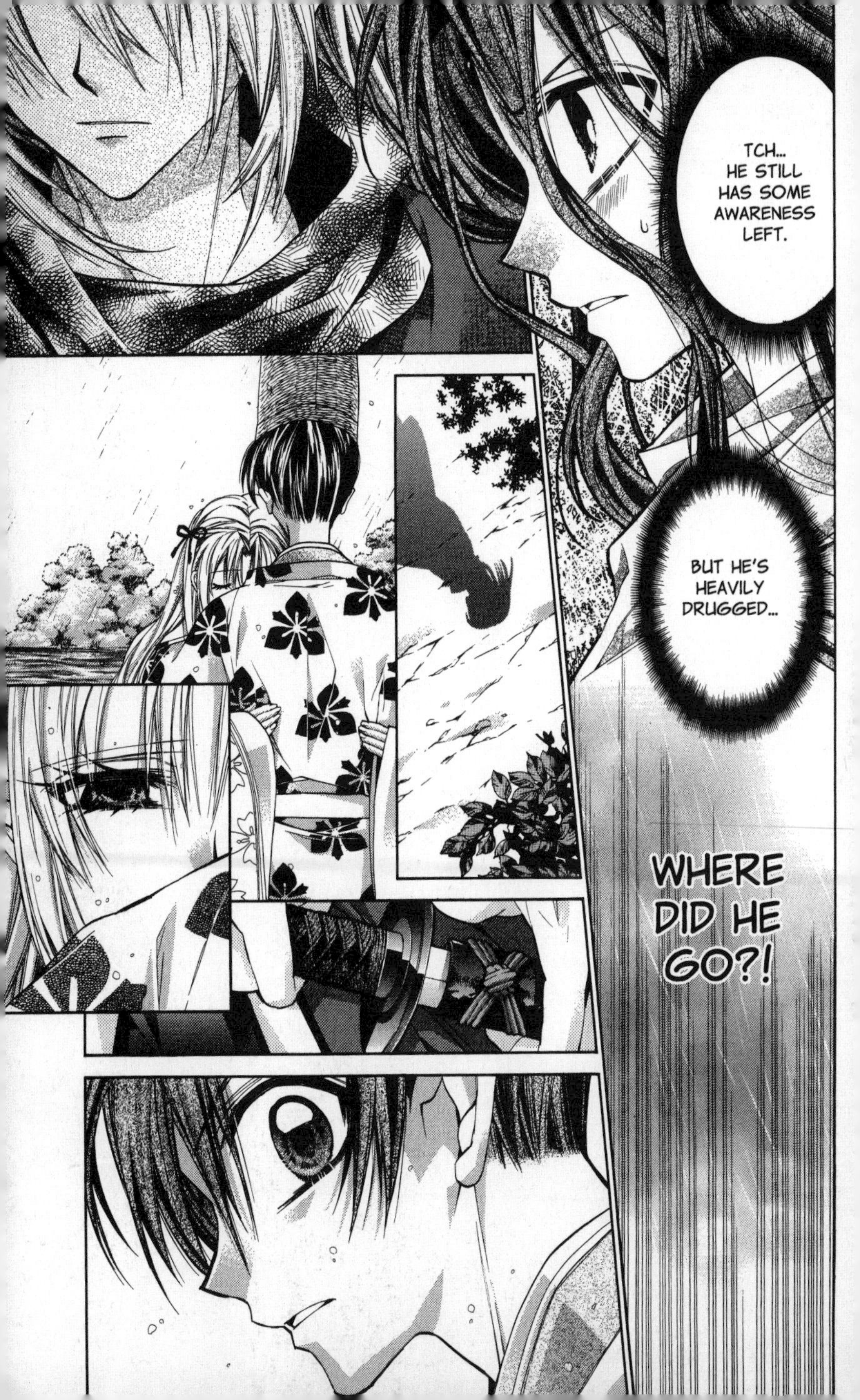
TCH... HE STILL HAS SOME AWARENESS LEFT.
BUT HE'S HEAVILY DRUGGED...
WHERE DID HE GO?!

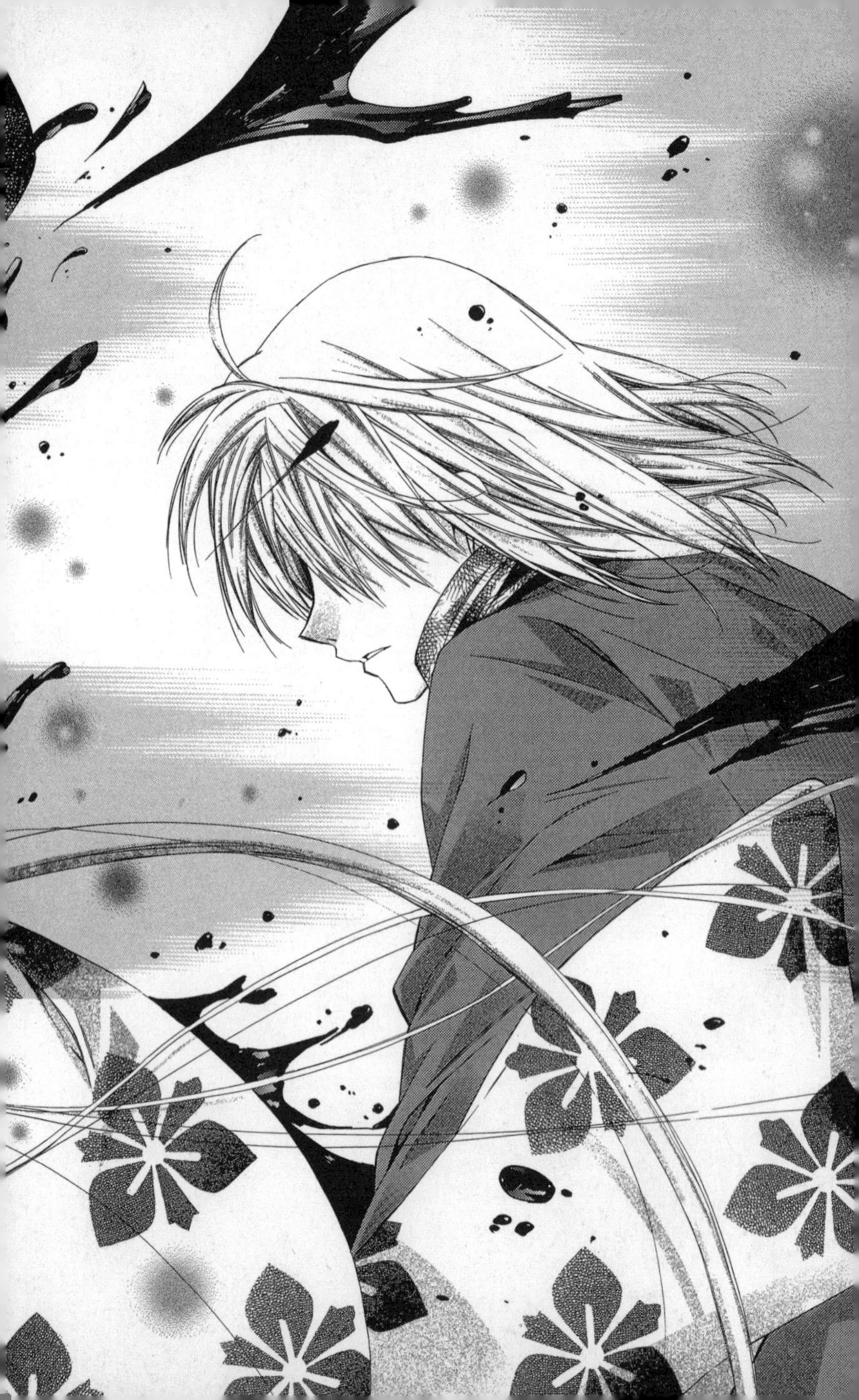

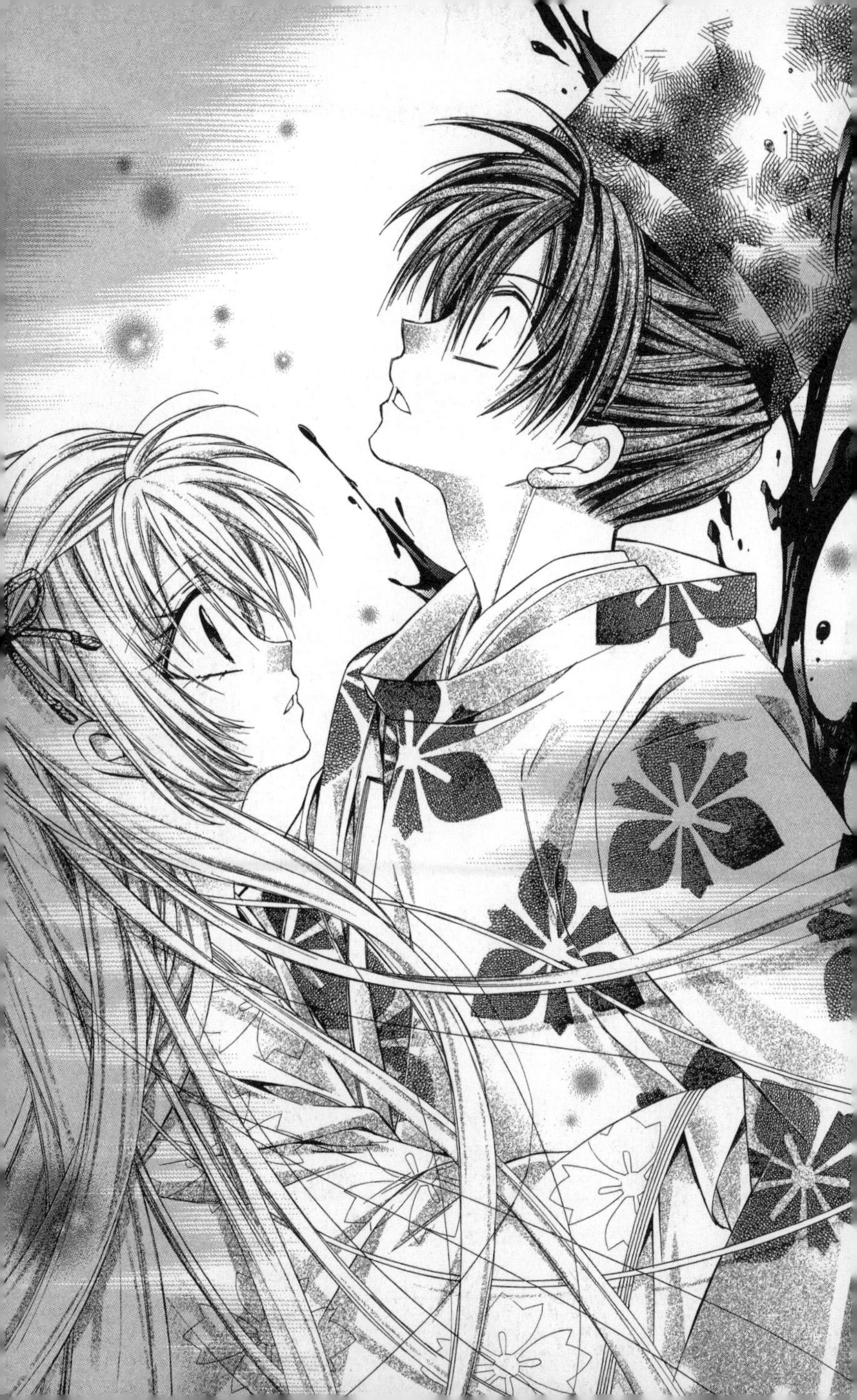

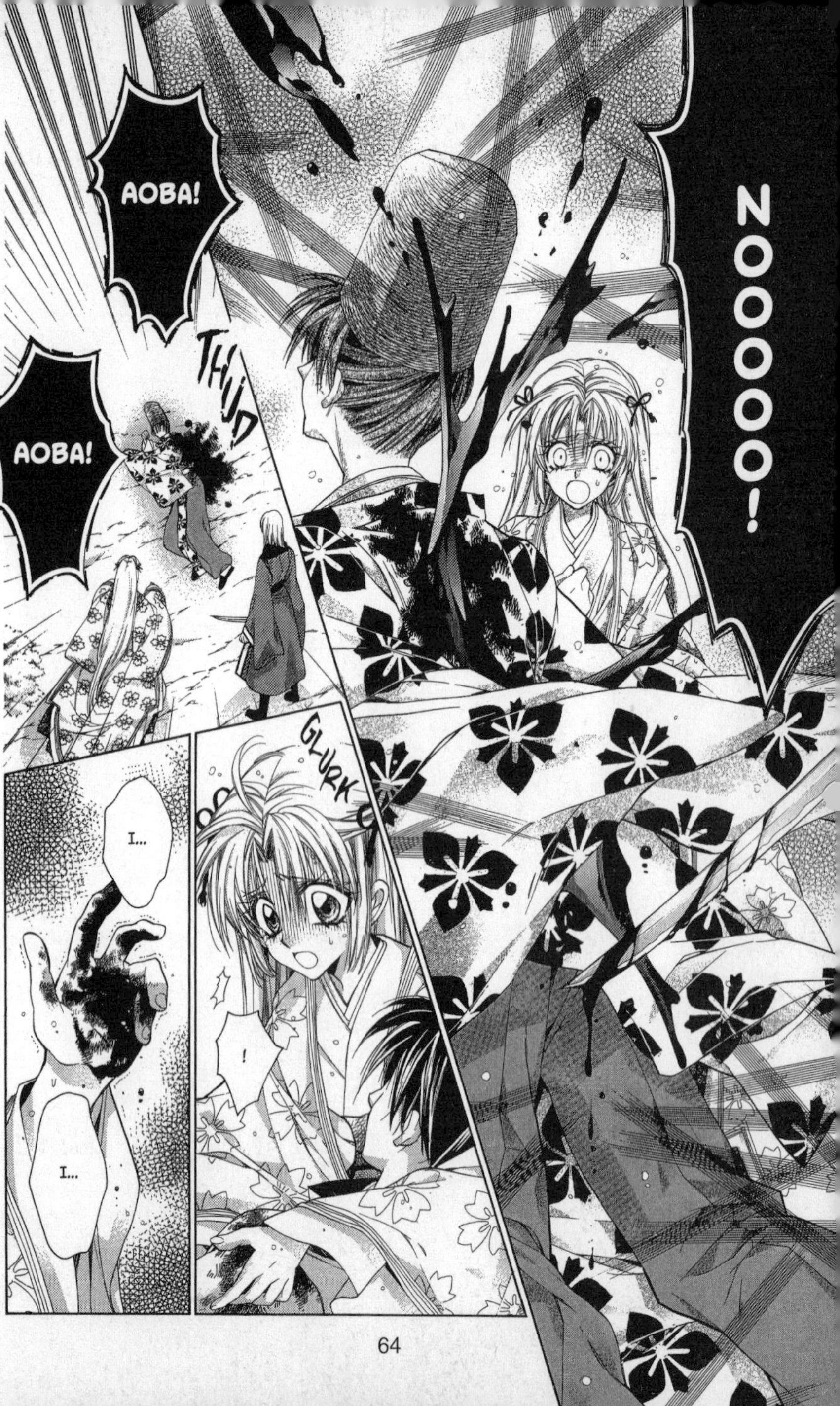
NOOOOO!
AOBA!
AOBA!
THUD!
GLURK
!
I...
I...

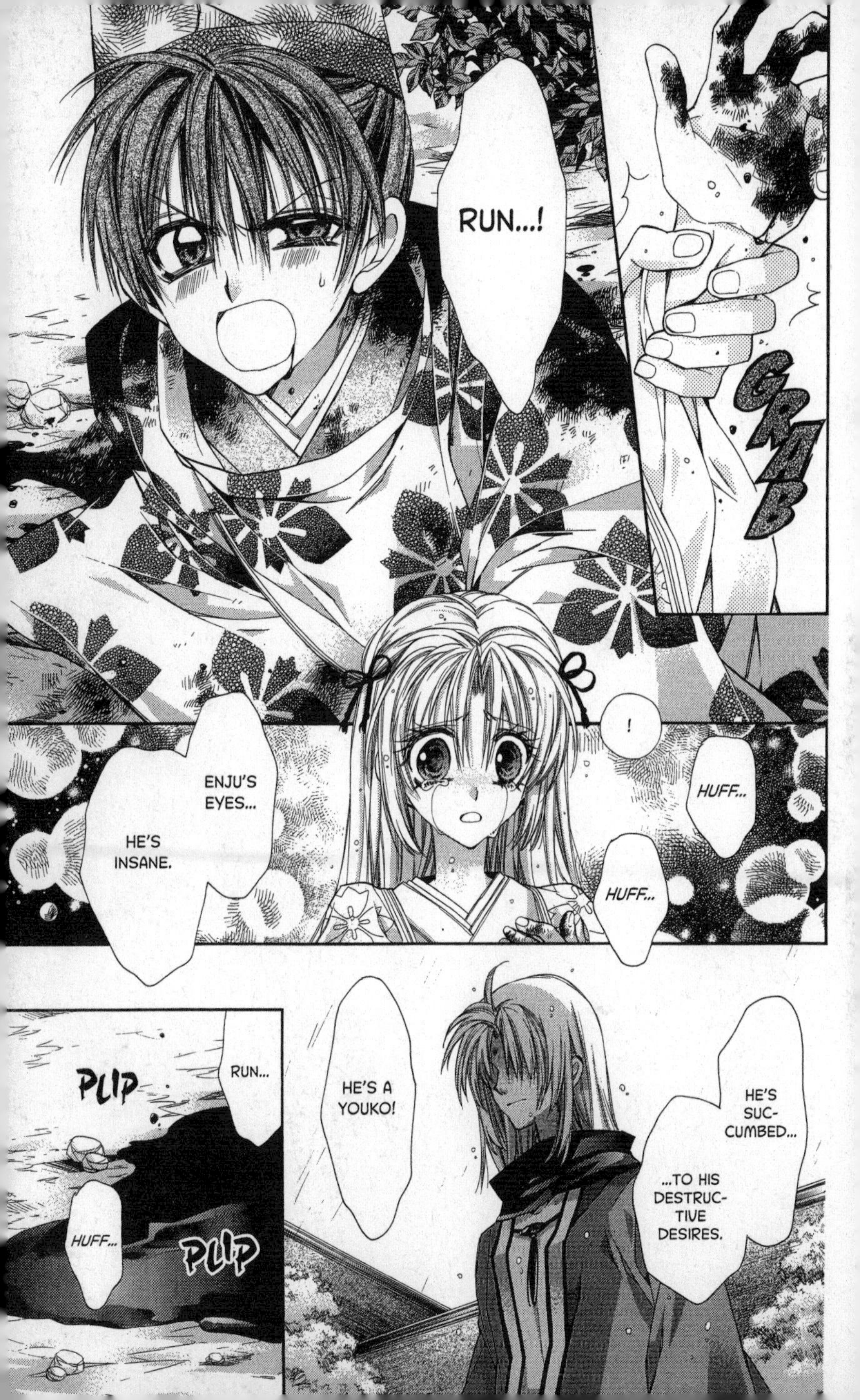
GRAB
RUN...!
!
HUFF...
HUFF...
ENJU'S EYES...
HE'S INSANE.
HE'S SUC-CUMBED...
...TO HIS DESTRUC-TIVE DESIRES.
HE'S A YOUKO!
RUN...
PLIP
PLIP
HUFF...

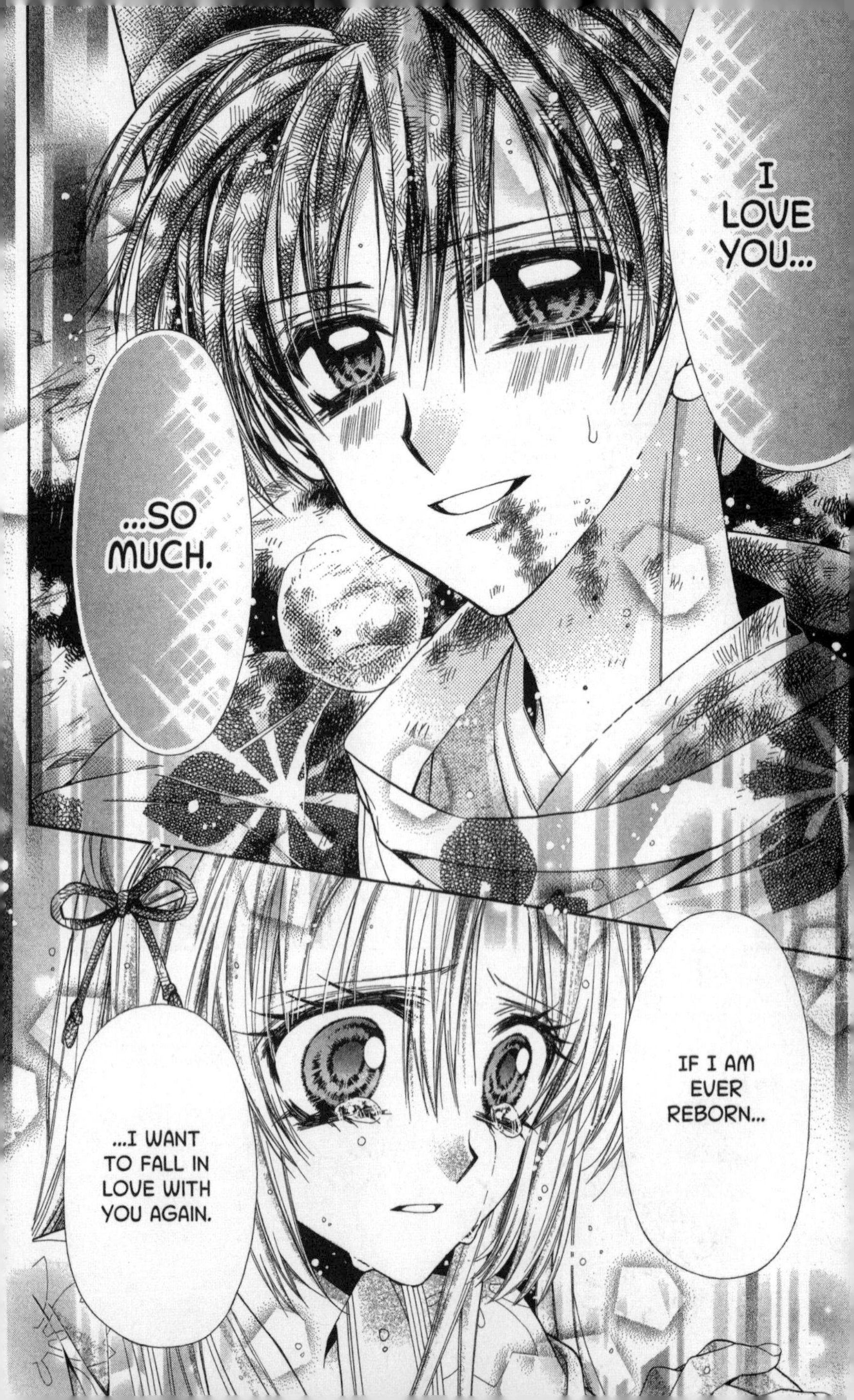
I LOVE YOU...
...SO MUCH.
IF I AM EVER REBORN...
...I WANT TO FALL IN LOVE WITH YOU AGAIN.

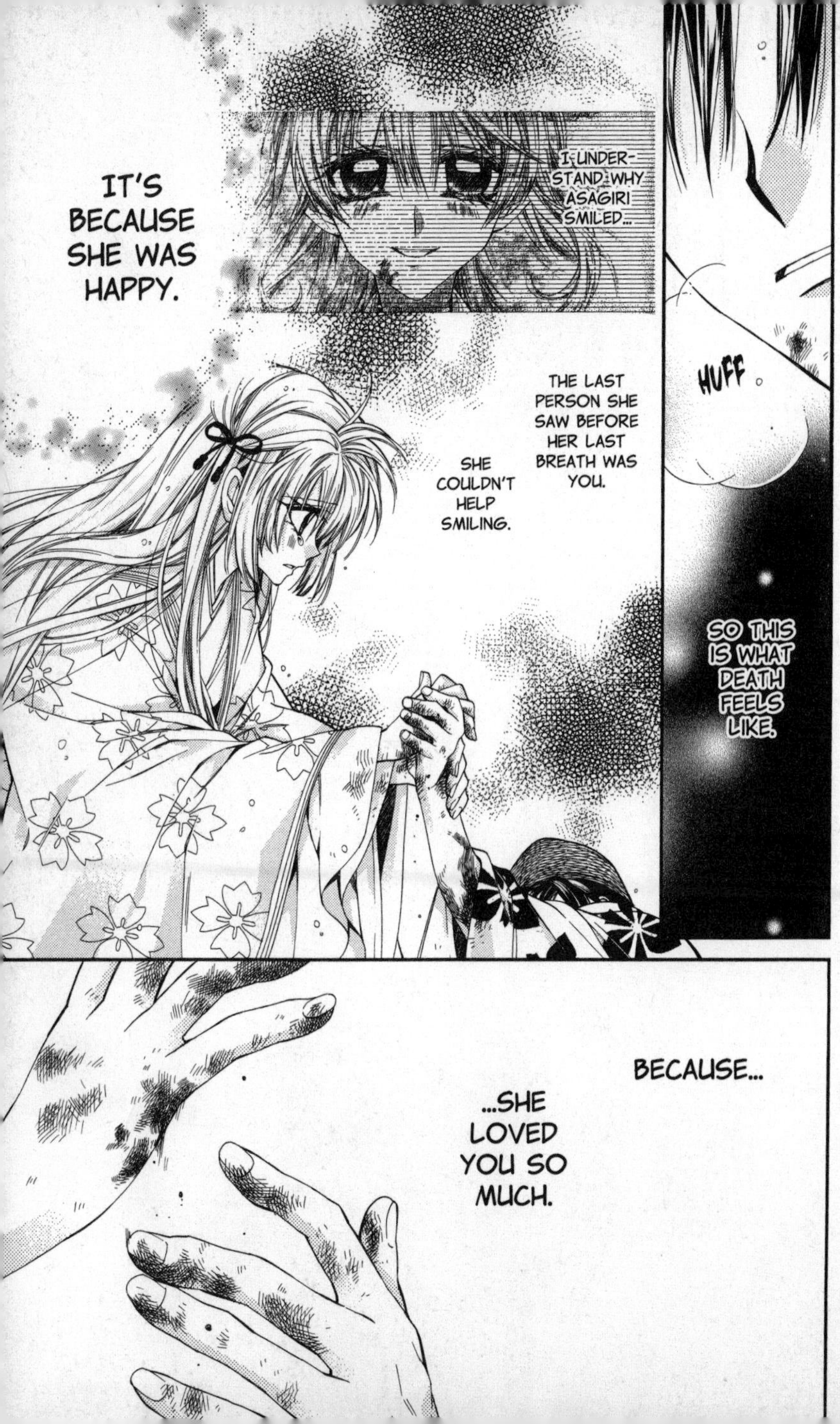
HUFF
SO THIS IS WHAT DEATH FEELS LIKE.
I UNDER-STAND WHY ASAGIRI SMILED...
IT'S BECAUSE SHE WAS HAPPY.
THE LAST PERSON SHE SAW BEFORE HER LAST BREATH WAS YOU.
SHE COULDN'T HELP SMILING.
BECAUSE...
...SHE LOVED YOU SO MUCH.

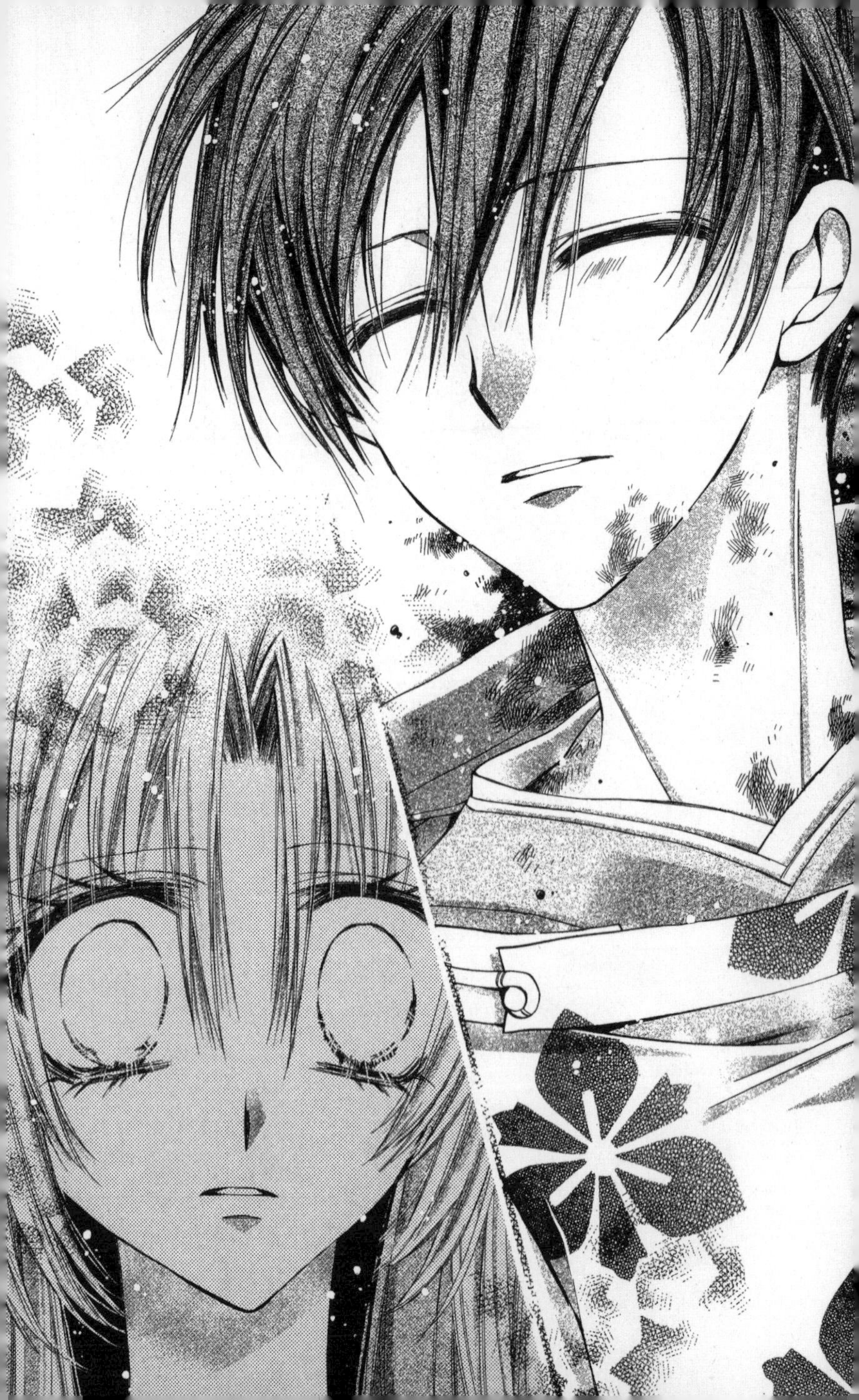

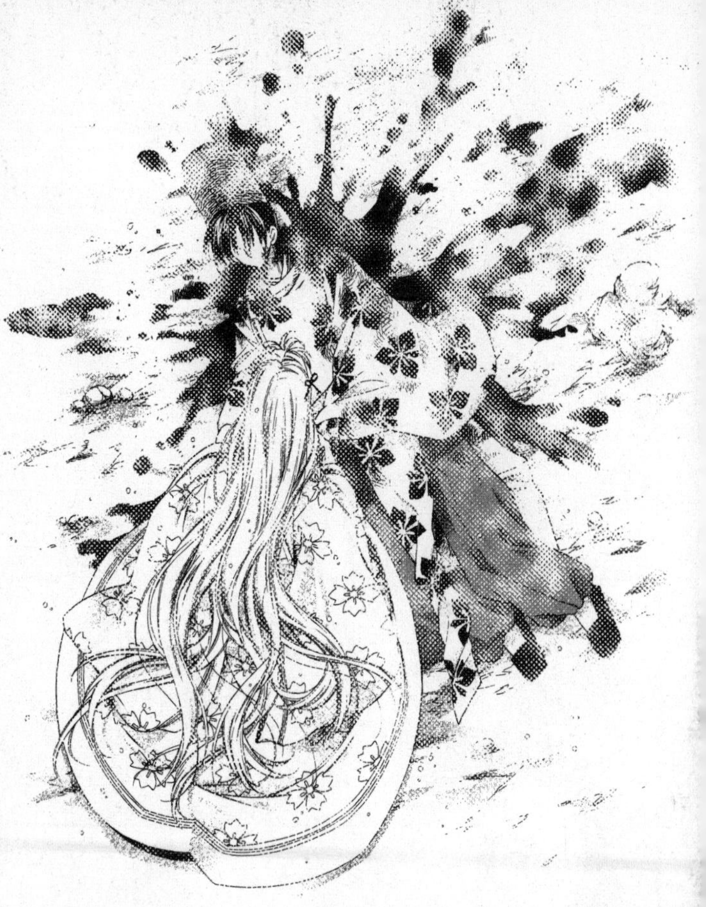

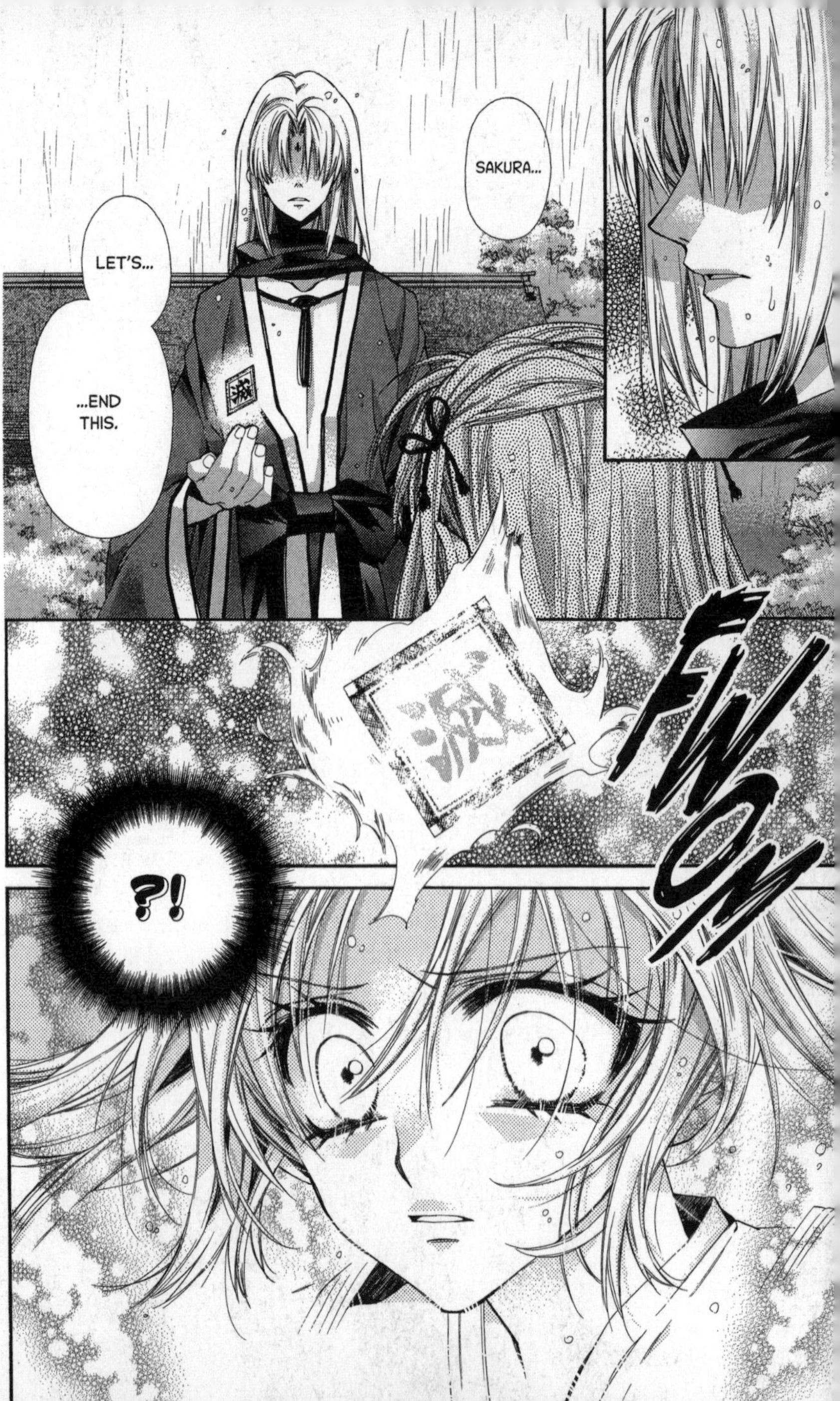
SAKURA...
LET'S...
...END THIS.
FWOOM
?!

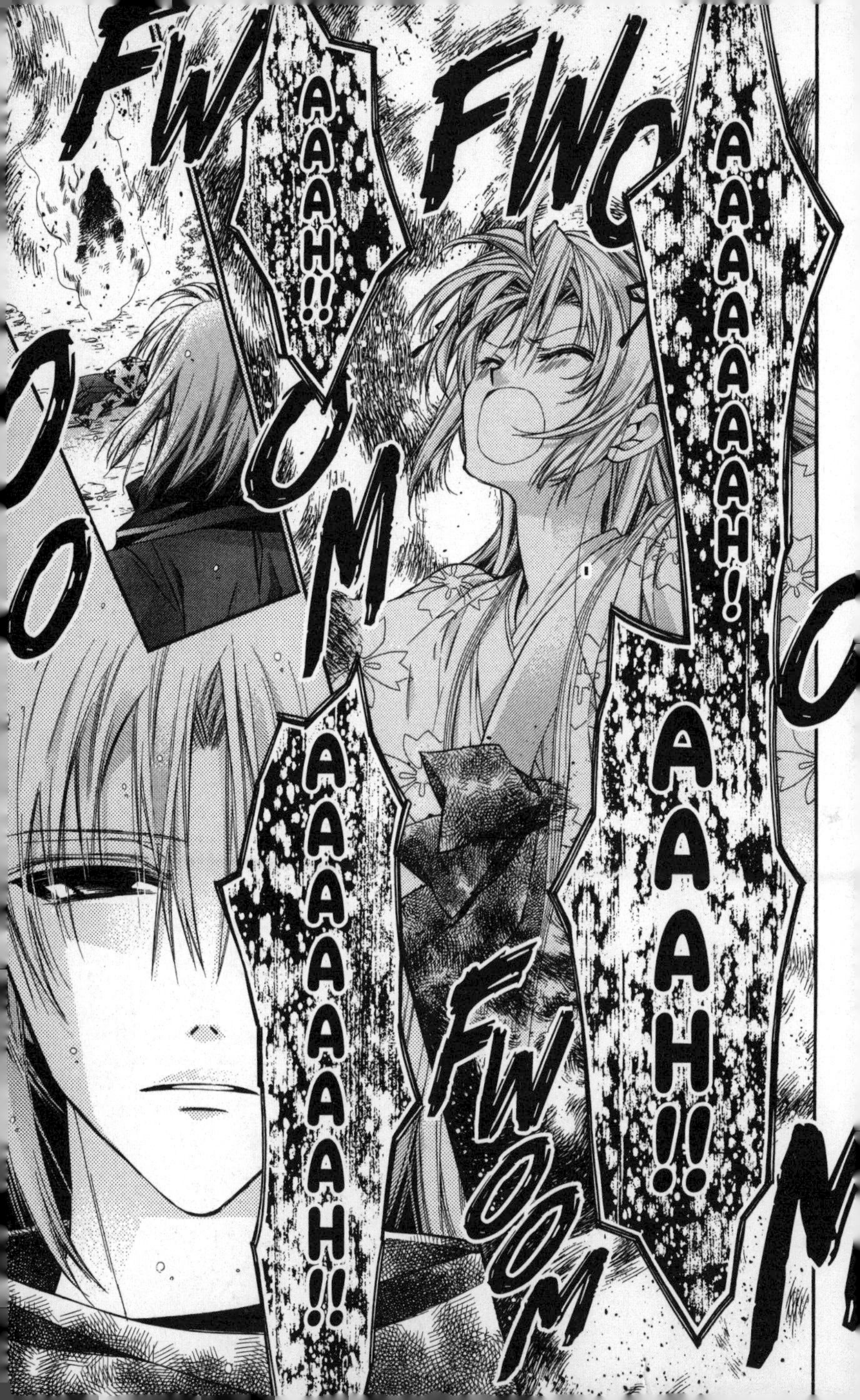
AAAAAAAAAH!
AAAAH!!
FWOOOM
AAAH!!
FWOOOM
AAAAAAAAAH!!
FWOOOM

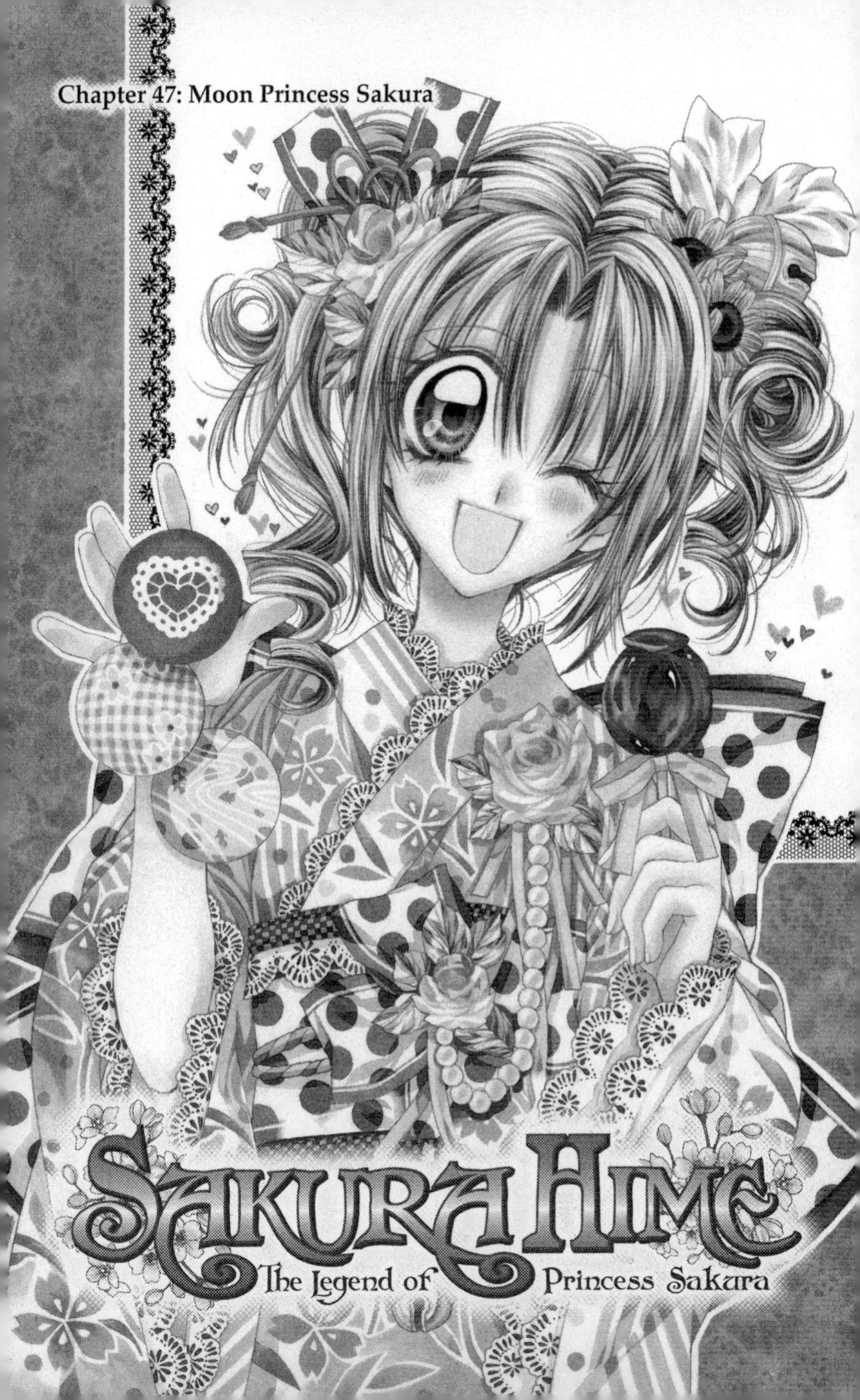
Chapter 47: Moon Princess Sakura
Sakura Hime
The Legend of Princess Sakura

Sakura Hime
The Legend of Princess Sakura

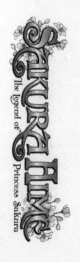

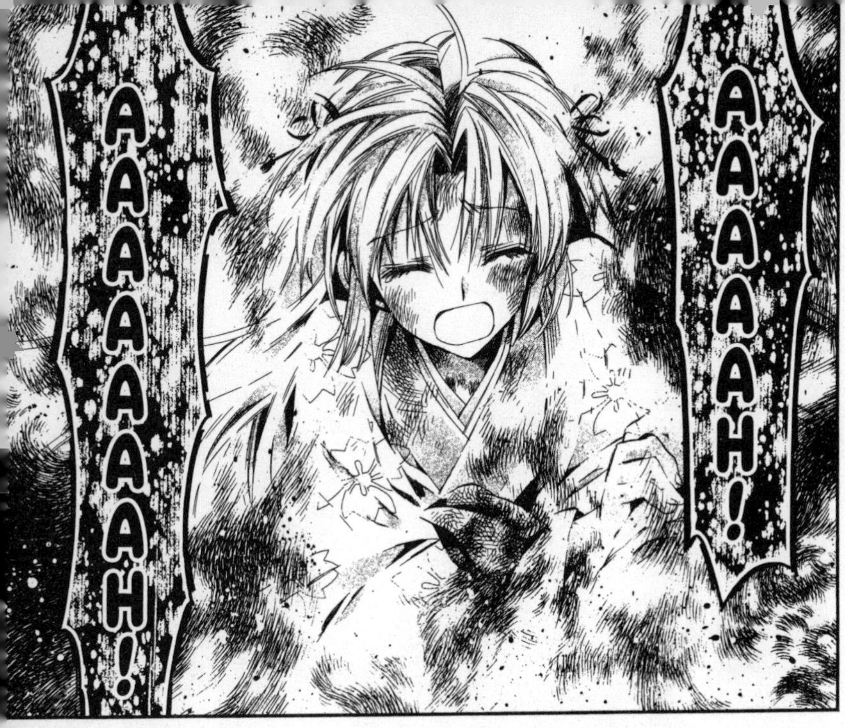
AAAAAH!
AAAAAAAH!

Chapter 47: Moon Princess Sakura

※ I'm giving away the story.

The story is reaching its climax. All the things I had been planning when I started working on this series have begun to appear. (Of course, there are many things that turned out differently than I had expected after I had drawn it.) Tearing apart the soul symbol seemed like a good way to show everyone (the readers) that Sakura had overcome her fate. I had been planning this scene from the start.

When I first came up with the soul symbols, I thought it'd be interesting if the symbols of two people combined to make a single word, but I didn't get around to doing that. The reason Enju ended up like this is because Rurijo is gone, but I don't think this would have occurred if he had realized his feelings earlier. (He loved Rurijo.) His head has basically "short-circuited" because he hadn't realized that. (This has nothing to do with the manga, but I'm so glad I could use a foreign word here.♥)

It turns out what Enju wanted was Sakura → little sister, and Rurijo → lover. I feel sorry for Enju...

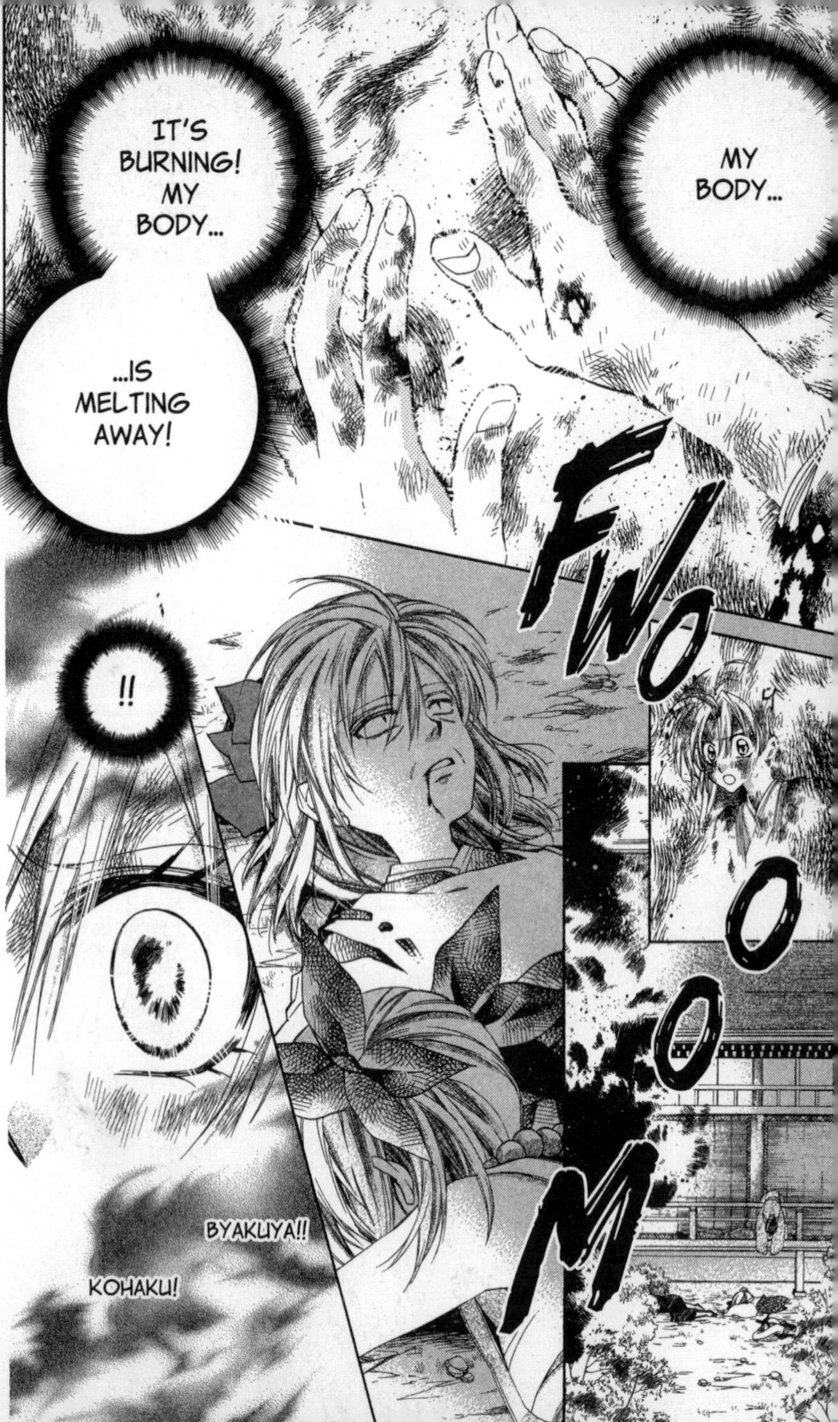
MY BODY...
IT'S BURNING! MY BODY...
...IS MELTING AWAY!
FWOOOOM
!!
BYAKUYA!!
KOHAKU!

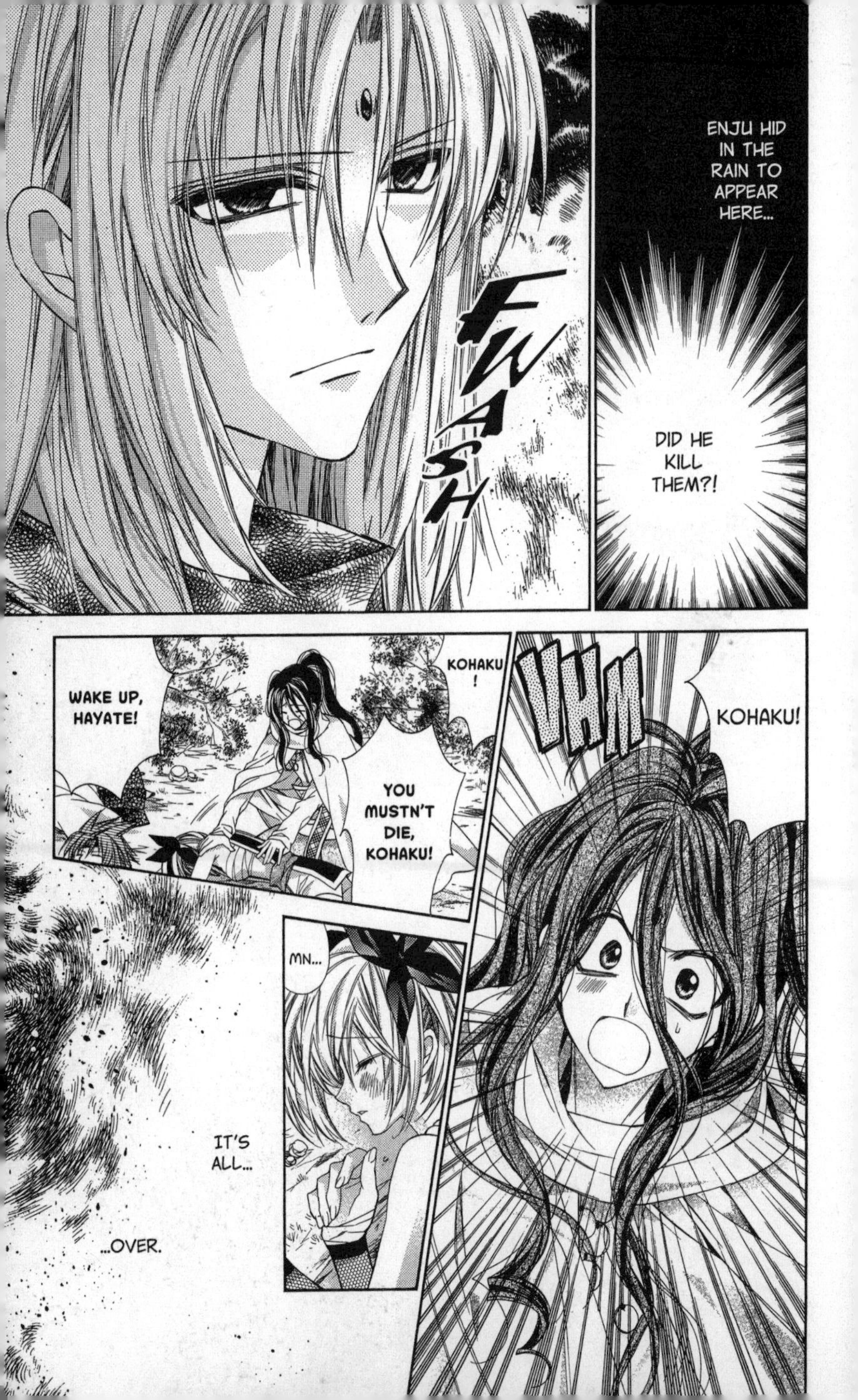
ENJU HID IN THE RAIN TO APPEAR HERE...
DID HE KILL THEM?!
FWASH
VHM
KOHAKU!
KOHAKU!
WAKE UP, HAYATE!
YOU MUSTN'T DIE, KOHAKU!
MN...
IT'S ALL...
...OVER.

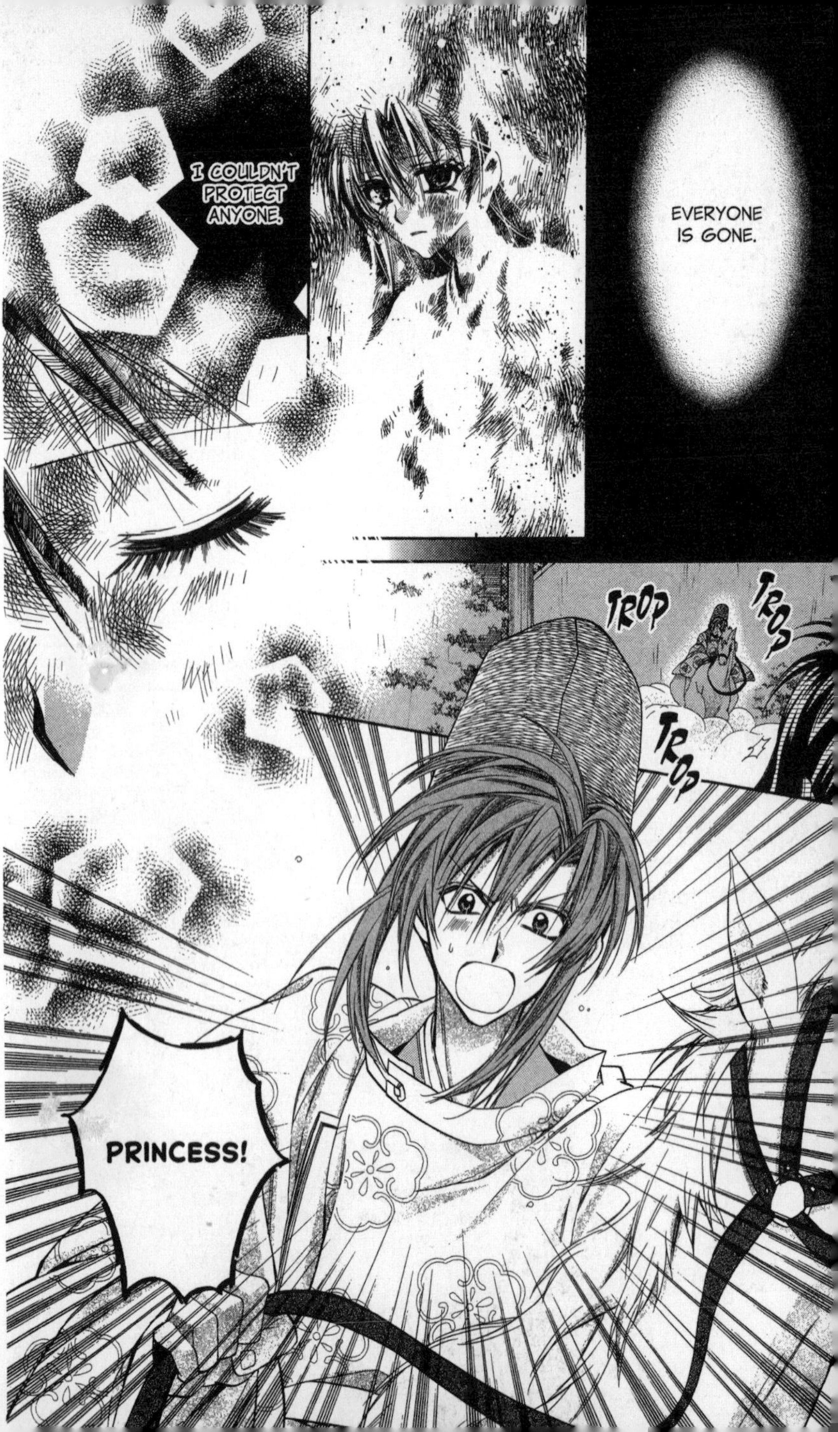
EVERYONE IS GONE.
I COULDN'T PROTECT ANYONE.
TROP
TROP
TROP
PRINCESS!

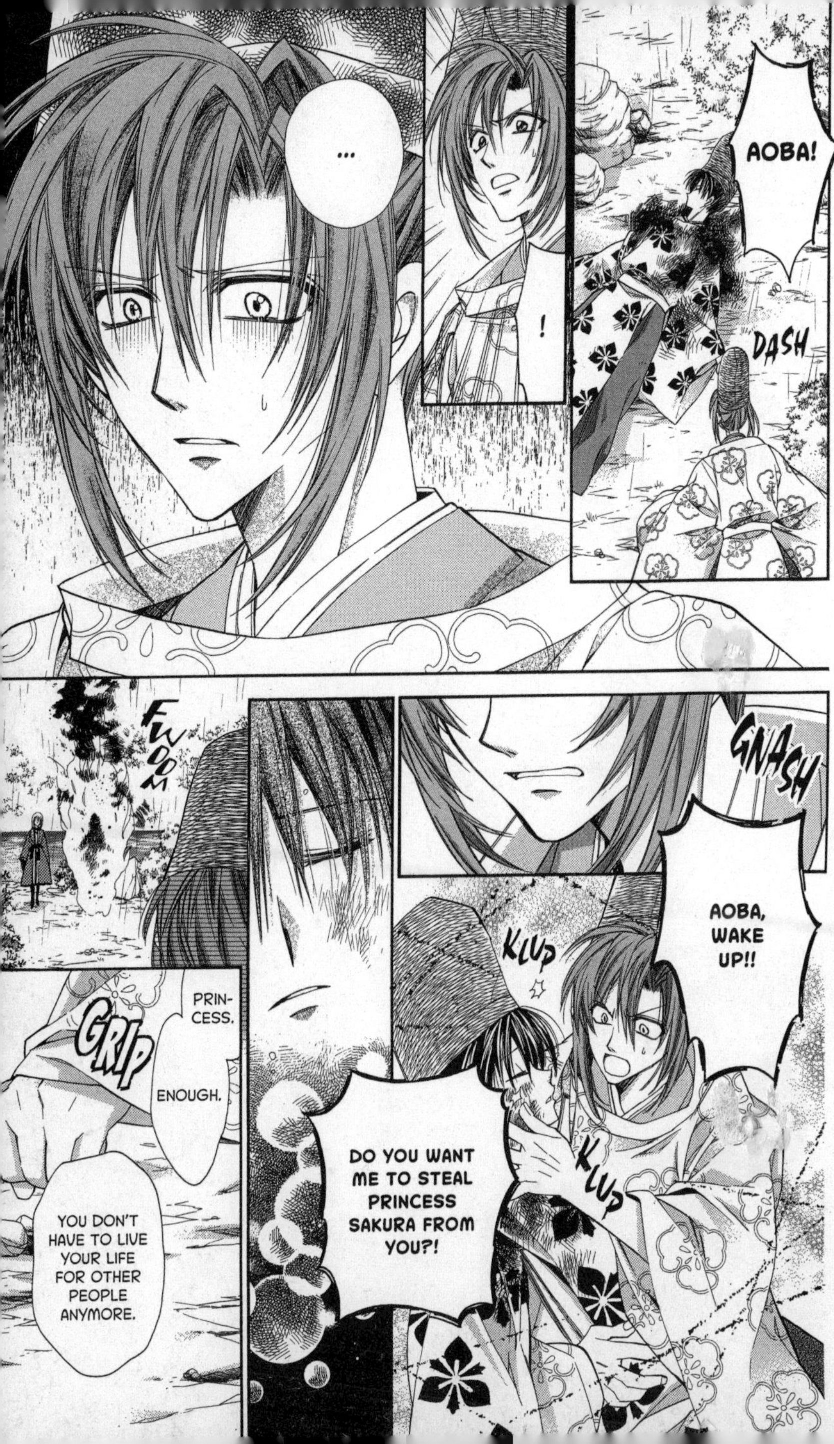
AOBA!
DASH
!
...
GNASH
AOBA, WAKE UP!!
KLUP
KLUP
DO YOU WANT ME TO STEAL PRINCESS SAKURA FROM YOU?!
FWOOOM
PRINCESS.
GRIP
ENOUGH.
YOU DON'T HAVE TO LIVE YOUR LIFE FOR OTHER PEOPLE ANYMORE.

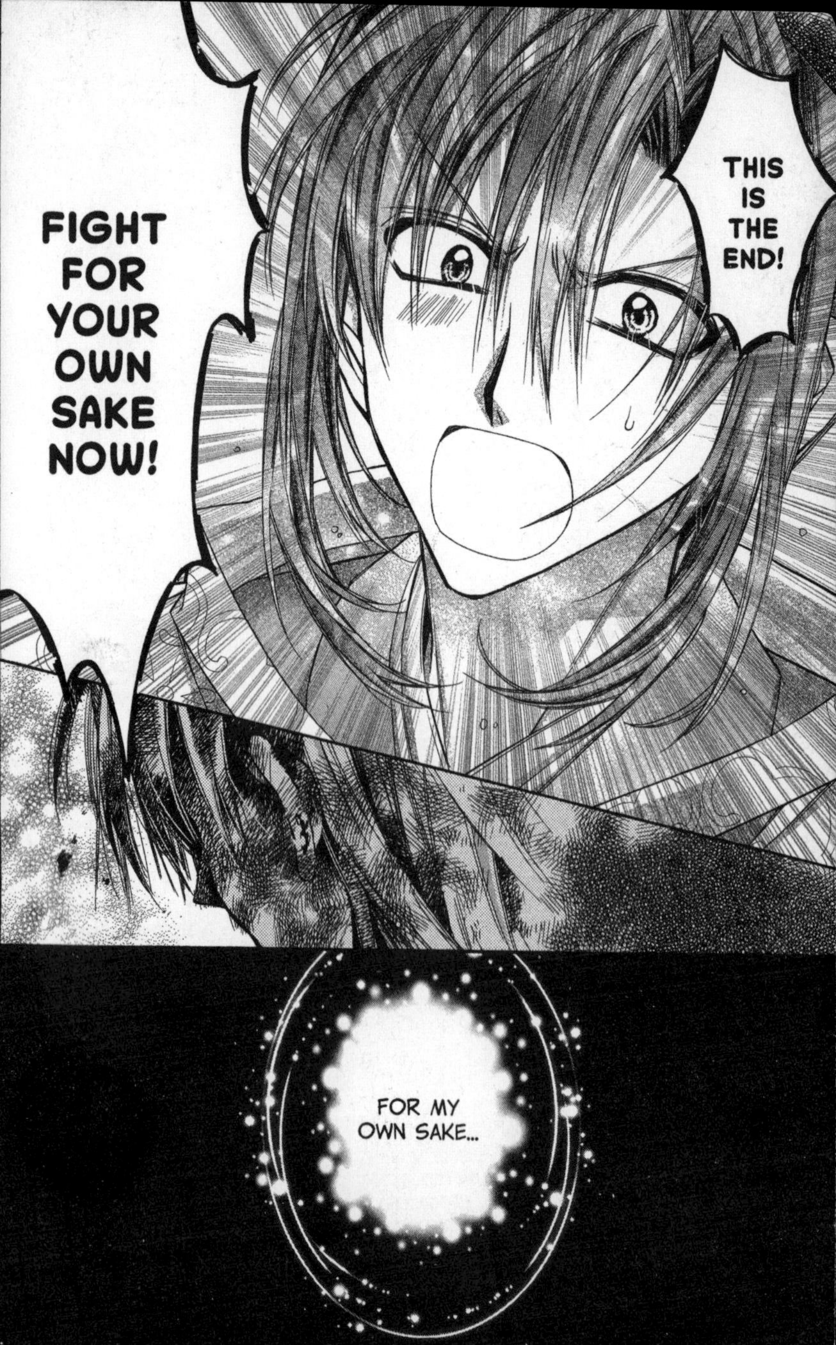
THIS IS THE END!
FIGHT FOR YOUR OWN SAKE NOW!
FOR MY OWN SAKE...

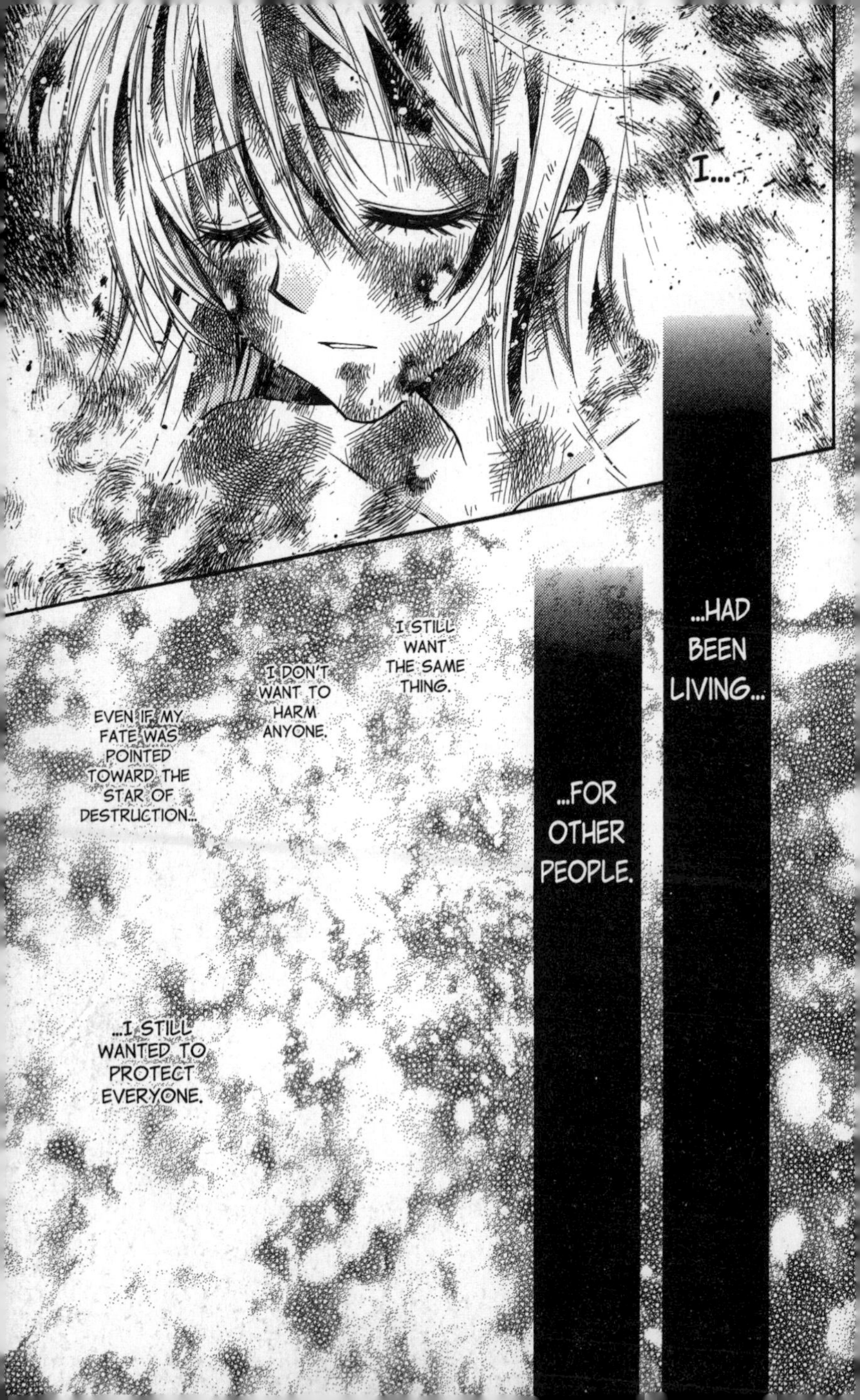
I...
...HAD BEEN LIVING...
...FOR OTHER PEOPLE.
I STILL WANT THE SAME THING.
I DON'T WANT TO HARM ANYONE.
EVEN IF MY FATE WAS POINTED TOWARD THE STAR OF DESTRUCTION...
...I STILL WANTED TO PROTECT EVERYONE.

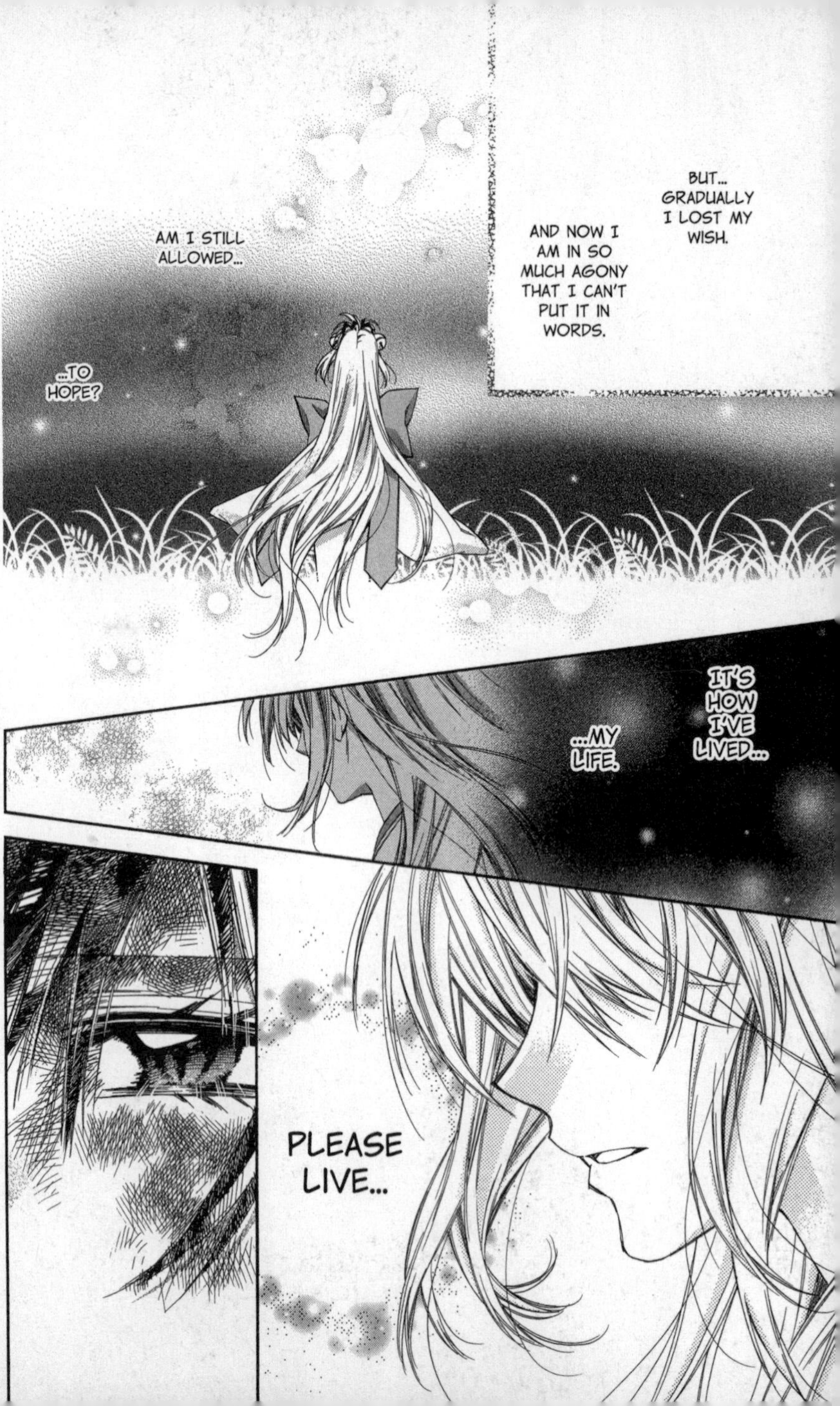
BUT... GRADUALLY I LOST MY WISH.
AND NOW I AM IN SO MUCH AGONY THAT I CAN'T PUT IT IN WORDS.
AM I STILL ALLOWED...
...TO HOPE?
IT'S HOW I'VE LIVED...
...MY LIFE.
PLEASE LIVE...

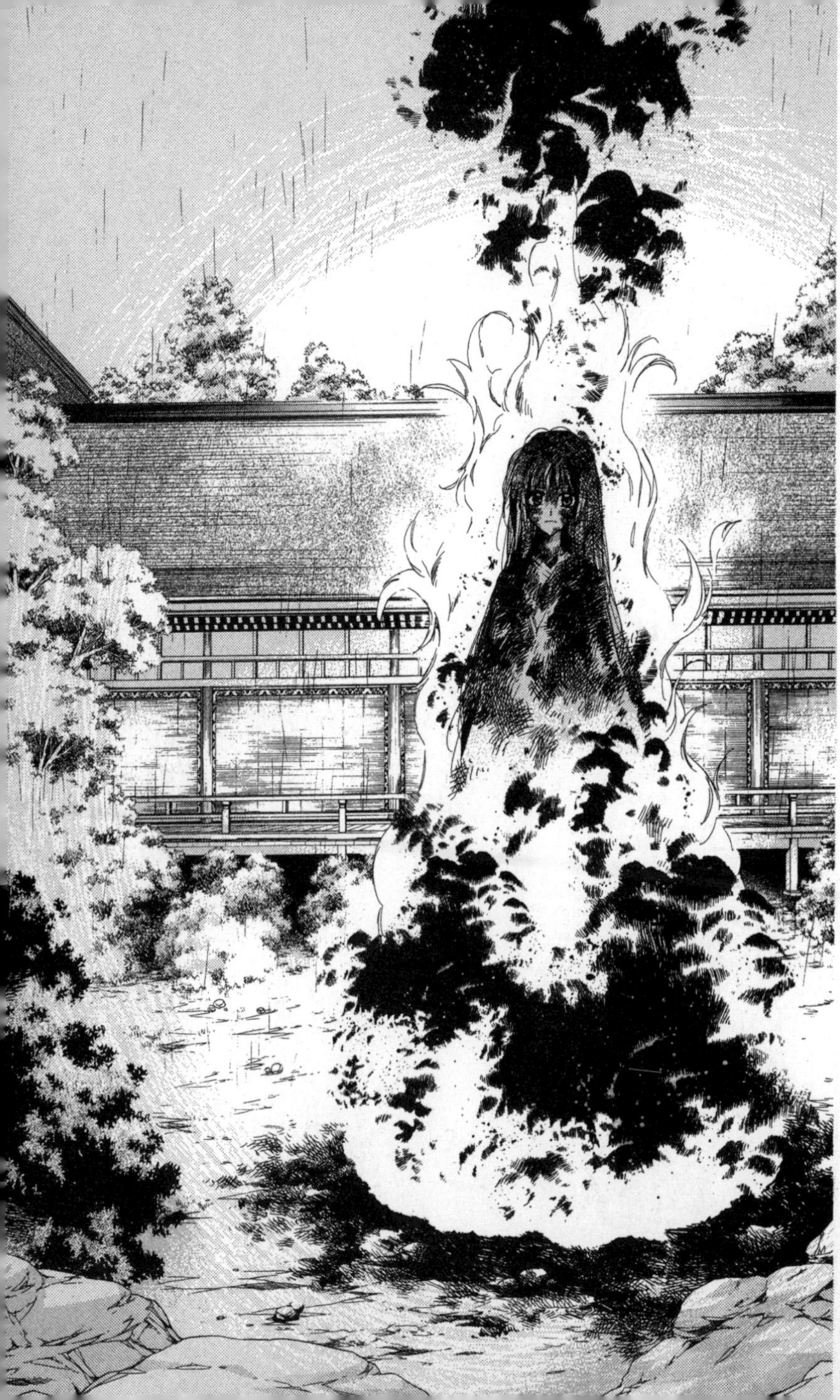

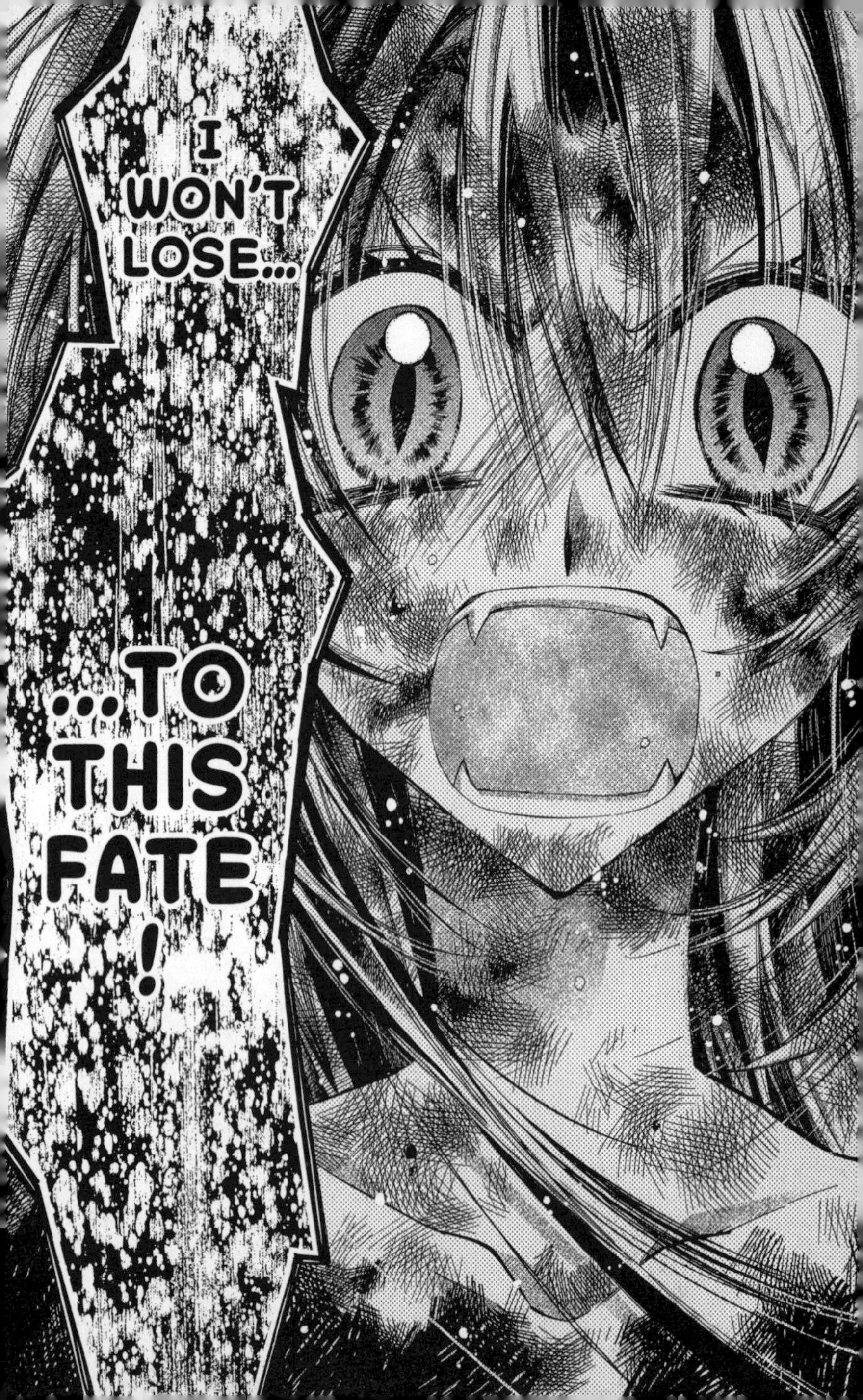
I WON'T LOSE...
...TO THIS FATE!

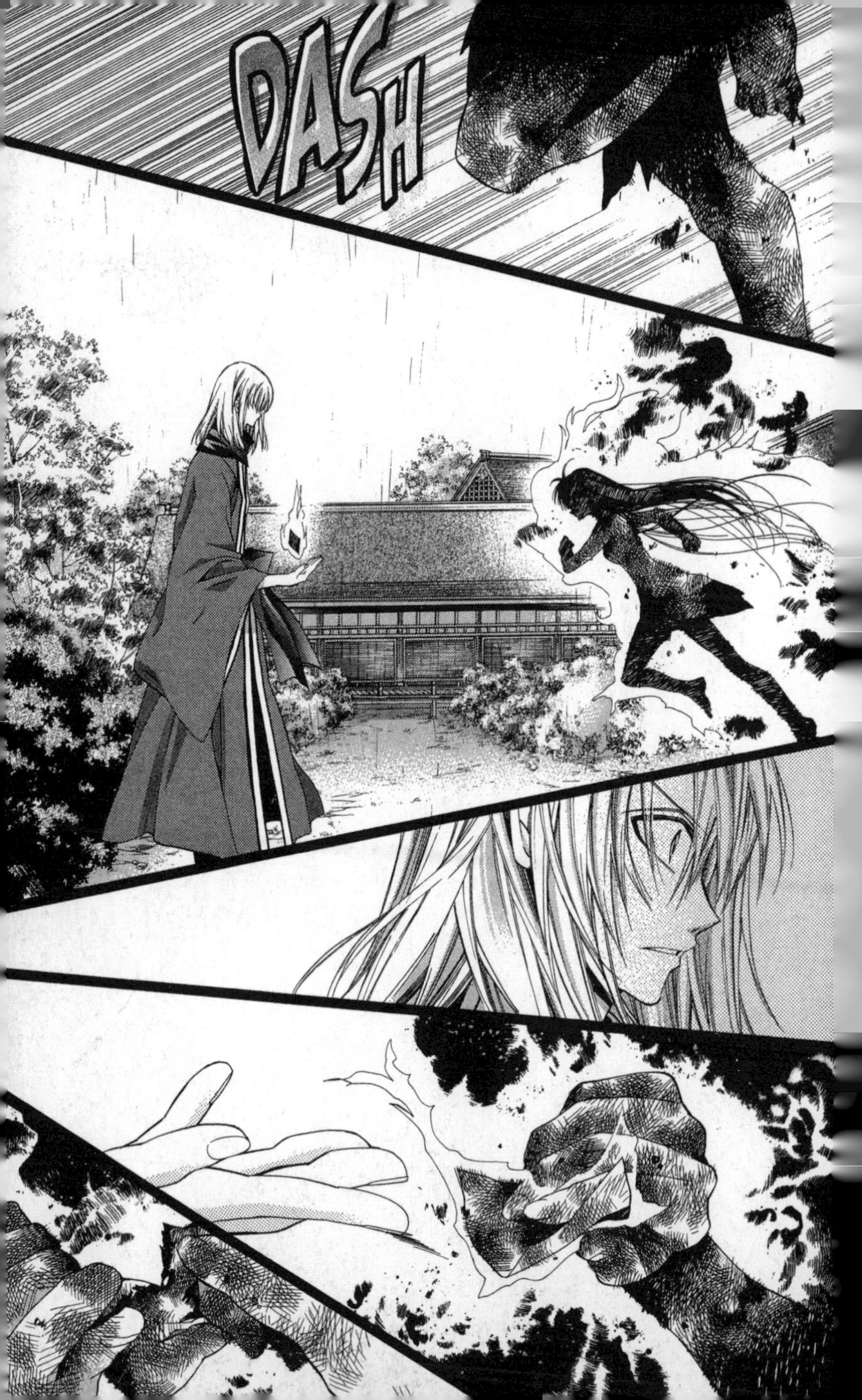
DASH

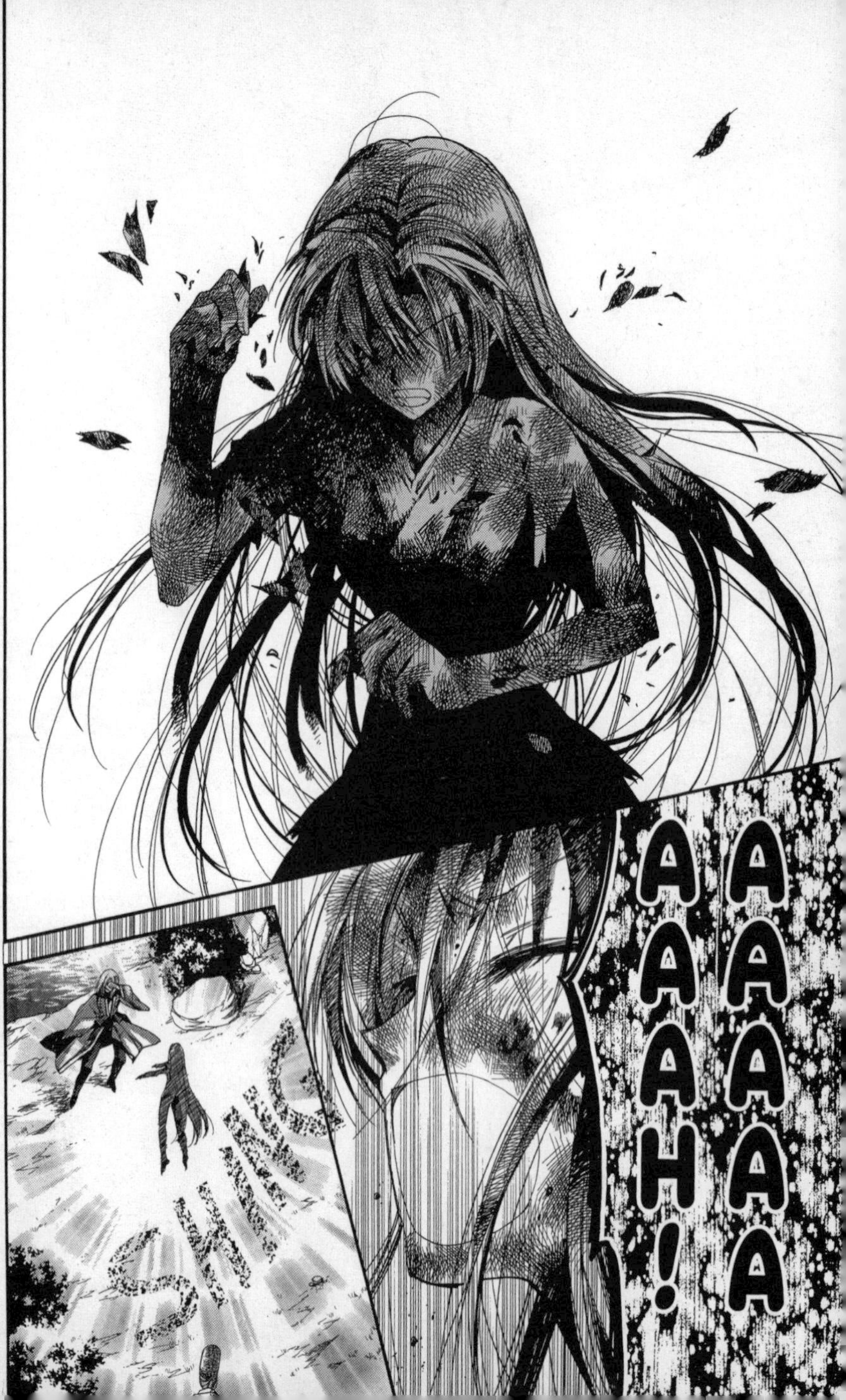
AAAAAA
AAAAH!
SHING

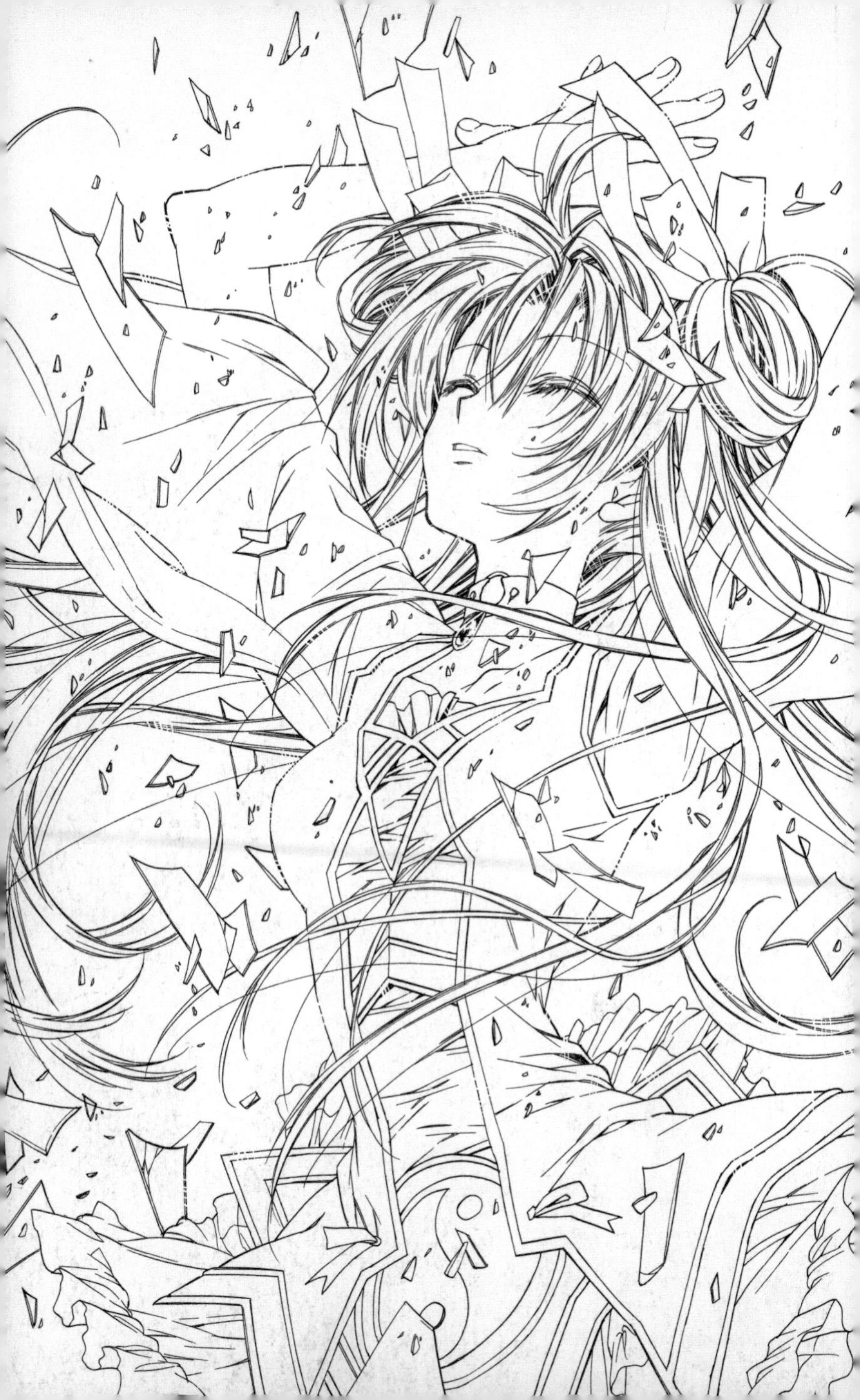

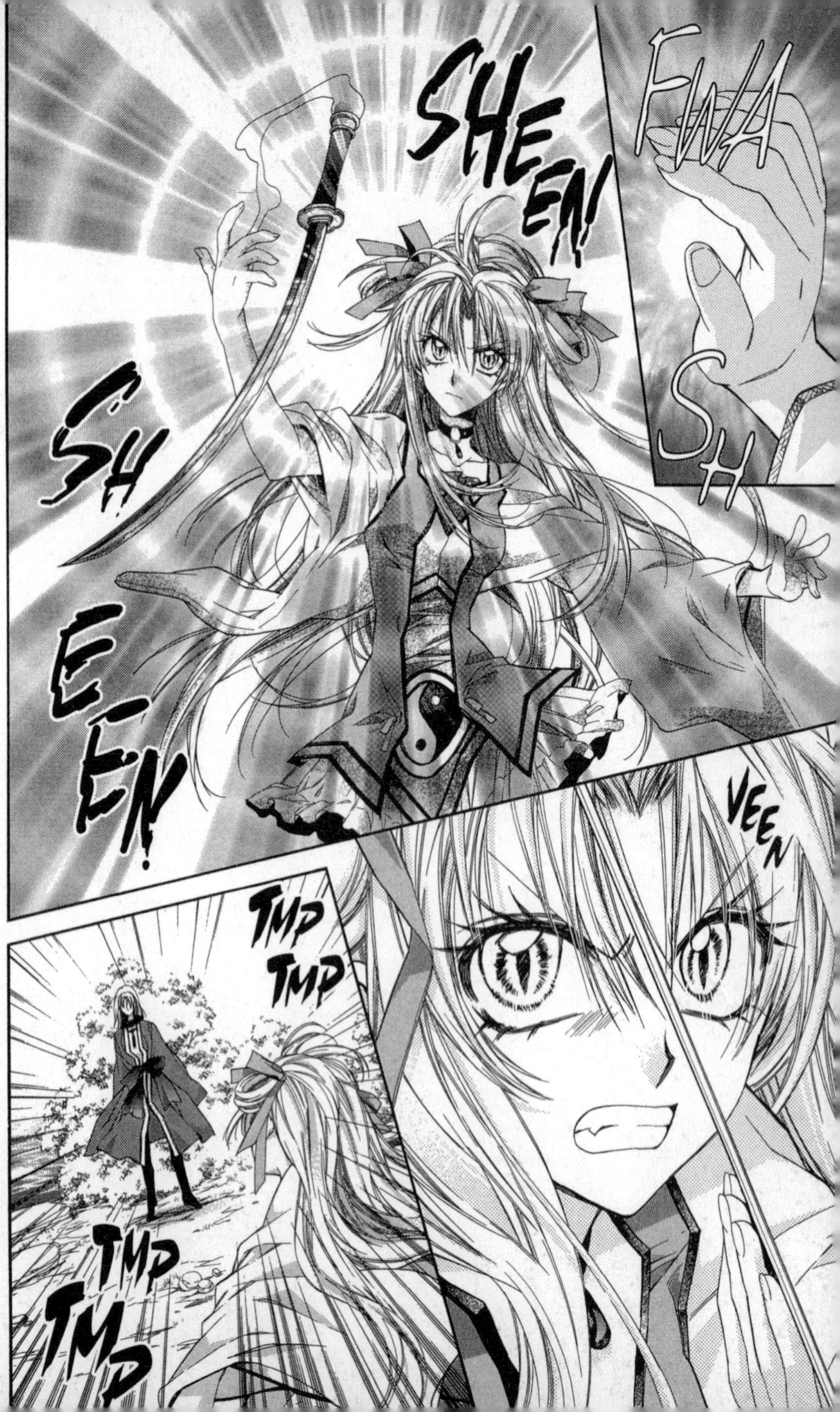
FWA
SH
SHEEN!
SH EEN!
VEEN
TMP TMP
TMP TMP

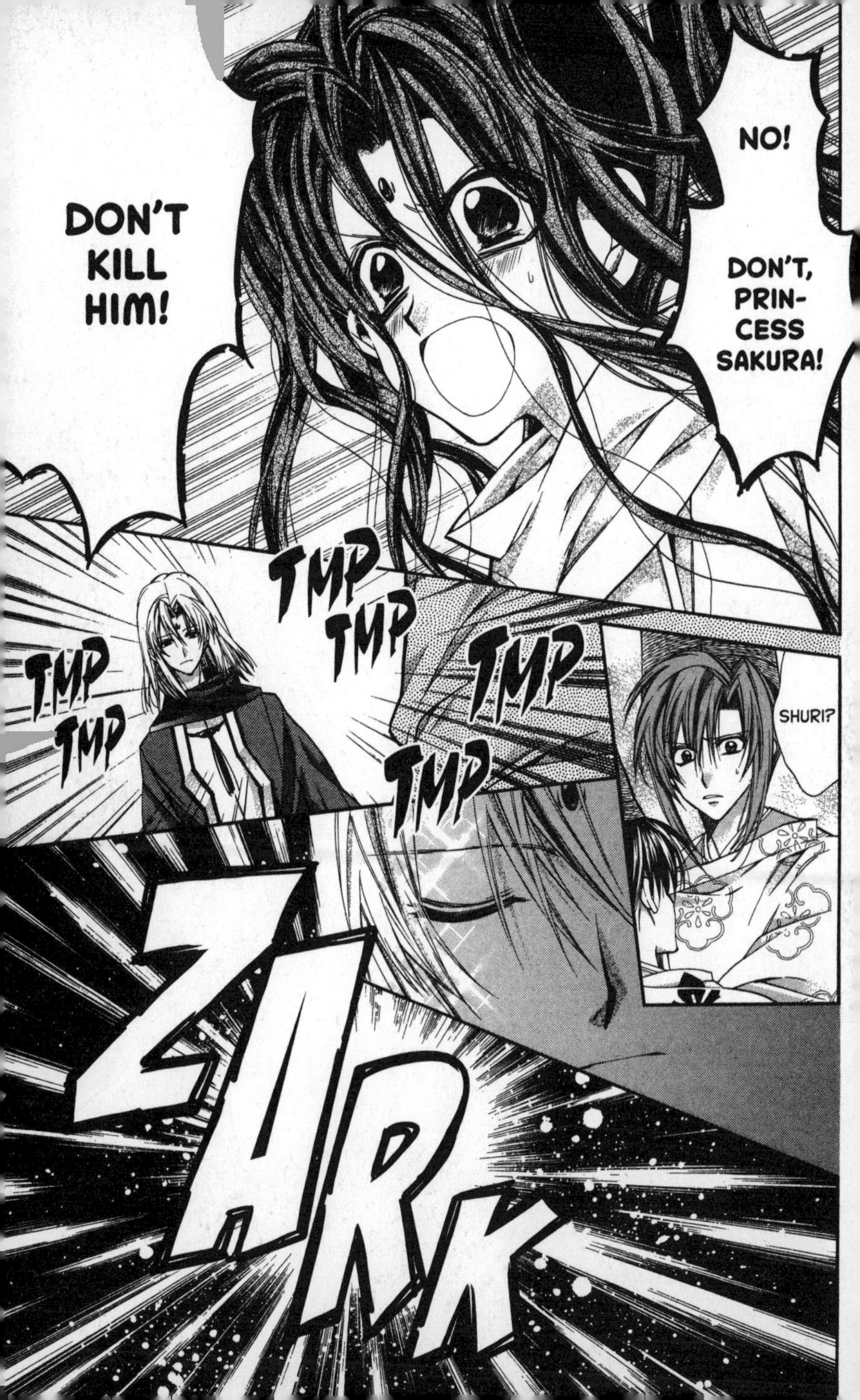
NO!
DON'T, PRIN-CESS SAKURA!
DON'T KILL HIM!
SHURI?
TMP TMP
TMP
TMP
TMP TMP
ZARK

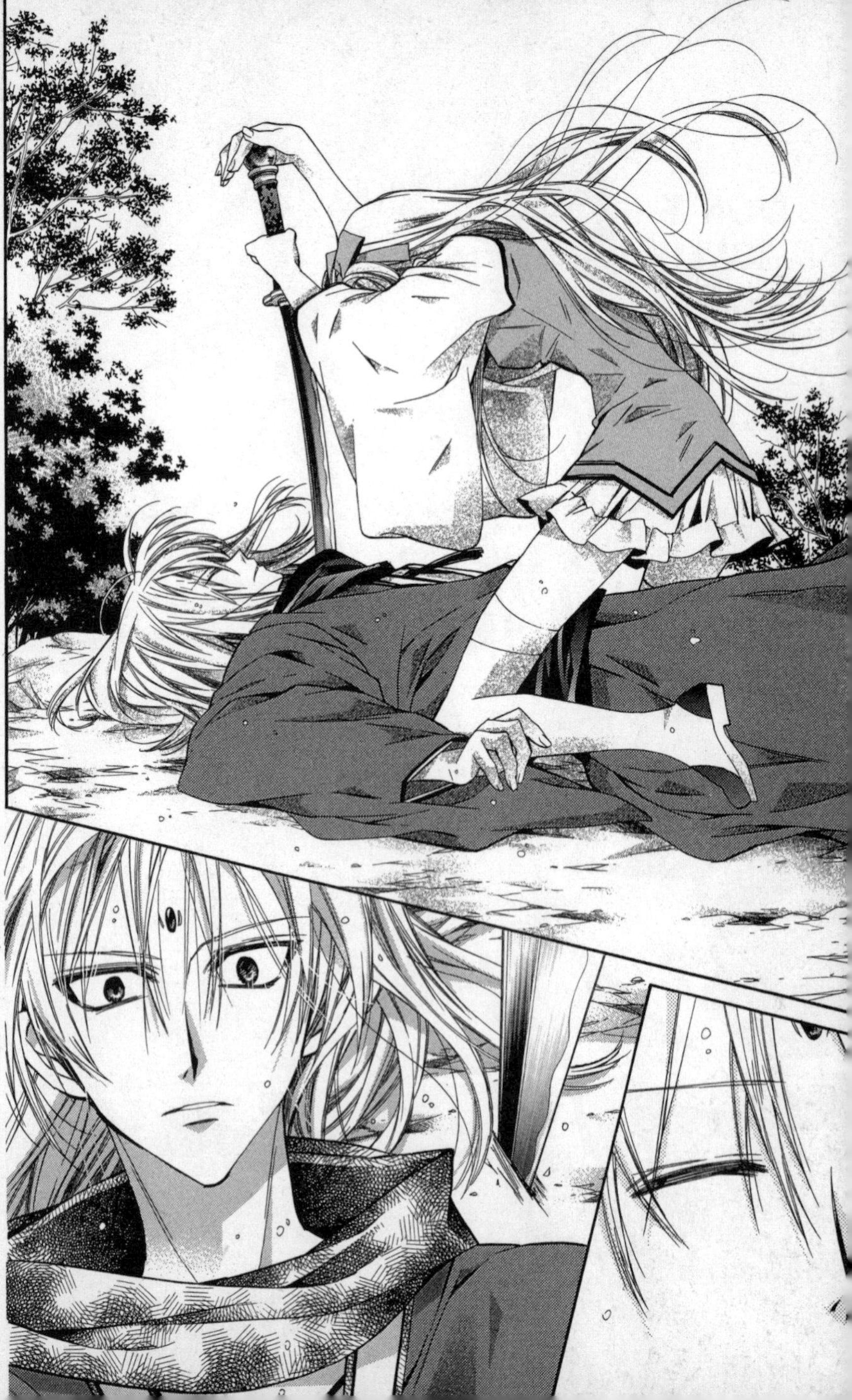

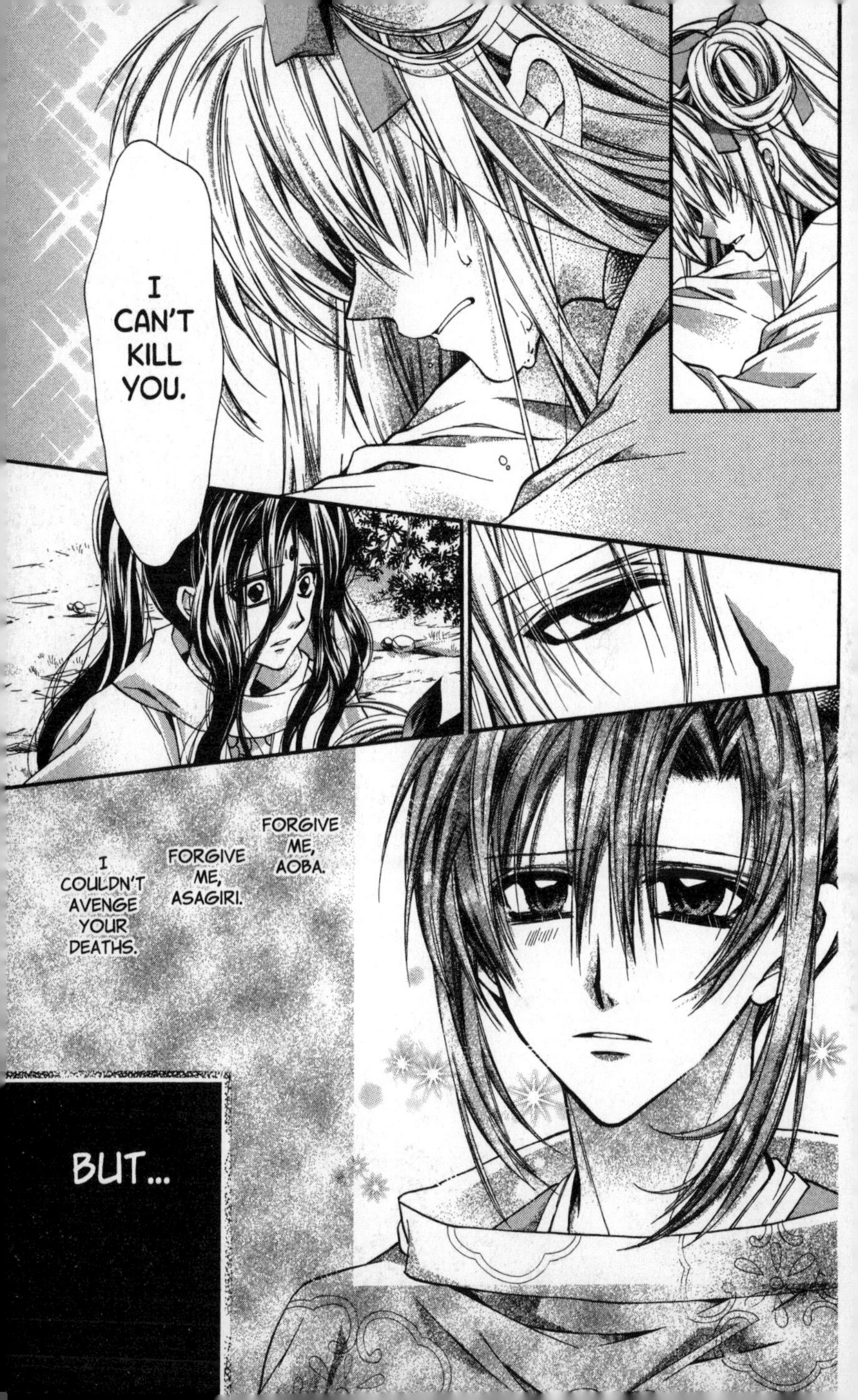
I CAN'T KILL YOU.
FORGIVE ME, AOBA.
FORGIVE ME, ASAGIRI.
I COULDN'T AVENGE YOUR DEATHS.
BUT...

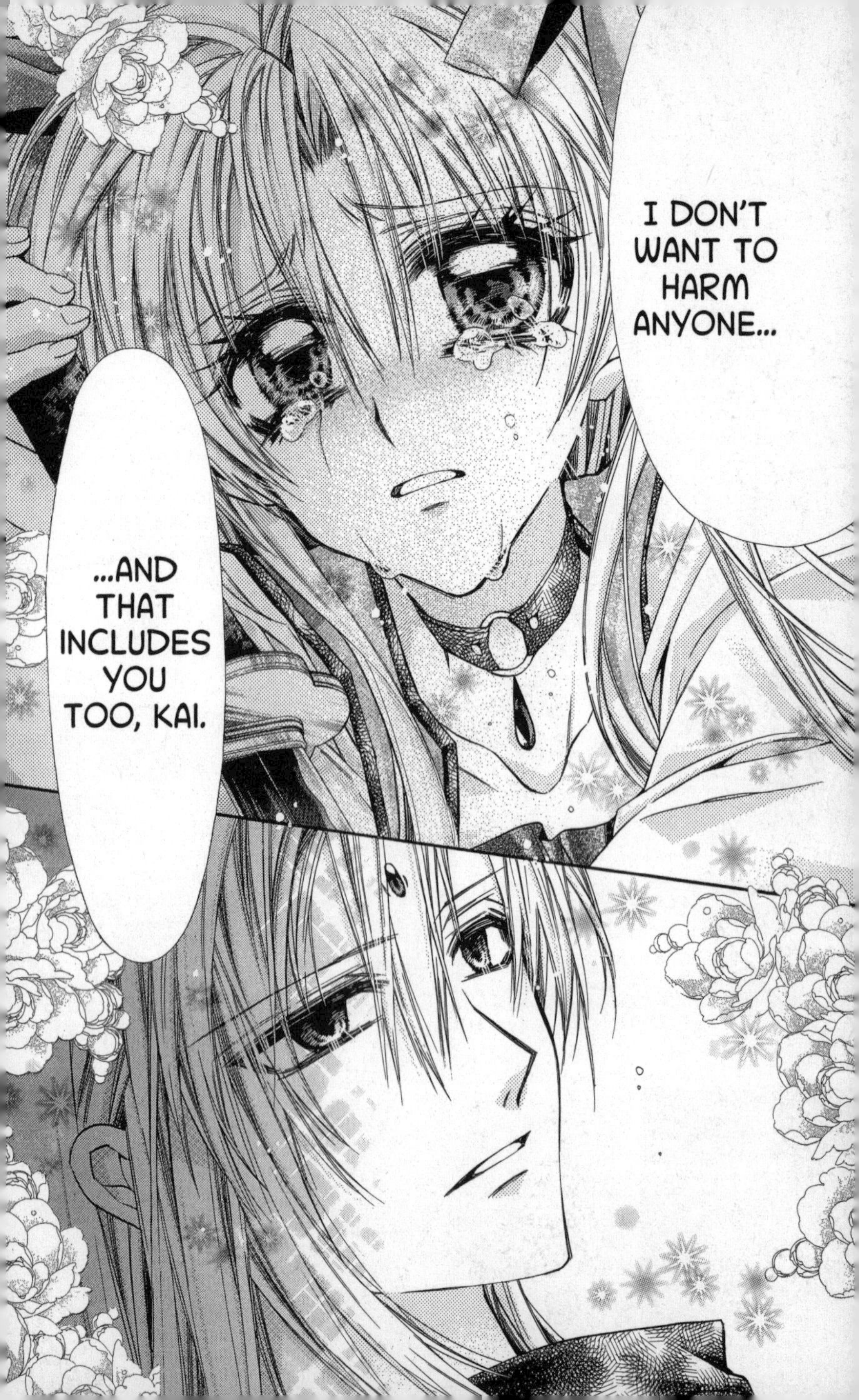
I DON'T WANT TO HARM ANYONE...
...AND THAT INCLUDES YOU TOO, KAI.

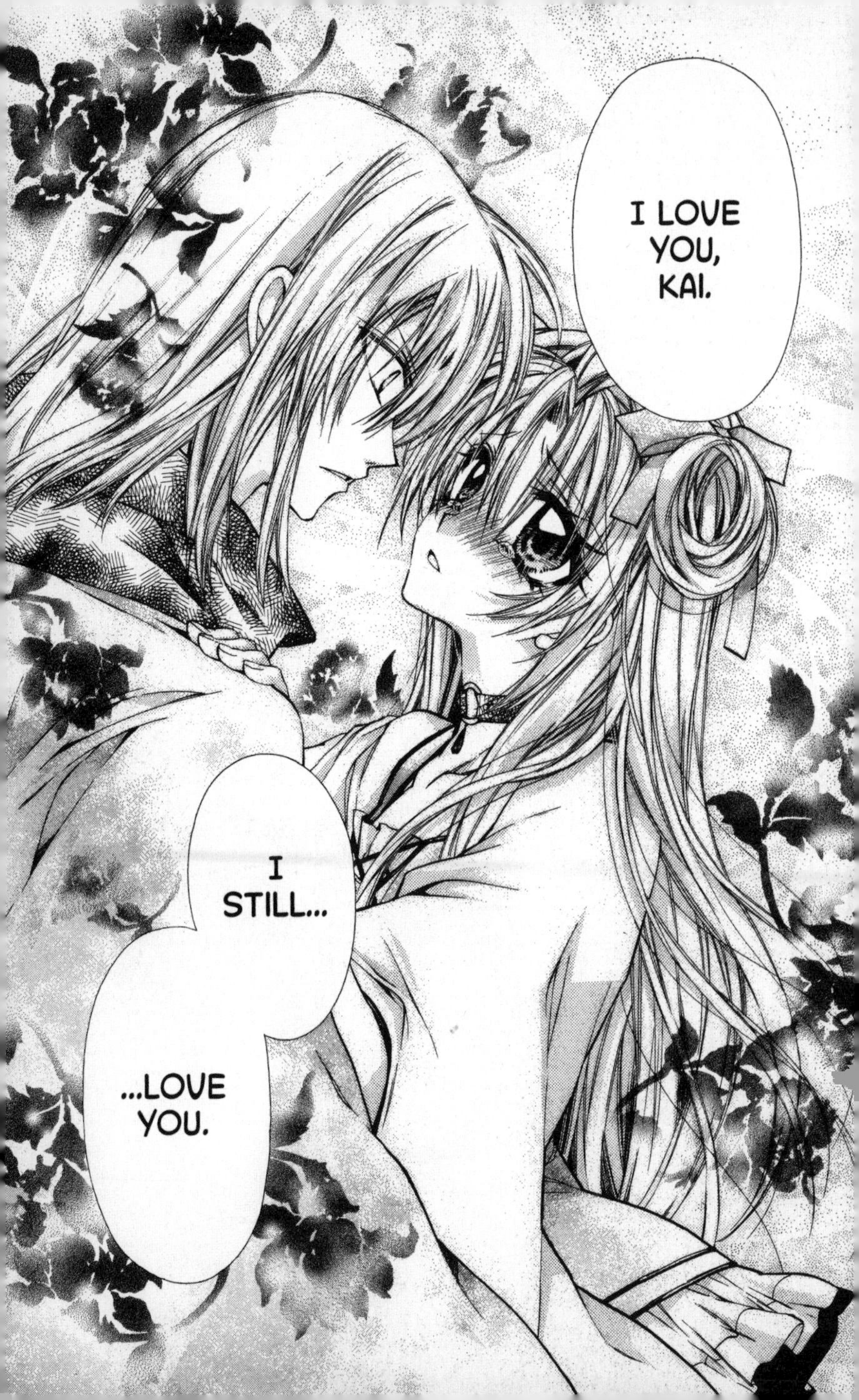
I LOVE YOU, KAI.
I STILL...
...LOVE YOU.

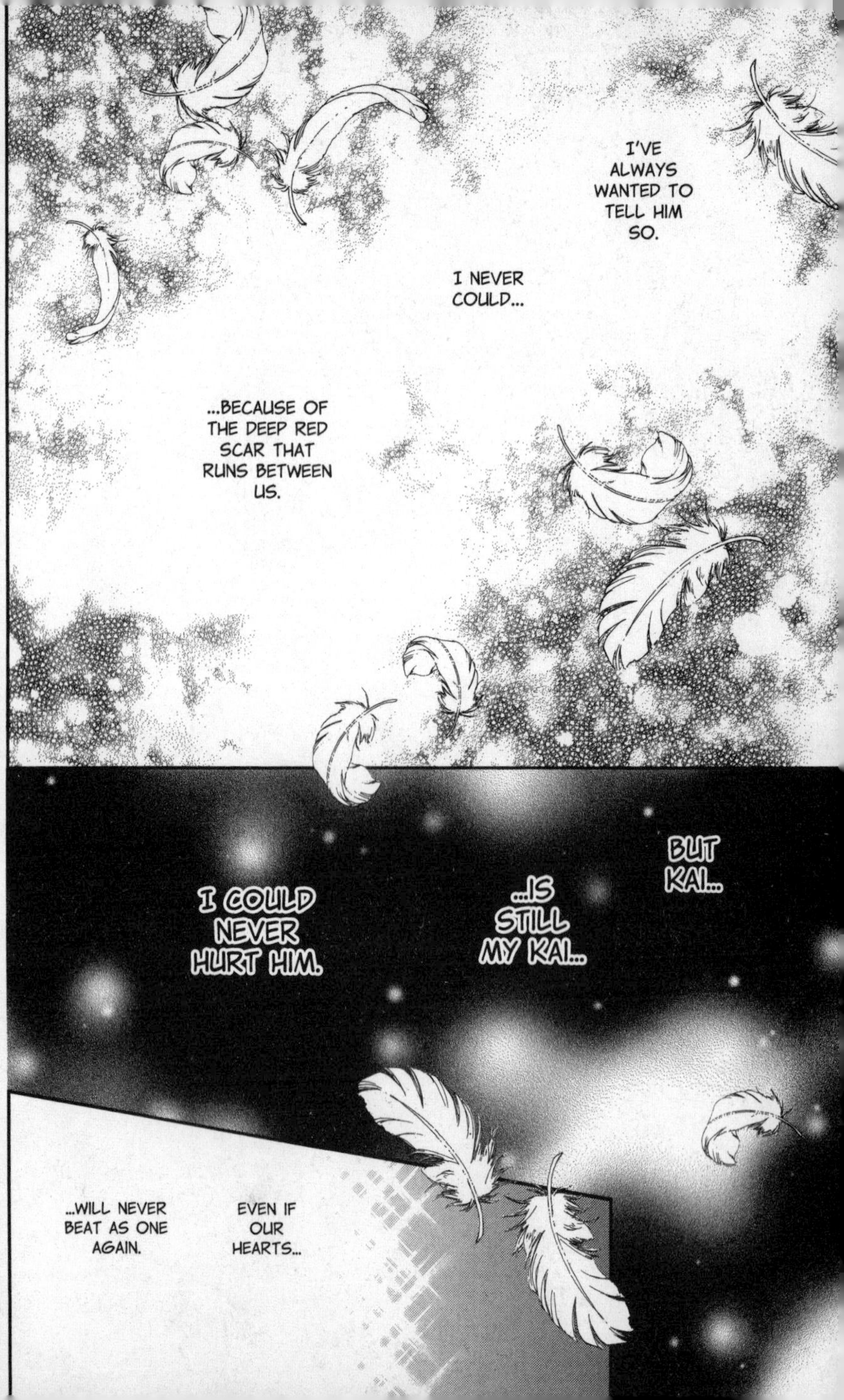
I'VE ALWAYS WANTED TO TELL HIM SO.
I NEVER COULD...
...BECAUSE OF THE DEEP RED SCAR THAT RUNS BETWEEN US.
BUT KAI...
...IS STILL MY KAI...
I COULD NEVER HURT HIM.
EVEN IF OUR HEARTS...
...WILL NEVER BEAT AS ONE AGAIN.

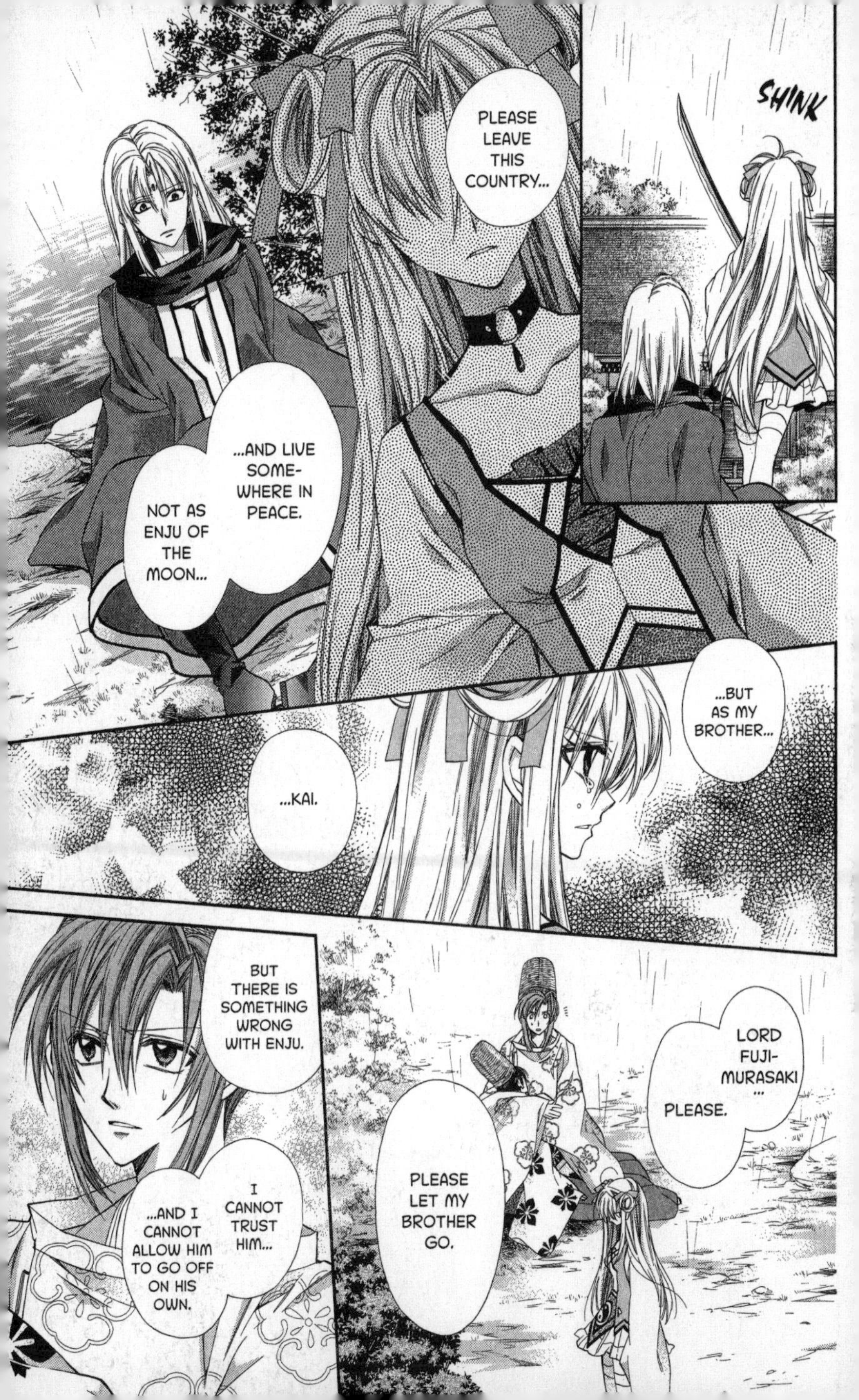
SHINK
PLEASE LEAVE THIS COUNTRY...
...AND LIVE SOME-WHERE IN PEACE.
NOT AS ENJU OF THE MOON...
...BUT AS MY BROTHER...
...KAI.
LORD FUJI-MURASAKI...
PLEASE.
PLEASE LET MY BROTHER GO.
BUT THERE IS SOMETHING WRONG WITH ENJU.
I CANNOT TRUST HIM...
...AND I CANNOT ALLOW HIM TO GO OFF ON HIS OWN.

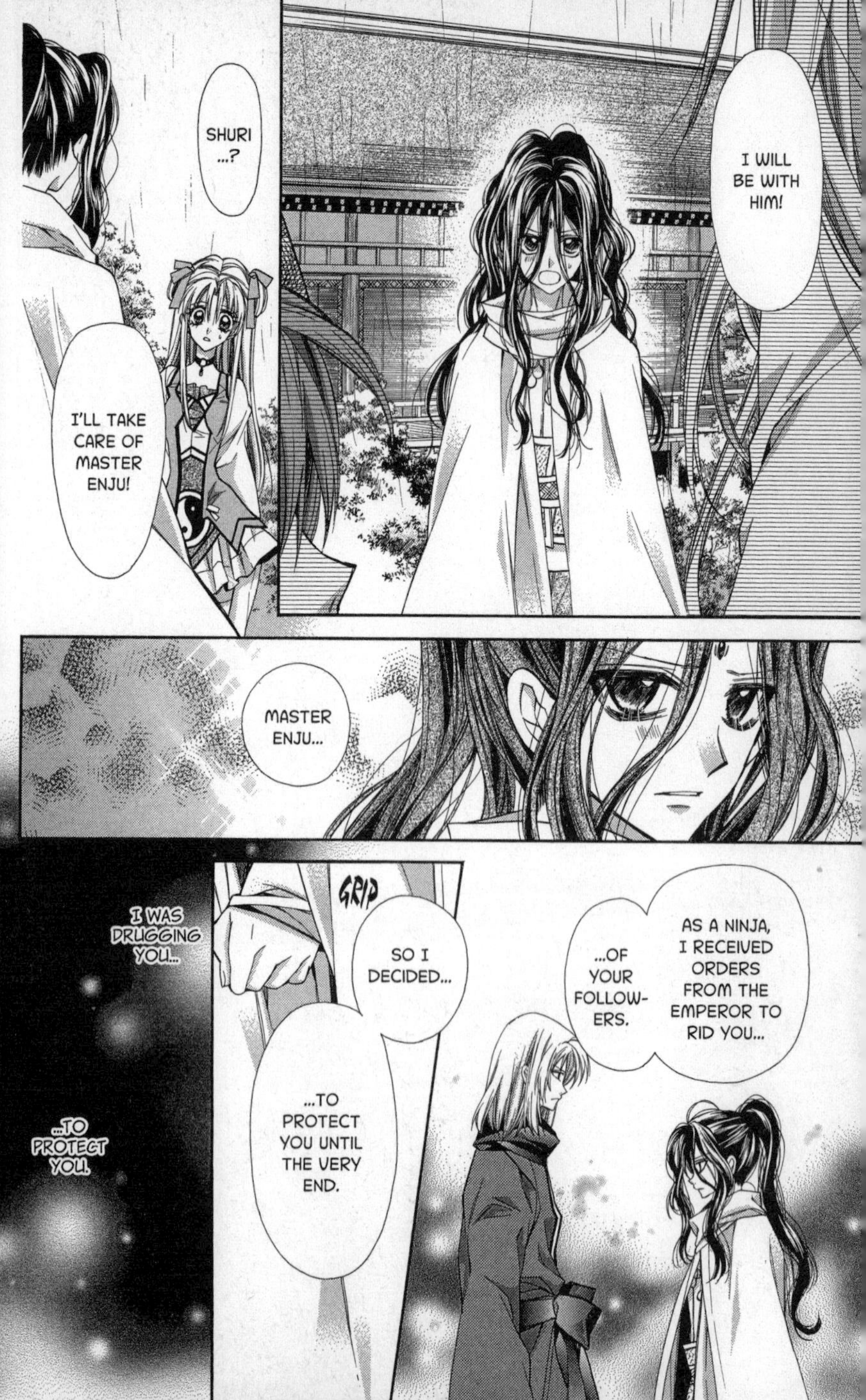
I WILL BE WITH HIM!
SHURI ...?
I'LL TAKE CARE OF MASTER ENJU!
MASTER ENJU...
AS A NINJA, I RECEIVED ORDERS FROM THE EMPEROR TO RID YOU...
...OF YOUR FOLLOW-ERS.
GRIP
SO I DECIDED...
...TO PROTECT YOU UNTIL THE VERY END.
I WAS DRUGGING YOU...
...TO PROTECT YOU.

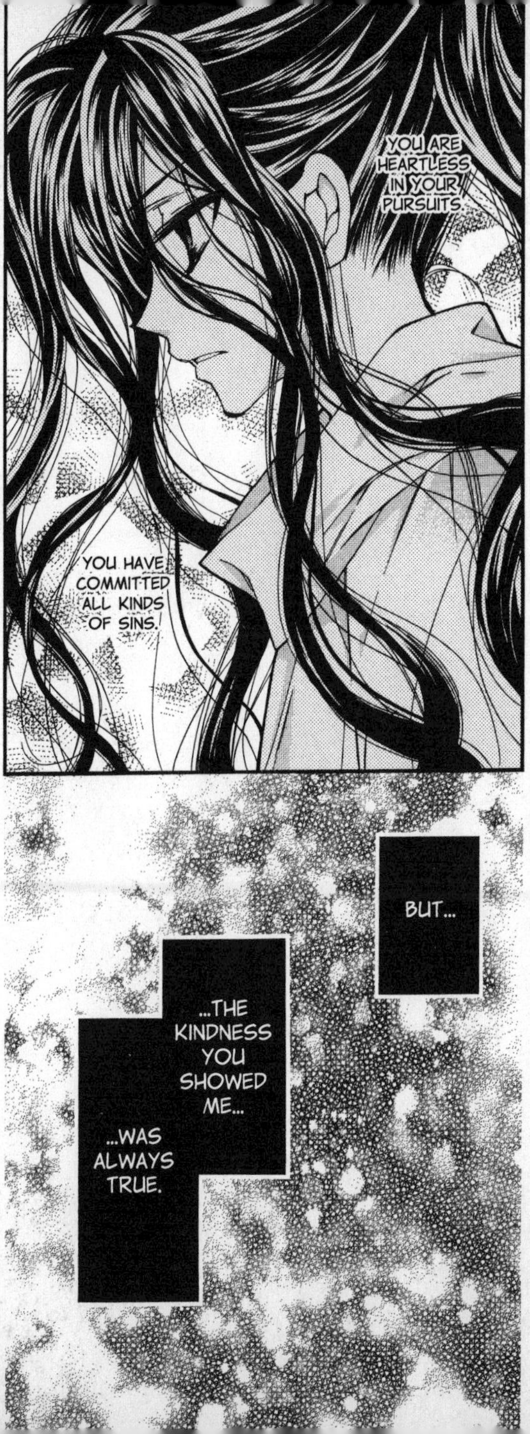
YOU ARE HEARTLESS IN YOUR PURSUITS.
YOU HAVE COMMITTED ALL KINDS OF SINS.
BUT...
...THE KINDNESS YOU SHOWED ME...
...WAS ALWAYS TRUE.

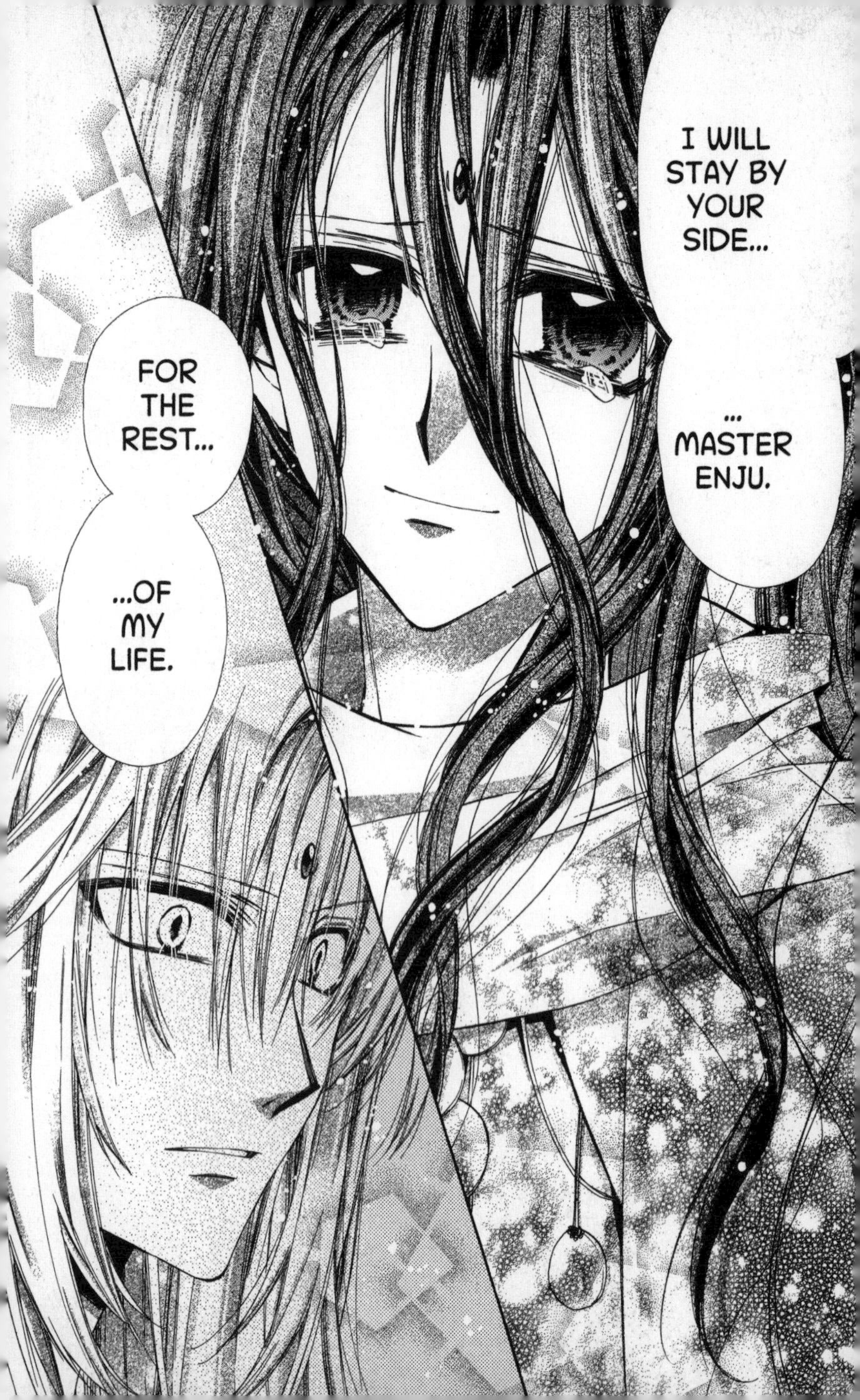
I WILL STAY BY YOUR SIDE...
...MASTER ENJU.
FOR THE REST...
...OF MY LIFE.

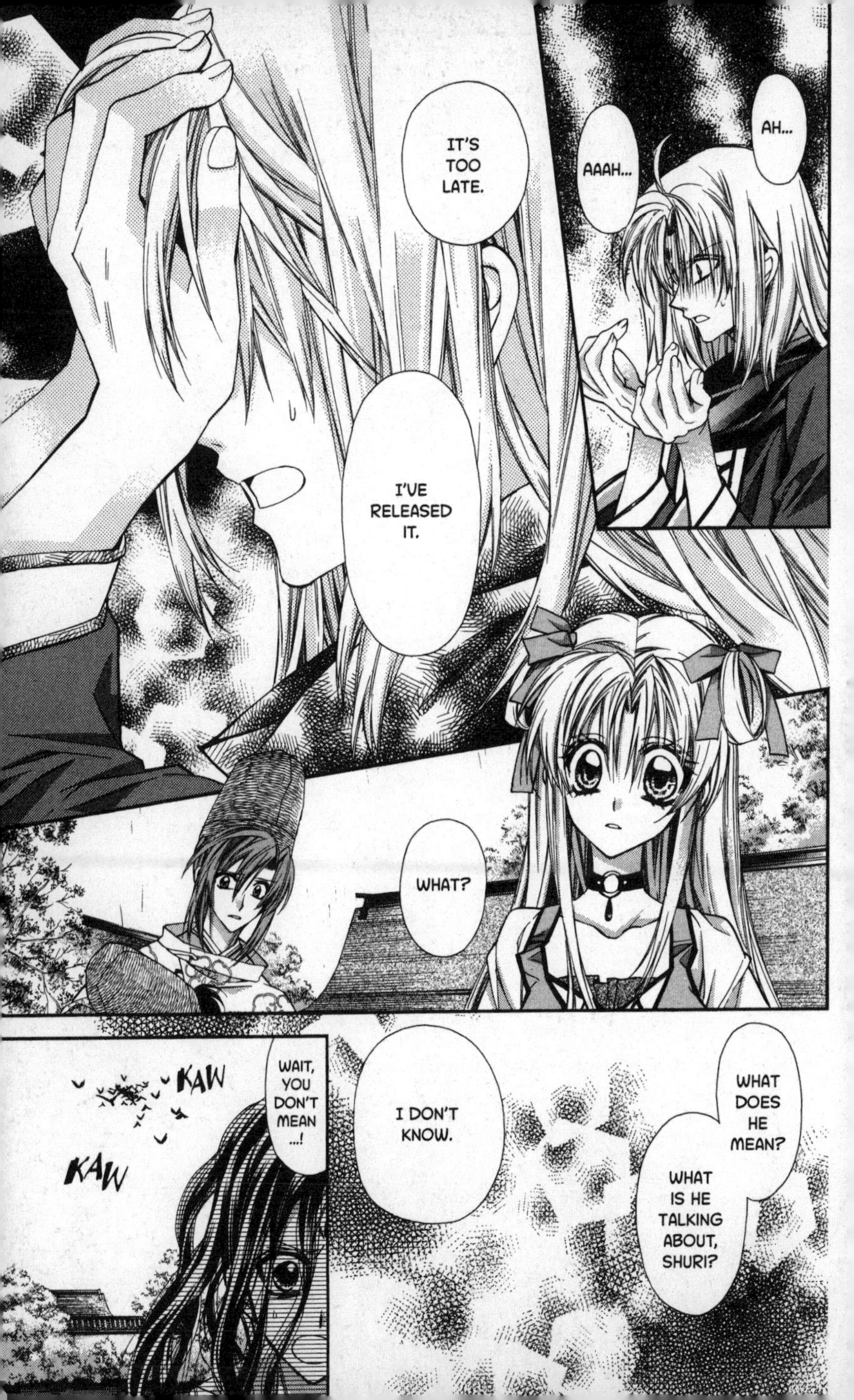

AH...
AAAH...
IT'S TOO LATE.
I'VE RELEASED IT.
WHAT?
WHAT DOES HE MEAN?
WHAT IS HE TALKING ABOUT, SHURI?
I DON'T KNOW.
WAIT, YOU DON'T MEAN ...!
KAW
KAW

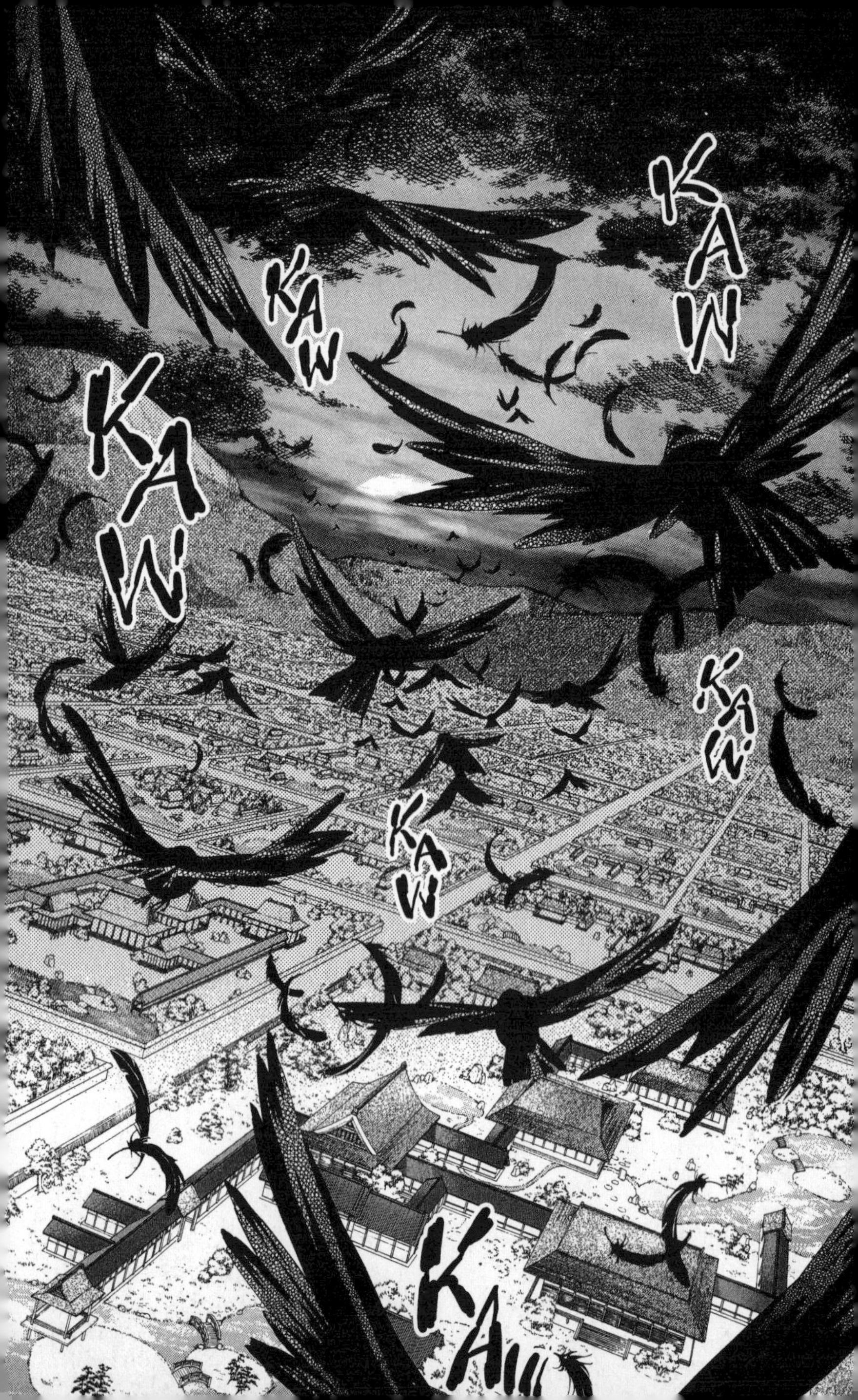
KAW
KAW
KAW
KAW
KAW
KA
KA

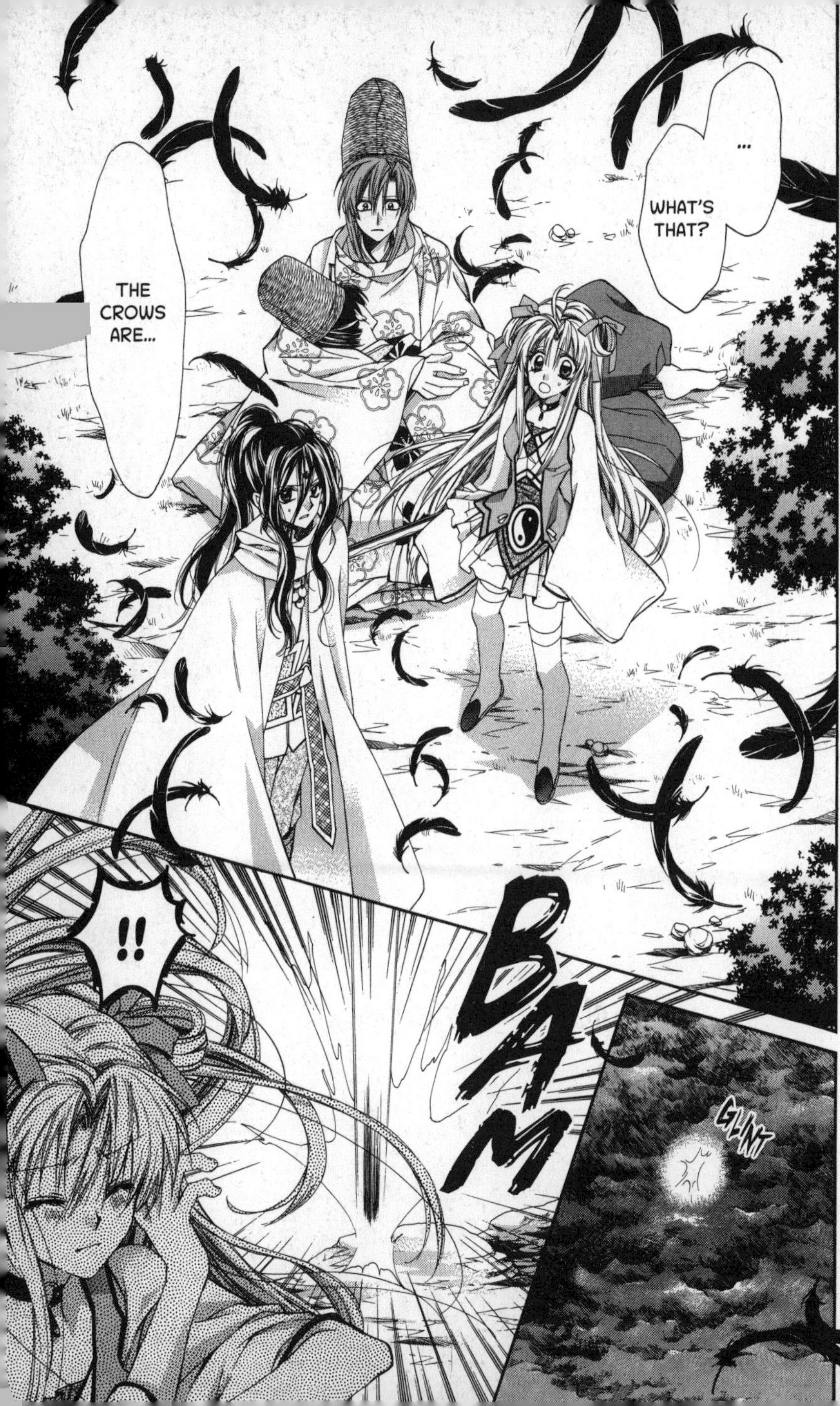
...
WHAT'S THAT?
THE CROWS ARE...
GLINT
BAM
!!

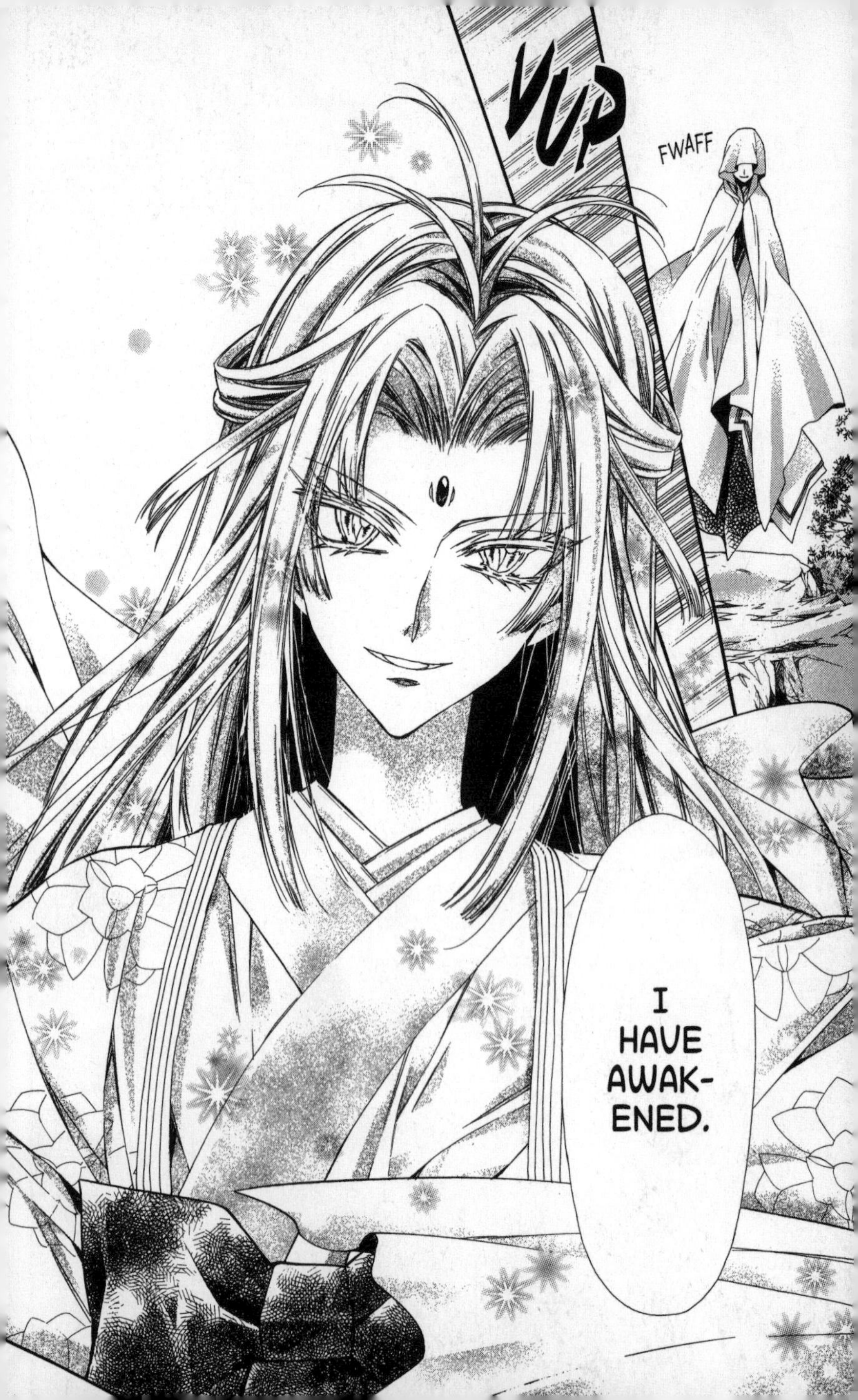
VUP
FWAFF
I HAVE AWAKENED.

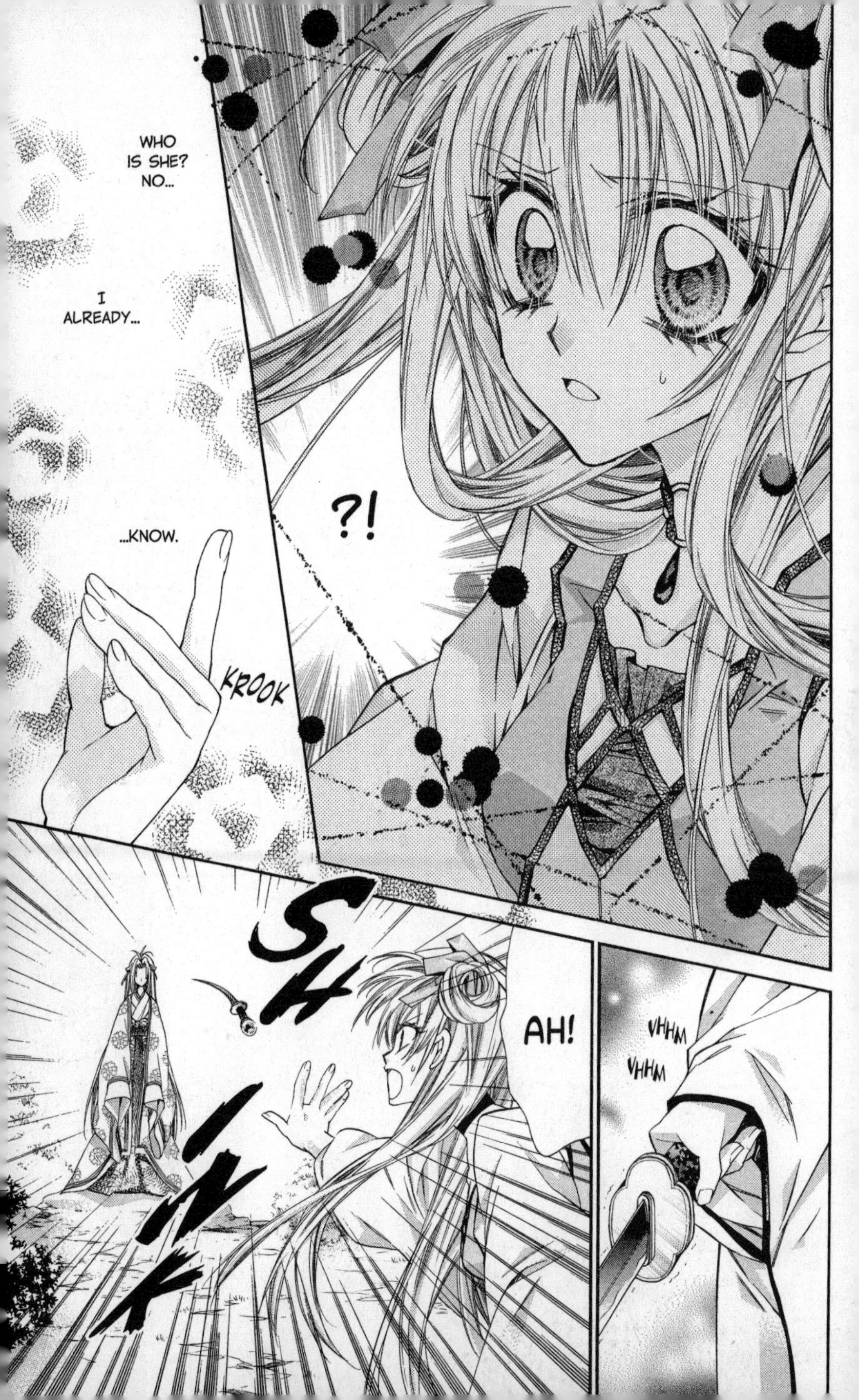
?!
WHO IS SHE? NO...
I ALREADY...
...KNOW.
KROOK
VHHM
VHHM
AH!
SHINK

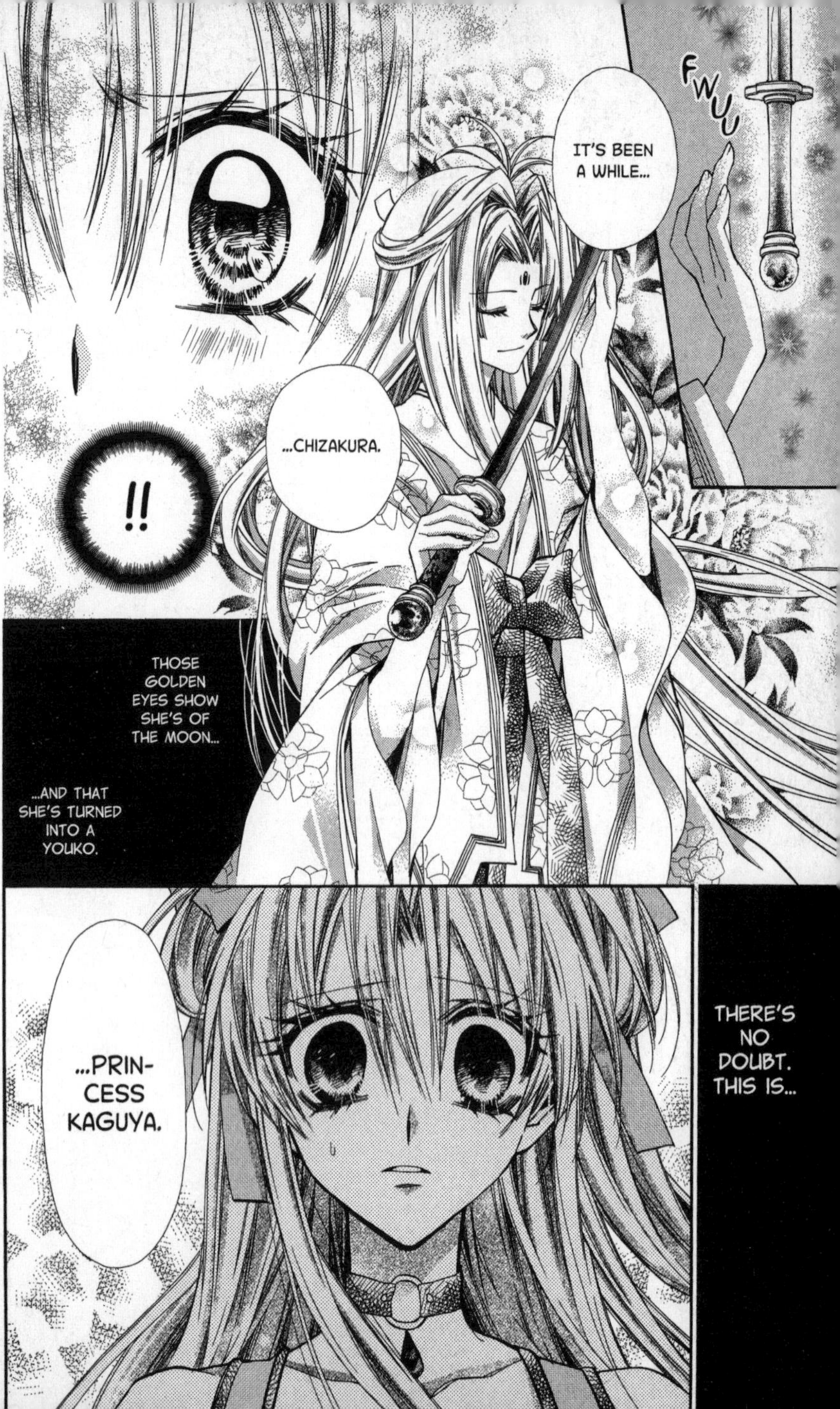
FWUU
IT'S BEEN A WHILE...
...CHIZAKURA.
!!
THOSE GOLDEN EYES SHOW SHE'S OF THE MOON...
...AND THAT SHE'S TURNED INTO A YOUKO.
THERE'S NO DOUBT. THIS IS...
...PRIN-CESS KAGUYA.

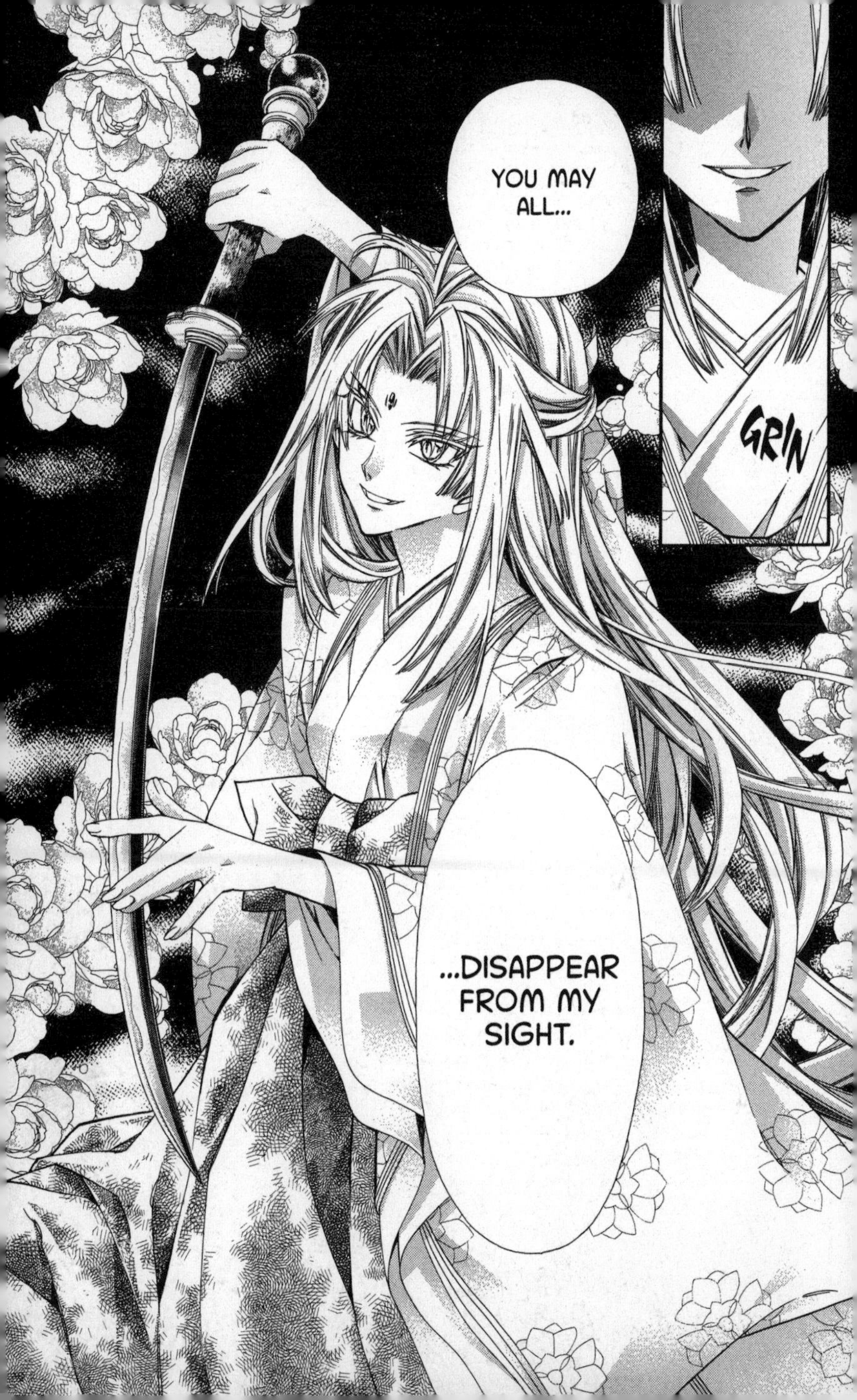
GRIN
YOU MAY ALL...
...DISAPPEAR FROM MY SIGHT.

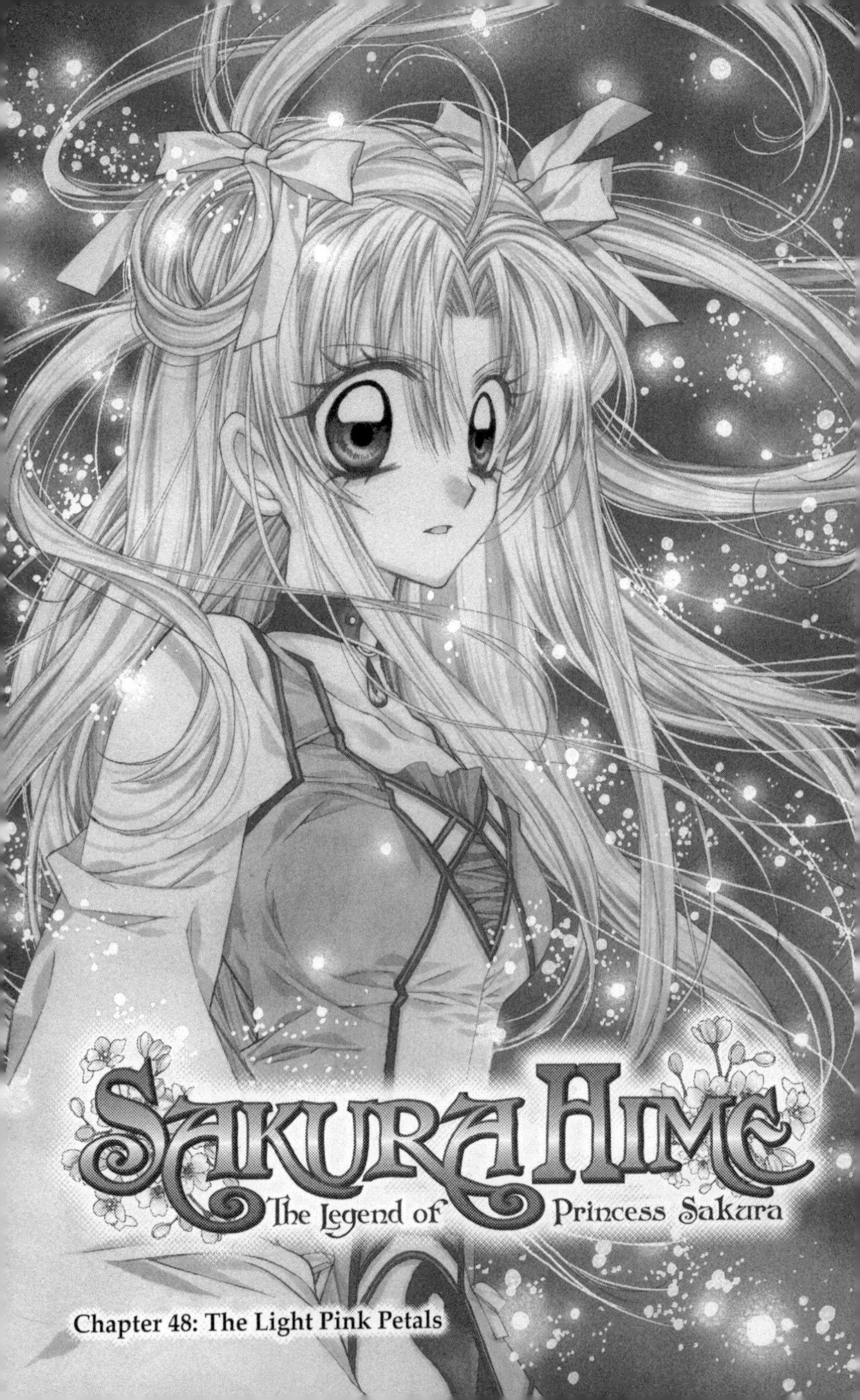
SAKURA HIME
The Legend of Princess Sakura
Chapter 48: The Light Pink Petals

Sakura Hime
The Legend of Princess Sakura

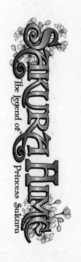

Chapter 48: The Light Pink Petals

※ I'm giving away the story.

Originally the chapter title was meant in Enju's point of view in reference to Sakura and Rurijo. But when I created the storyboard, it ended up becoming Sakura's point of view about the people who were killed by Chizakura. (I guess you can say the chapter title has many meanings.) ← I work on the chapter title illustration long before the storyboard. (Color illustrations take a long time to print.) I turn in the chapter title along with the illustration and give an estimate of what the chapter would be about, so I end up in a slight panic when I decide to make changes to the story.

I've written about how I've included all the ideas I wanted to draw in these chapters. The parting of Enju and Sakura was a scene I especially wanted to do, and I drew many scenes leading up to this one. (Like Enju's line saying how he would never mistake Sakura for Rurijo.)

I wanted to draw a scene in which Enju would protect and care for Sakura, and she would in turn care for him. This was to show they had finally been able to create a bond. But I never thought Kai would pop back up. I was so surprised when I drew it, and I felt a bit teary when I told my assistant, "Don't forget to add screentone to his hair."

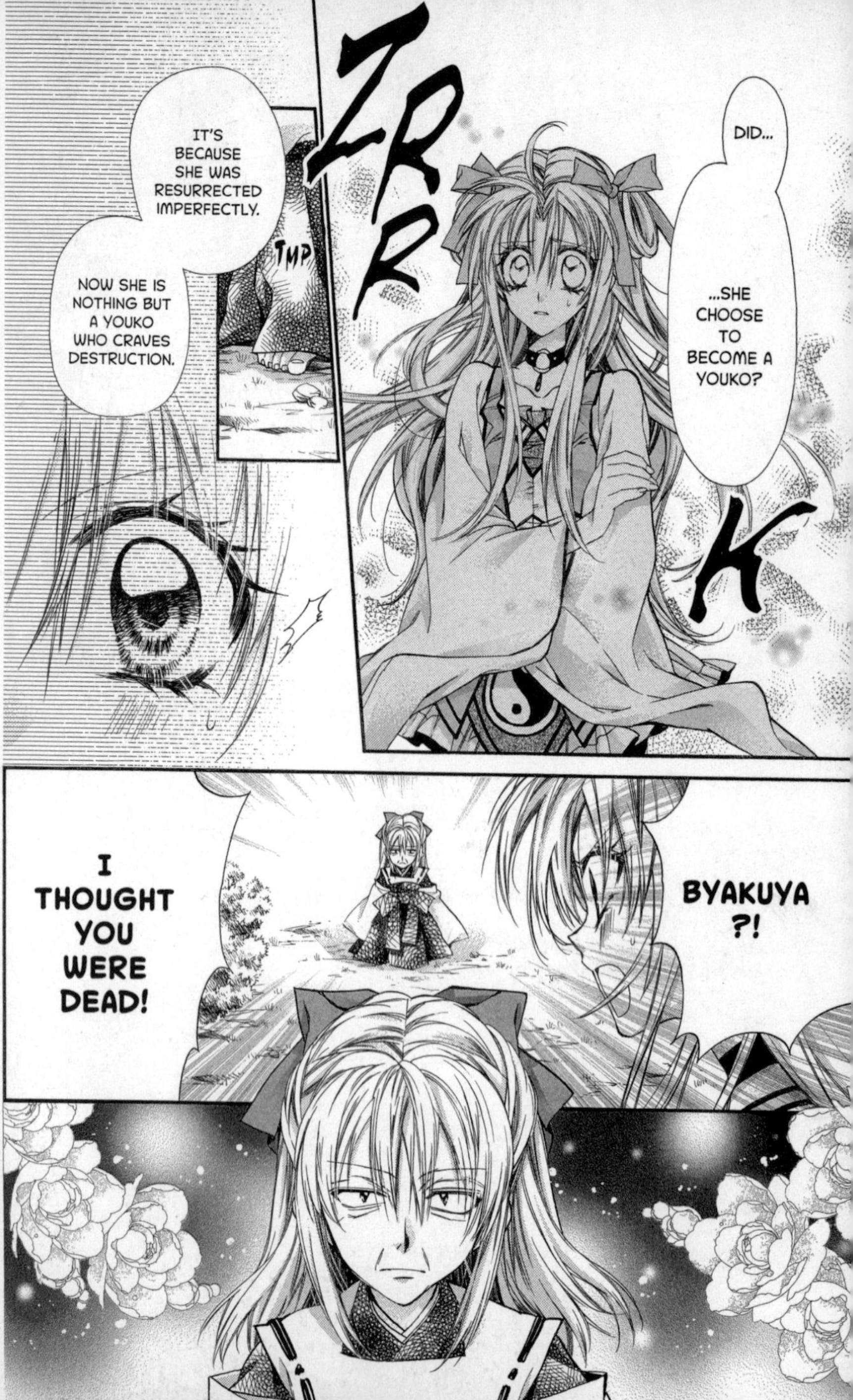
DID...
...SHE CHOOSE TO BECOME A YOUKO?
ZRR
K
TMP
IT'S BECAUSE SHE WAS RESURRECTED IMPERFECTLY.
NOW SHE IS NOTHING BUT A YOUKO WHO CRAVES DESTRUCTION.
BYAKUYA ?!
I THOUGHT YOU WERE DEAD!

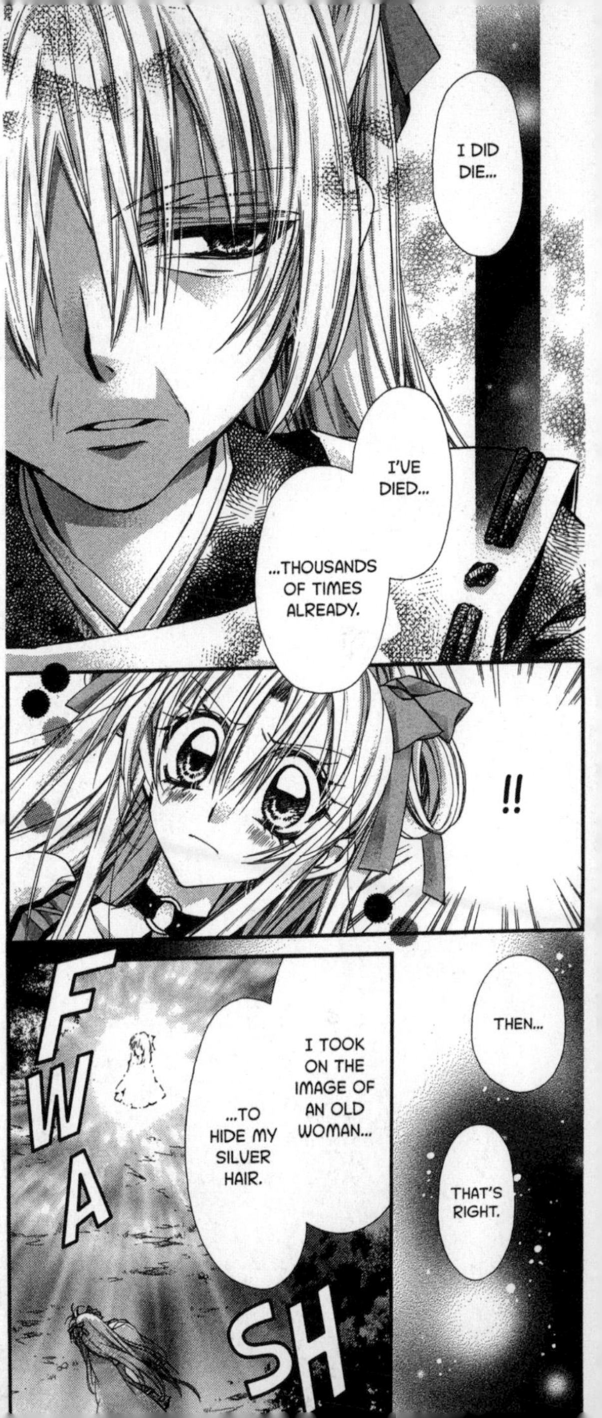
I DID DIE...
I'VE DIED...
...THOUSANDS OF TIMES ALREADY.
!!
THEN...
THAT'S RIGHT.
I TOOK ON THE IMAGE OF AN OLD WOMAN...
...TO HIDE MY SILVER HAIR.
FWASH

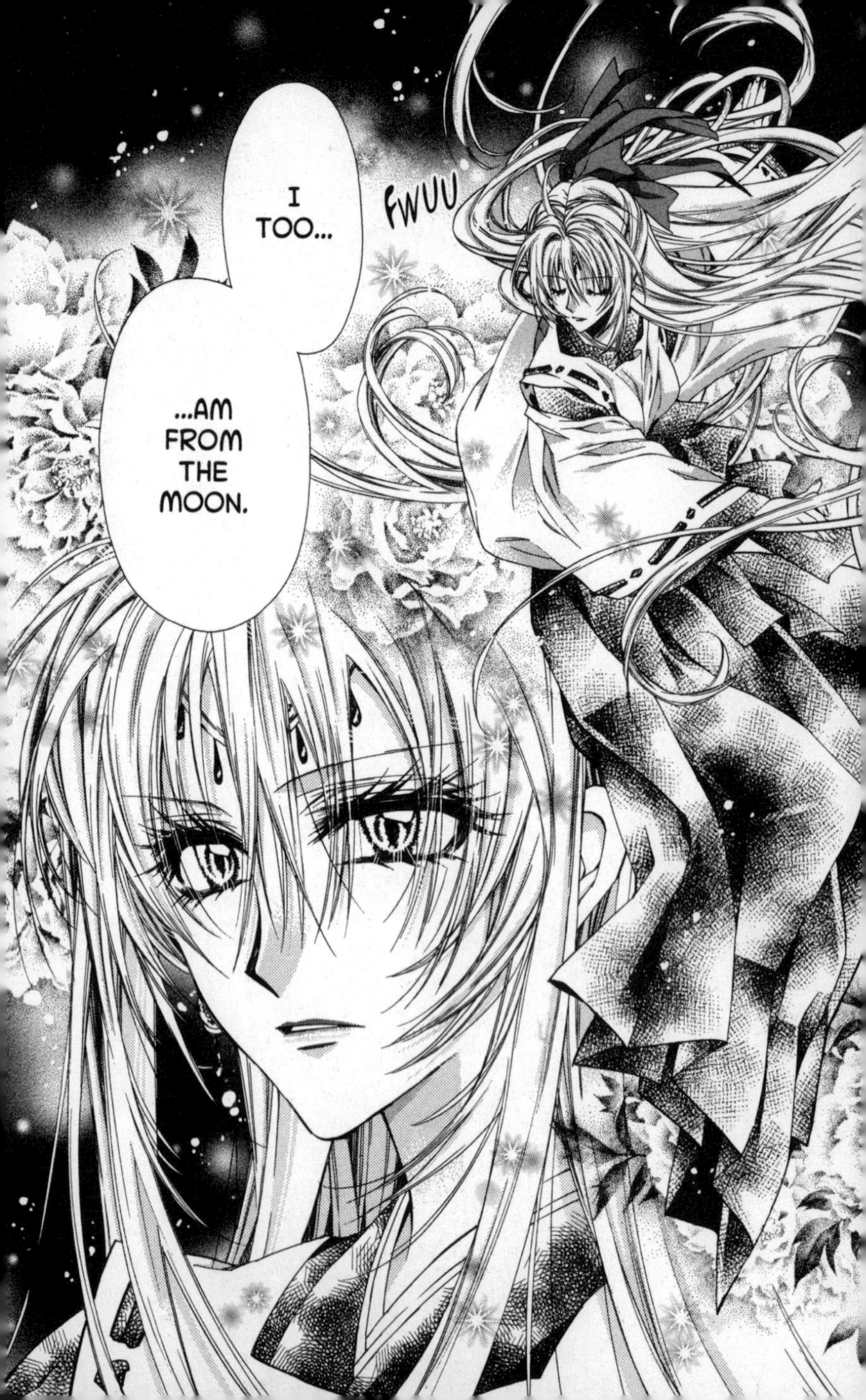
I TOO...
...AM FROM THE MOON.
FWUU

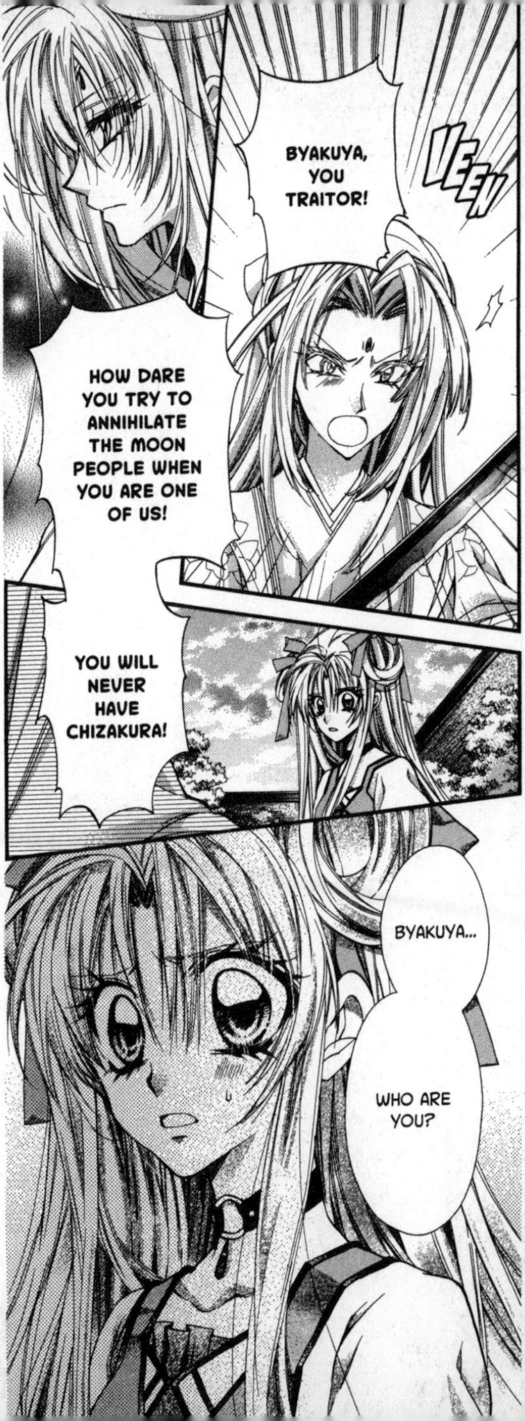
BYAKUYA, YOU TRAITOR!
VEEN
HOW DARE YOU TRY TO ANNIHILATE THE MOON PEOPLE WHEN YOU ARE ONE OF US!
YOU WILL NEVER HAVE CHIZAKURA!
BYAKUYA...
WHO ARE YOU?

See You Later

And so, this is the last sidebar.

So much has happened at *Ribon*...

And now I think of it, I feel I've been very blessed. I experienced many hardships too, but they are all important memories to me.

I might be thought of as a strange mangaka, but I have taken all my work seriously. I will continue to put everything into my manga. Of course I might create failures, but you never know how it'll turn out until you draw it.

Although I've left *Ribon*, I hope you will keep calling me Arinacchi like you've always done.

I hope you will continue to support me. ♥

December 2012
種村有菜
Arina Tanemura

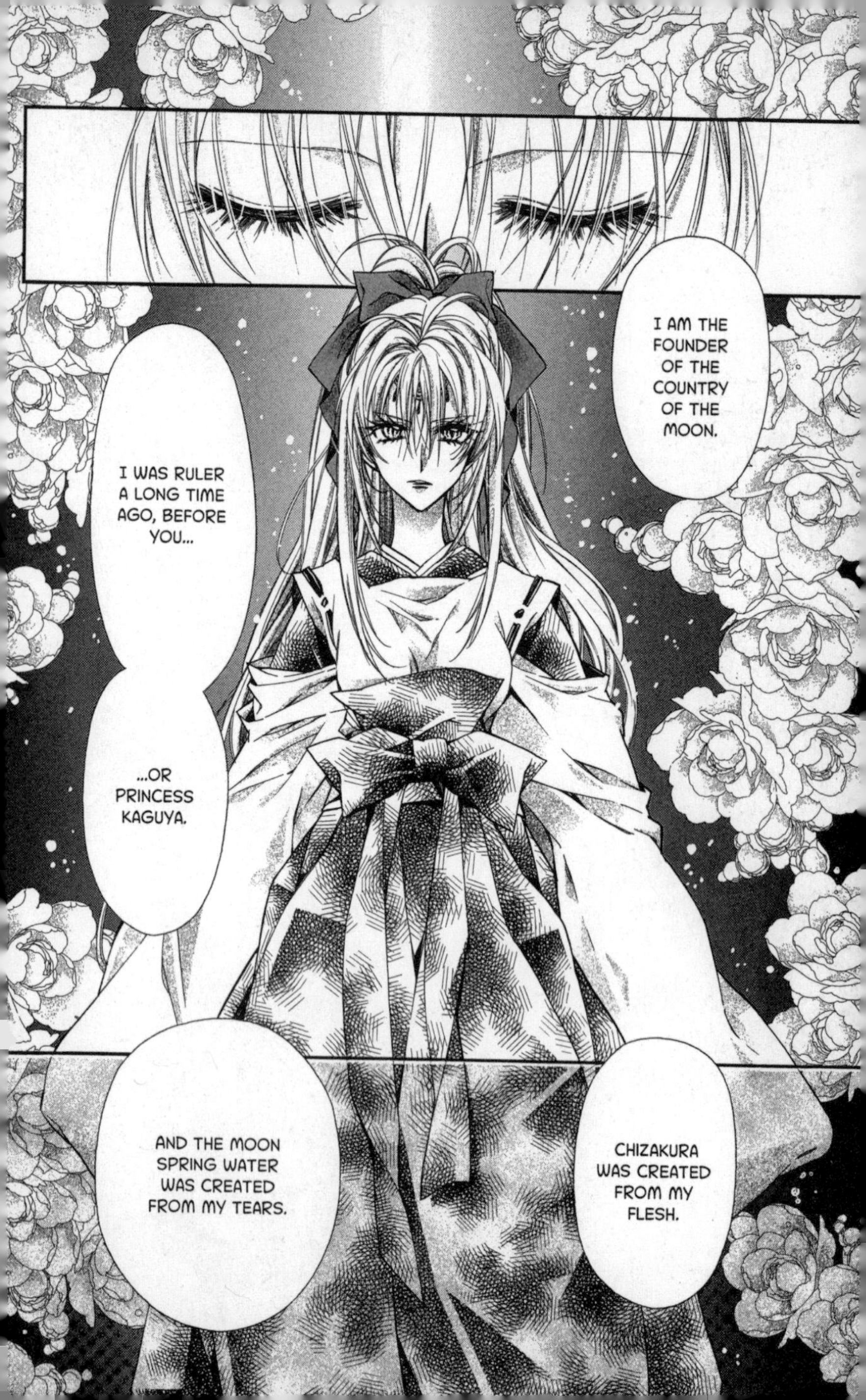
I AM THE FOUNDER OF THE COUNTRY OF THE MOON.
I WAS RULER A LONG TIME AGO, BEFORE YOU...
...OR PRINCESS KAGUYA.
CHIZAKURA WAS CREATED FROM MY FLESH.
AND THE MOON SPRING WATER WAS CREATED FROM MY TEARS.

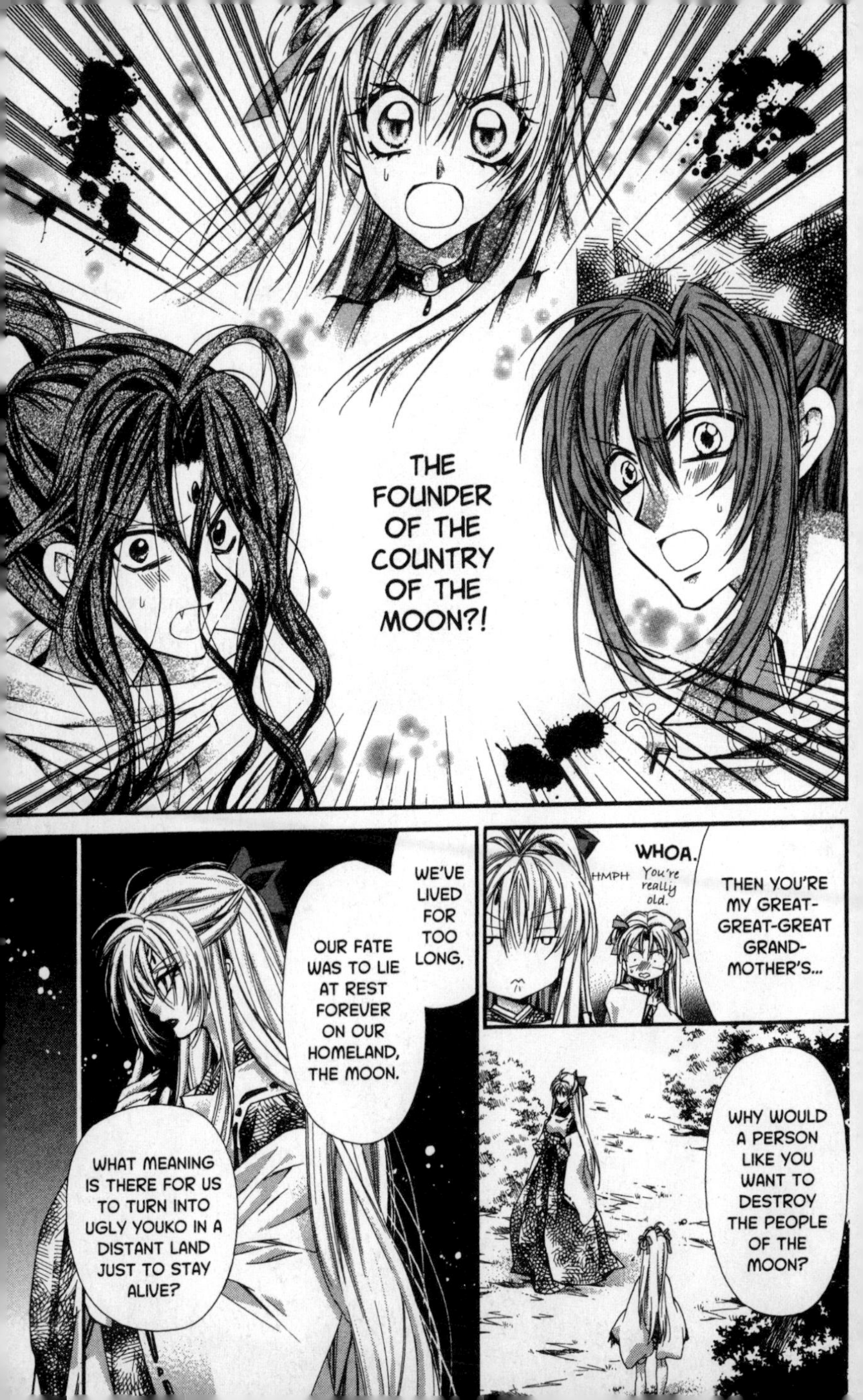
THE FOUNDER OF THE COUNTRY OF THE MOON?!
THEN YOU'RE MY GREAT-GREAT-GREAT GRAND-MOTHER'S...
WHOA.
You're really old.
HMPH
WHY WOULD A PERSON LIKE YOU WANT TO DESTROY THE PEOPLE OF THE MOON?
WE'VE LIVED FOR TOO LONG.
OUR FATE WAS TO LIE AT REST FOREVER ON OUR HOMELAND, THE MOON.
WHAT MEANING IS THERE FOR US TO TURN INTO UGLY YOUKO IN A DISTANT LAND JUST TO STAY ALIVE?

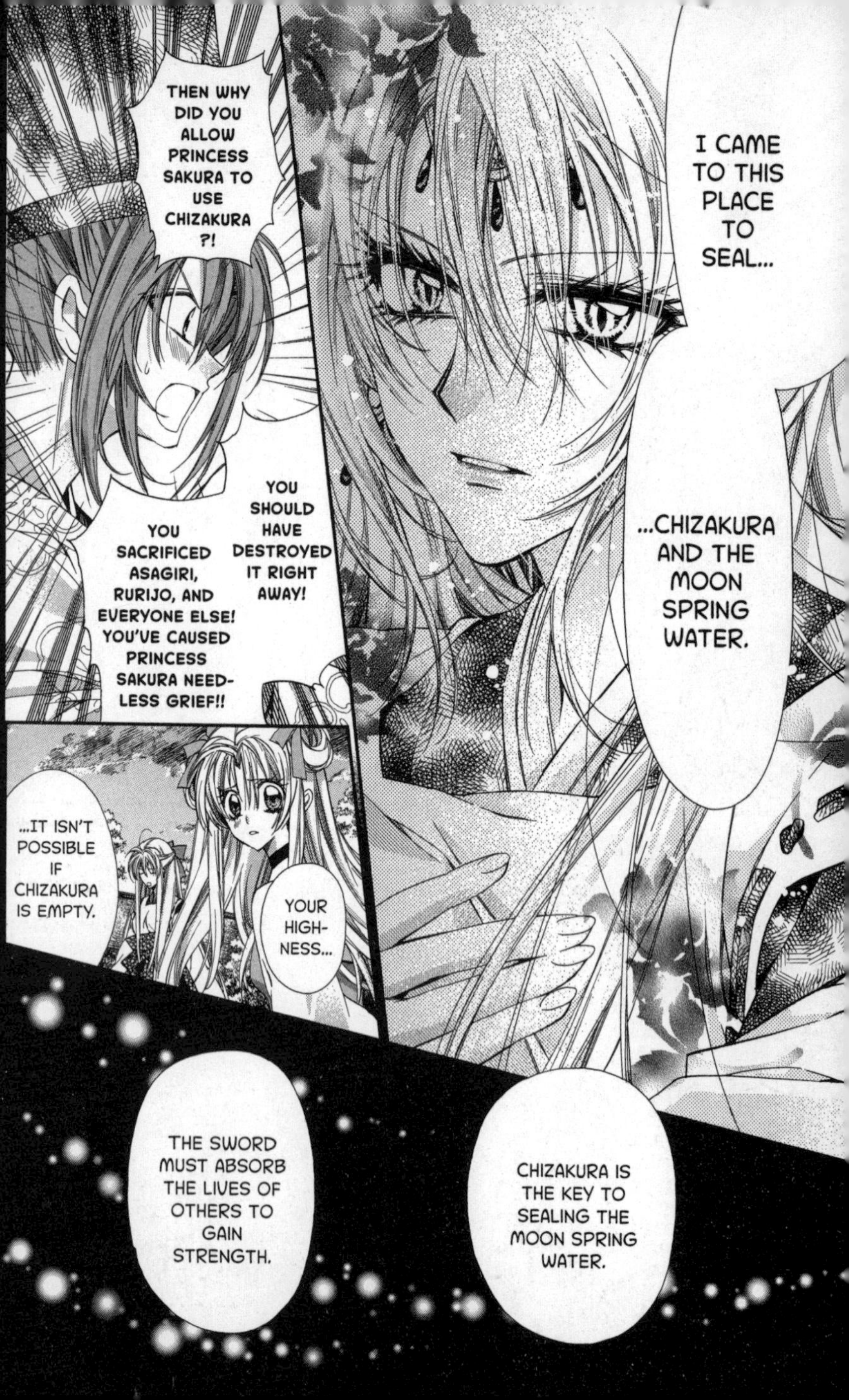
I CAME TO THIS PLACE TO SEAL...
...CHIZAKURA AND THE MOON SPRING WATER.
THEN WHY DID YOU ALLOW PRINCESS SAKURA TO USE CHIZAKURA?!
YOU SHOULD HAVE DESTROYED IT RIGHT AWAY!
YOU SACRIFICED ASAGIRI, RURIJO, AND EVERYONE ELSE! YOU'VE CAUSED PRINCESS SAKURA NEEDLESS GRIEF!!
YOUR HIGHNESS...
...IT ISN'T POSSIBLE IF CHIZAKURA IS EMPTY.
CHIZAKURA IS THE KEY TO SEALING THE MOON SPRING WATER.
THE SWORD MUST ABSORB THE LIVES OF OTHERS TO GAIN STRENGTH.

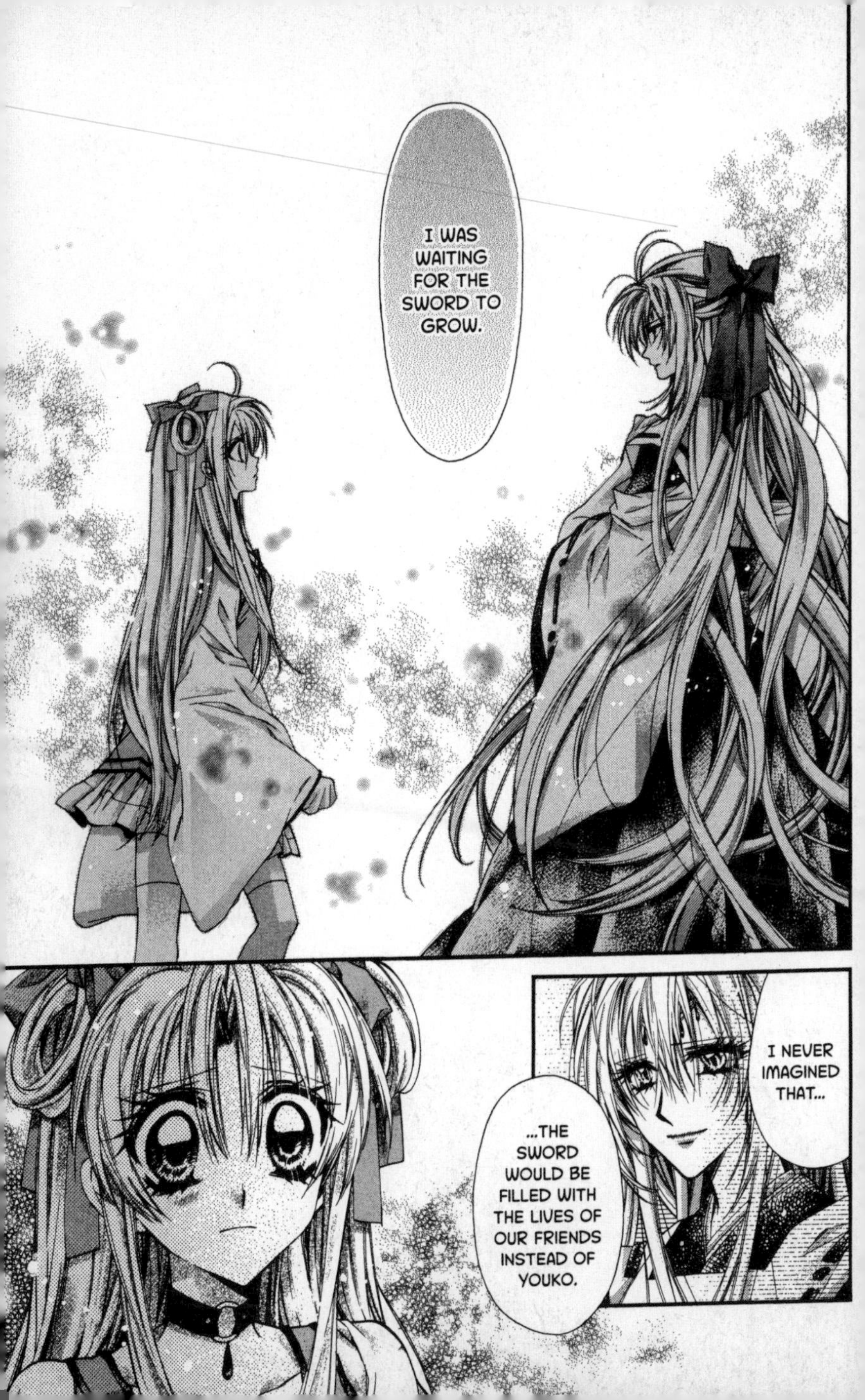
I WAS WAITING FOR THE SWORD TO GROW.
I NEVER IMAGINED THAT...
...THE SWORD WOULD BE FILLED WITH THE LIVES OF OUR FRIENDS INSTEAD OF YOUKO.

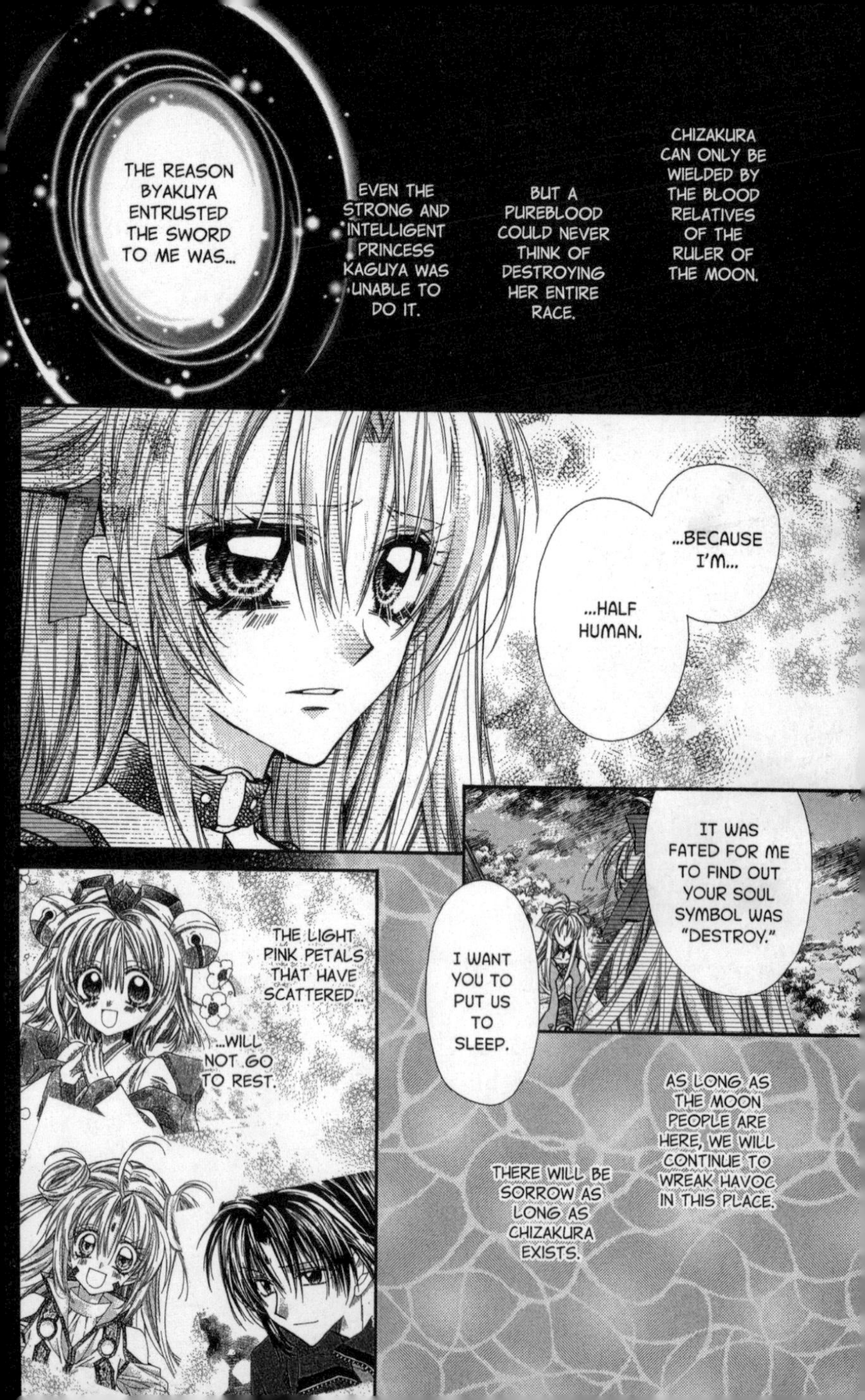
CHIZAKURA CAN ONLY BE WIELDED BY THE BLOOD RELATIVES OF THE RULER OF THE MOON.
BUT A PUREBLOOD COULD NEVER THINK OF DESTROYING HER ENTIRE RACE.
EVEN THE STRONG AND INTELLIGENT PRINCESS KAGUYA WAS UNABLE TO DO IT.
THE REASON BYAKUYA ENTRUSTED THE SWORD TO ME WAS...
...BECAUSE I'M...
...HALF HUMAN.
IT WAS FATED FOR ME TO FIND OUT YOUR SOUL SYMBOL WAS "DESTROY."
I WANT YOU TO PUT US TO SLEEP.
AS LONG AS THE MOON PEOPLE ARE HERE, WE WILL CONTINUE TO WREAK HAVOC IN THIS PLACE.
THERE WILL BE SORROW AS LONG AS CHIZAKURA EXISTS.
THE LIGHT PINK PETALS THAT HAVE SCATTERED...
...WILL NOT GO TO REST.

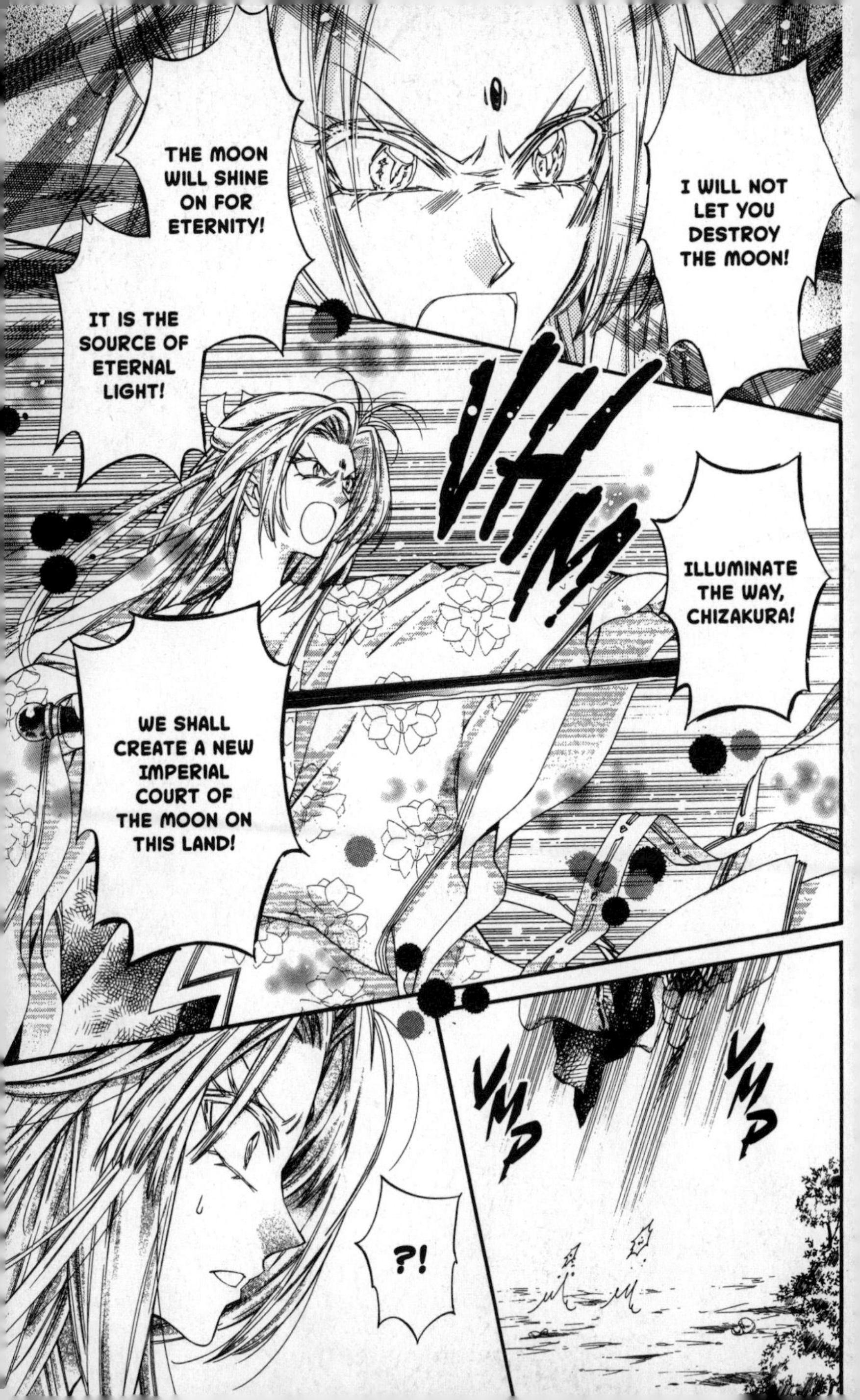
I WILL NOT LET YOU DESTROY THE MOON!
THE MOON WILL SHINE ON FOR ETERNITY!
IT IS THE SOURCE OF ETERNAL LIGHT!
VHM
ILLUMINATE THE WAY, CHIZAKURA!
WE SHALL CREATE A NEW IMPERIAL COURT OF THE MOON ON THIS LAND!
VMP
VMP
?!

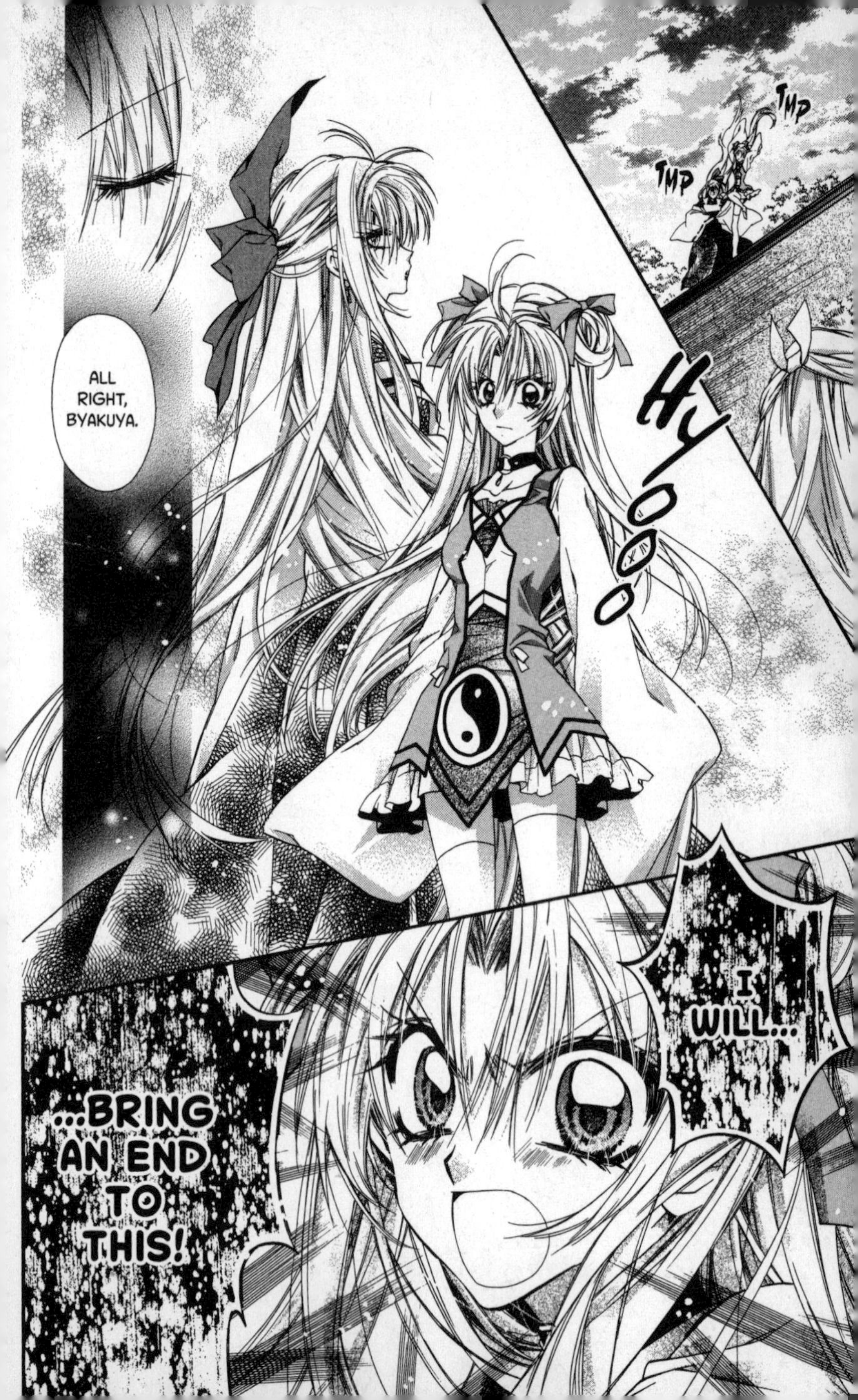
TMP
TMP
HYOOOO
ALL RIGHT, BYAKUYA.
I WILL...
...BRING AN END TO THIS!

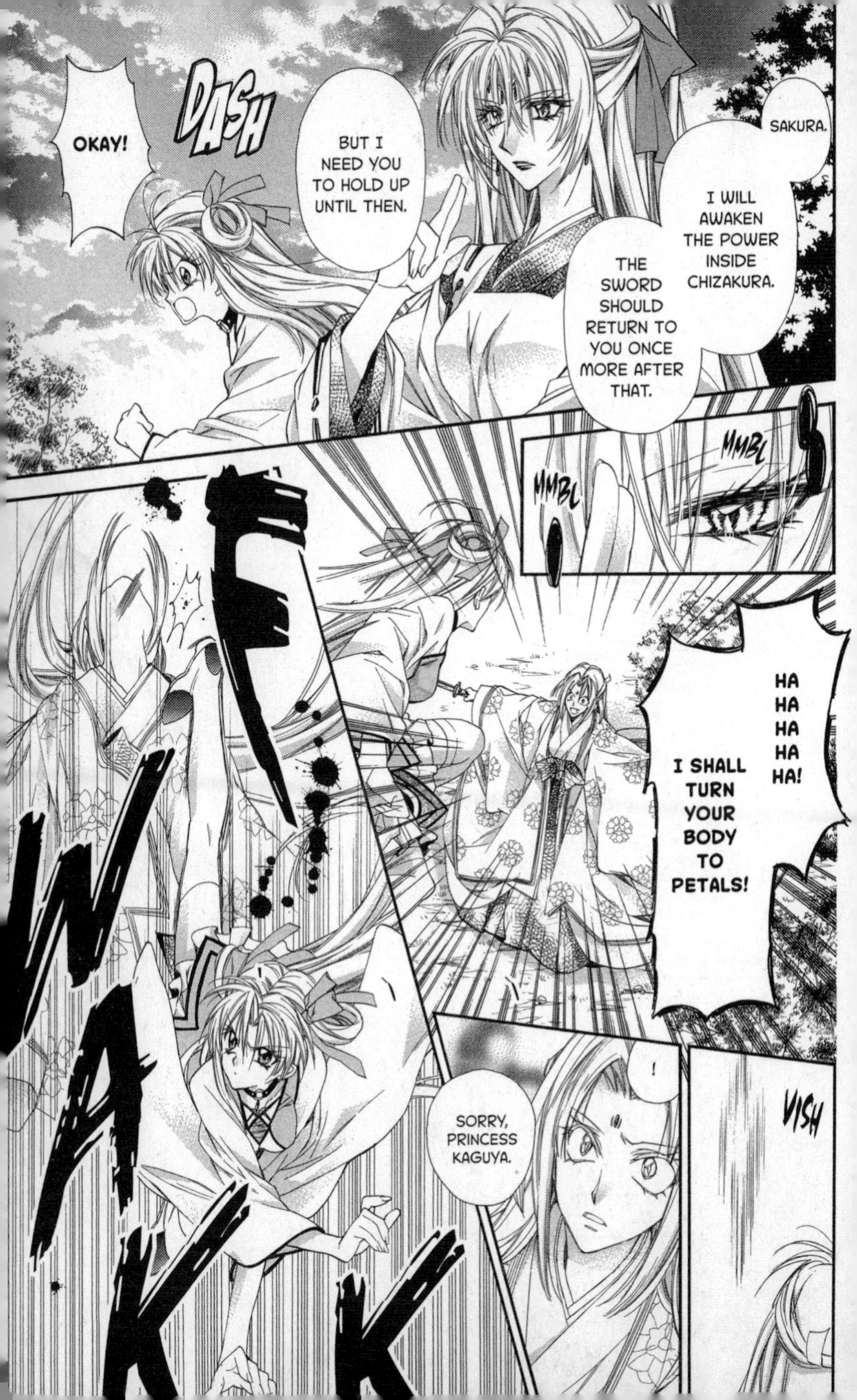
SAKURA.
I WILL AWAKEN THE POWER INSIDE CHIZAKURA.
THE SWORD SHOULD RETURN TO YOU ONCE MORE AFTER THAT.
BUT I NEED YOU TO HOLD UP UNTIL THEN.
DASH
OKAY!
MMBL
MMBL
HA HA HA HA HA!
I SHALL TURN YOUR BODY TO PETALS!
VISH
!
SORRY, PRINCESS KAGUYA.
WAKK

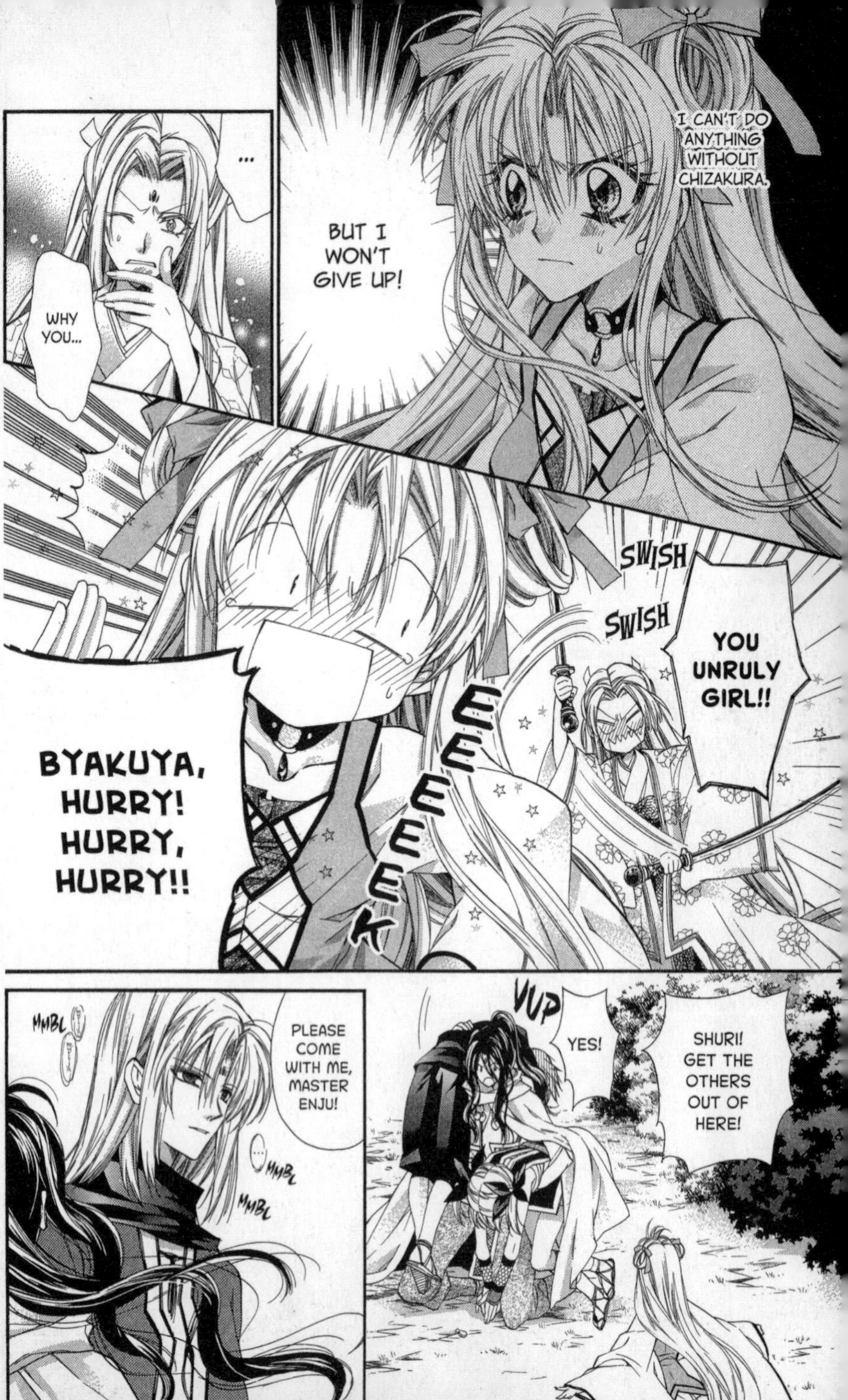
I CAN'T DO ANYTHING WITHOUT CHIZAKURA.
BUT I WON'T GIVE UP!
...
WHY YOU...
SWISH
SWISH
YOU UNRULY GIRL!!
EEEEEEK
BYAKUYA, HURRY! HURRY, HURRY!!
VUP
SHURI! GET THE OTHERS OUT OF HERE!
YES!
PLEASE COME WITH ME, MASTER ENJU!
MMBL
...
MMBL
MMBL

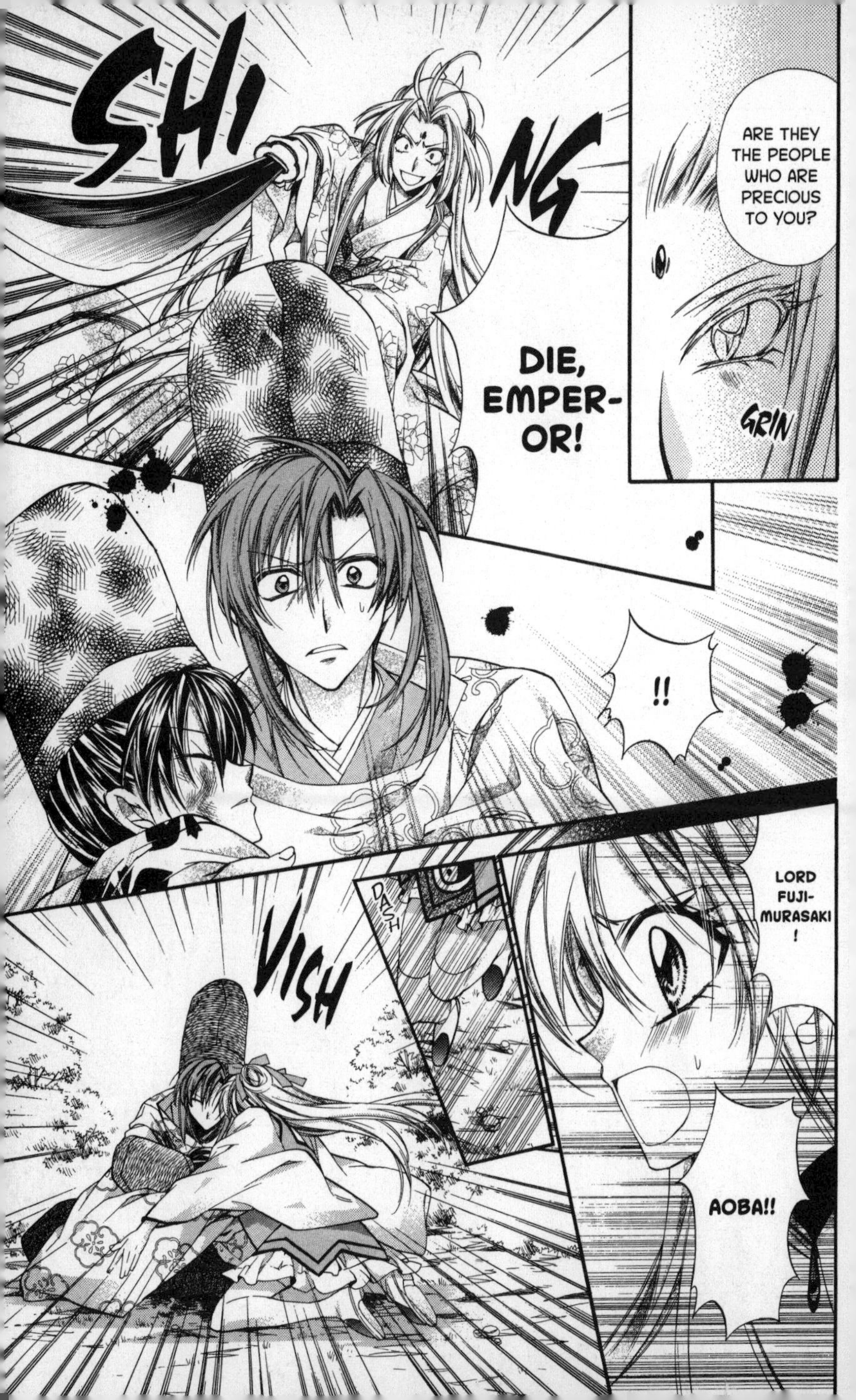
ARE THEY THE PEOPLE WHO ARE PRECIOUS TO YOU?
GRIN
SHHING
DIE, EMPER-OR!
!!
LORD FUJI-MURASAKI!
AOBA!!
DASH
VISH

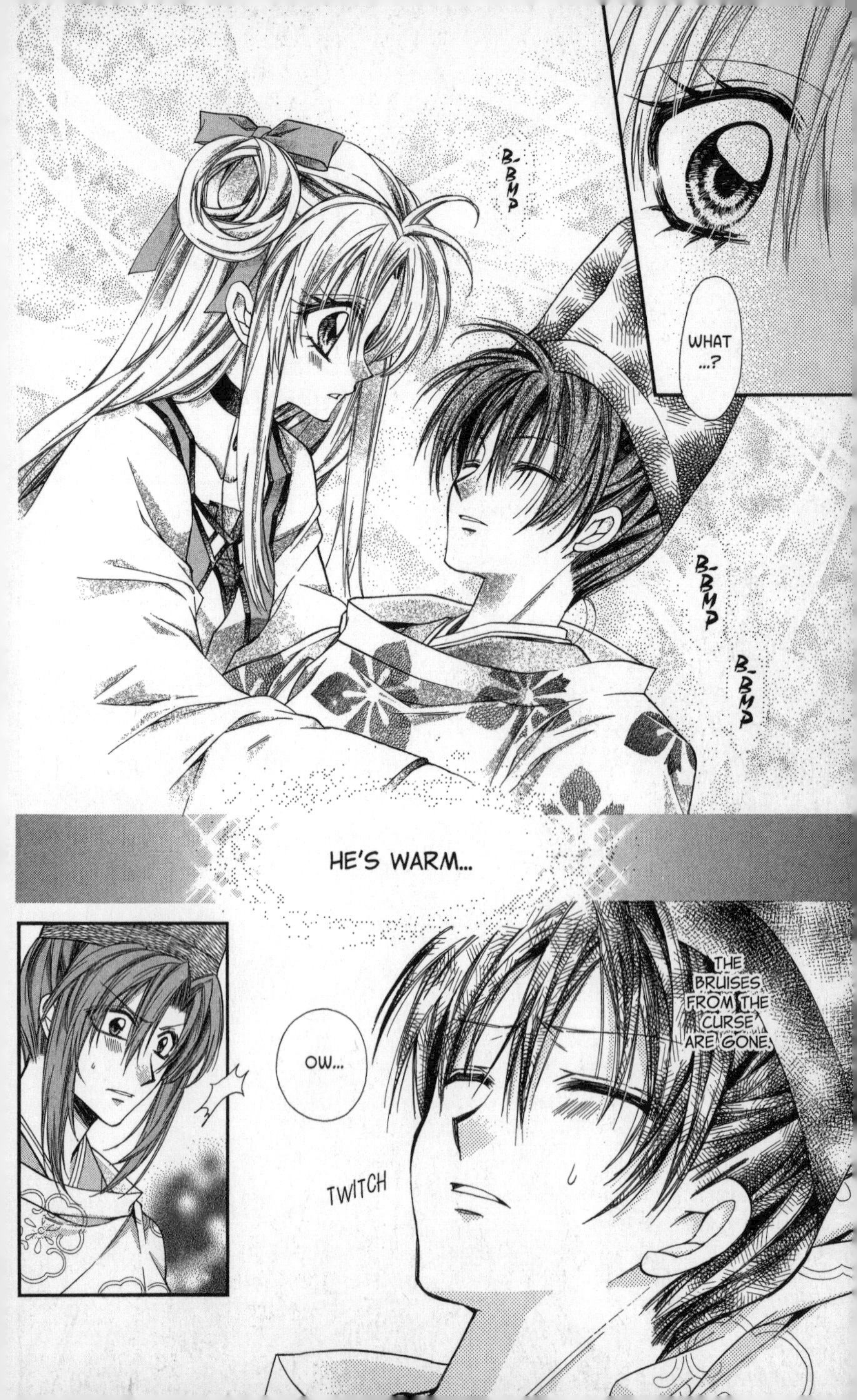
WHAT ...?
B-BMP
B-BMP
B-BMP
HE'S WARM...
THE BRUISES FROM THE CURSE ARE GONE.
OW...
TWITCH

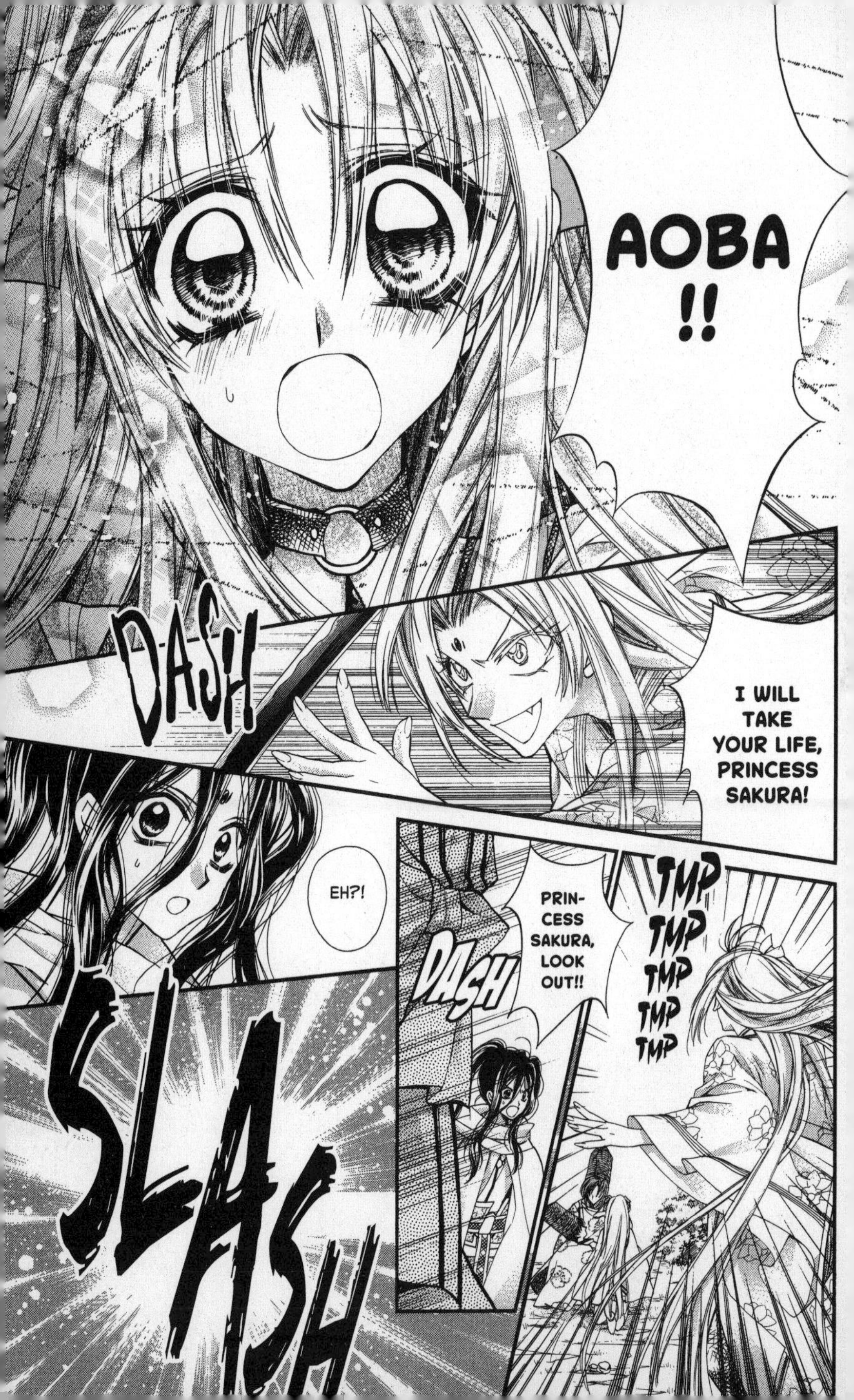
AOBA !!
I WILL TAKE YOUR LIFE, PRINCESS SAKURA!
DASH
TMP TMP TMP TMP TMP
PRIN-CESS SAKURA, LOOK OUT!!
DASH
EH?!
SLASH

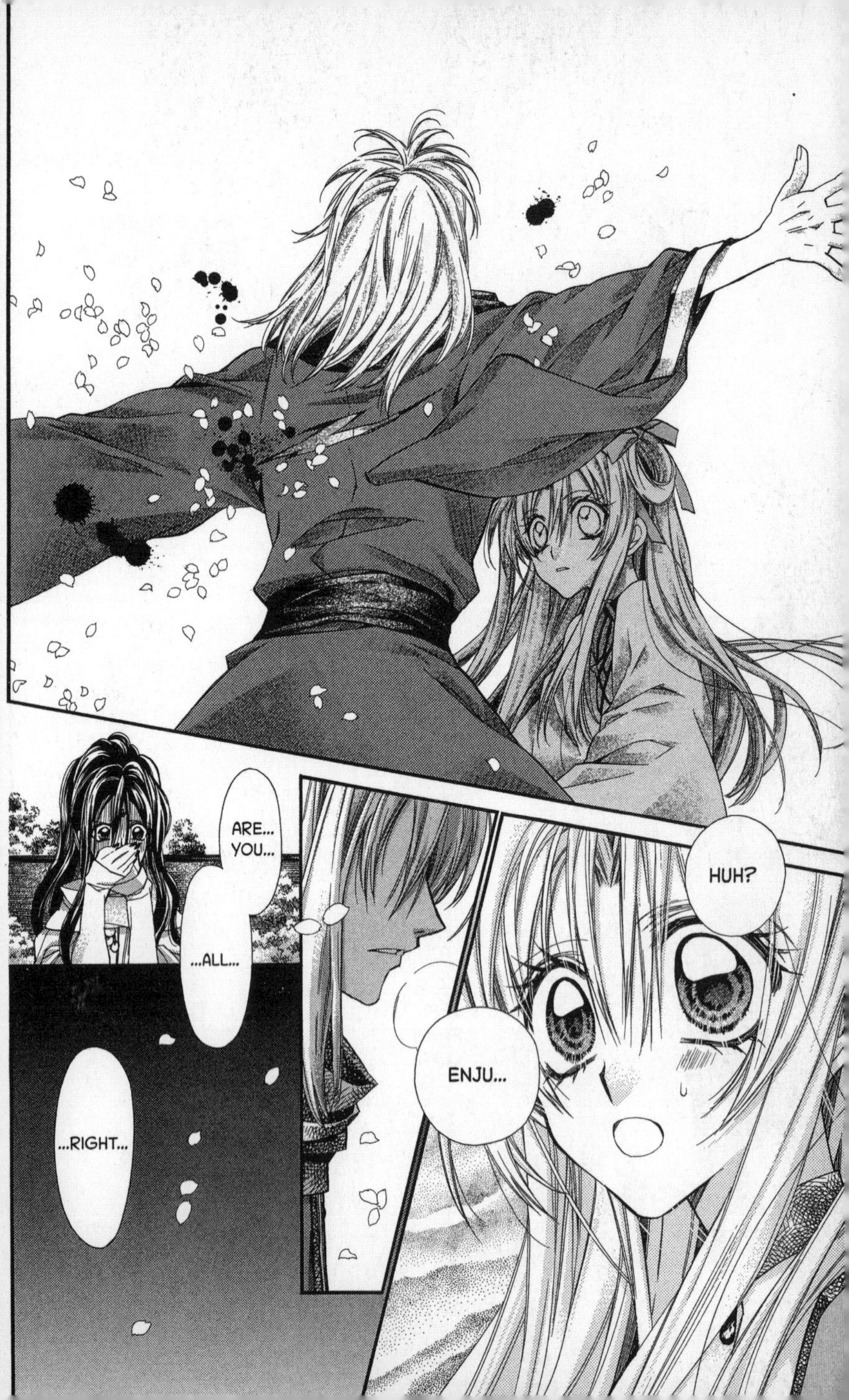
HUH?
ENJU...
ARE... YOU...
...ALL...
...RIGHT...

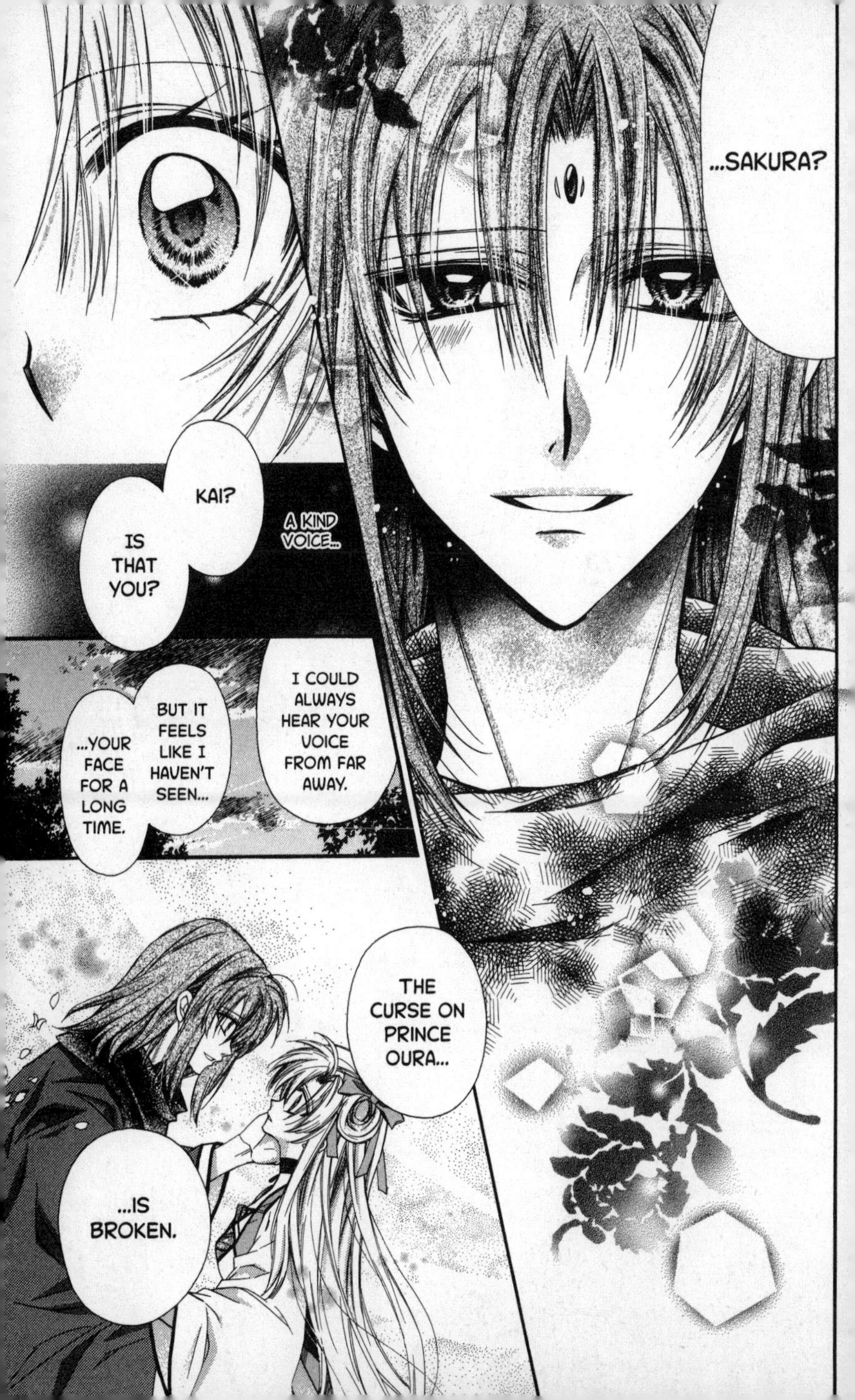
...SAKURA?
A KIND VOICE...
KAI? IS THAT YOU?
I COULD ALWAYS HEAR YOUR VOICE FROM FAR AWAY.
BUT IT FEELS LIKE I HAVEN'T SEEN...
...YOUR FACE FOR A LONG TIME.
THE CURSE ON PRINCE OURA...
...IS BROKEN.

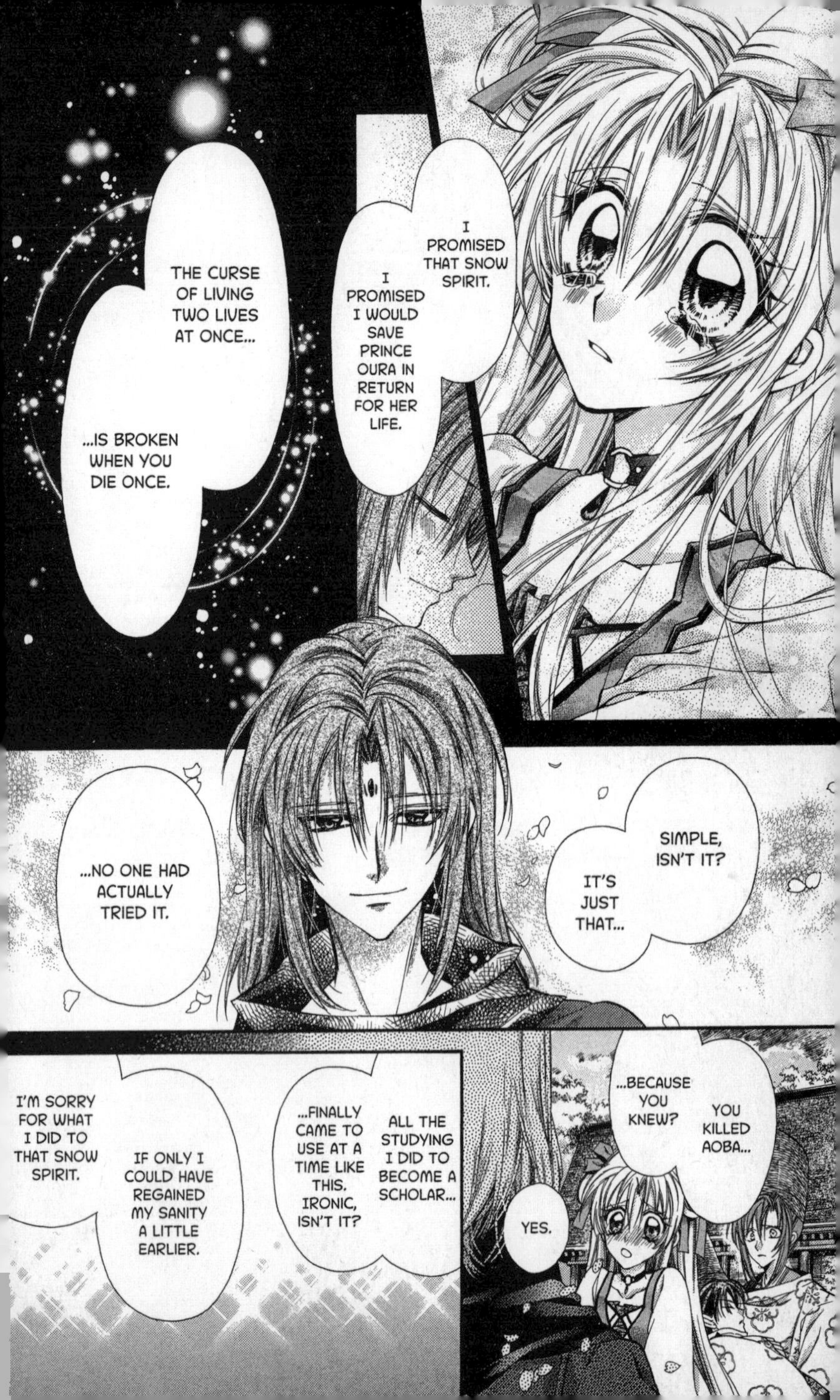
I PROMISED THAT SNOW SPIRIT.
I PROMISED I WOULD SAVE PRINCE OURA IN RETURN FOR HER LIFE.
THE CURSE OF LIVING TWO LIVES AT ONCE...
...IS BROKEN WHEN YOU DIE ONCE.
SIMPLE, ISN'T IT?
IT'S JUST THAT...
...NO ONE HAD ACTUALLY TRIED IT.
YOU KILLED AOBA...
...BECAUSE YOU KNEW?
YES.
ALL THE STUDYING I DID TO BECOME A SCHOLAR...
...FINALLY CAME TO USE AT A TIME LIKE THIS. IRONIC, ISN'T IT?
IF ONLY I COULD HAVE REGAINED MY SANITY A LITTLE EARLIER.
I'M SORRY FOR WHAT I DID TO THAT SNOW SPIRIT.

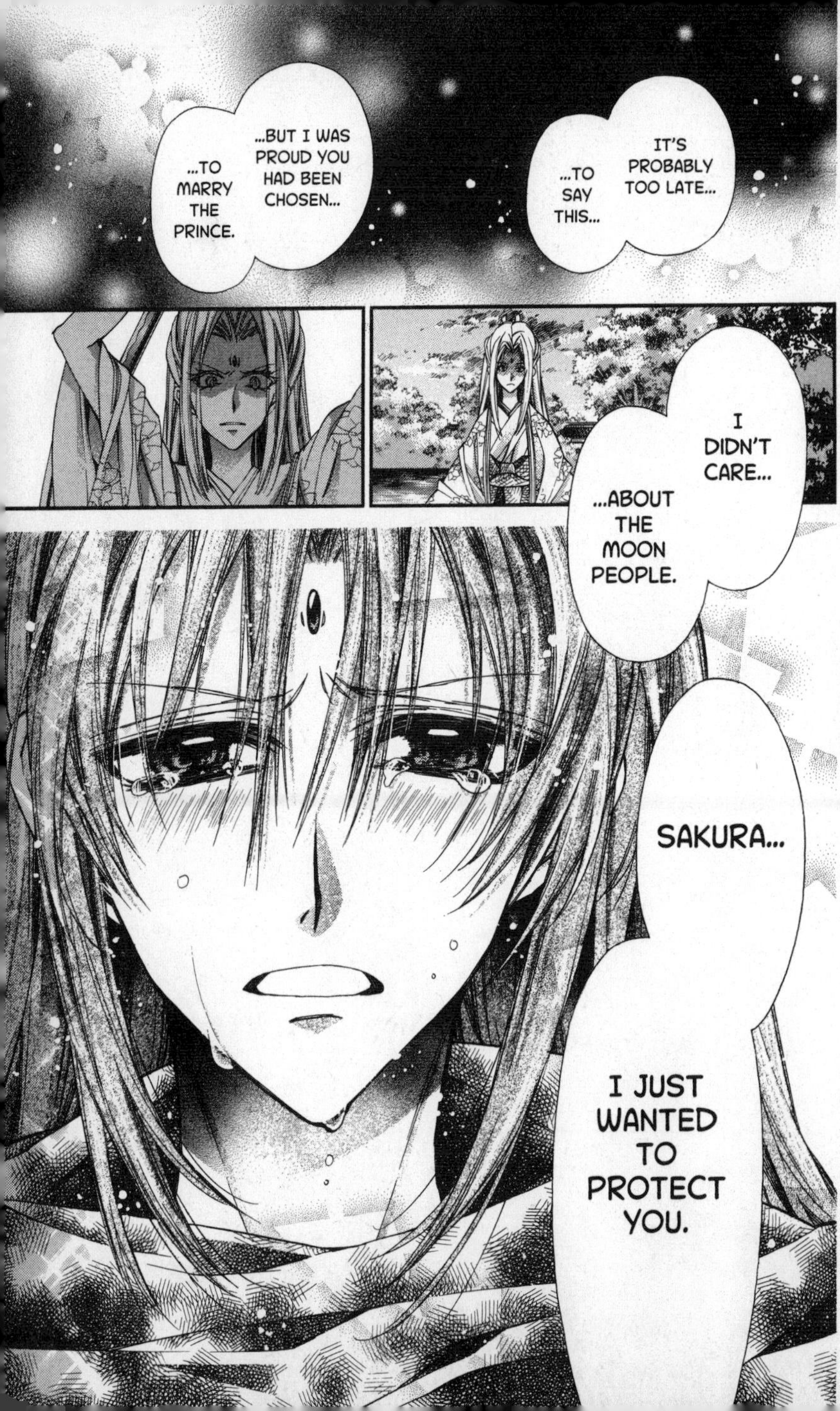

IT'S PROBABLY TOO LATE...
...TO SAY THIS...
...BUT I WAS PROUD YOU HAD BEEN CHOSEN...
...TO MARRY THE PRINCE.
I DIDN'T CARE...
...ABOUT THE MOON PEOPLE.
SAKURA...
I JUST WANTED TO PROTECT YOU.

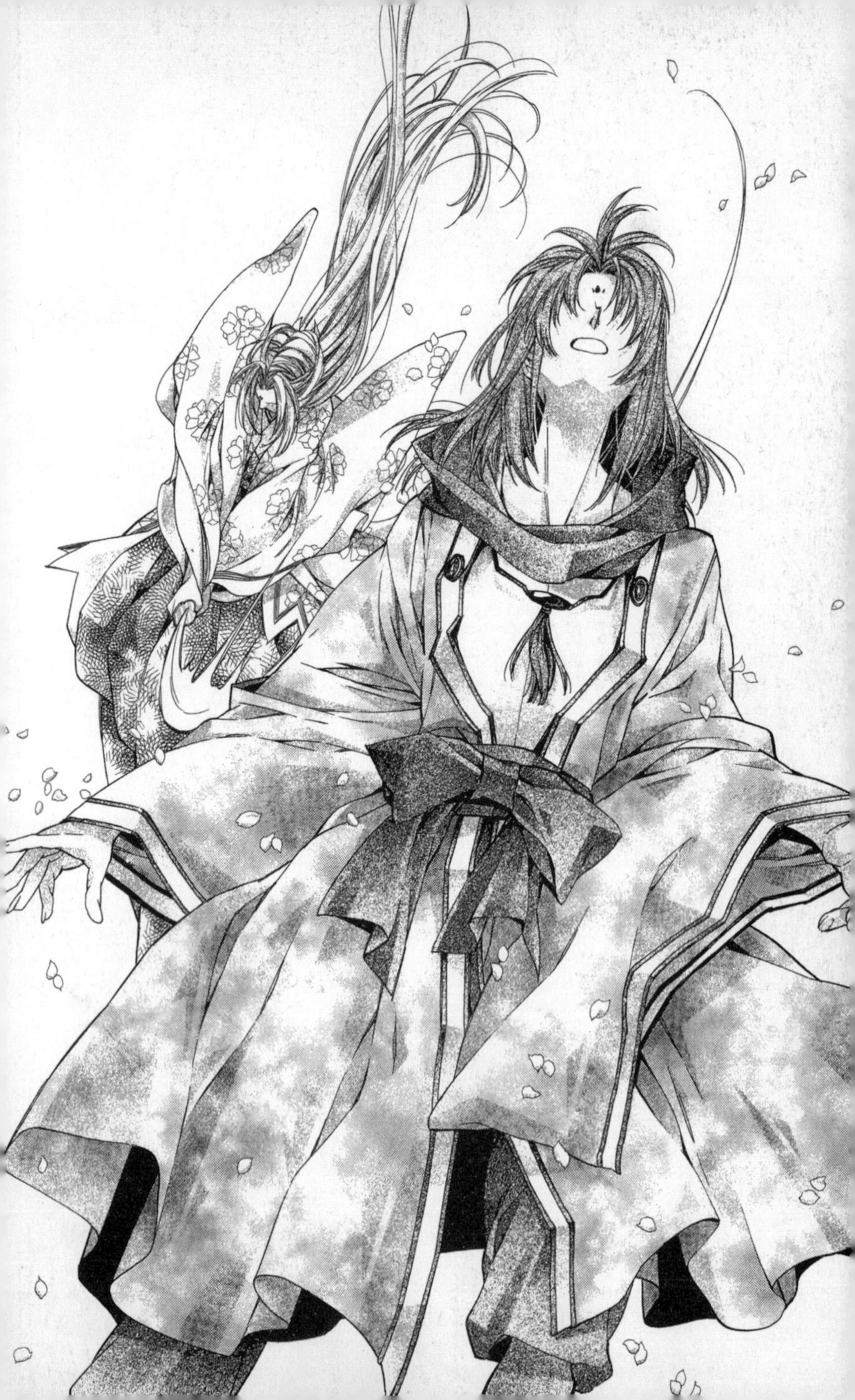

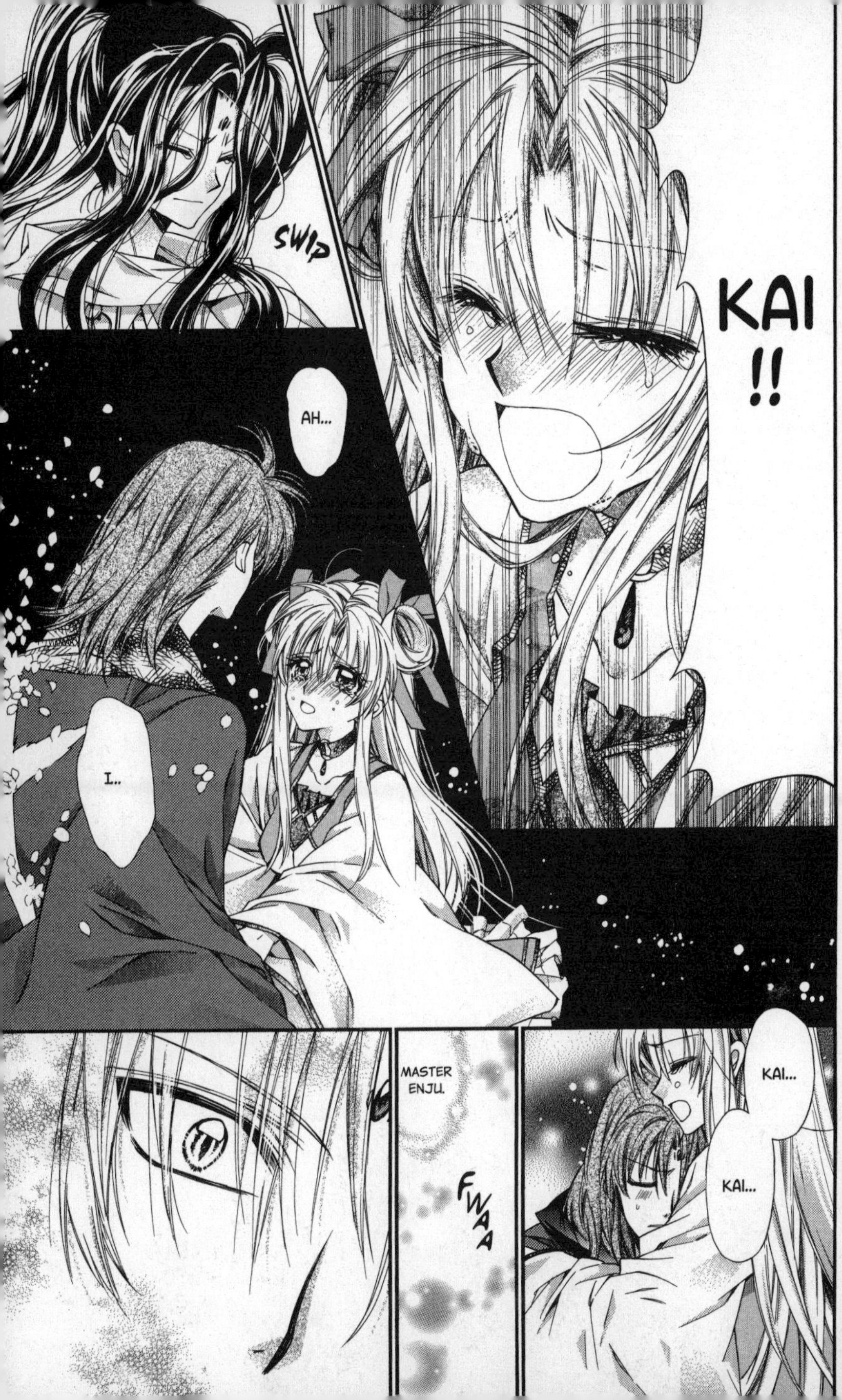
KAI !!
SWIP
AH...
I..
KAI...
KAI...
MASTER ENJU.
FWAA

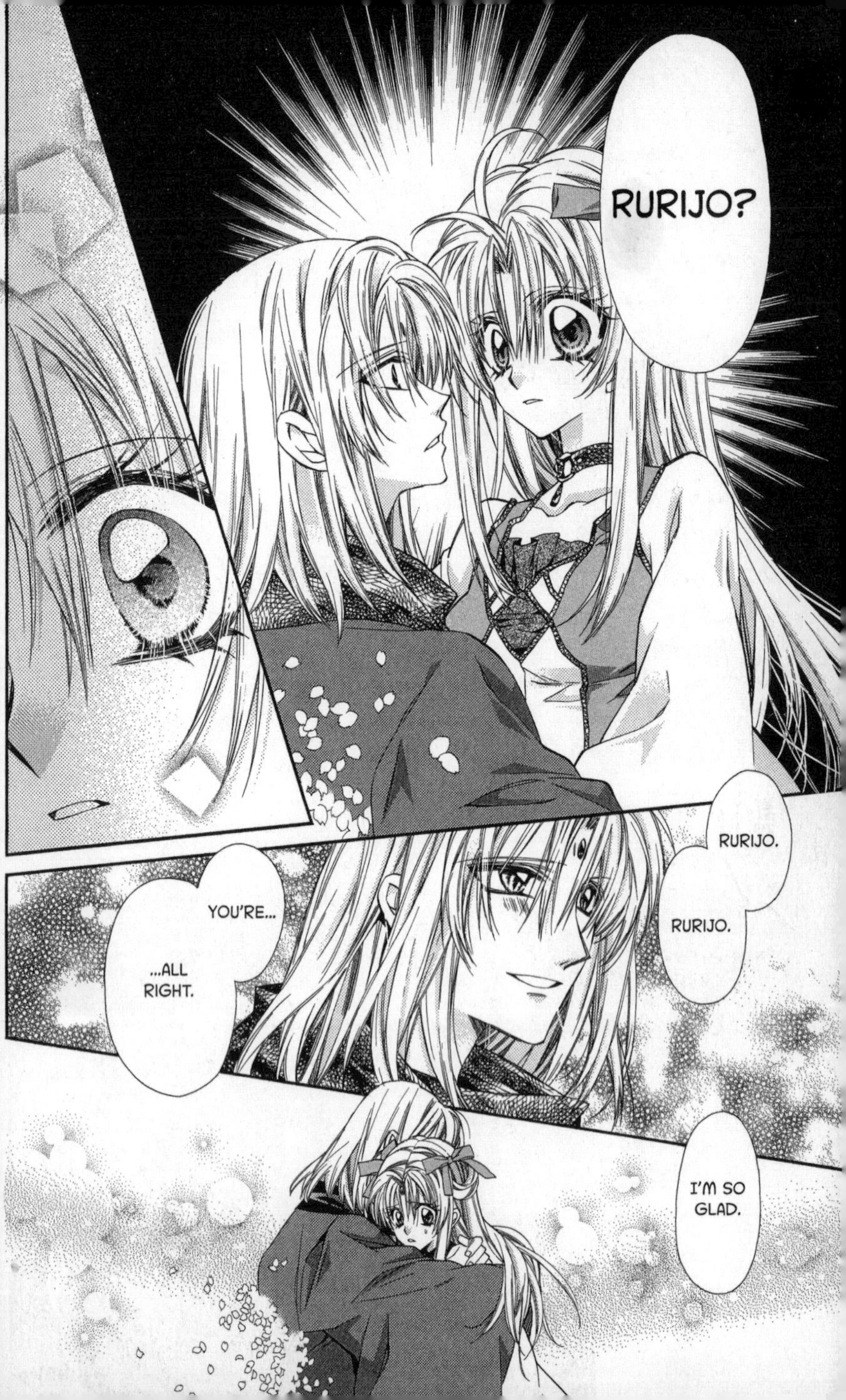
RURIJO?
RURIJO.
RURIJO.
YOU'RE...
...ALL RIGHT.
I'M SO GLAD.

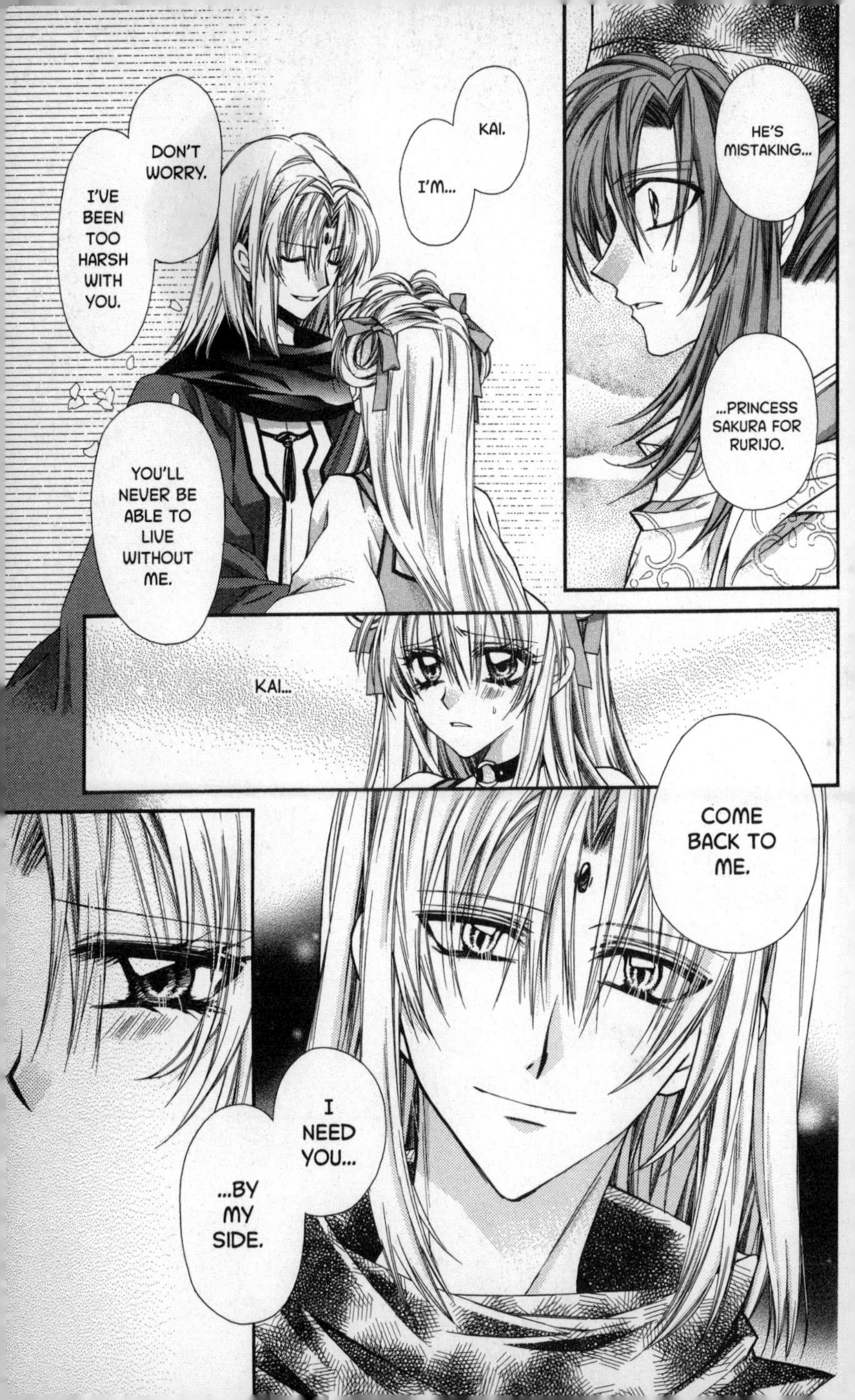
HE'S MISTAKING...
...PRINCESS SAKURA FOR RURIJO.
KAI.
I'M...
DON'T WORRY.
I'VE BEEN TOO HARSH WITH YOU.
YOU'LL NEVER BE ABLE TO LIVE WITHOUT ME.
KAI...
COME BACK TO ME.
I NEED YOU...
...BY MY SIDE.

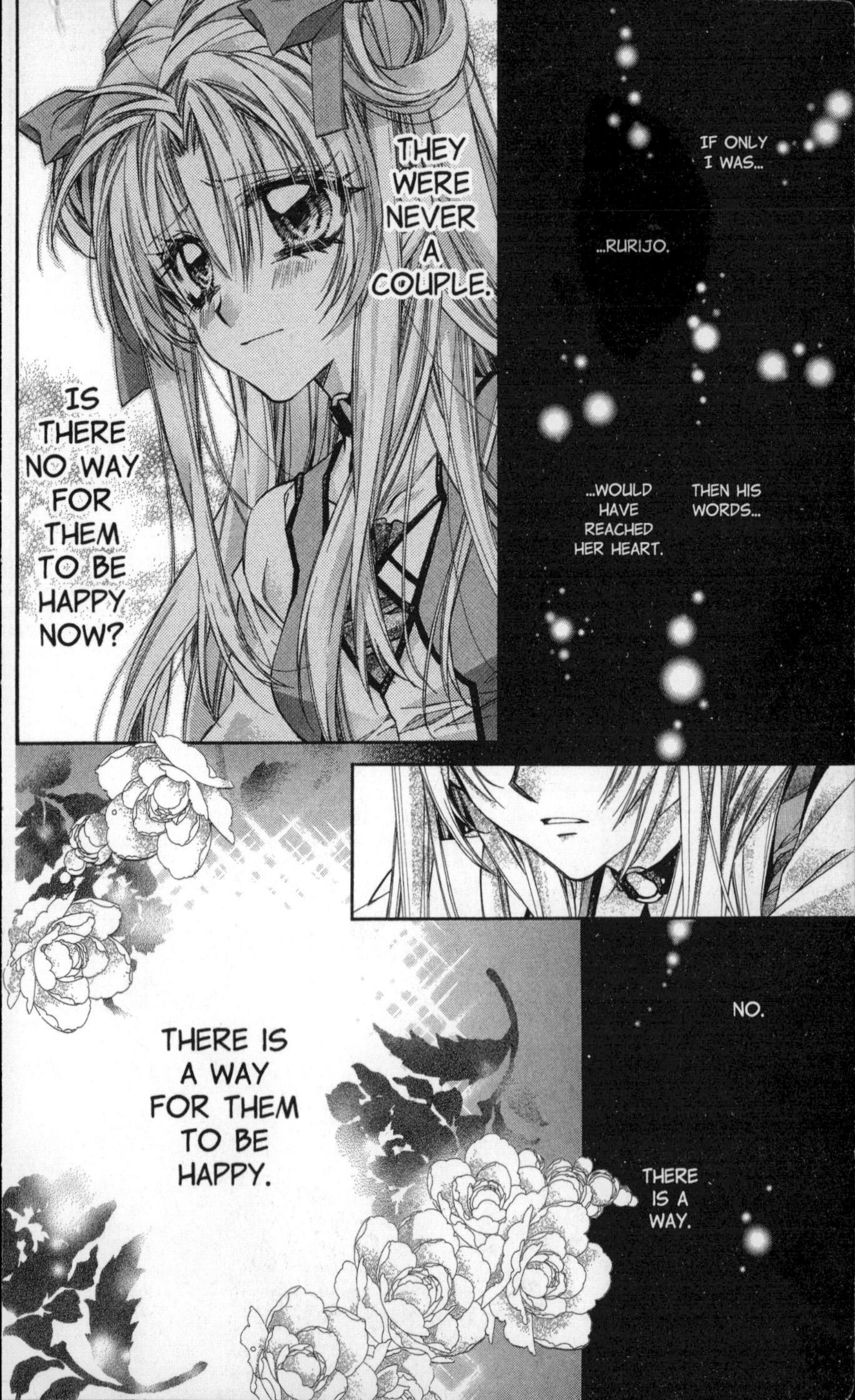
IF ONLY I WAS...
...RURIJO.
THEN HIS WORDS...
...WOULD HAVE REACHED HER HEART.
THEY WERE NEVER A COUPLE.
IS THERE NO WAY FOR THEM TO BE HAPPY NOW?
NO.
THERE IS A WAY.
THERE IS A WAY FOR THEM TO BE HAPPY.

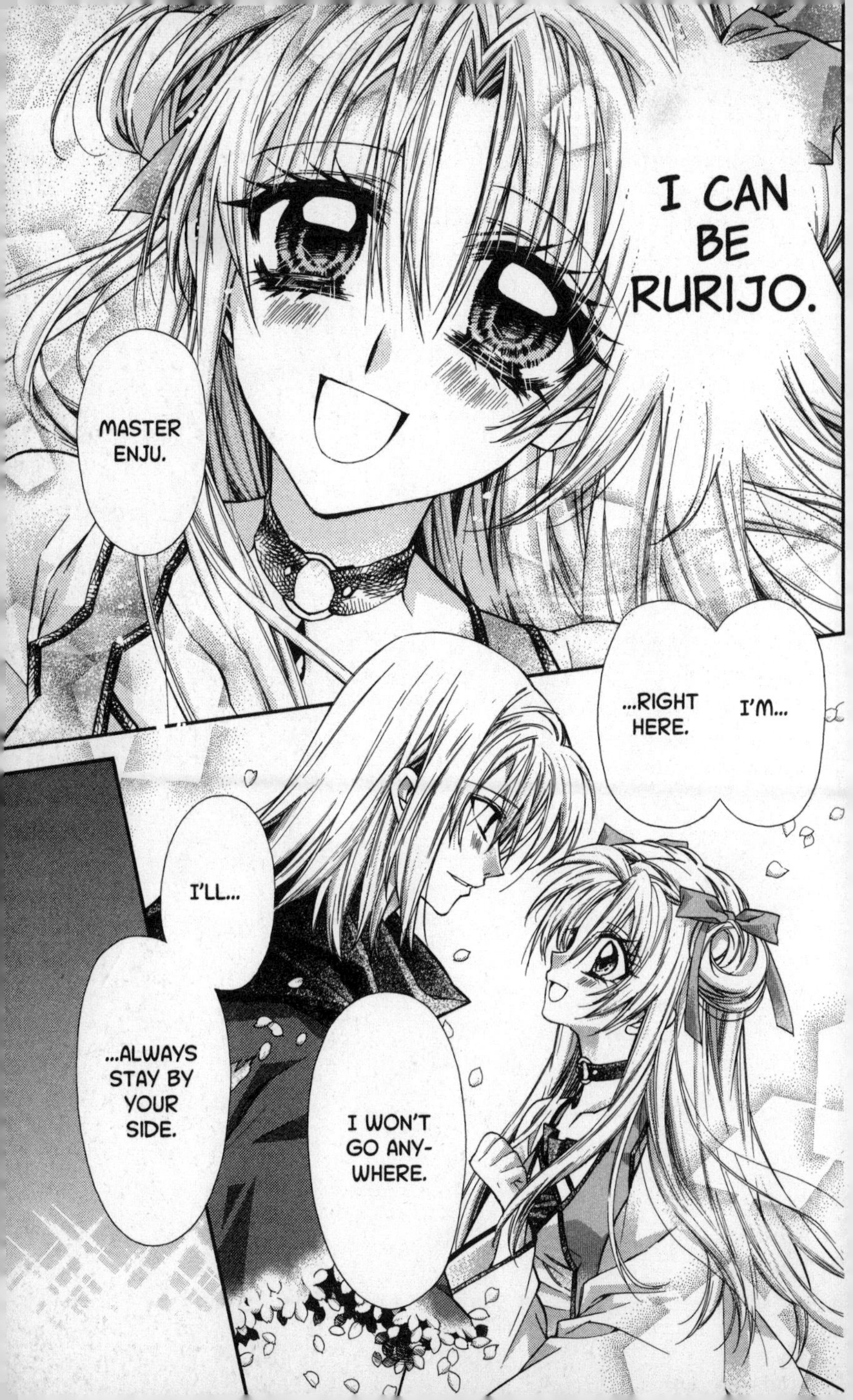
I CAN BE RURIJO.
MASTER ENJU.
I'M...
...RIGHT HERE.
I'LL...
...ALWAYS STAY BY YOUR SIDE.
I WON'T GO ANY-WHERE.

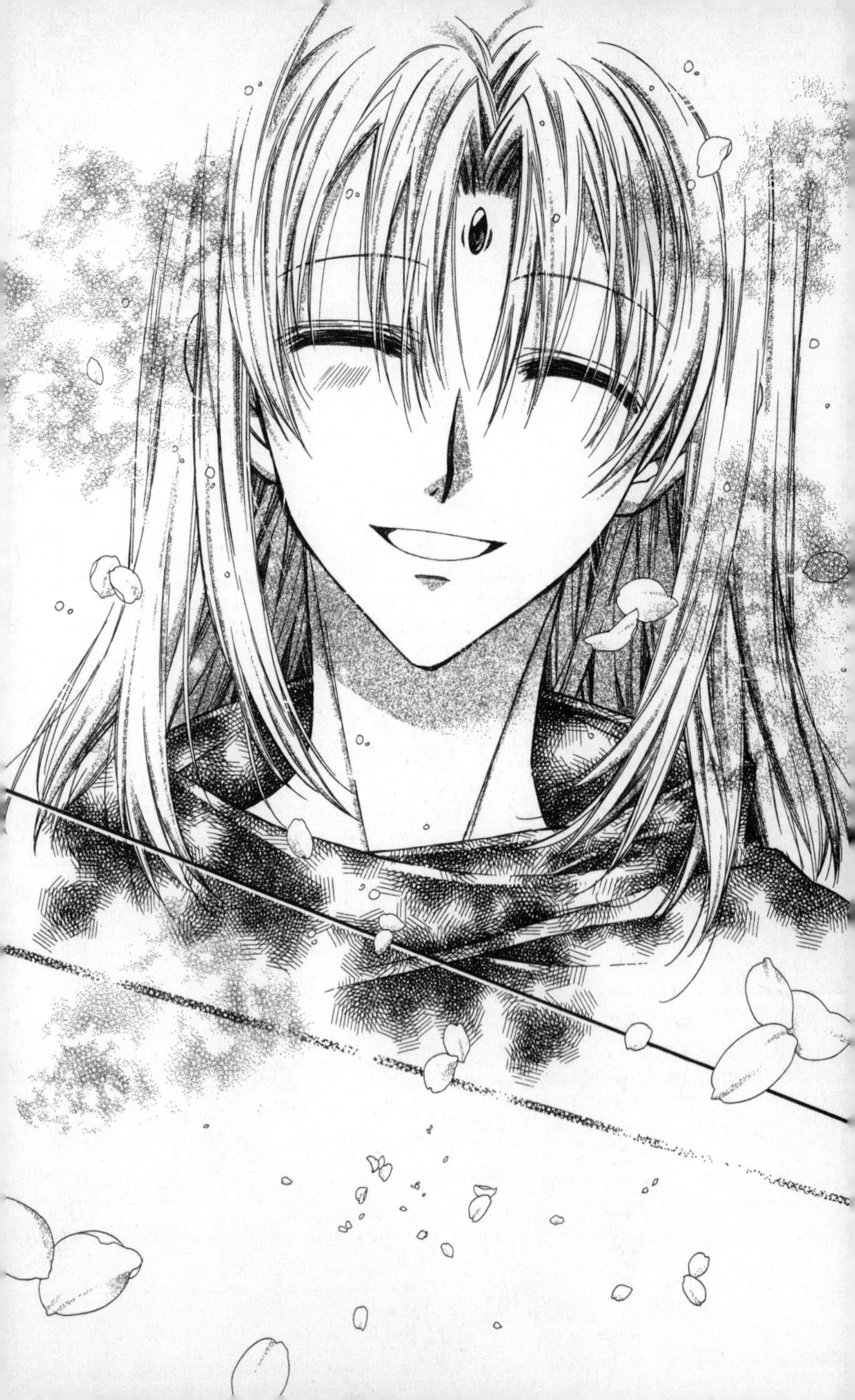

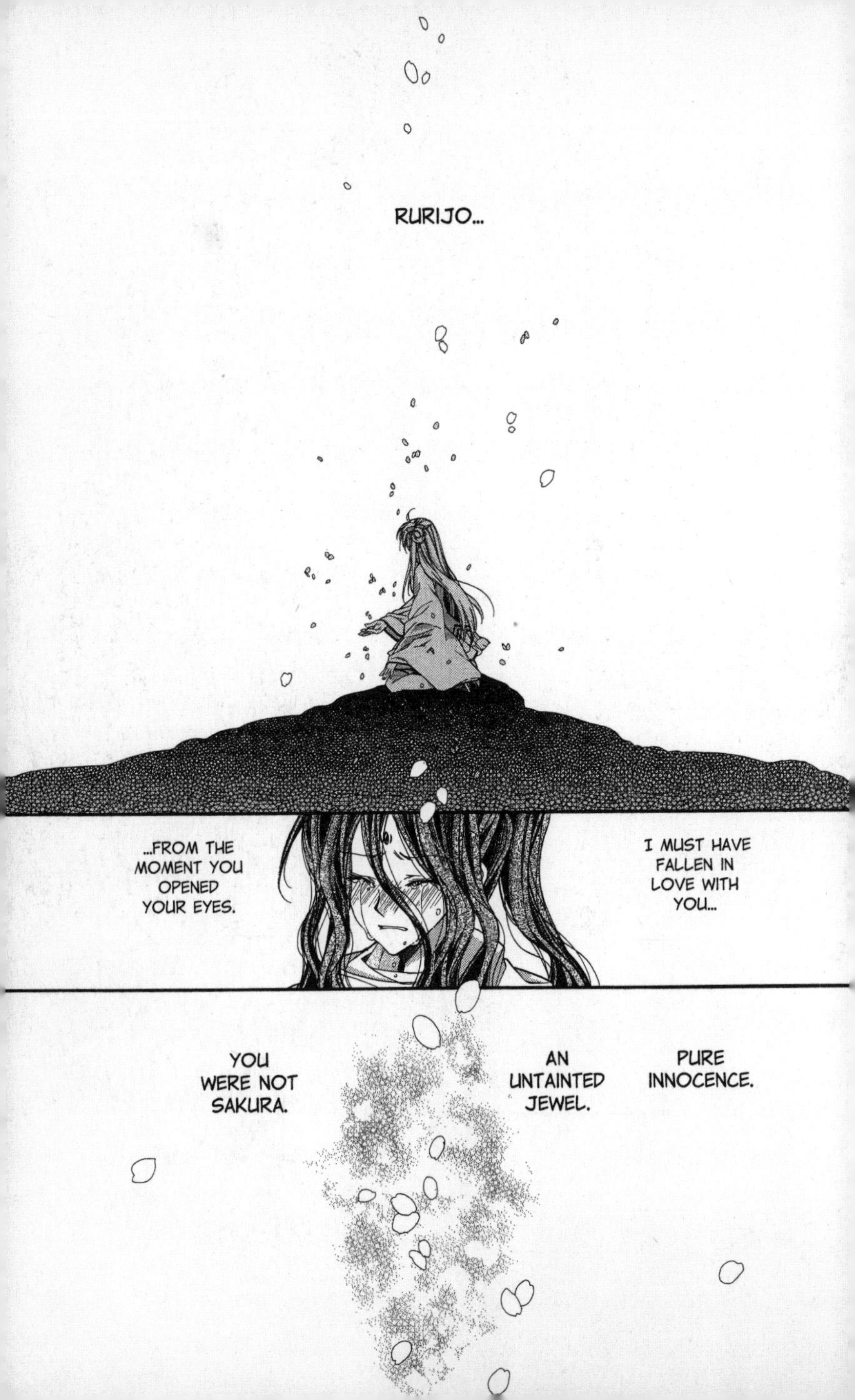
RURIJO...
I MUST HAVE FALLEN IN LOVE WITH YOU...
...FROM THE MOMENT YOU OPENED YOUR EYES.
PURE INNOCENCE.
AN UNTAINTED JEWEL.
YOU WERE NOT SAKURA.

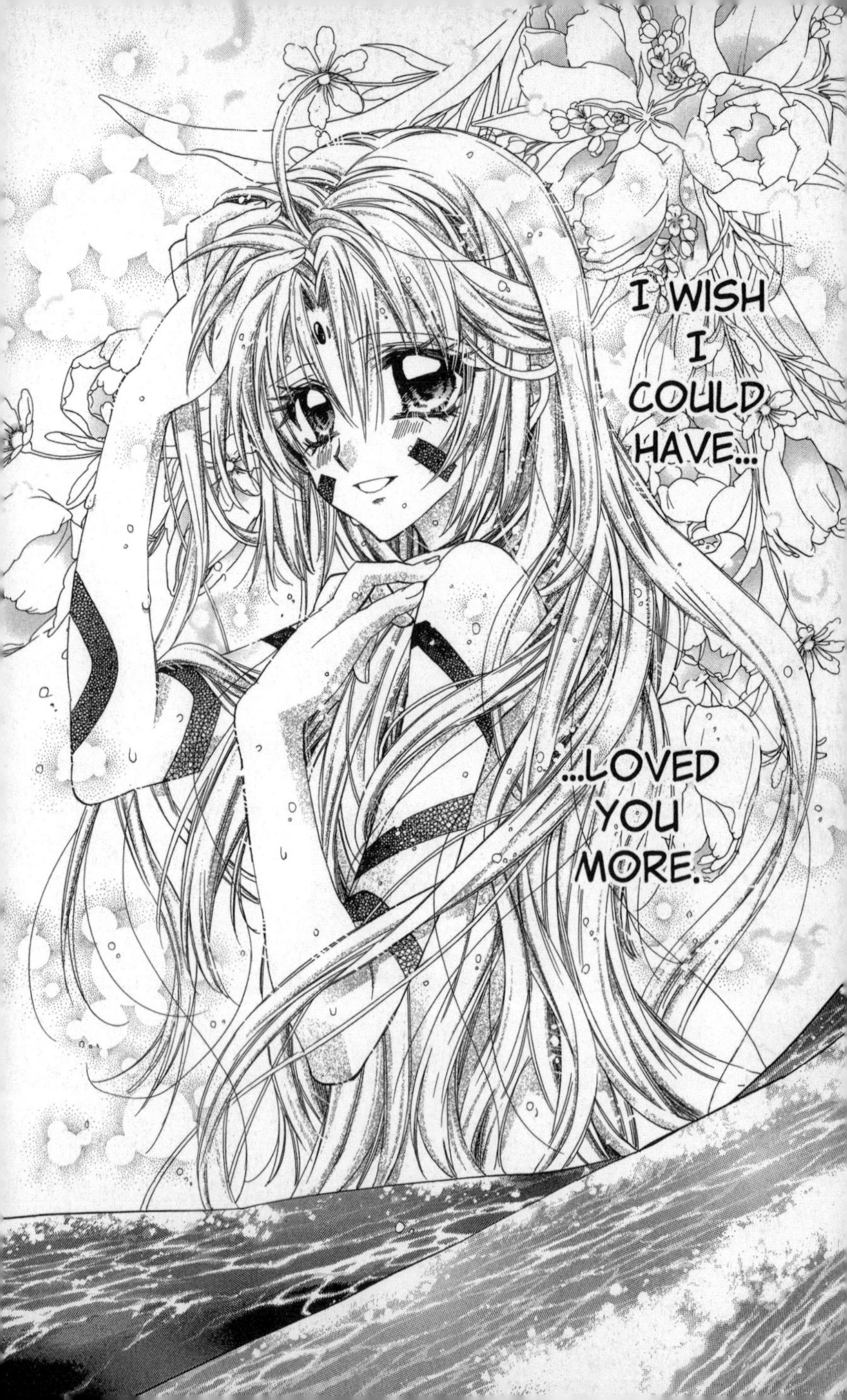
I WISH I COULD HAVE...
...LOVED YOU MORE.

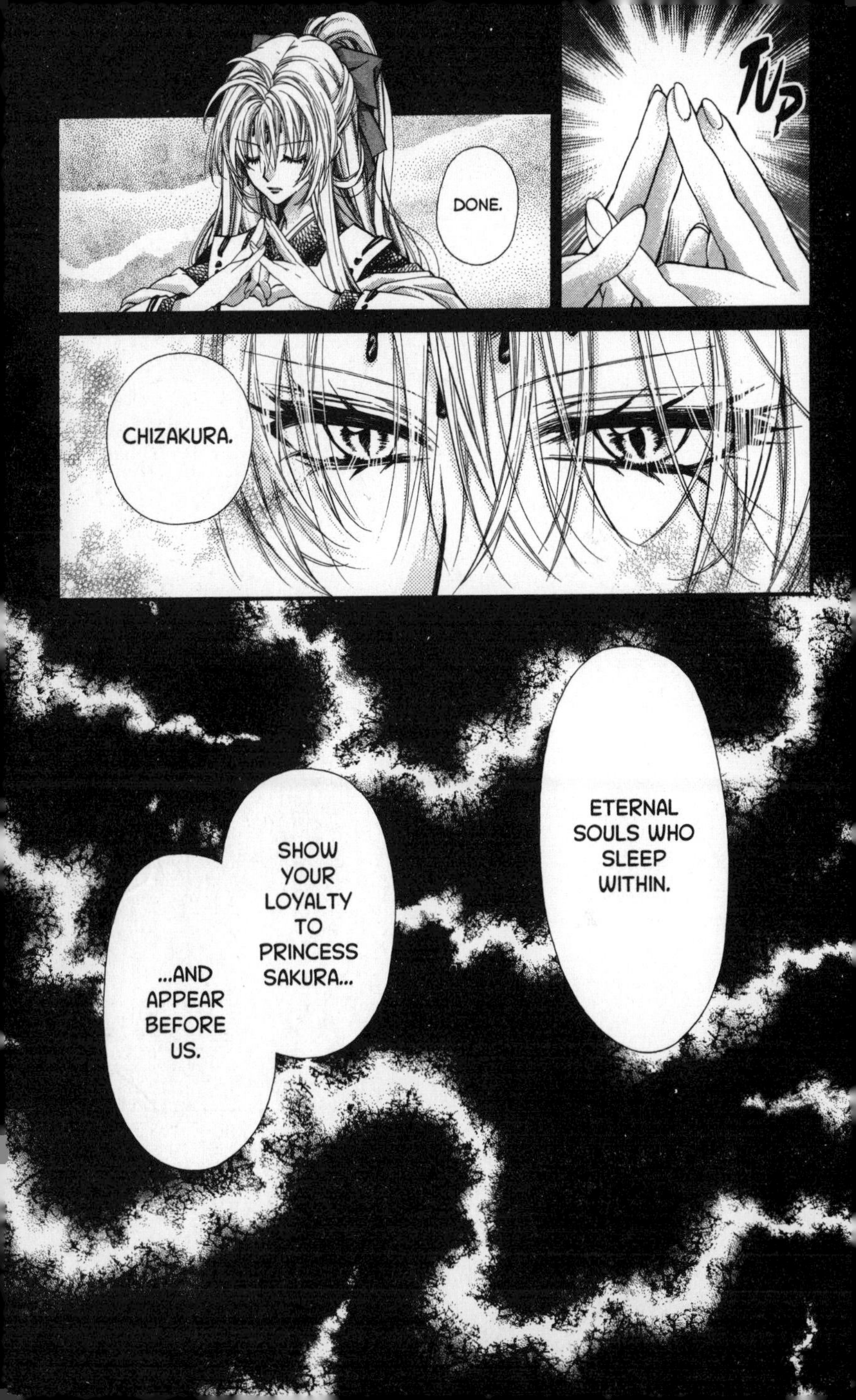
TUP
DONE.
CHIZAKURA.
ETERNAL SOULS WHO SLEEP WITHIN.
SHOW YOUR LOYALTY TO PRINCESS SAKURA...
...AND APPEAR BEFORE US.

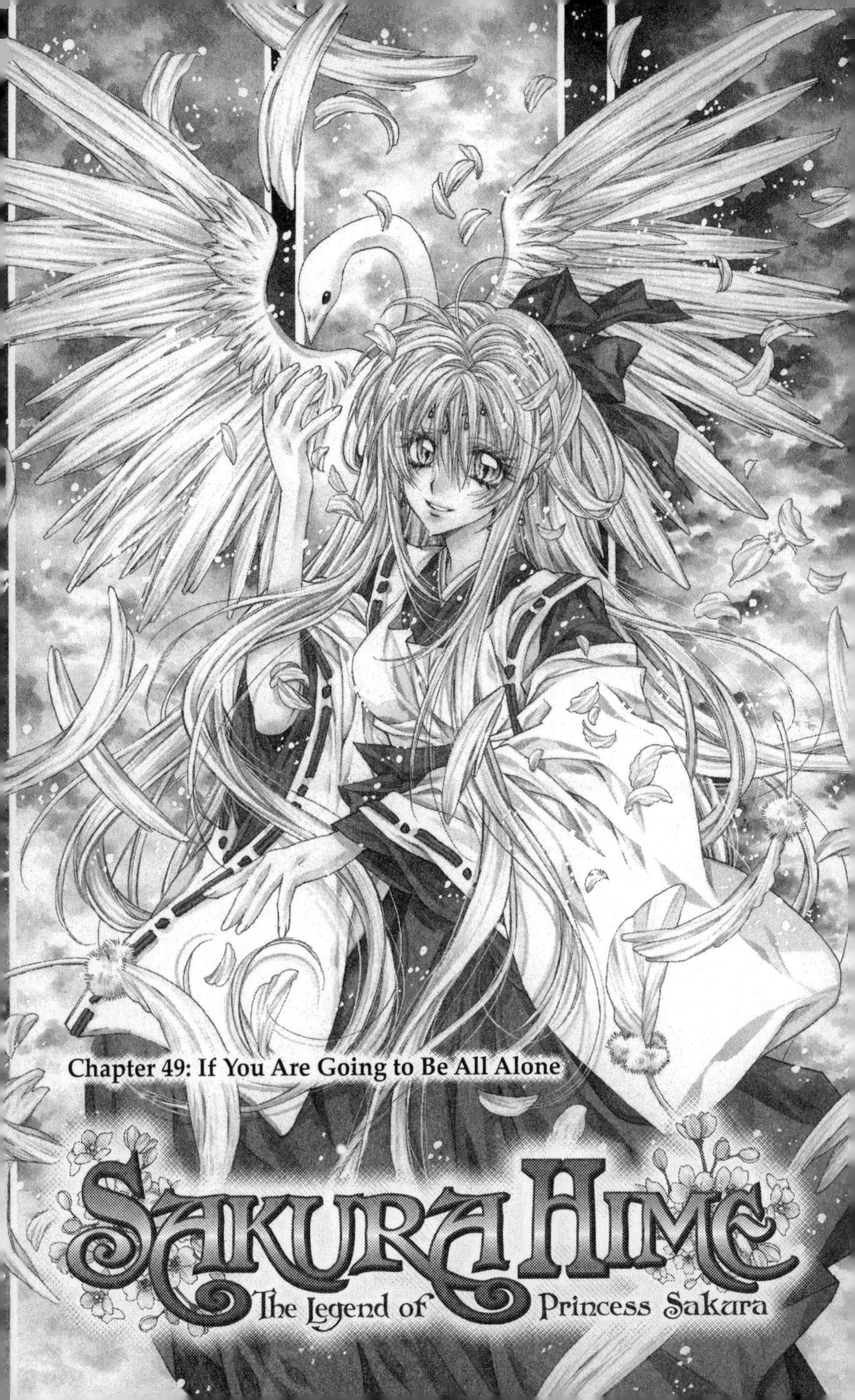
Chapter 49: If You Are Going to Be All Alone
SAKURA HIME
The Legend of Princess Sakura

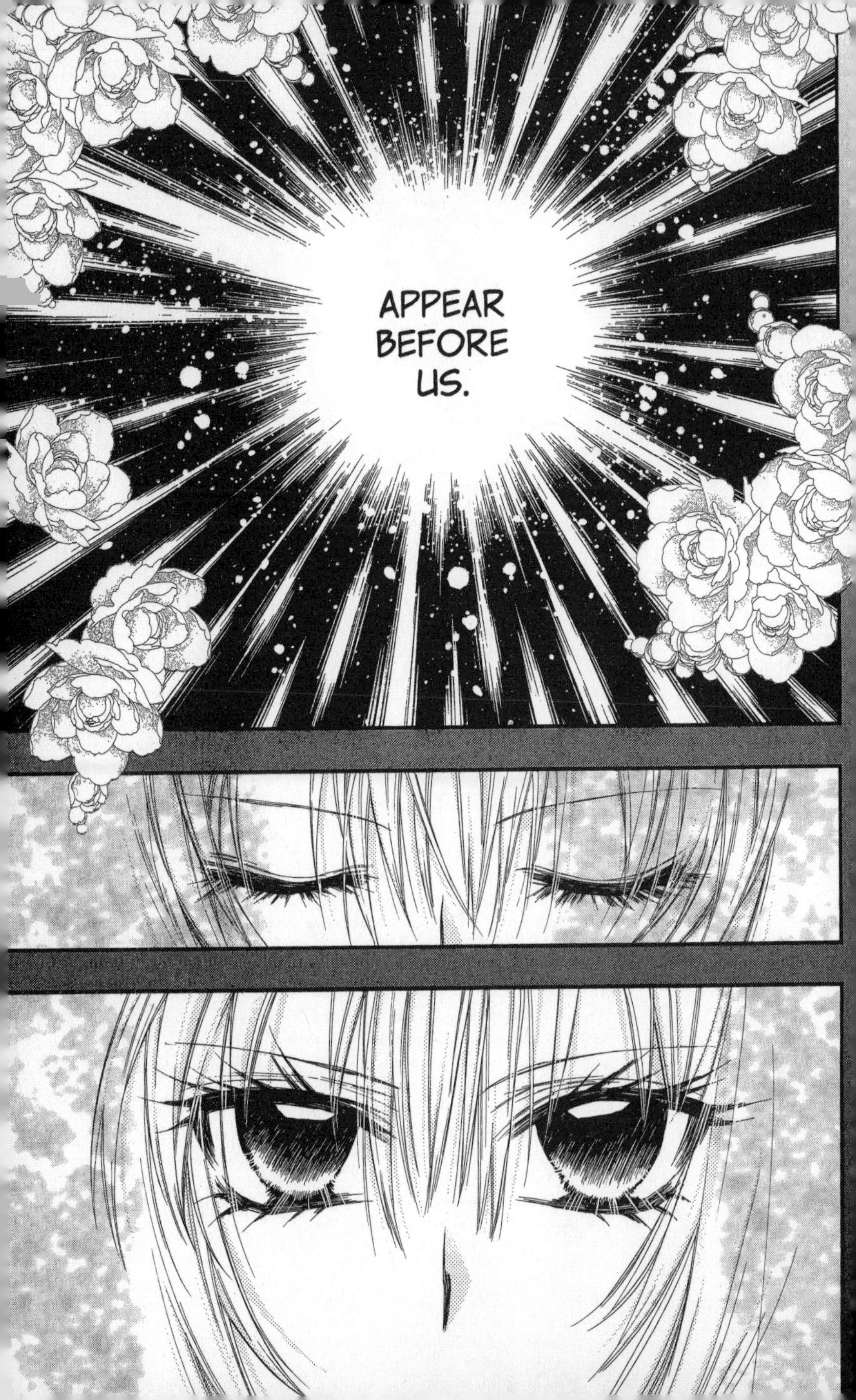
APPEAR BEFORE US.

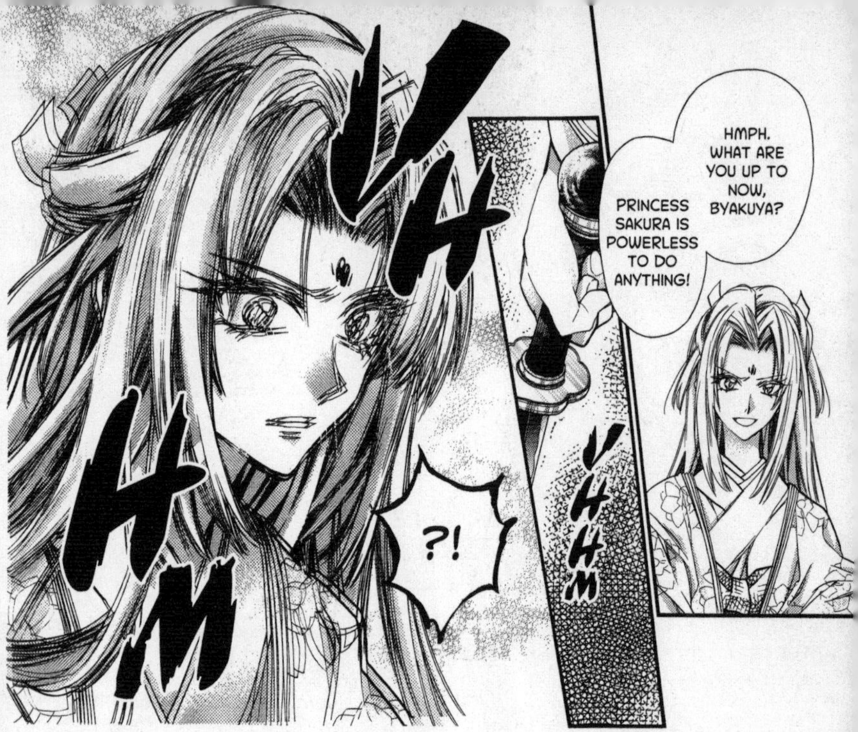
HMPH. WHAT ARE YOU UP TO NOW, BYAKUYA?
PRINCESS SAKURA IS POWERLESS TO DO ANYTHING!
?!

Chapter 49: If You Are Going to Be All Alone

※ I'm giving away the story.
All the people who had been sealed inside Chizakura come out. This is possible only because Princess Kaguya had come out of the sword. My assistants asked me why Enju wasn't among them, so I replied, "Um, he hasn't gone through the registration procedures yet." "Registration procedures?! ξ" They seemed really surprised. (laugh) But I'm sure a lot happens inside that sword.
Originally I had imagined Sakura to be tired of everything around her and unable to smile anymore. But when I was working on this chapter, Sakura was still smiling and she still had hope for the future. That was when I realized I had been the one who was unable to smile. I'd been going through a lot, and there was a time when I asked for this series to be put on hiatus. But after drawing the last scene of this chapter, I realized I was able to continue this series because Sakura was the main character. Her smile saved me.
I was able to smile after drawing Sakura, who smiled so easily to say, "I'm all right."

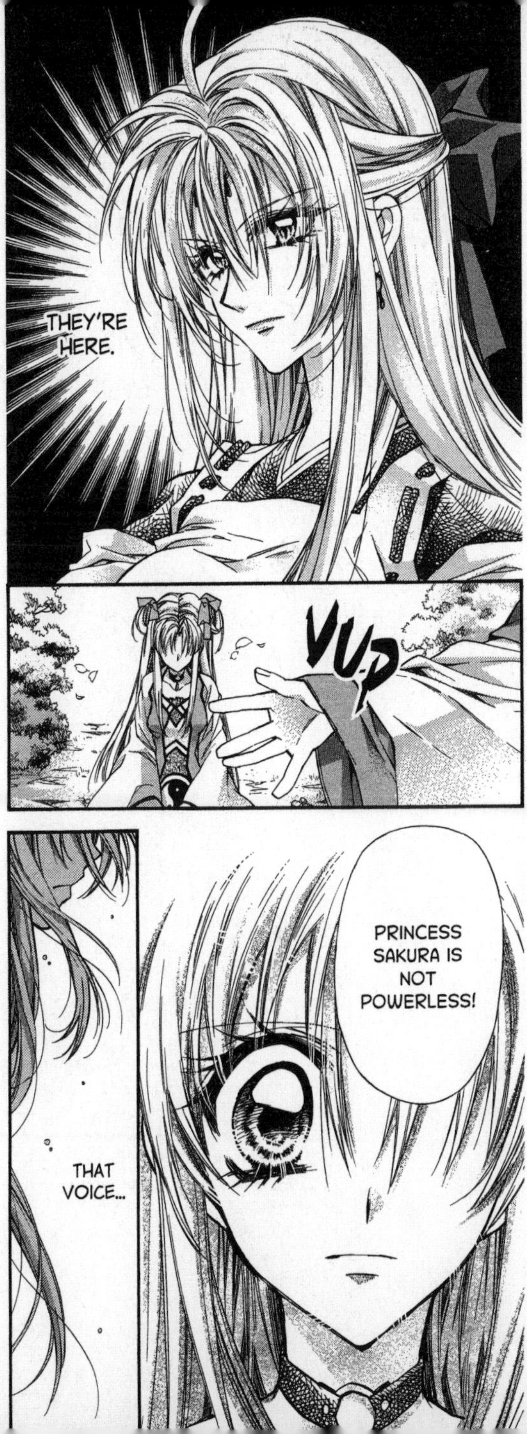
THEY'RE HERE.
VUD
PRINCESS SAKURA IS NOT POWERLESS!
THAT VOICE...

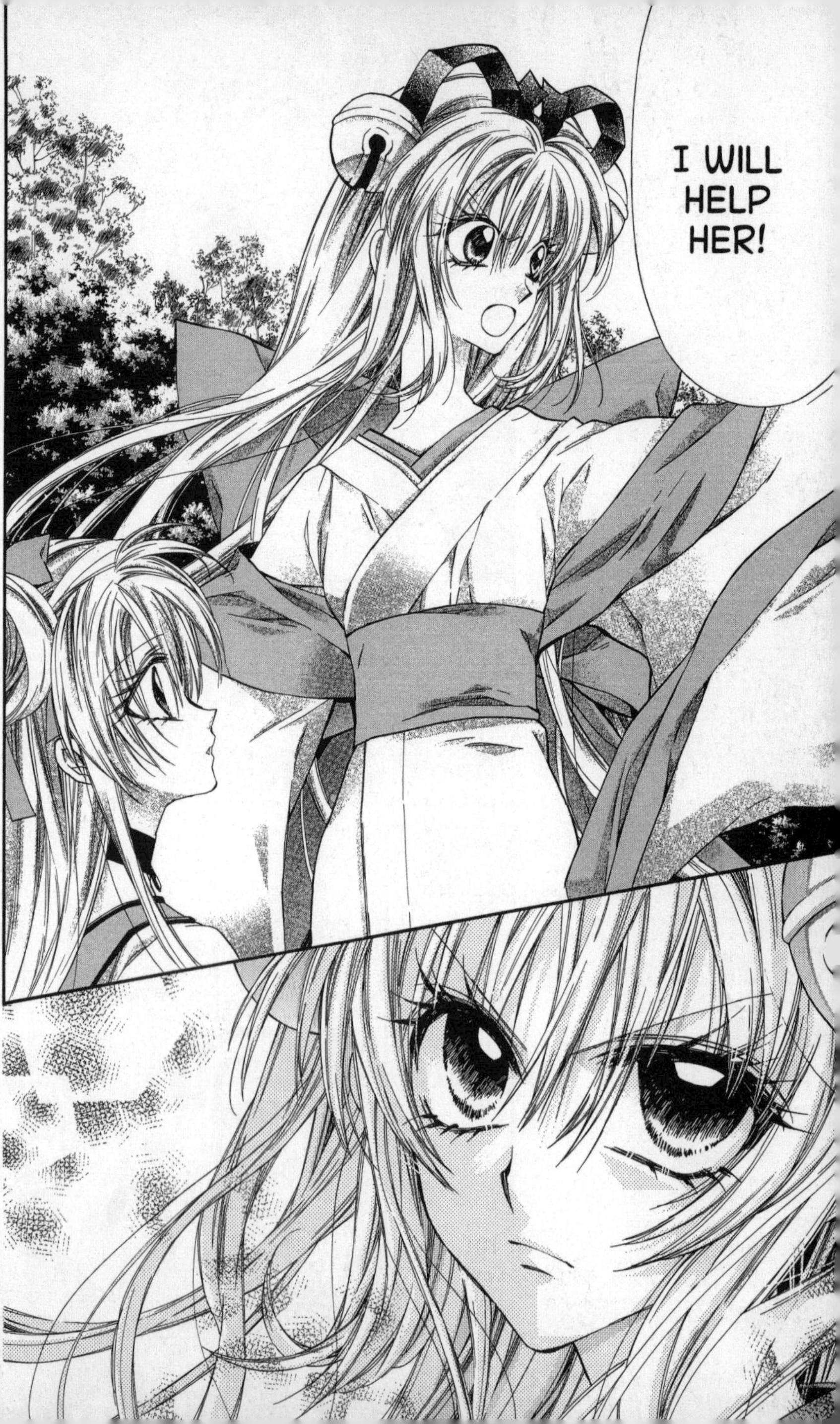
I WILL HELP HER!

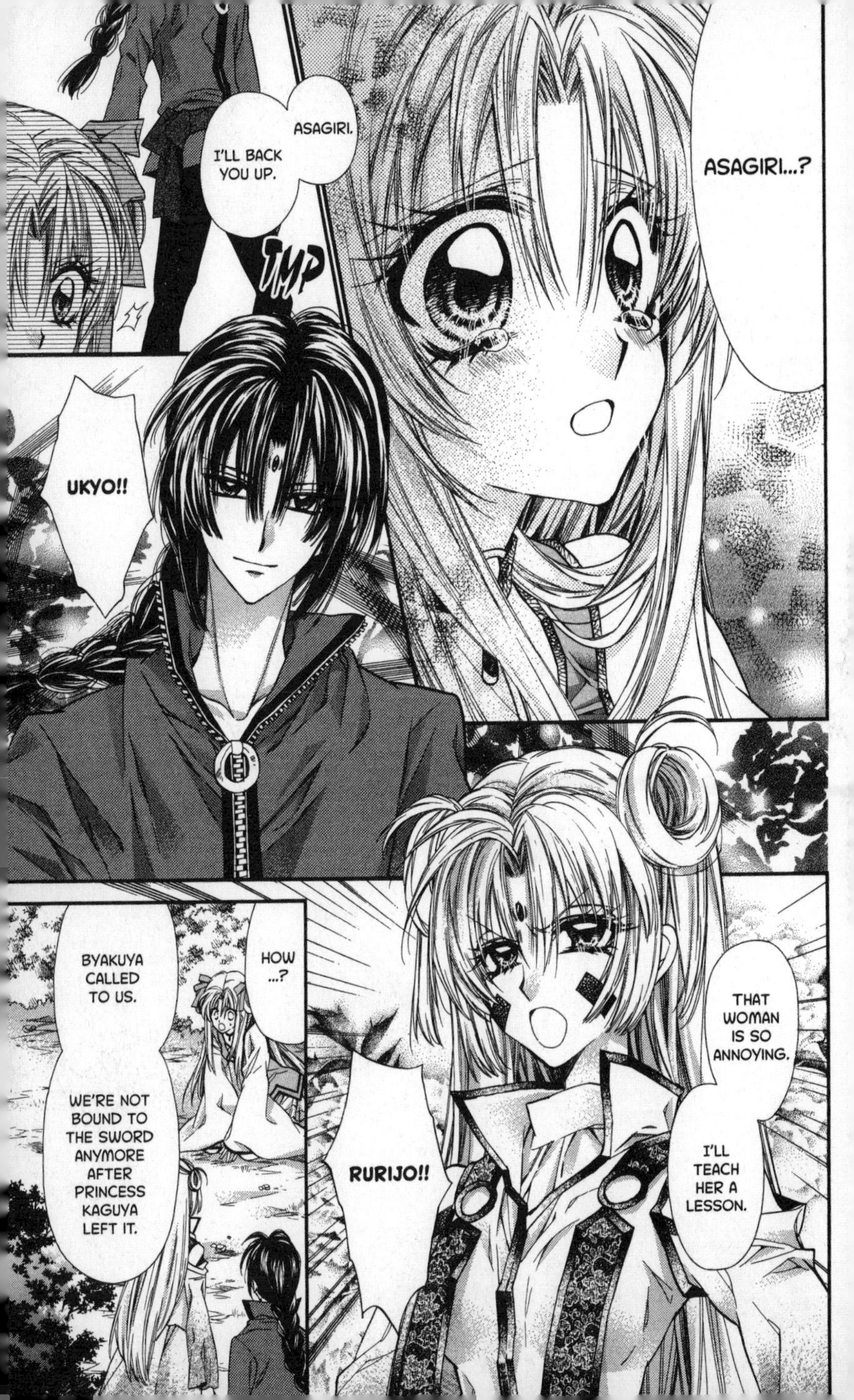
ASAGIRI...?
ASAGIRI.
I'LL BACK YOU UP.
TMP
UKYO!!
THAT WOMAN IS SO ANNOYING.
I'LL TEACH HER A LESSON.
RURIJO!!
HOW ...?
BYAKUYA CALLED TO US.
WE'RE NOT BOUND TO THE SWORD ANYMORE AFTER PRINCESS KAGUYA LEFT IT.

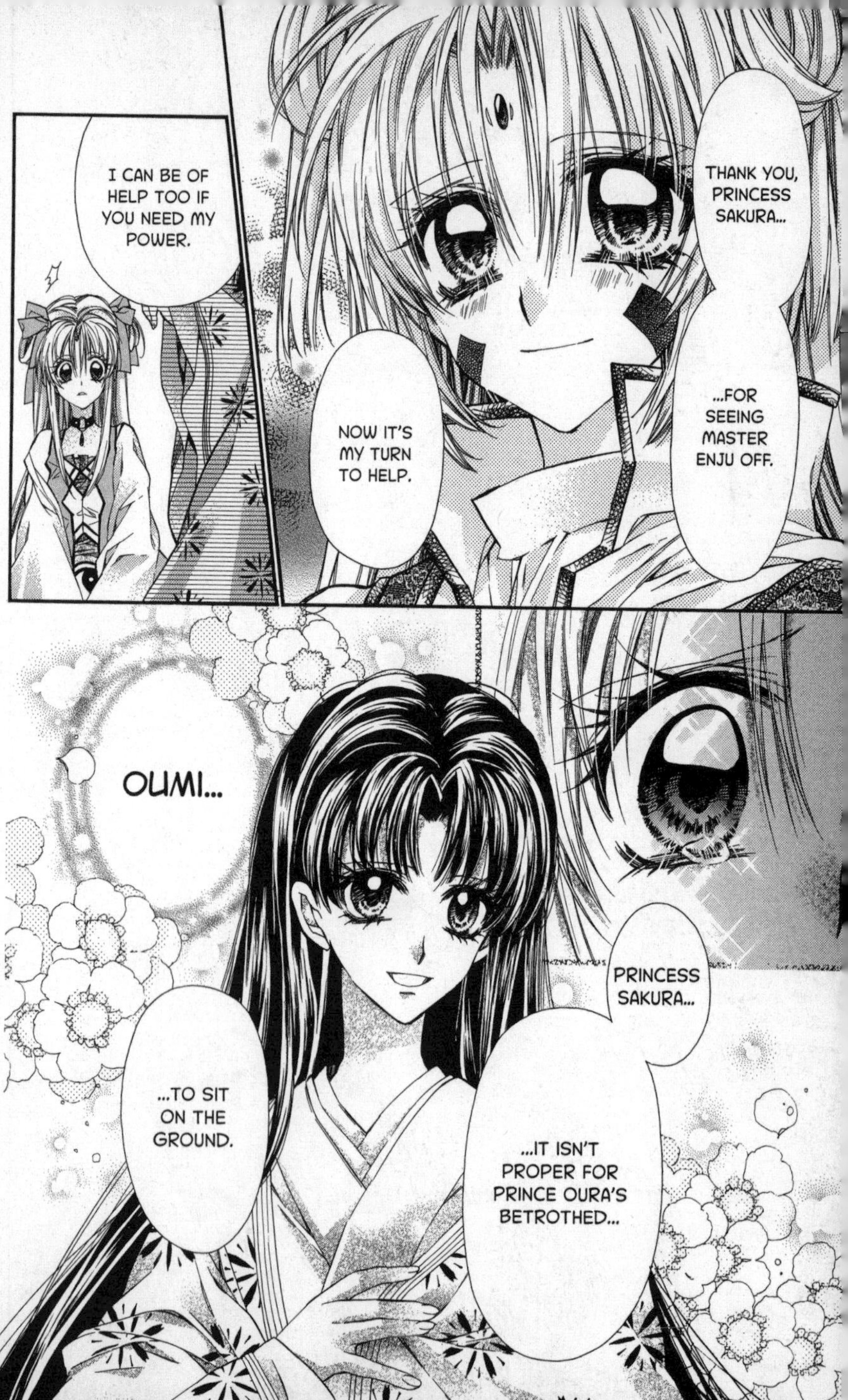

THANK YOU, PRINCESS SAKURA...
...FOR SEEING MASTER ENJU OFF.
NOW IT'S MY TURN TO HELP.
I CAN BE OF HELP TOO IF YOU NEED MY POWER.
OUMI...
PRINCESS SAKURA...
...IT ISN'T PROPER FOR PRINCE OURA'S BETROTHED...
...TO SIT ON THE GROUND.

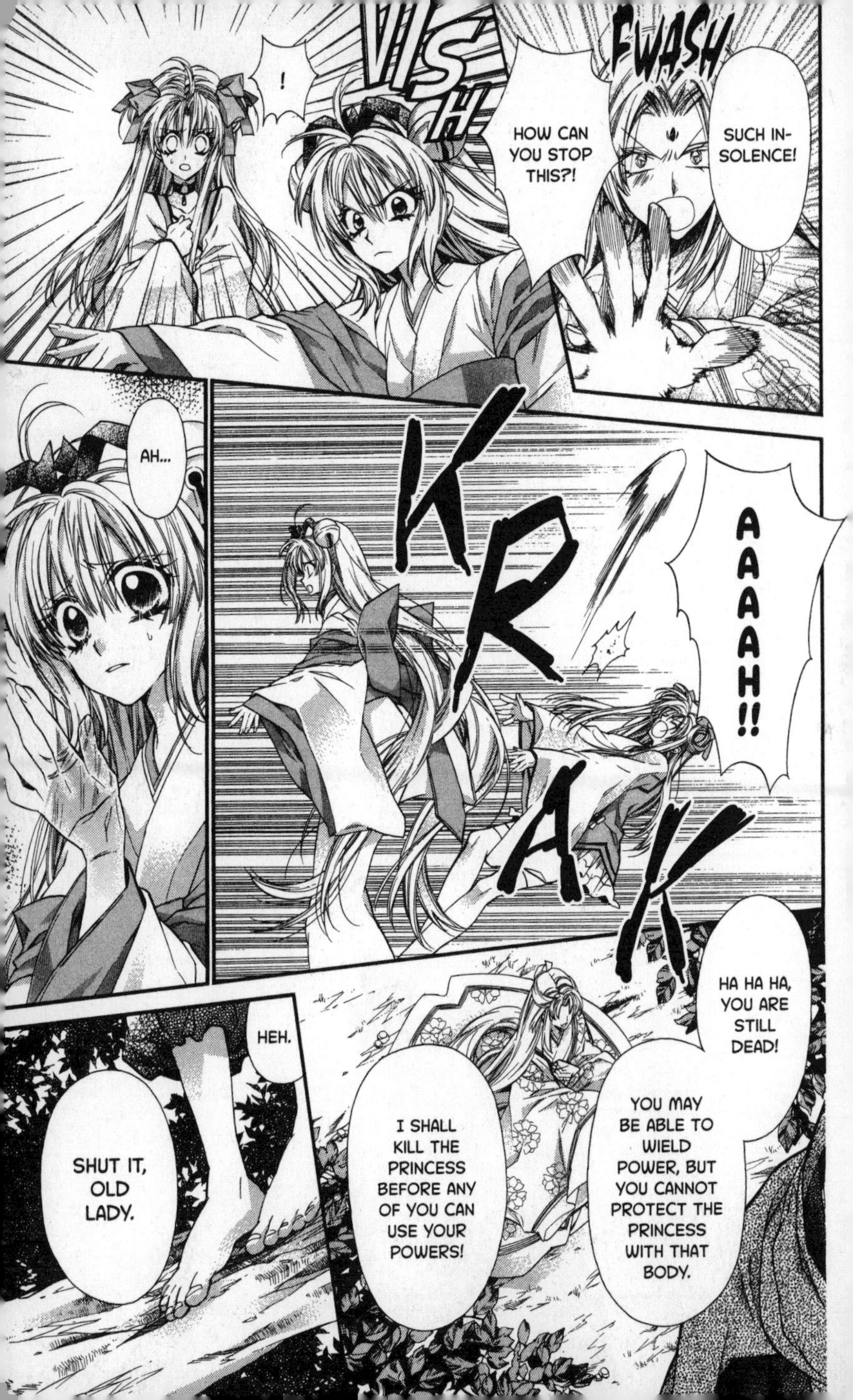
FWASH
SUCH IN-SOLENCE!
HOW CAN YOU STOP THIS?!
VISH
!
AAAAAH!!
KRAK
AH...
HA HA HA, YOU ARE STILL DEAD!
YOU MAY BE ABLE TO WIELD POWER, BUT YOU CANNOT PROTECT THE PRINCESS WITH THAT BODY.
I SHALL KILL THE PRINCESS BEFORE ANY OF YOU CAN USE YOUR POWERS!
HEH.
SHUT IT, OLD LADY.

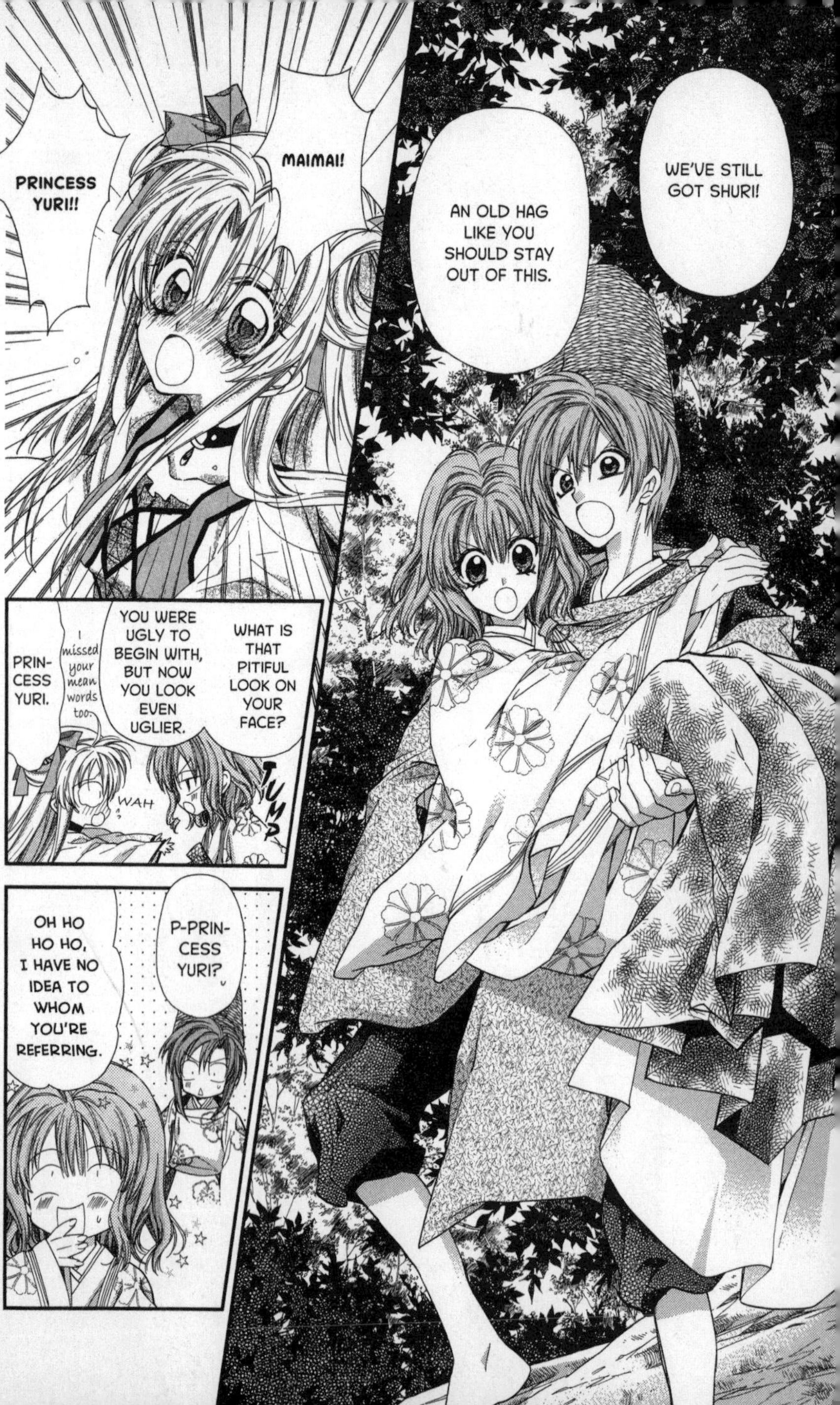
WE'VE STILL GOT SHURI!
AN OLD HAG LIKE YOU SHOULD STAY OUT OF THIS.
MAIMAI!
PRINCESS YURI!!
WHAT IS THAT PITIFUL LOOK ON YOUR FACE?
YOU WERE UGLY TO BEGIN WITH, BUT NOW YOU LOOK EVEN UGLIER.
I missed your mean words too.
PRIN-CESS YURI.
TUMP
WAH
P-PRIN-CESS YURI?
OH HO HO HO, I HAVE NO IDEA TO WHOM YOU'RE REFERRING.

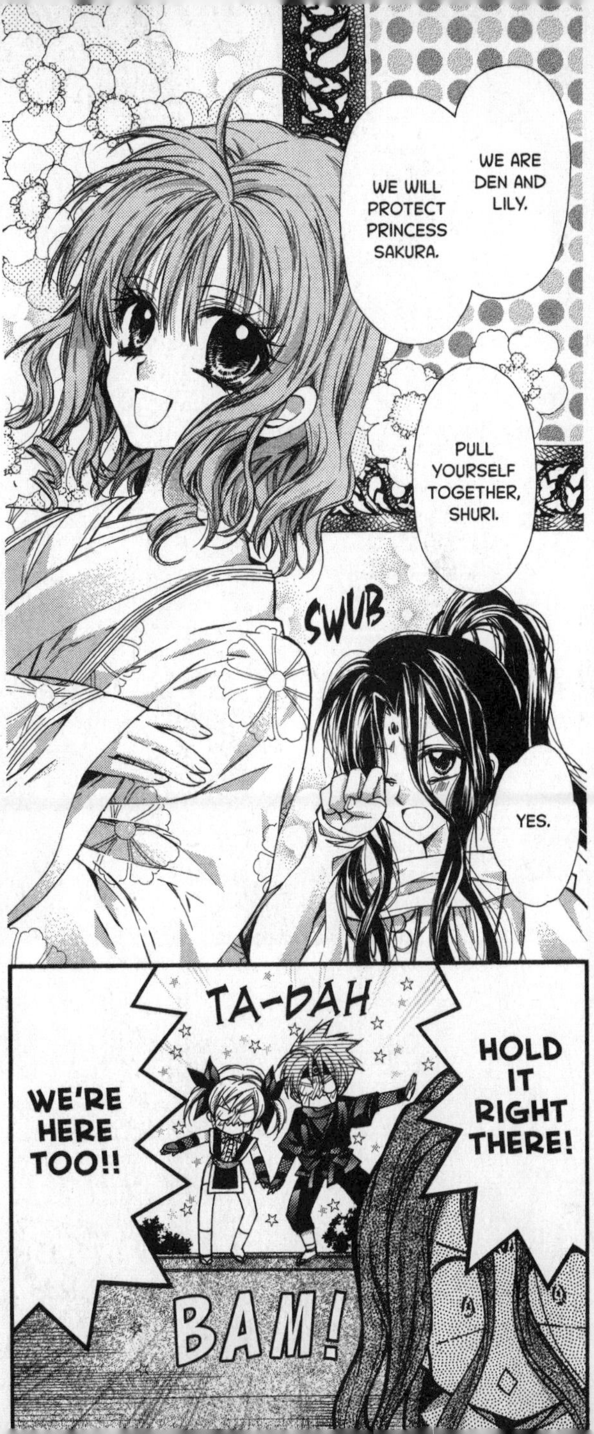
WE ARE DEN AND LILY.
WE WILL PROTECT PRINCESS SAKURA.
PULL YOURSELF TOGETHER, SHURI.
SWUB
YES.
HOLD IT RIGHT THERE!
TA-DAH
WE'RE HERE TOO!!
BAM!

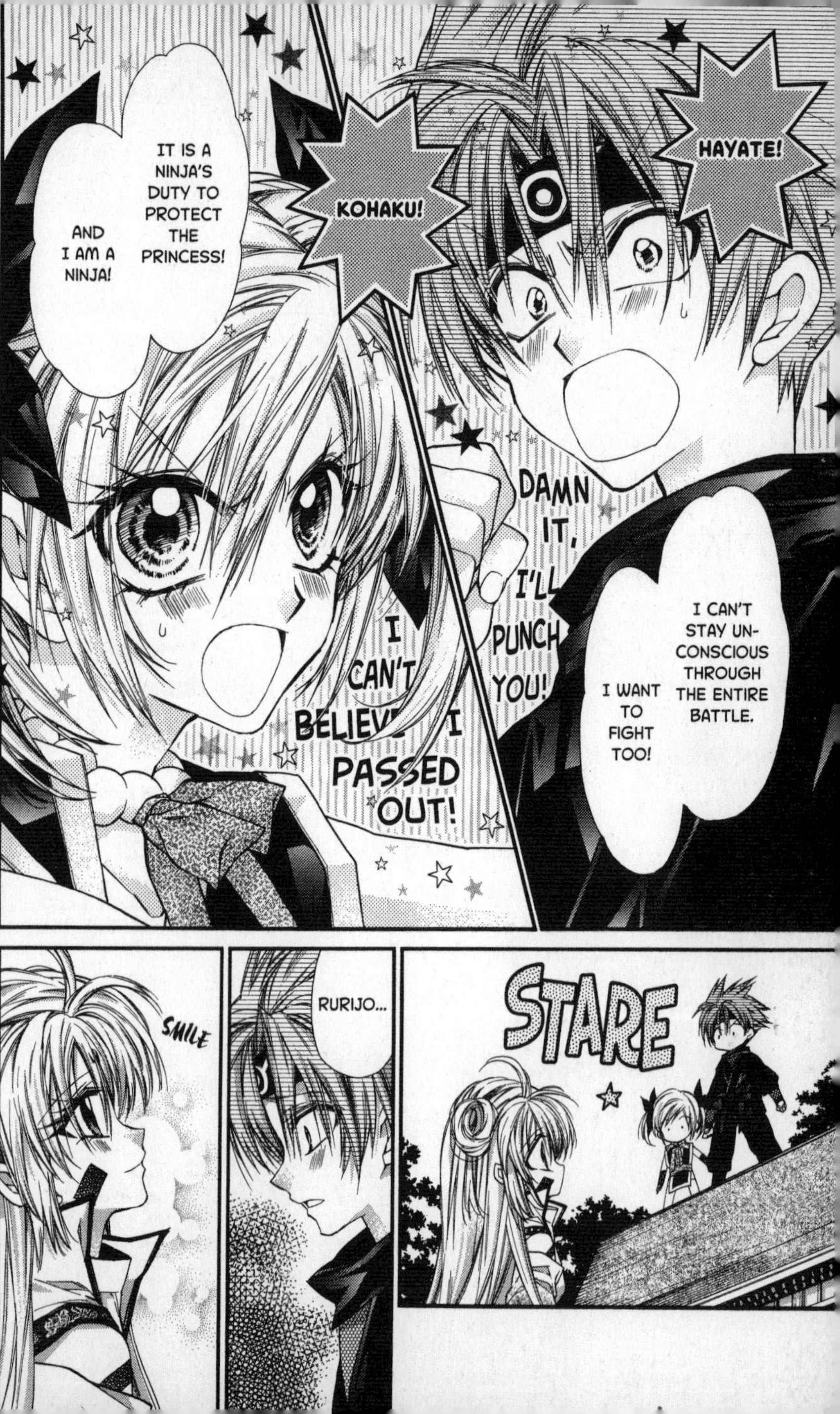
HAYATE!
KOHAKU!
DAMN IT, I'LL PUNCH YOU!
I CAN'T STAY UN-CONSCIOUS THROUGH THE ENTIRE BATTLE.
I WANT TO FIGHT TOO!
IT IS A NINJA'S DUTY TO PROTECT THE PRINCESS!
AND I AM A NINJA!
I CAN'T BELIEVE I PASSED OUT!
STARE
RURIJO...
SMILE

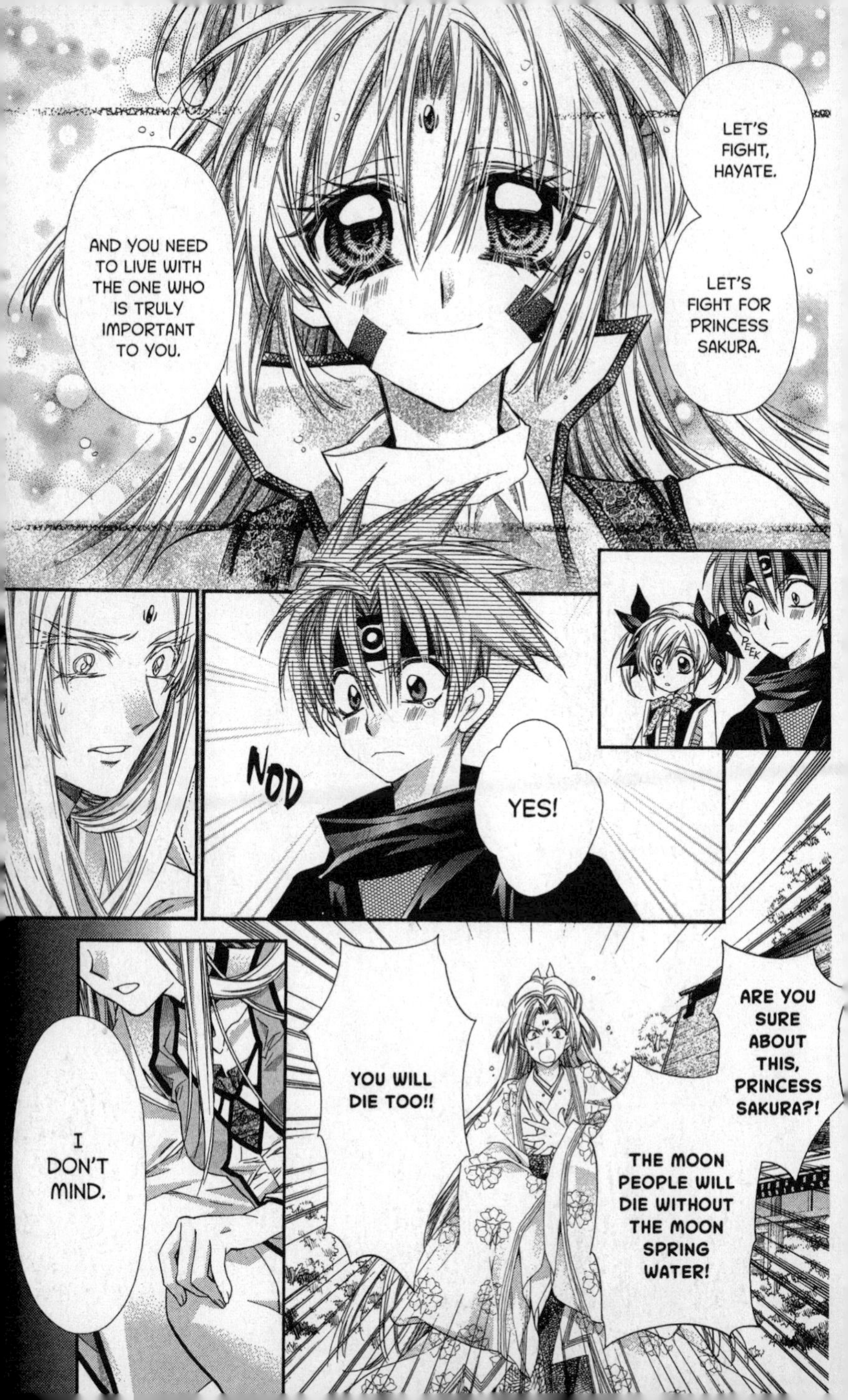
LET'S FIGHT, HAYATE.
LET'S FIGHT FOR PRINCESS SAKURA.
AND YOU NEED TO LIVE WITH THE ONE WHO IS TRULY IMPORTANT TO YOU.
PEEK
NOD
YES!
ARE YOU SURE ABOUT THIS, PRINCESS SAKURA?!
THE MOON PEOPLE WILL DIE WITHOUT THE MOON SPRING WATER!
YOU WILL DIE TOO!!
I DON'T MIND.

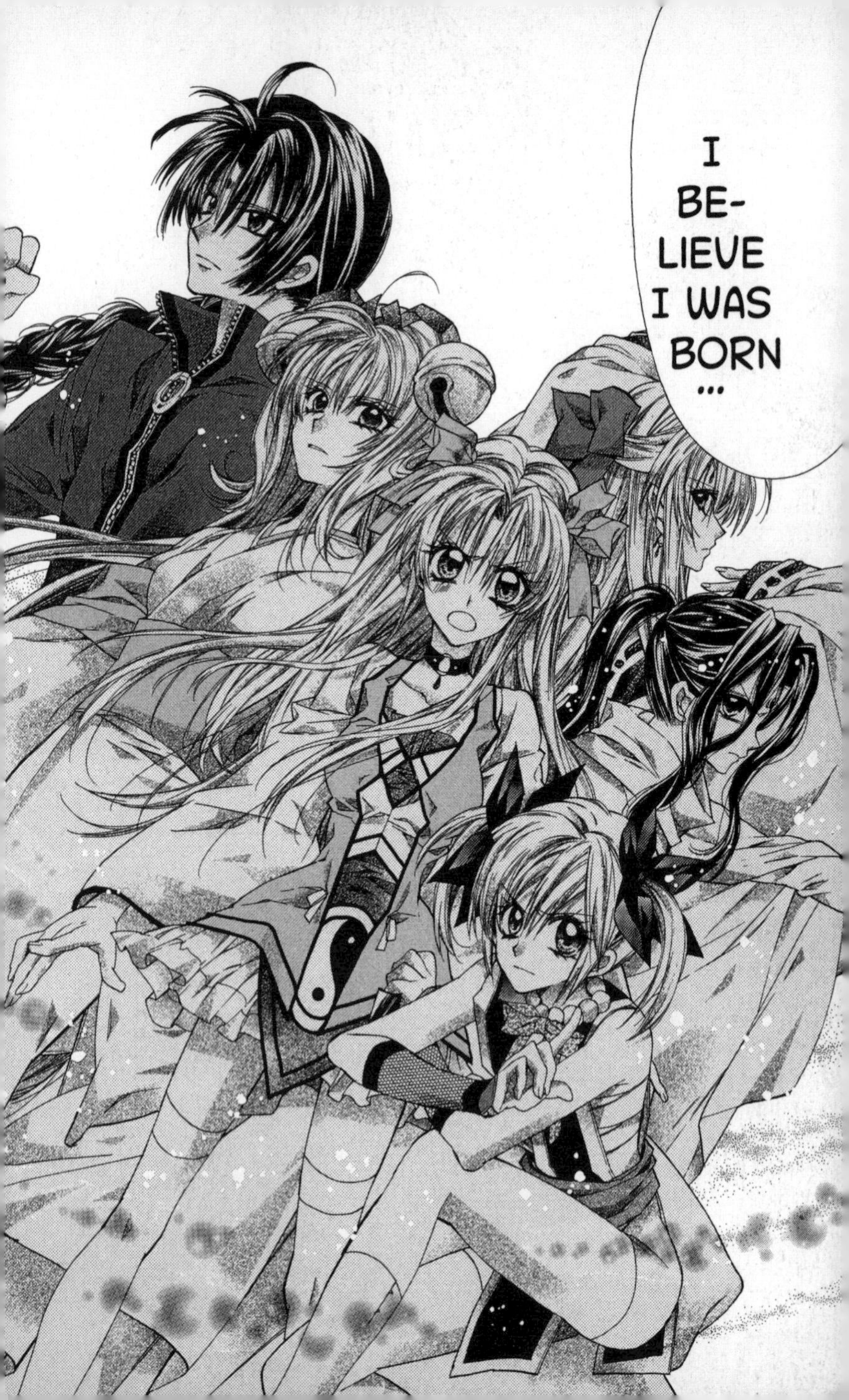
I BE-LIEVE I WAS BORN ...

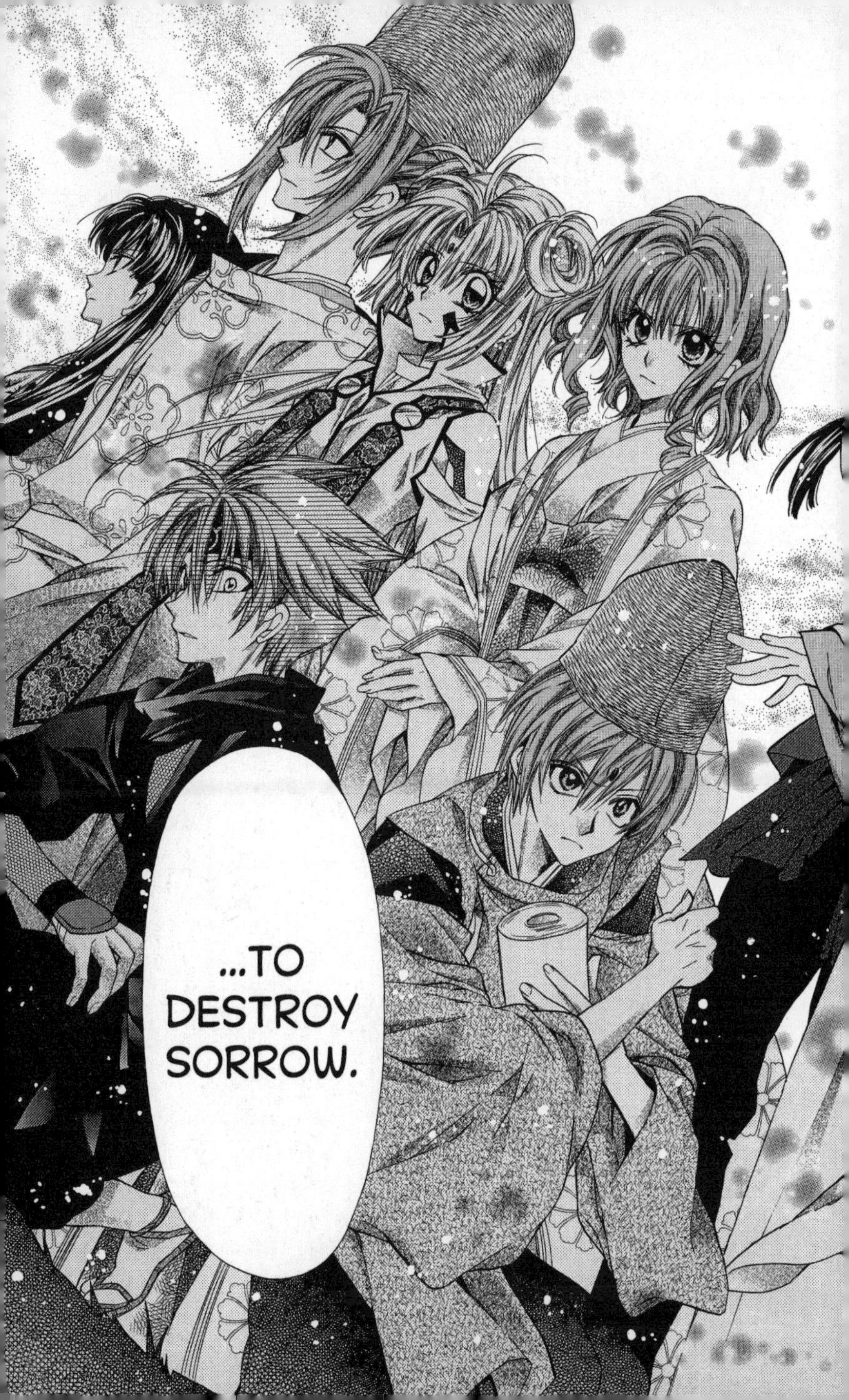
...TO DESTROY SORROW.

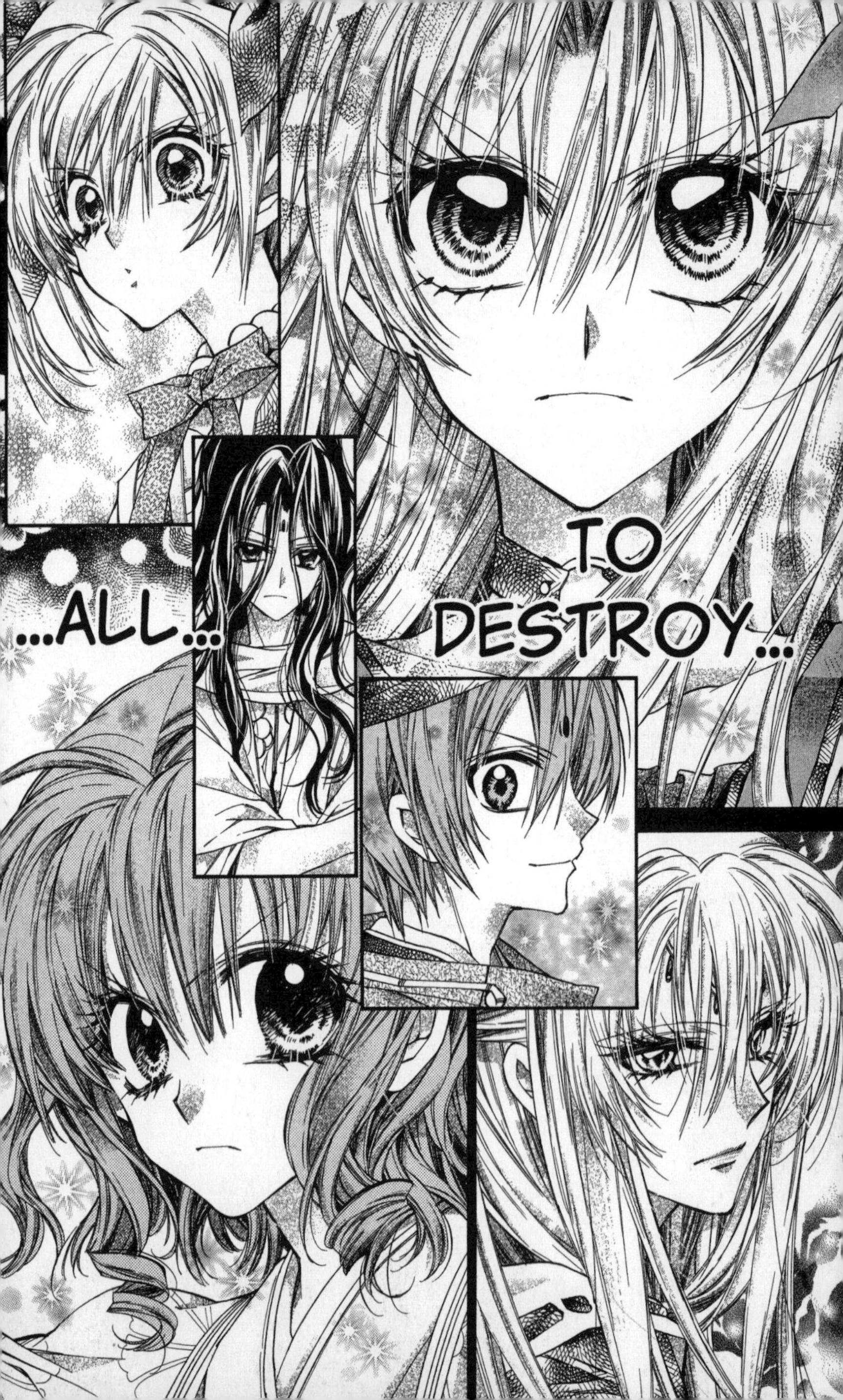
TO DESTROY...
...ALL...

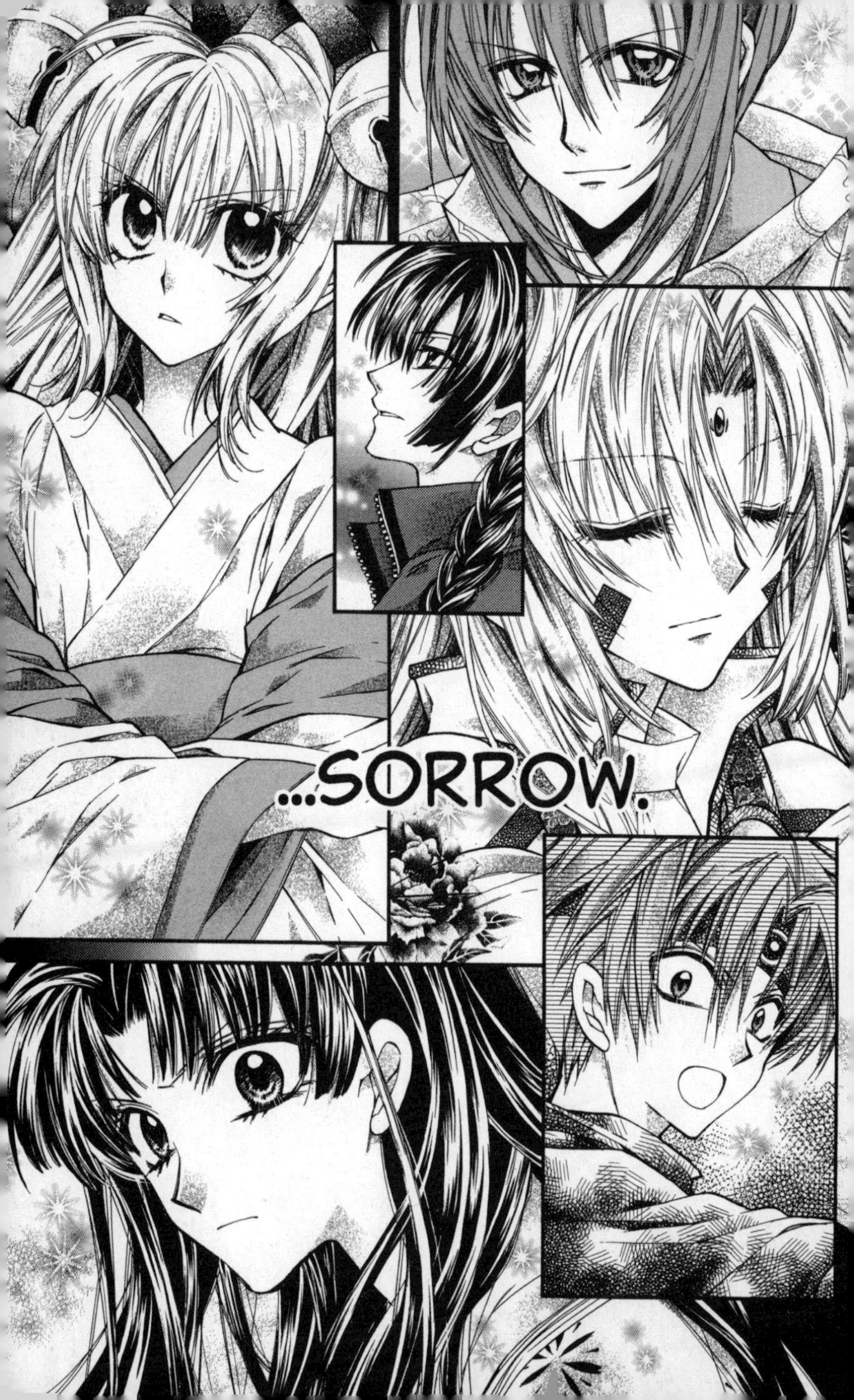
...SORROW.

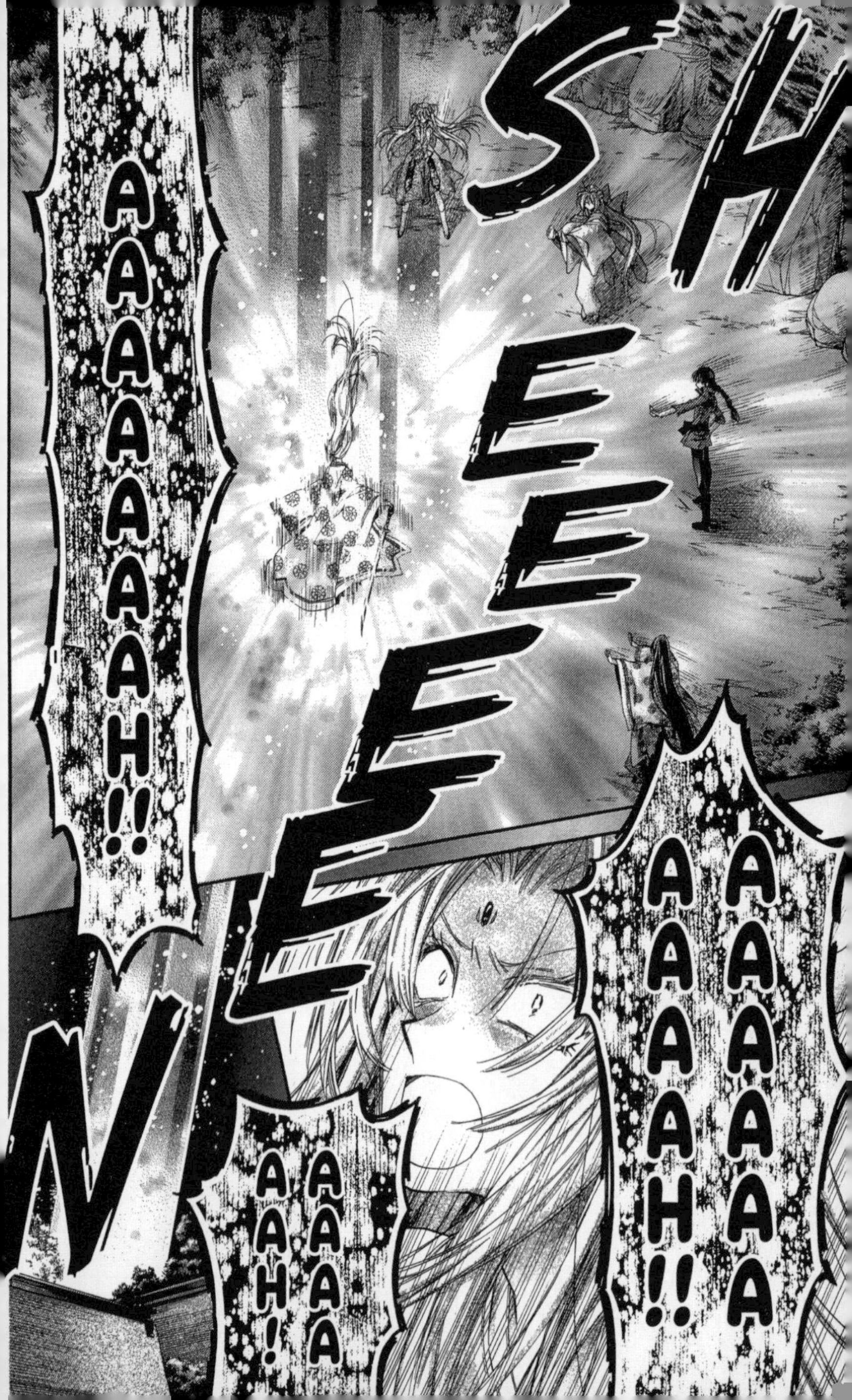
SHEEEEEEN
AAAAAAAAH!!
AAAAAAAAAAAAAAAH!!
AAAAAAAAAH!

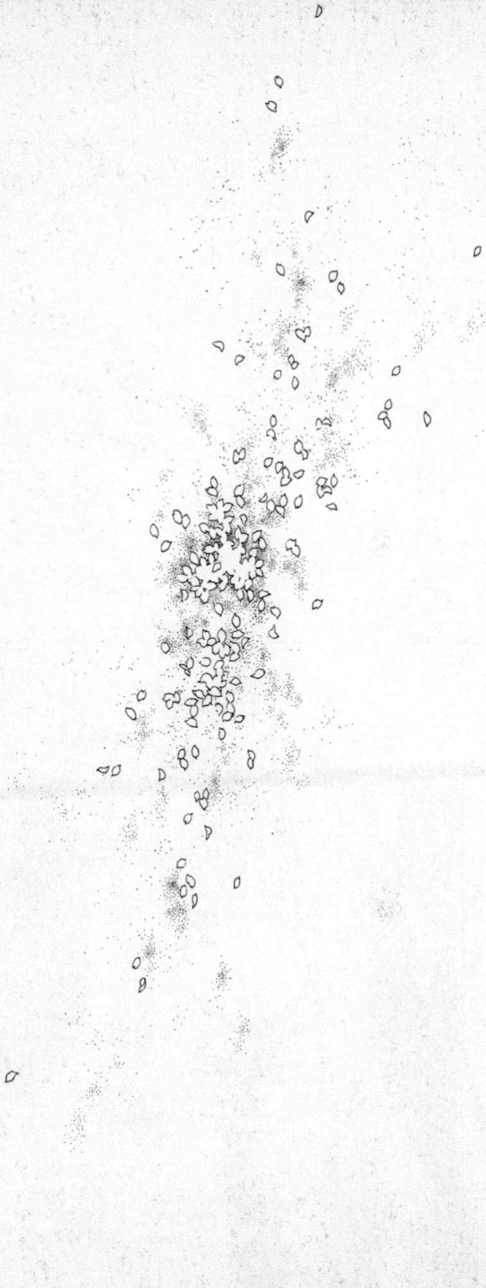

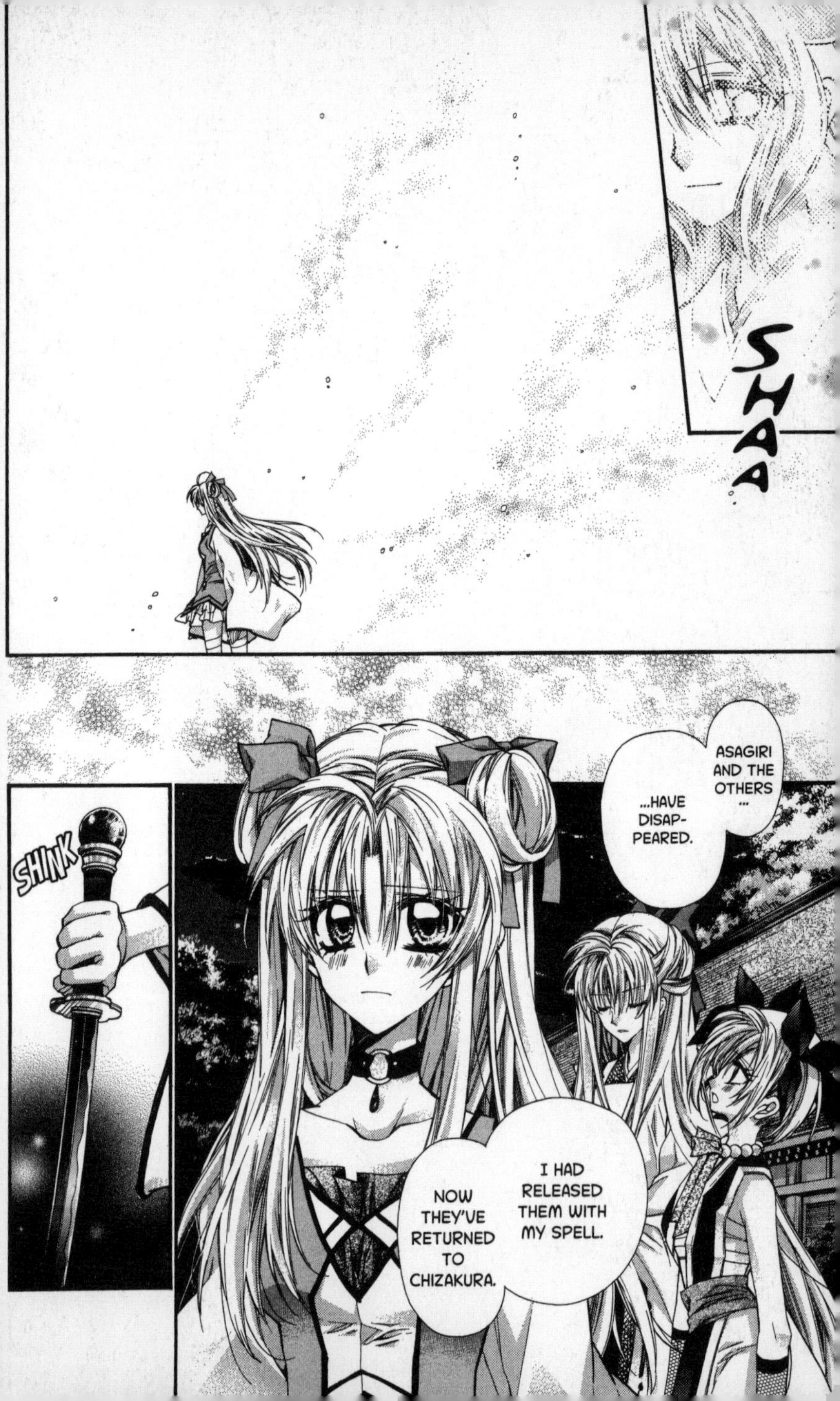
SHAA
ASAGIRI AND THE OTHERS ...
...HAVE DISAP-PEARED.
I HAD RELEASED THEM WITH MY SPELL.
NOW THEY'VE RETURNED TO CHIZAKURA.
SHINK

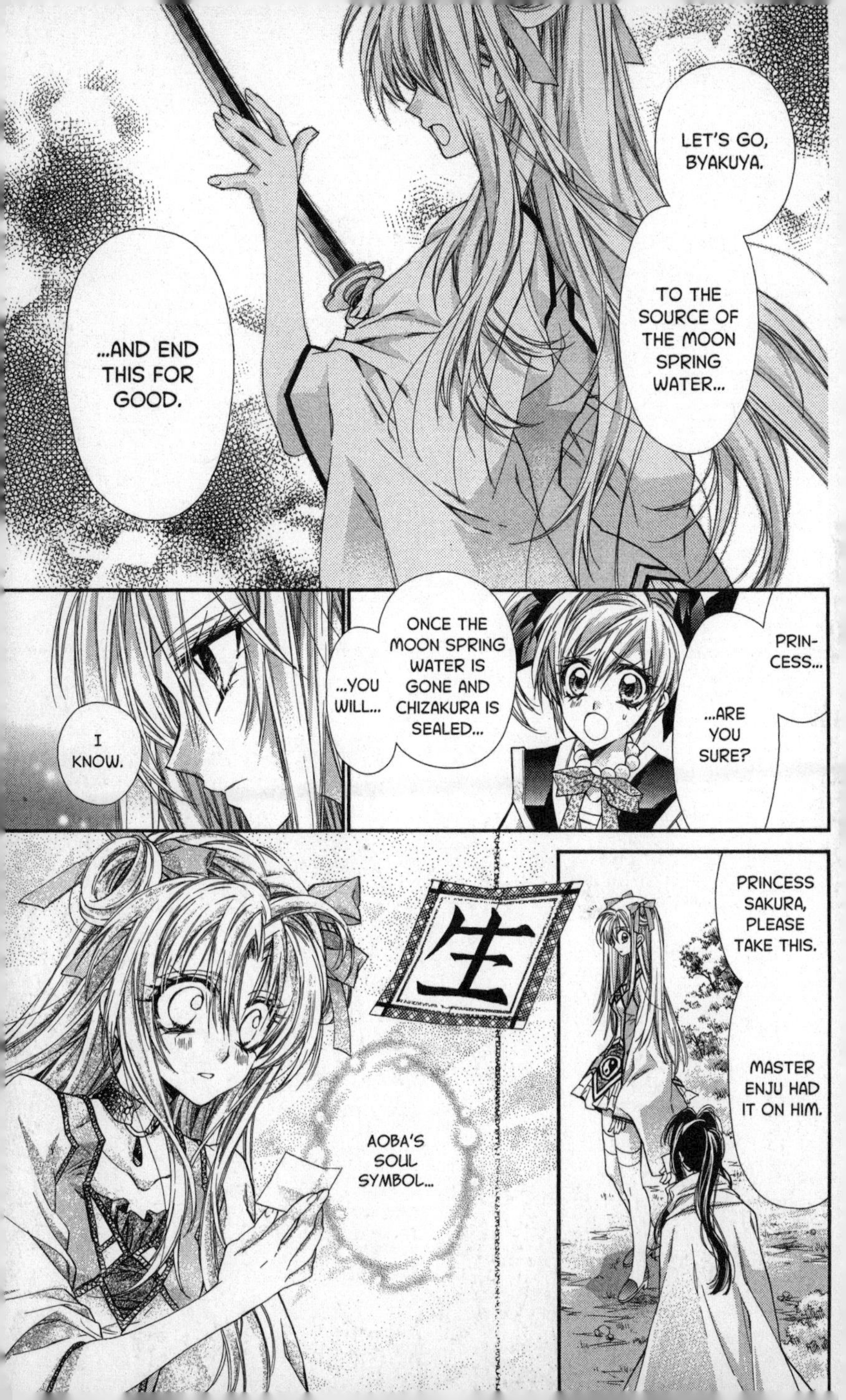
LET'S GO, BYAKUYA.
TO THE SOURCE OF THE MOON SPRING WATER...
...AND END THIS FOR GOOD.
PRIN-CESS...
...ARE YOU SURE?
ONCE THE MOON SPRING WATER IS GONE AND CHIZAKURA IS SEALED...
...YOU WILL...
I KNOW.
PRINCESS SAKURA, PLEASE TAKE THIS.
MASTER ENJU HAD IT ON HIM.
生
AOBA'S SOUL SYMBOL...

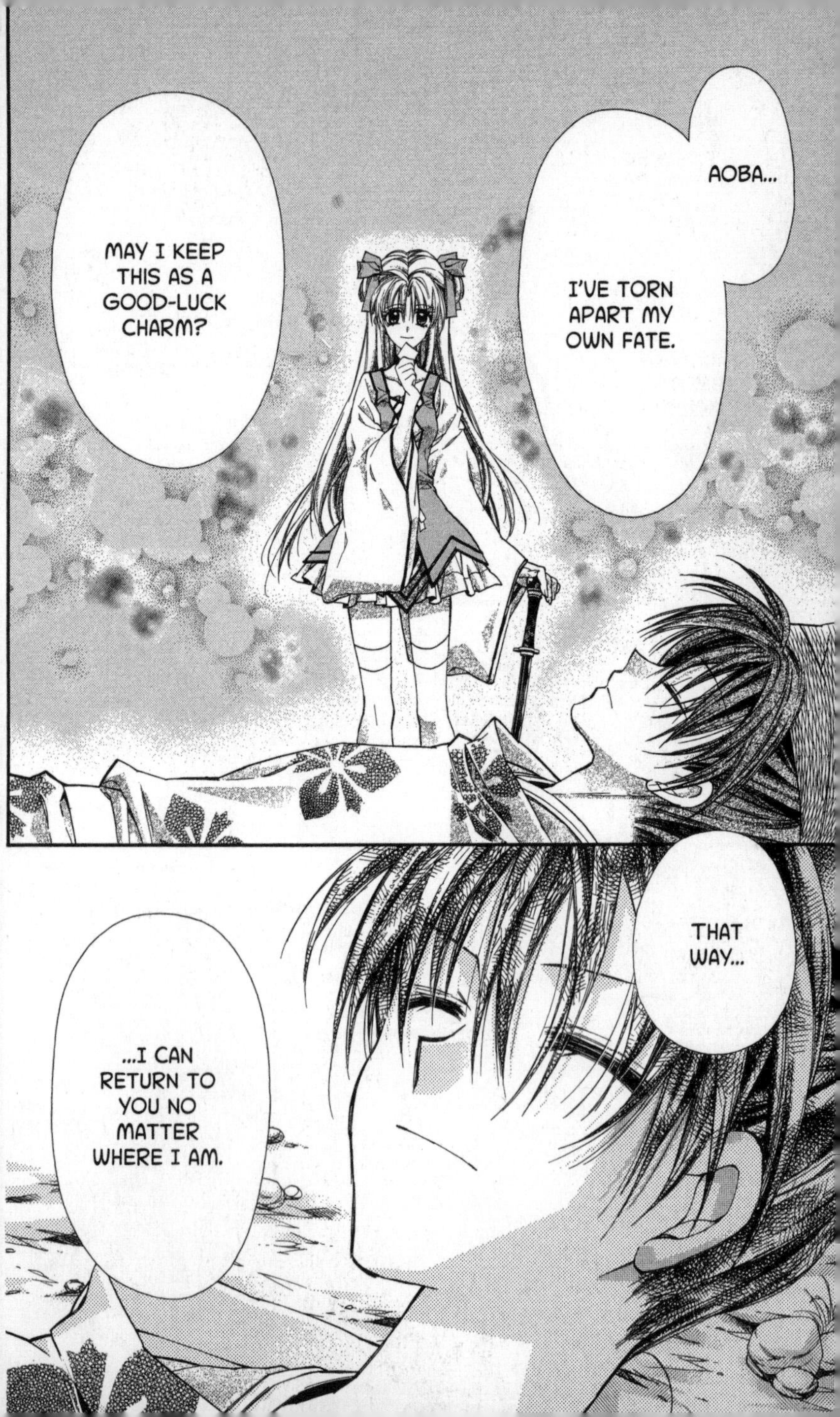
AOBA...
I'VE TORN APART MY OWN FATE.
MAY I KEEP THIS AS A GOOD-LUCK CHARM?
THAT WAY...
...I CAN RETURN TO YOU NO MATTER WHERE I AM.

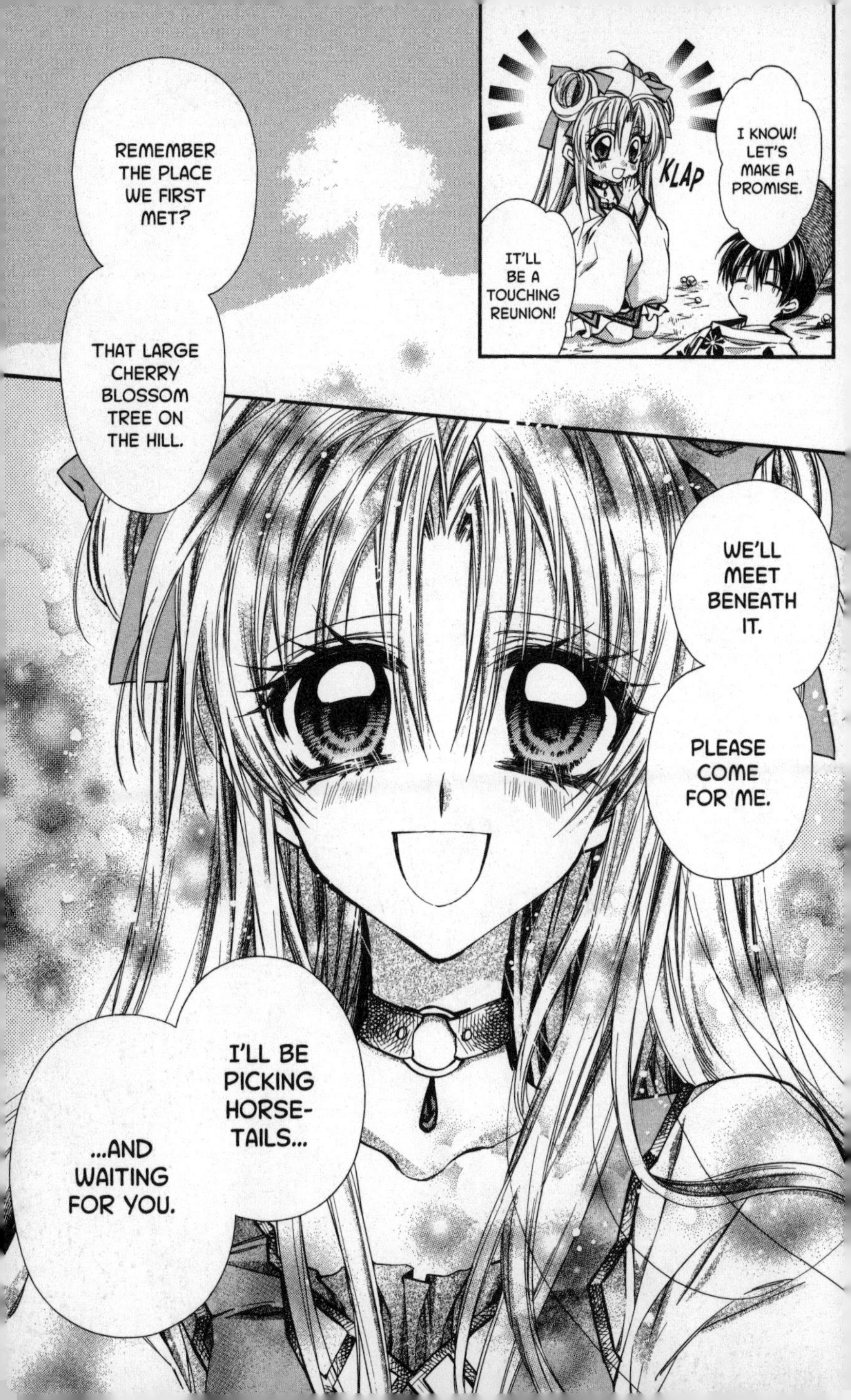
I KNOW! LET'S MAKE A PROMISE.
KLAP
IT'LL BE A TOUCHING REUNION!
REMEMBER THE PLACE WE FIRST MET?
THAT LARGE CHERRY BLOSSOM TREE ON THE HILL.
WE'LL MEET BENEATH IT.
PLEASE COME FOR ME.
I'LL BE PICKING HORSE-TAILS...
...AND WAITING FOR YOU.

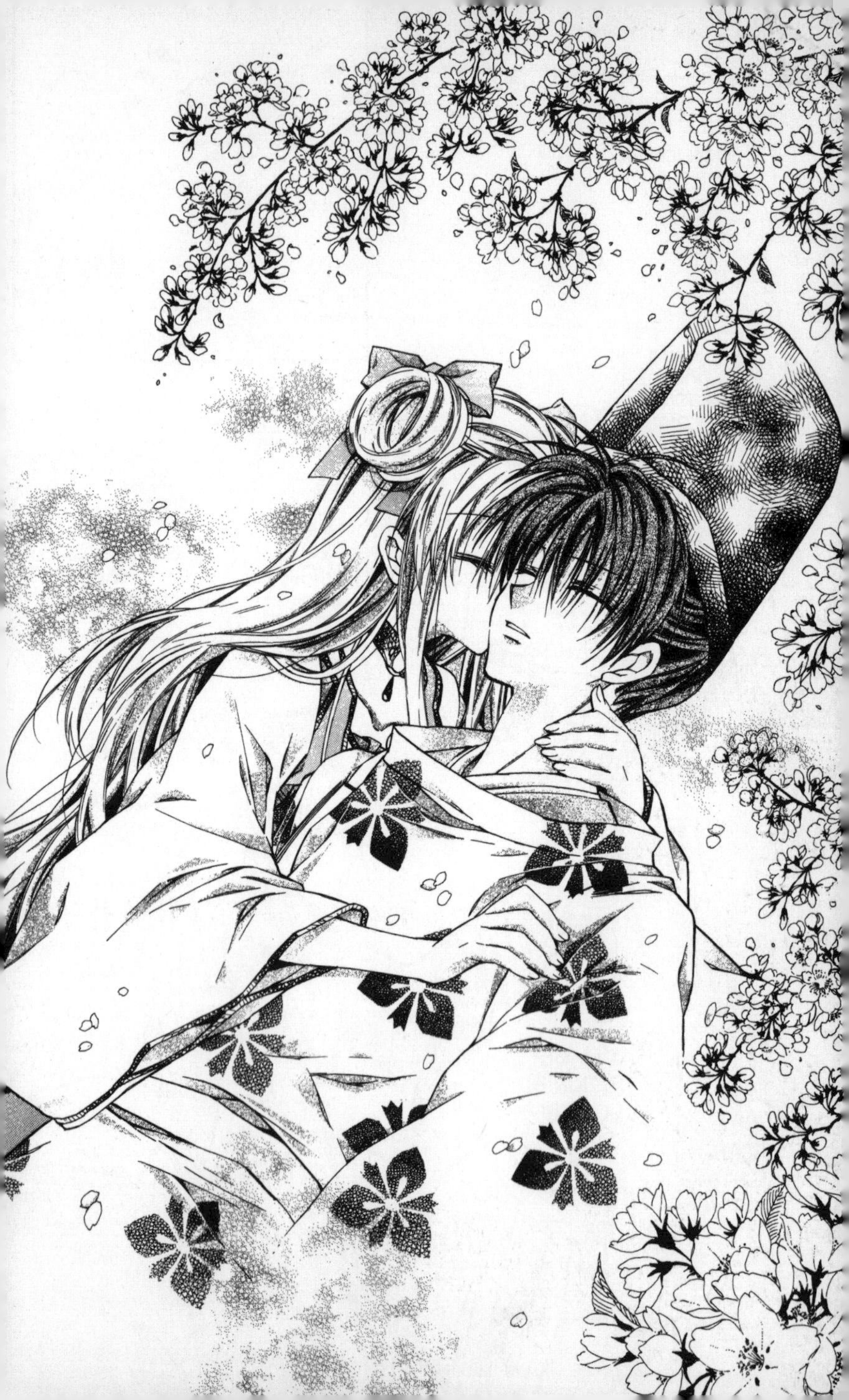

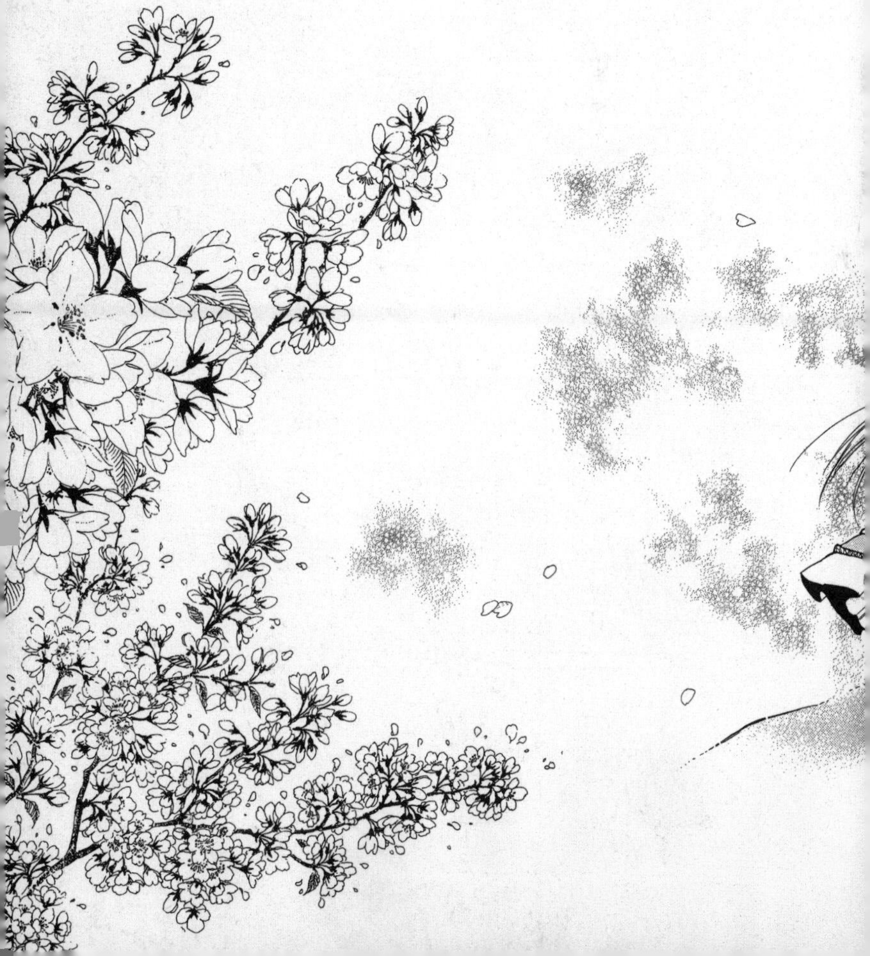

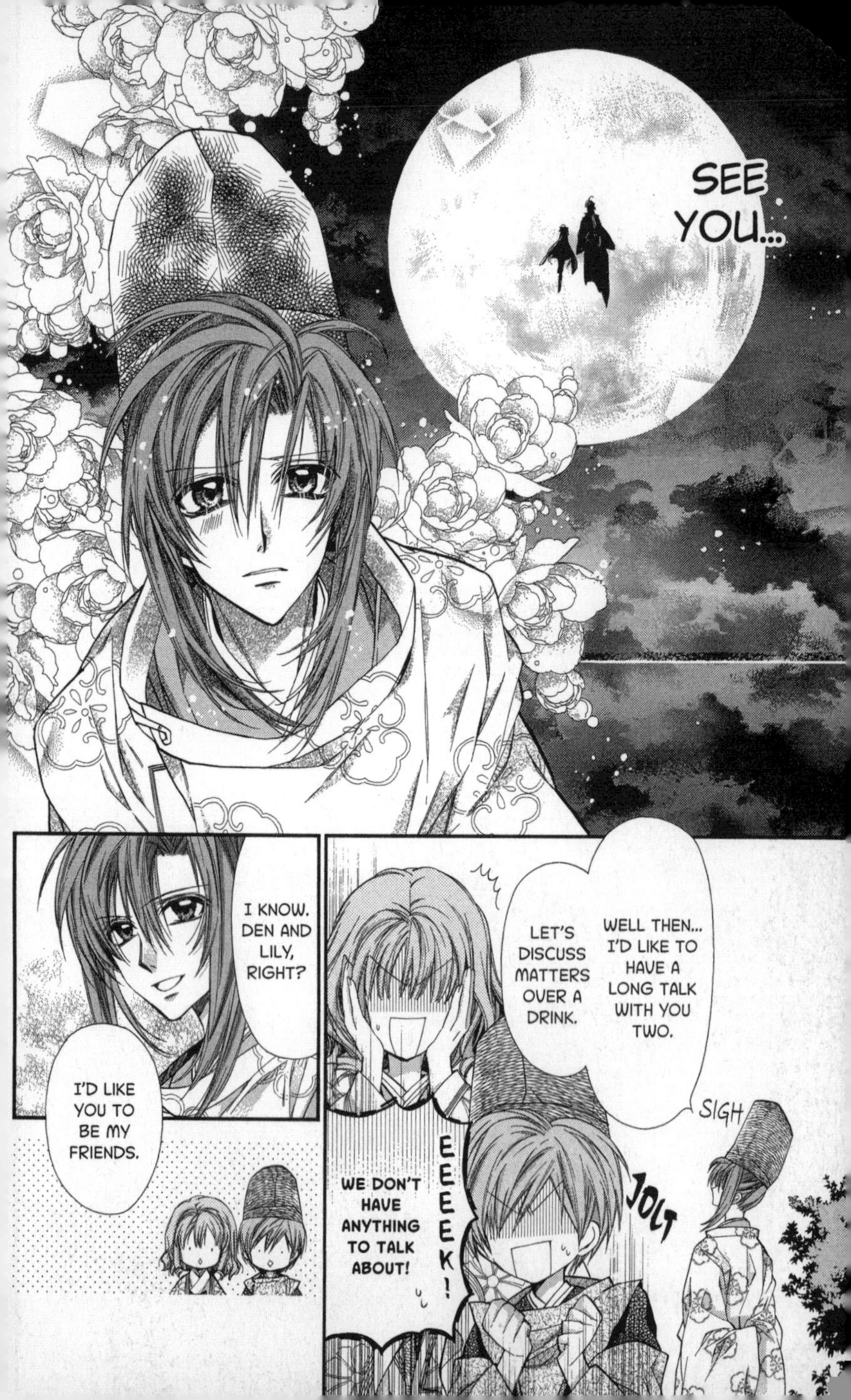
SEE YOU...
WELL THEN... I'D LIKE TO HAVE A LONG TALK WITH YOU TWO.
LET'S DISCUSS MATTERS OVER A DRINK.
SIGH
JOLT
EEEEEK!
WE DON'T HAVE ANYTHING TO TALK ABOUT!
I KNOW. DEN AND LILY, RIGHT?
I'D LIKE YOU TO BE MY FRIENDS.

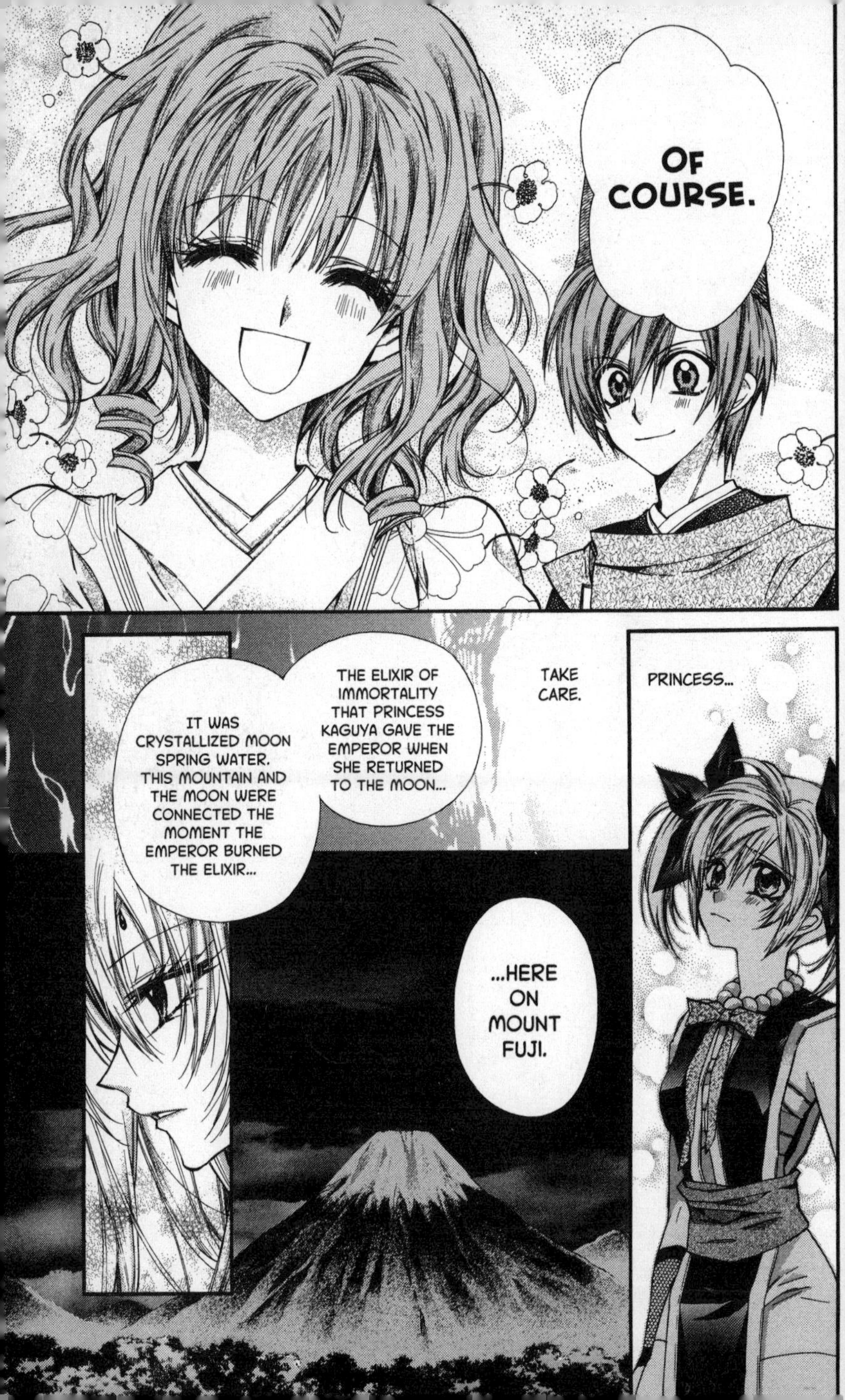
OF COURSE.
PRINCESS...
TAKE CARE.
THE ELIXIR OF IMMORTALITY THAT PRINCESS KAGUYA GAVE THE EMPEROR WHEN SHE RETURNED TO THE MOON...
IT WAS CRYSTALLIZED MOON SPRING WATER. THIS MOUNTAIN AND THE MOON WERE CONNECTED THE MOMENT THE EMPEROR BURNED THE ELIXIR...
...HERE ON MOUNT FUJI.

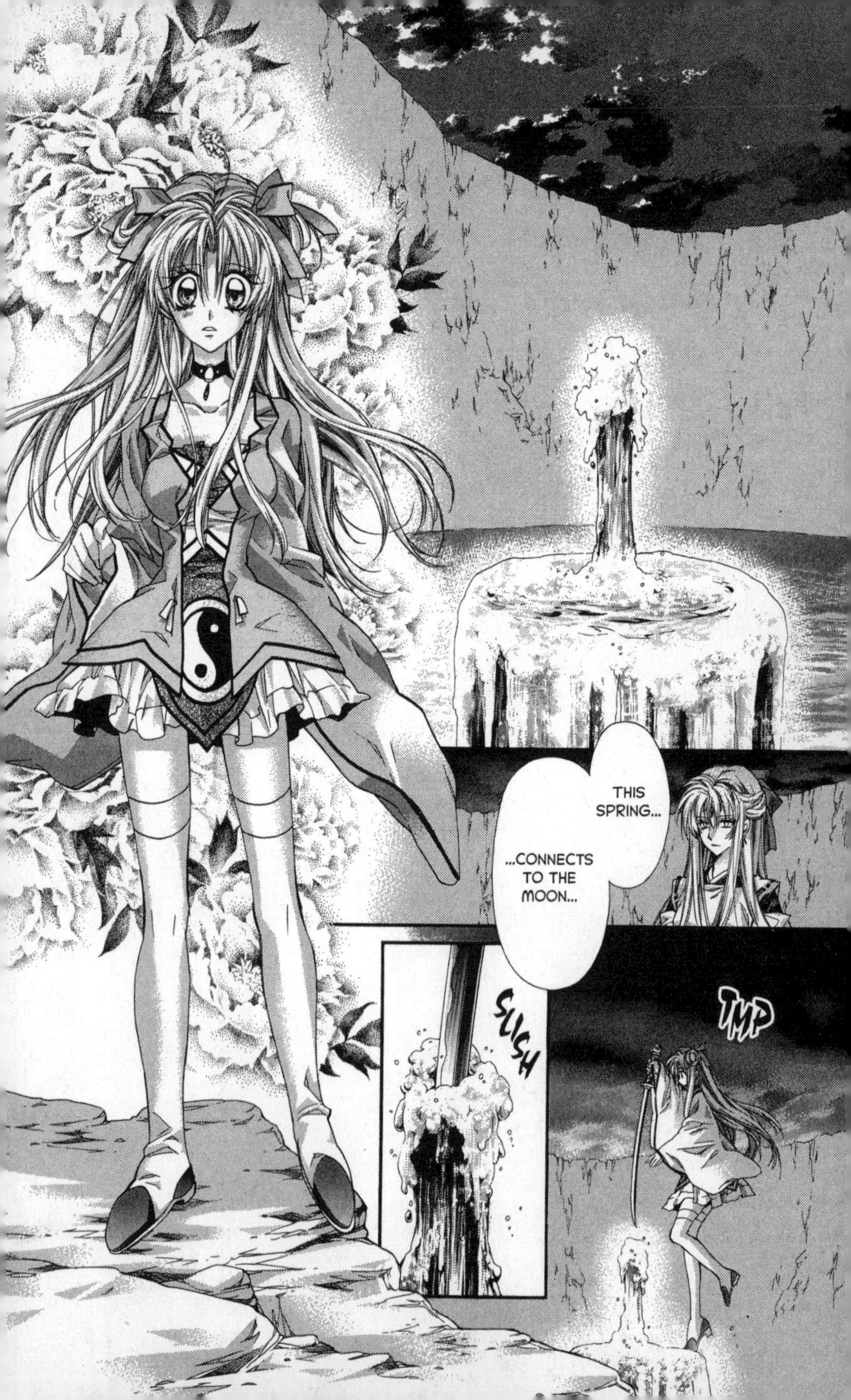
THIS SPRING...
...CONNECTS TO THE MOON...
TMP
SLISH

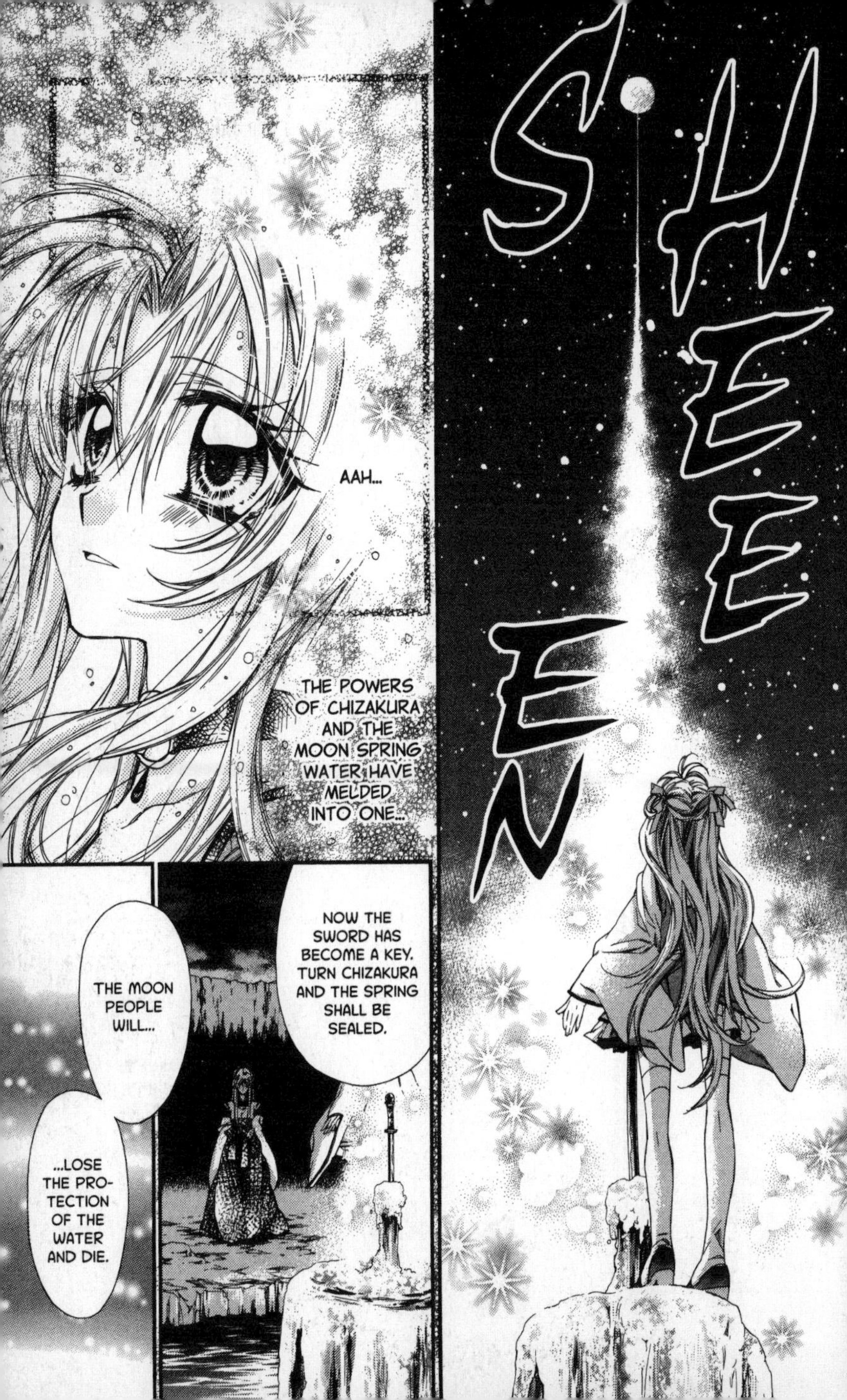
SHEEEN
AAH...
THE POWERS OF CHIZAKURA AND THE MOON SPRING WATER HAVE MELDED INTO ONE...
NOW THE SWORD HAS BECOME A KEY. TURN CHIZAKURA AND THE SPRING SHALL BE SEALED.
THE MOON PEOPLE WILL...
...LOSE THE PROTECTION OF THE WATER AND DIE.

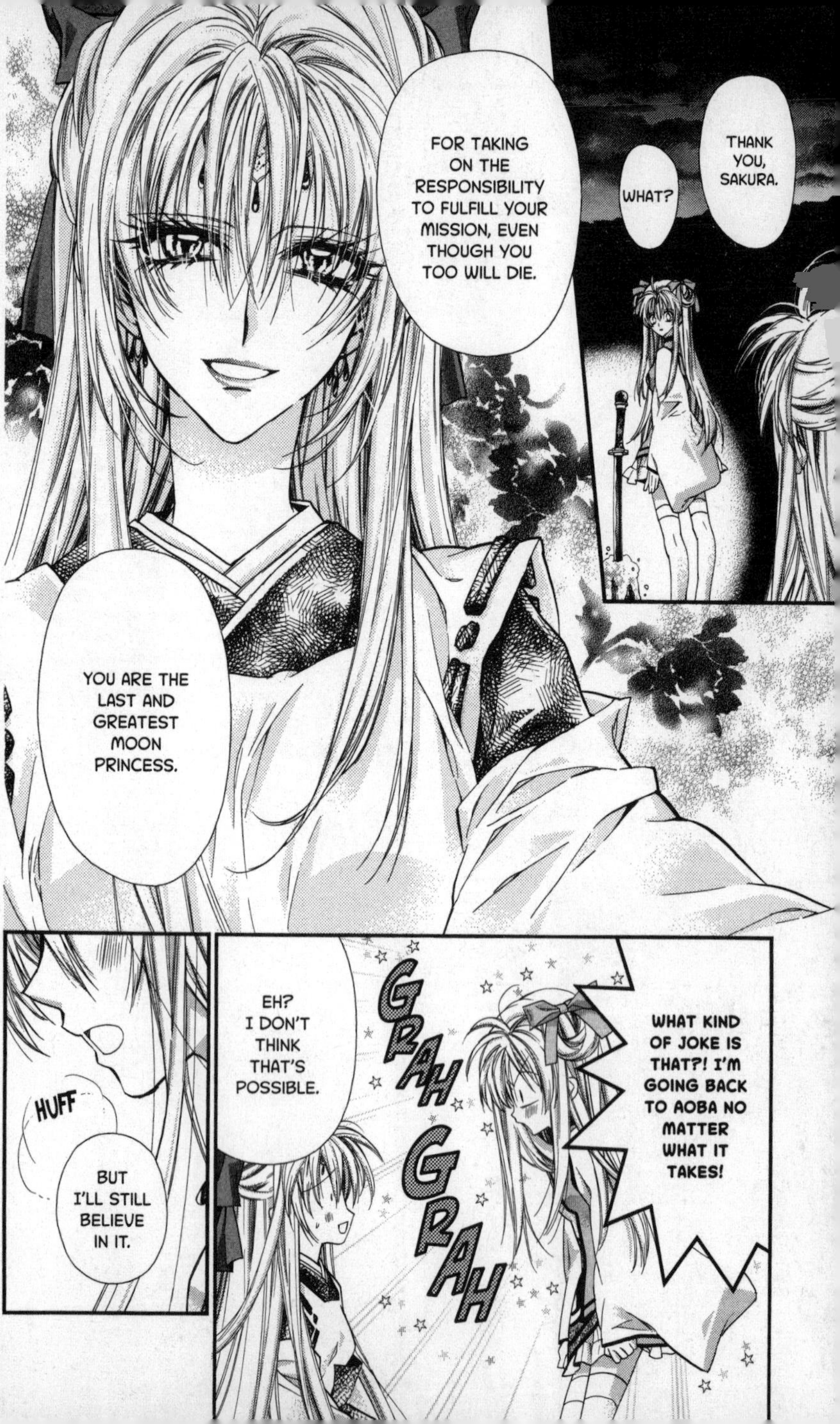
THANK YOU, SAKURA.
WHAT?
FOR TAKING ON THE RESPONSIBILITY TO FULFILL YOUR MISSION, EVEN THOUGH YOU TOO WILL DIE.
YOU ARE THE LAST AND GREATEST MOON PRINCESS.
WHAT KIND OF JOKE IS THAT?! I'M GOING BACK TO AOBA NO MATTER WHAT IT TAKES!
GRAH
GRAH
EH? I DON'T THINK THAT'S POSSIBLE.
HUFF
BUT I'LL STILL BELIEVE IN IT.

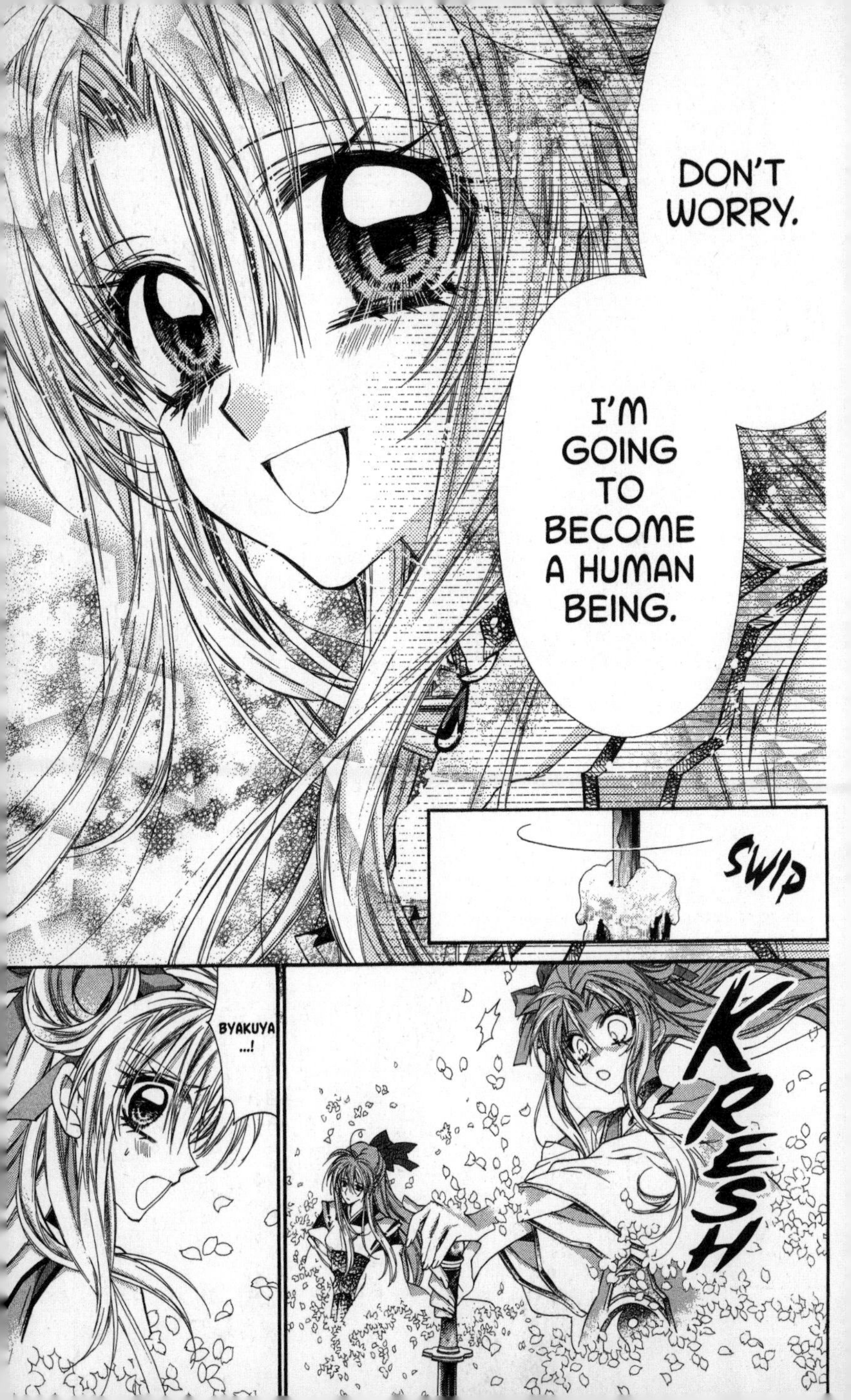
DON'T WORRY.
I'M GOING TO BECOME A HUMAN BEING.
SWIP
KRESH
BYAKUYA ...!

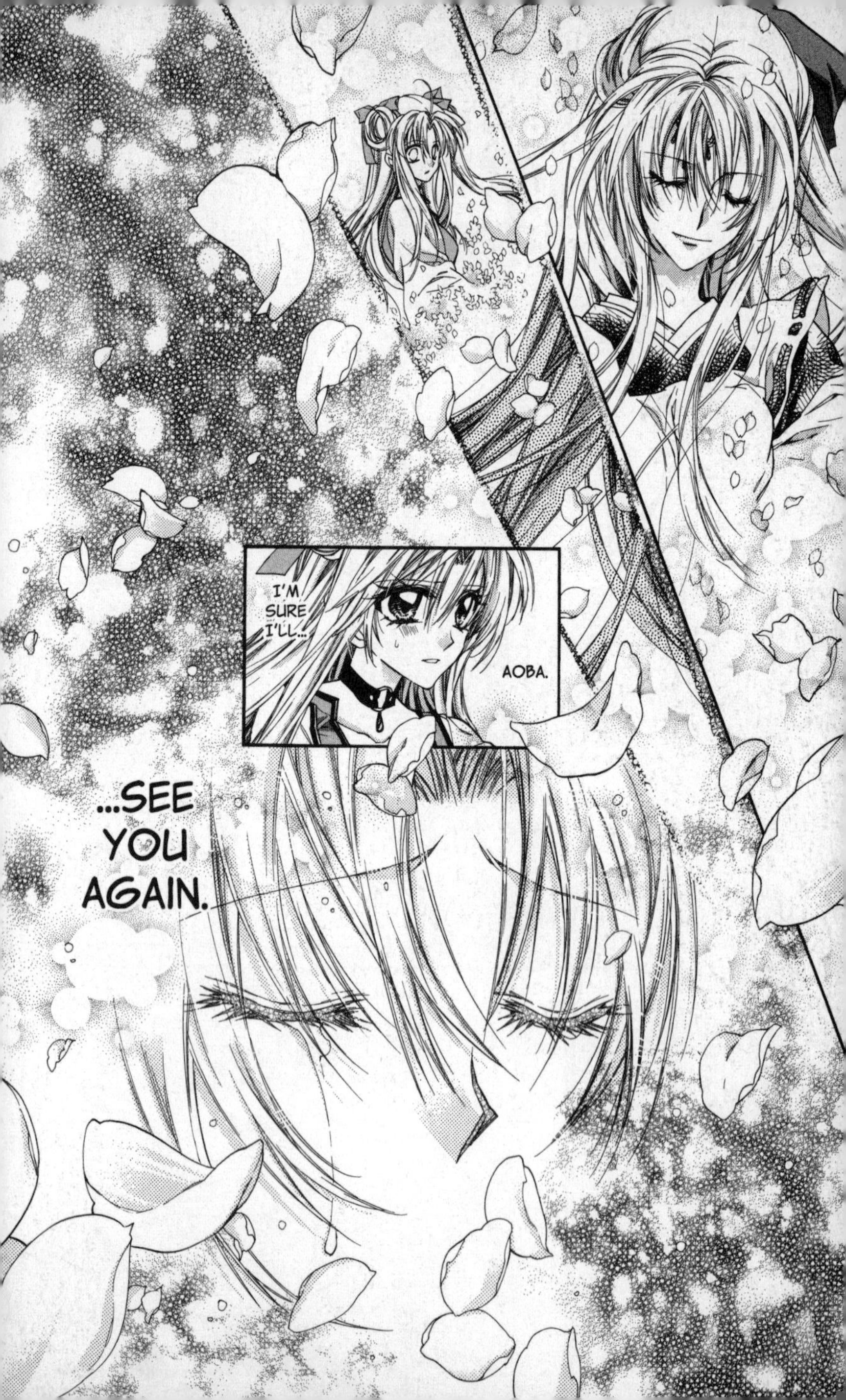
I'M SURE I'LL...
AOBA.
...SEE YOU AGAIN.

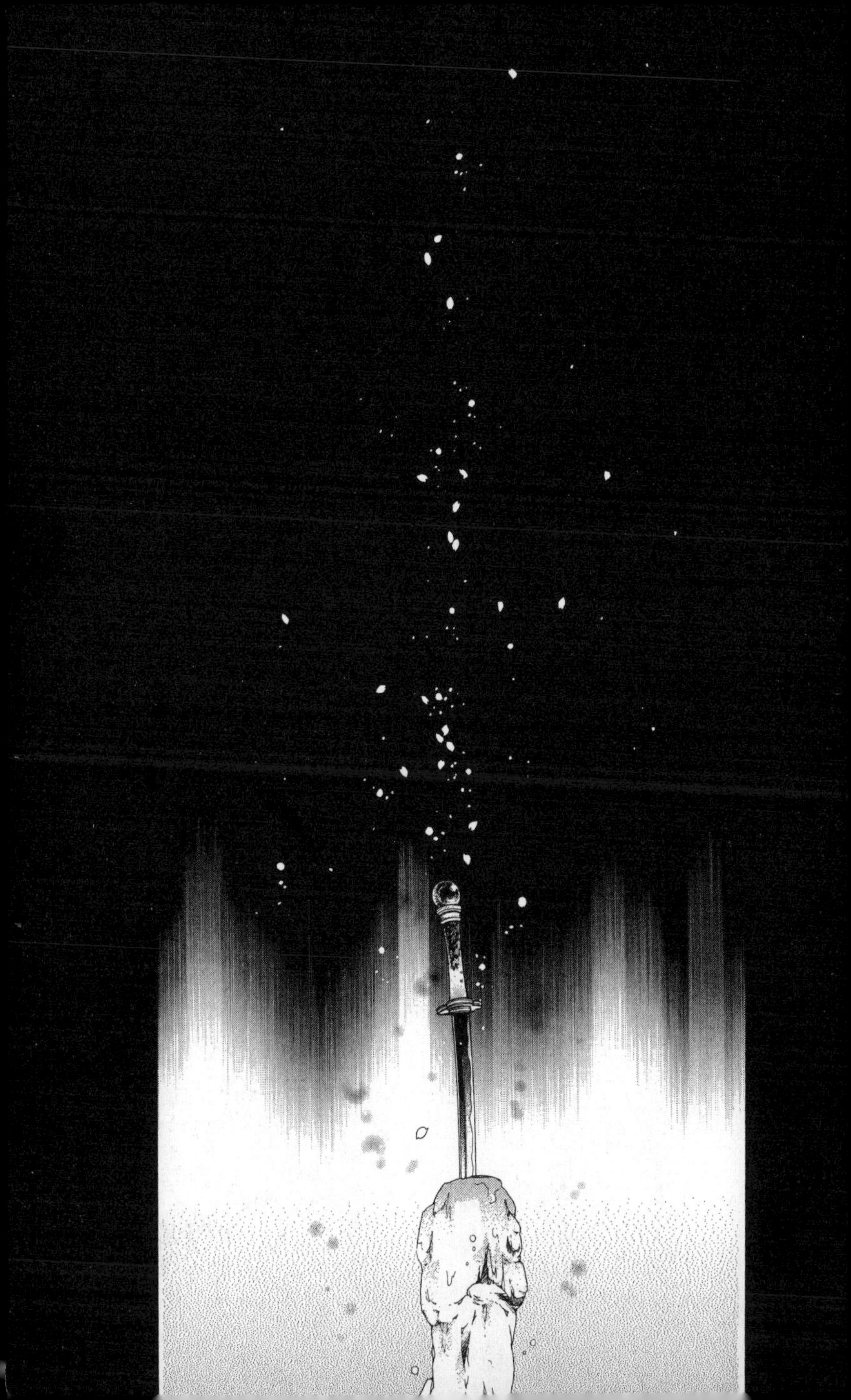

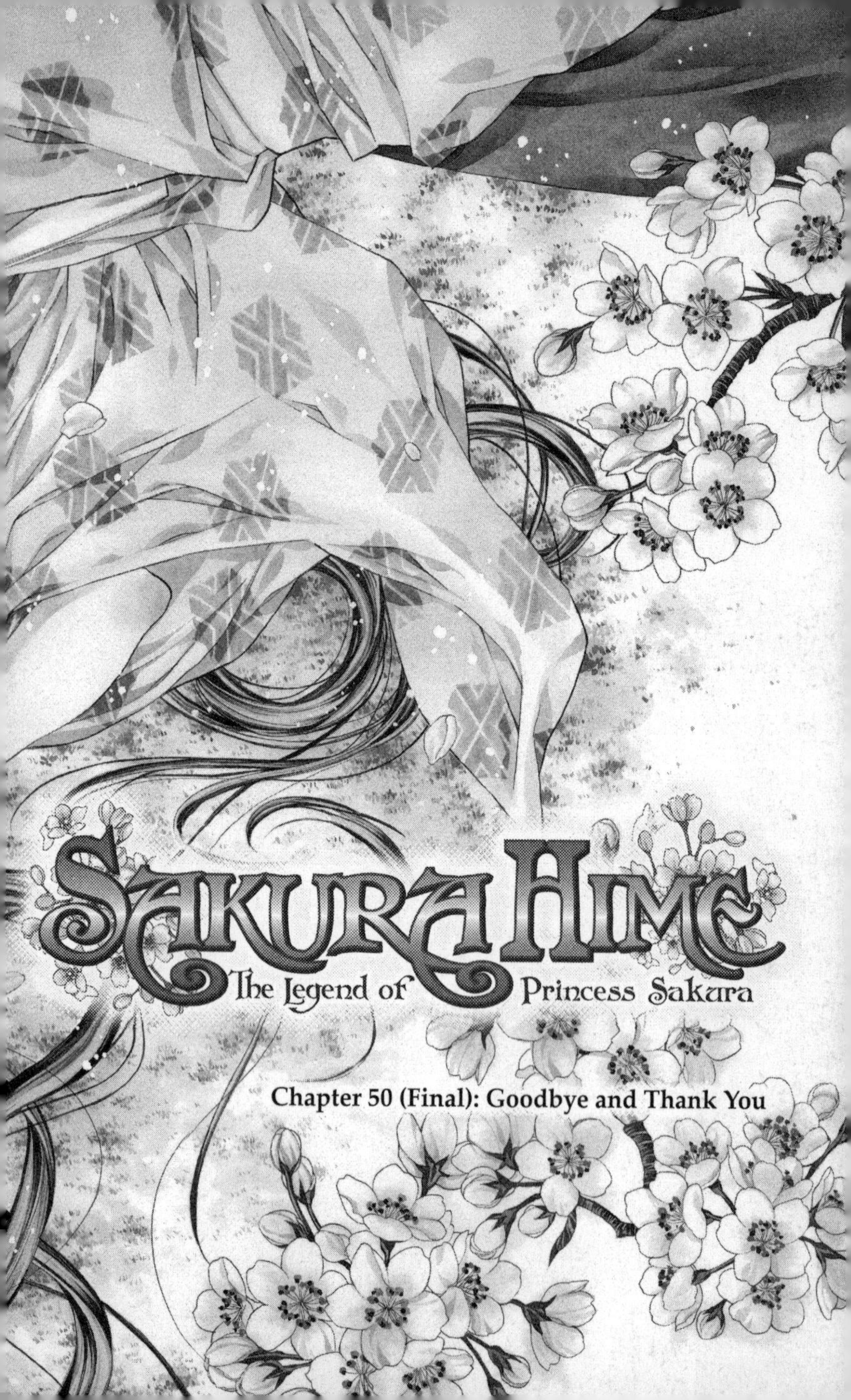
SAKURA HIME
The Legend of Princess Sakura
Chapter 50 (Final): Goodbye and Thank You

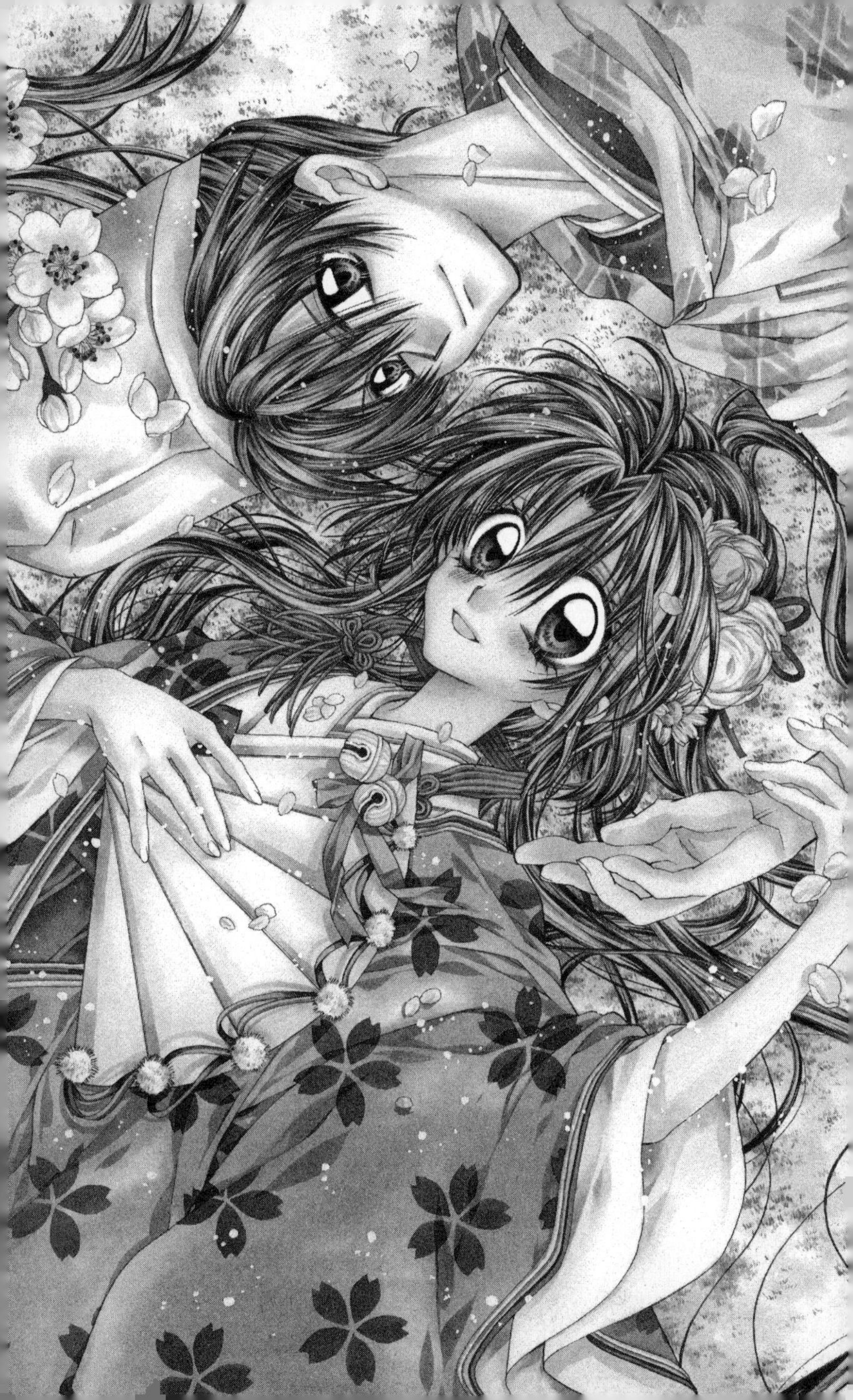

Sakura Hime
The Legend of Princess Sakura

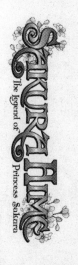

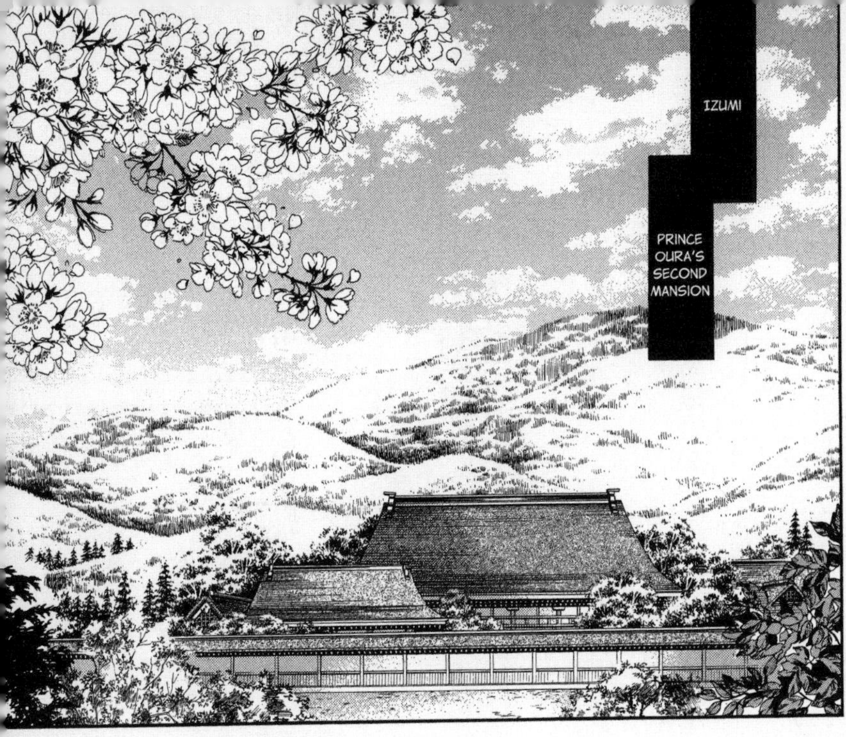
IZUMI
PRINCE OURA'S SECOND MANSION

Chapter 50: Goodbye and Thank You

※I'm giving away the story.
This is the final chapter. While working on this, I felt this story was based on the bond between Asagiri and Sakura.
To live, the reason to live... I too am human, so I have been asking myself that question often. And this is the answer I've currently come up with.
I might change my thoughts tomorrow, or I might not. After all, I'm a living being. To be honest, Kohaku, Hayate, Shuri, and Maimai's lives were in danger too, but I consider their lives not to be over yet, so I hope they will continue leading a happy life.

As for Sakura's hair, this was something I thought of at the very beginning when I was planning this series. It's a touching scene to end the series. I will not publish my work in *Ribon* again, and I may never work on a series as long as this again either. The last monologue is a mixture of Sakura's thoughts and my own.
I need to search for that something too.

Thank you very much!

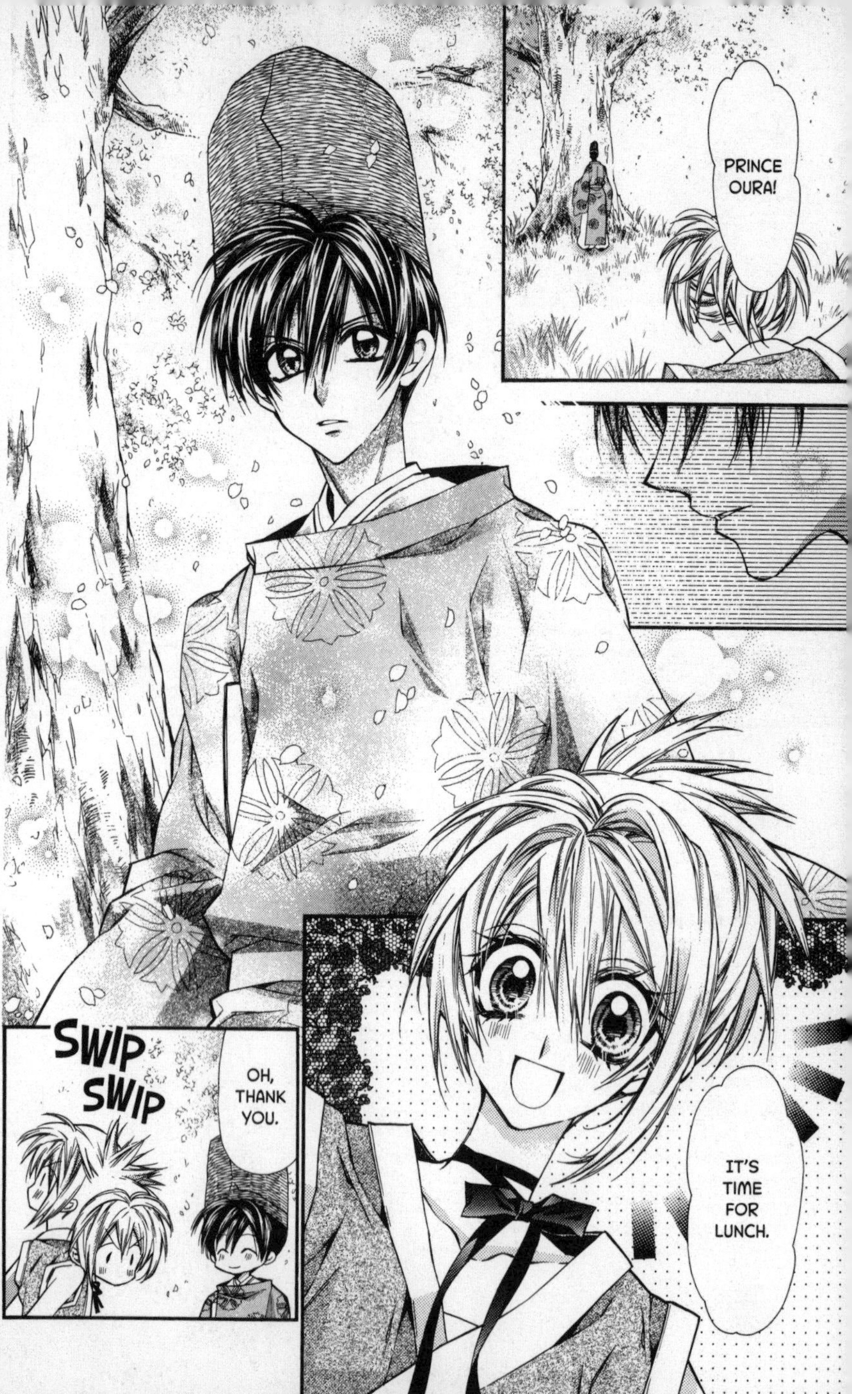
PRINCE OURA!
IT'S TIME FOR LUNCH.
SWIP SWIP
OH, THANK YOU.

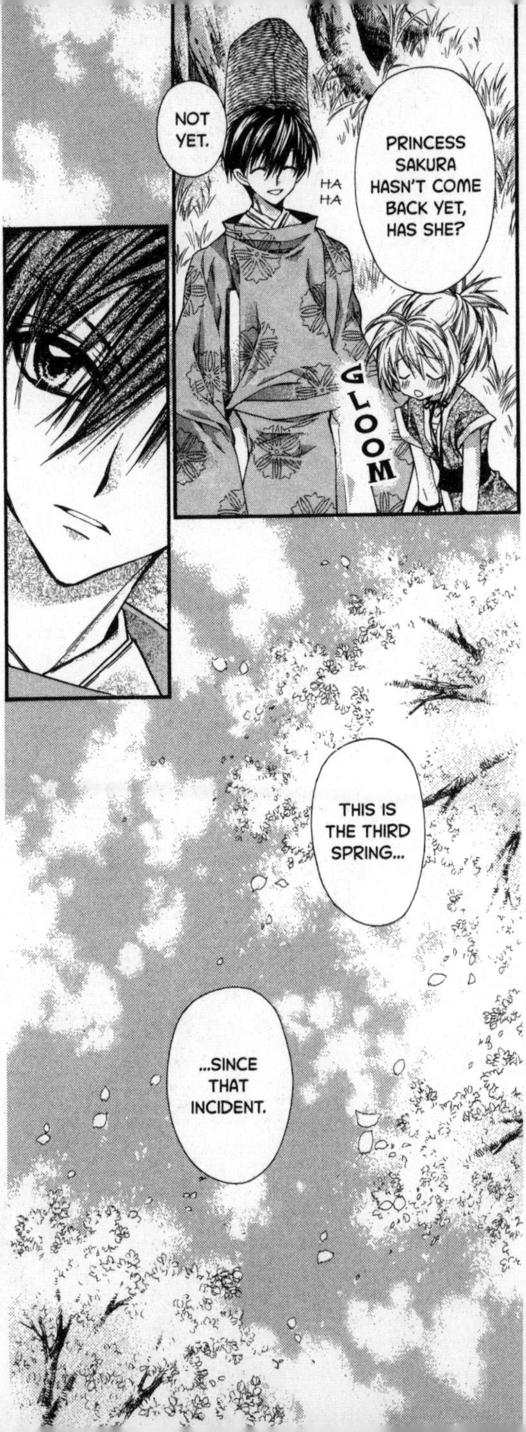
PRINCESS SAKURA HASN'T COME BACK YET, HAS SHE?
HA HA
NOT YET.
GLOOM
THIS IS THE THIRD SPRING...
...SINCE THAT INCIDENT.

Special Thanks

To the best staff who have supported me to the very end. Thank you very much!

Nakame
Momo-chan

Matsun
Hii-chan
Mari
Ikurun
Naho Minami-san
Yogurt-chan
Acchan
Rena-san
Miichi

And all the staff on *Sakura-Hime: The Legend of Princess Sakura*

Shueisha Ribon Editorial Department
Ammonite, Inc.
Kawatani Design
Sobisha

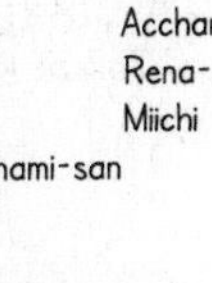

BOW

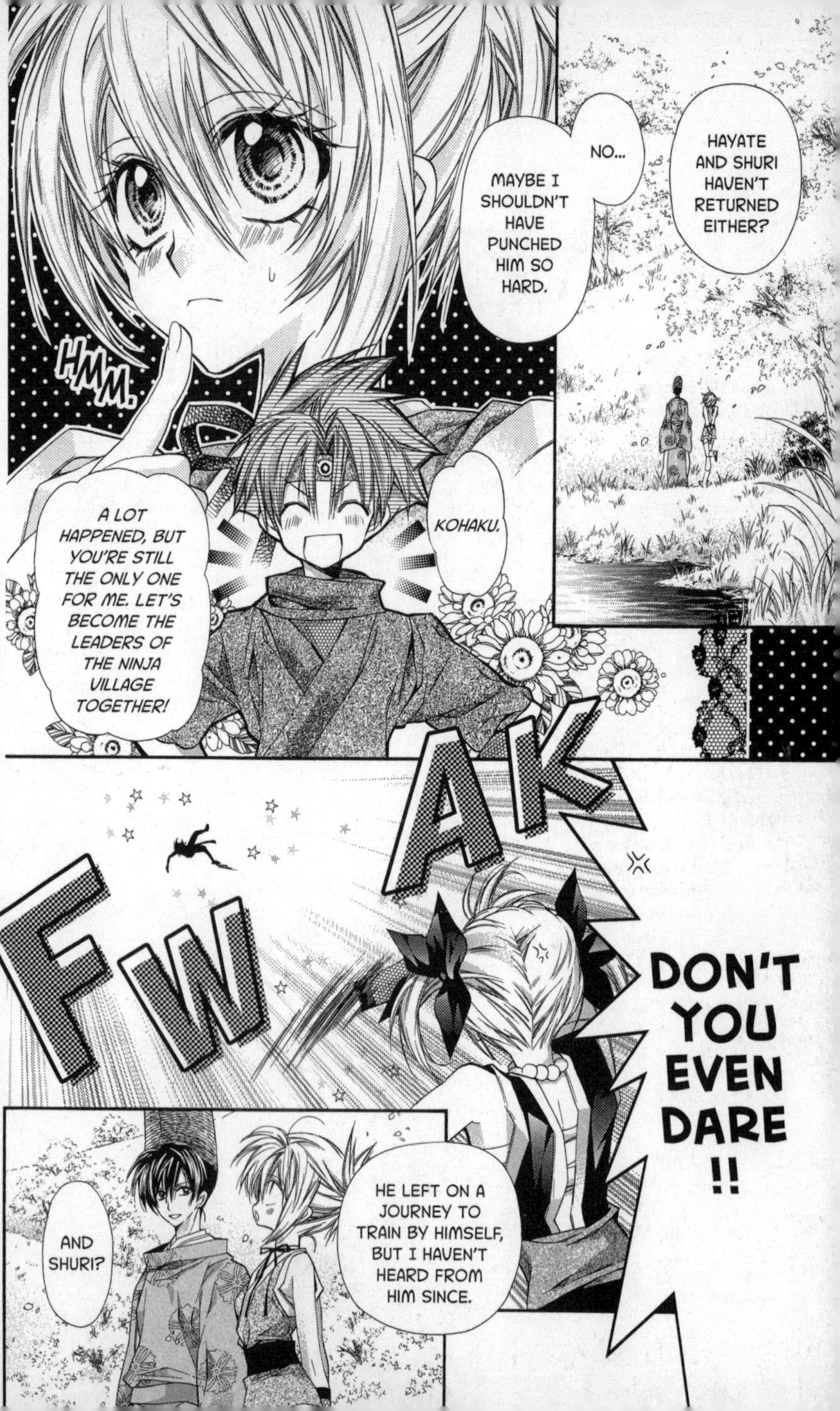
HAYATE AND SHURI HAVEN'T RETURNED EITHER?
NO...
MAYBE I SHOULDN'T HAVE PUNCHED HIM SO HARD.
HMM.
KOHAKU.
A LOT HAPPENED, BUT YOU'RE STILL THE ONLY ONE FOR ME. LET'S BECOME THE LEADERS OF THE NINJA VILLAGE TOGETHER!
DON'T YOU EVEN DARE!!
FWAK
HE LEFT ON A JOURNEY TO TRAIN BY HIMSELF, BUT I HAVEN'T HEARD FROM HIM SINCE.
AND SHURI?

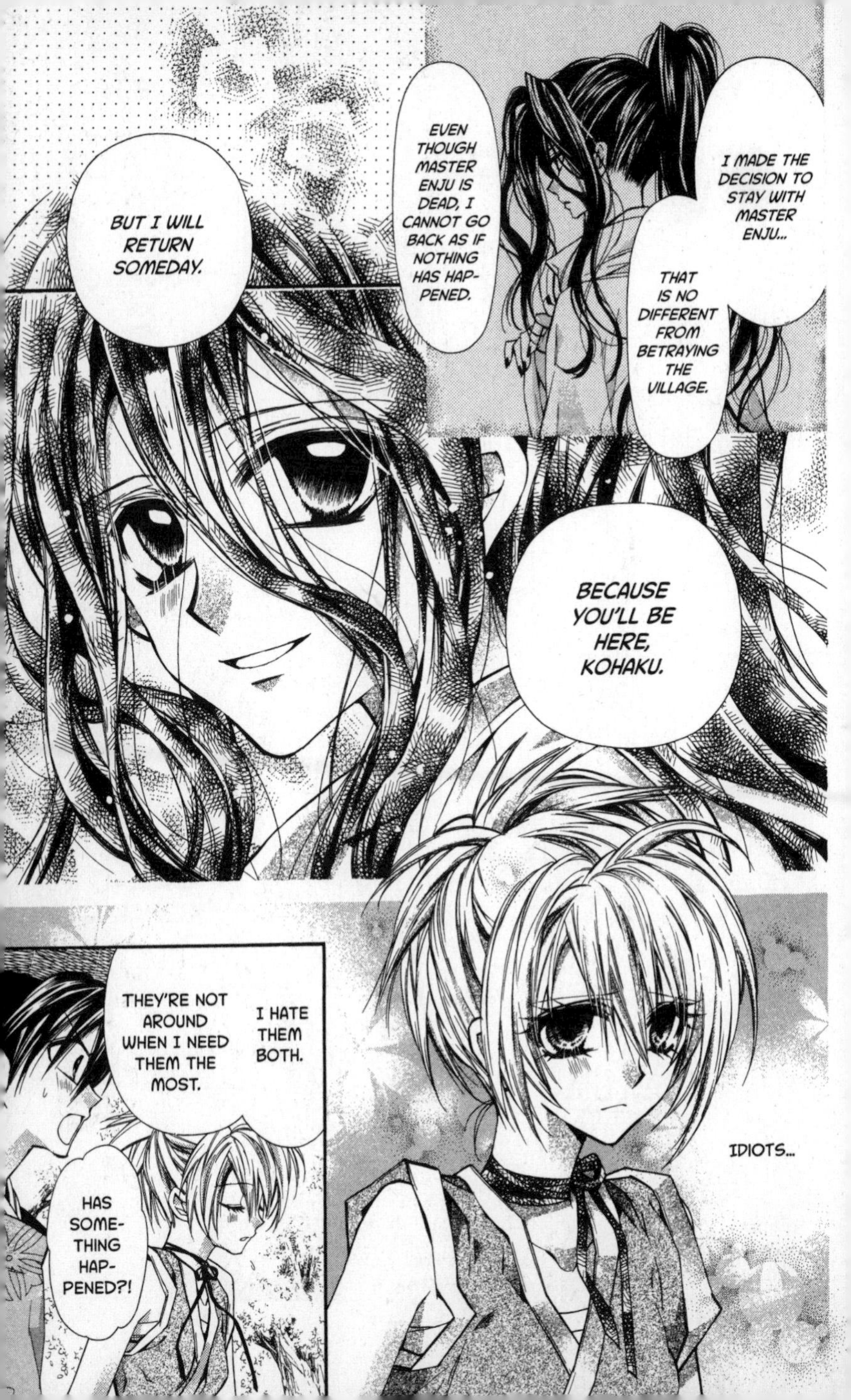
I MADE THE DECISION TO STAY WITH MASTER ENJU...
THAT IS NO DIFFERENT FROM BETRAYING THE VILLAGE.
EVEN THOUGH MASTER ENJU IS DEAD, I CANNOT GO BACK AS IF NOTHING HAS HAP-PENED.
BUT I WILL RETURN SOMEDAY.
BECAUSE YOU'LL BE HERE, KOHAKU.
IDIOTS...
I HATE THEM BOTH.
THEY'RE NOT AROUND WHEN I NEED THEM THE MOST.
HAS SOME-THING HAP-PENED?!

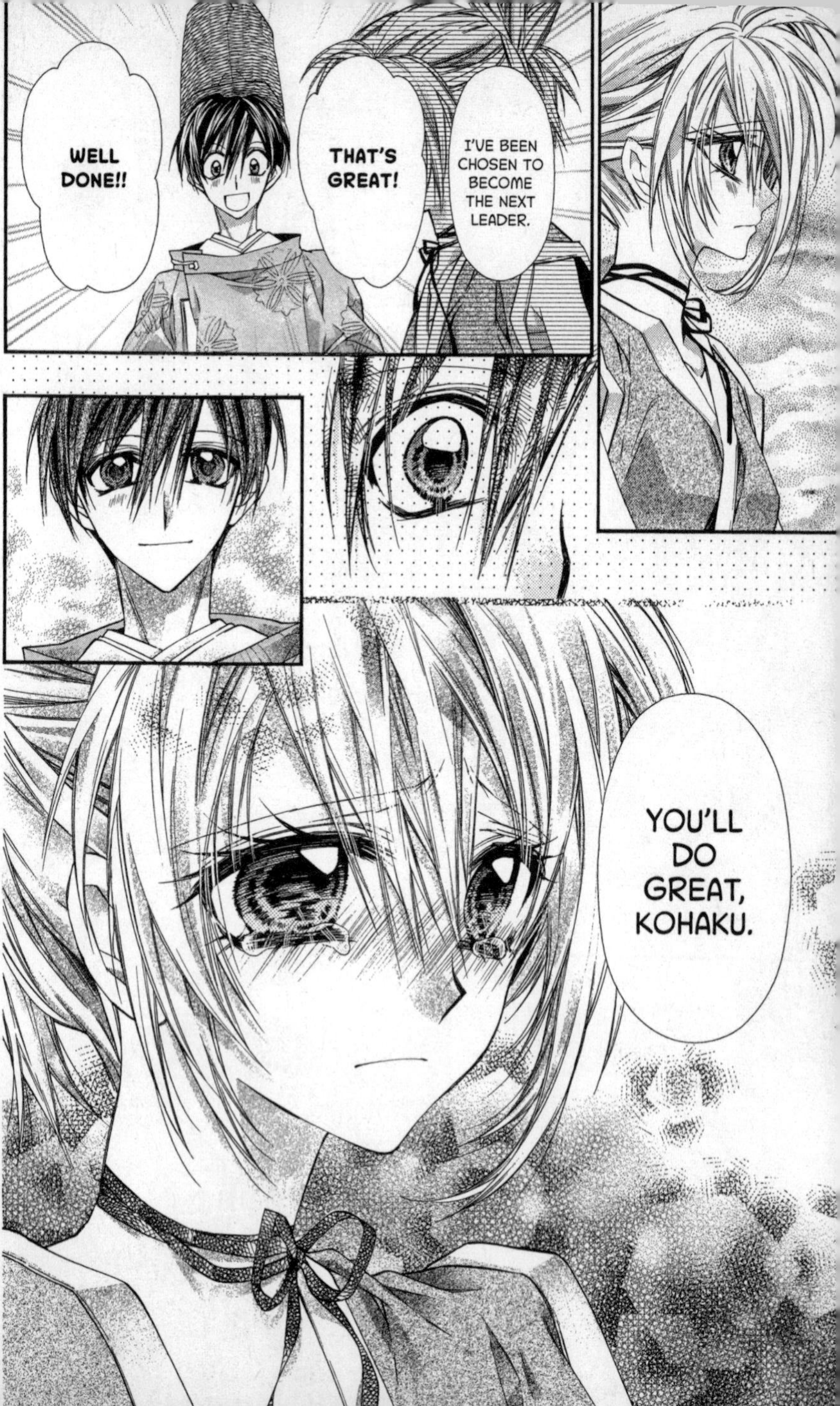
I'VE BEEN CHOSEN TO BECOME THE NEXT LEADER.
THAT'S GREAT!
WELL DONE!!
YOU'LL DO GREAT, KOHAKU.

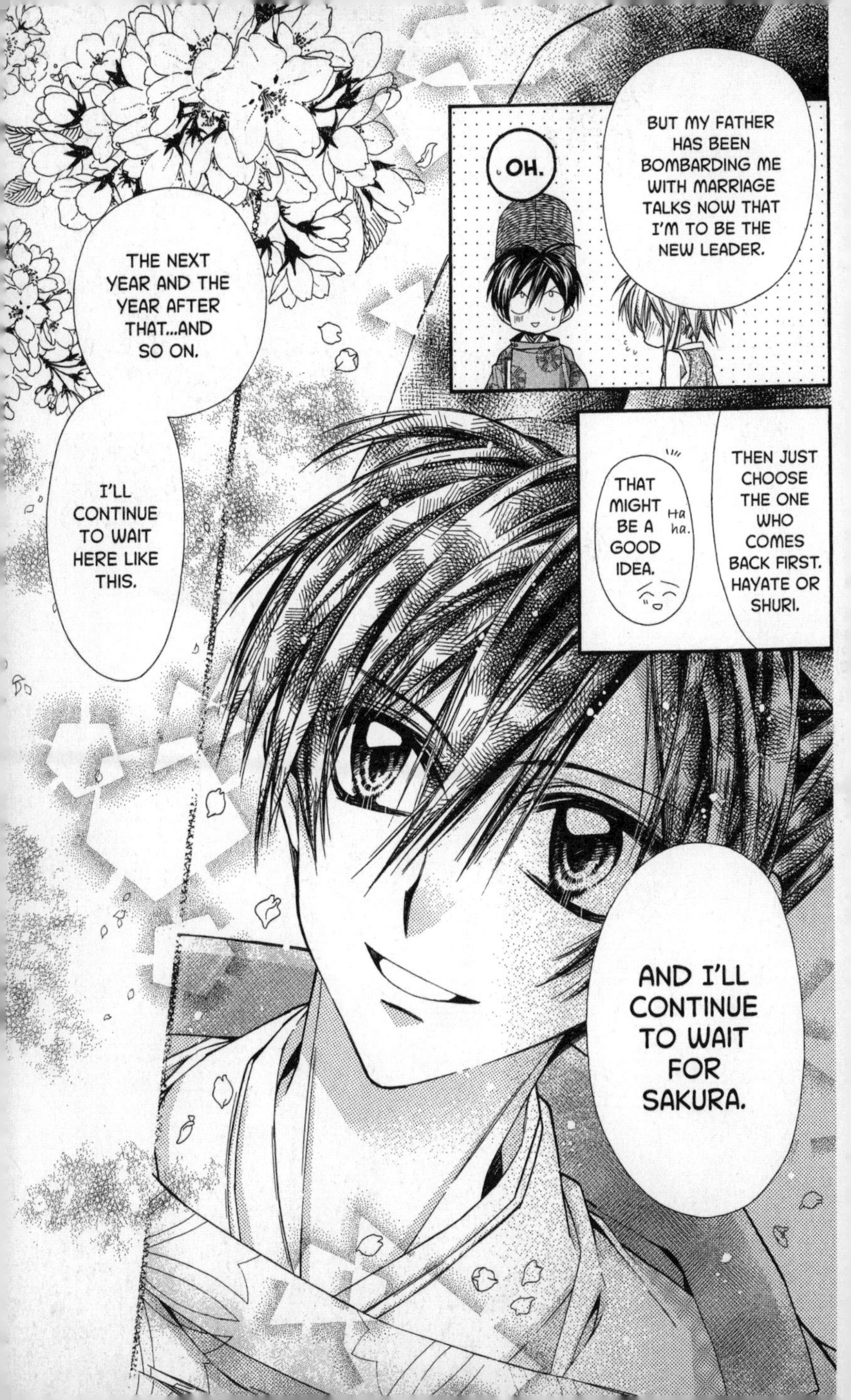
BUT MY FATHER HAS BEEN BOMBARDING ME WITH MARRIAGE TALKS NOW THAT I'M TO BE THE NEW LEADER.
OH.
THEN JUST CHOOSE THE ONE WHO COMES BACK FIRST. HAYATE OR SHURI.
THAT MIGHT BE A GOOD IDEA.
Ha ha.
THE NEXT YEAR AND THE YEAR AFTER THAT...AND SO ON.
I'LL CONTINUE TO WAIT HERE LIKE THIS.
AND I'LL CONTINUE TO WAIT FOR SAKURA.

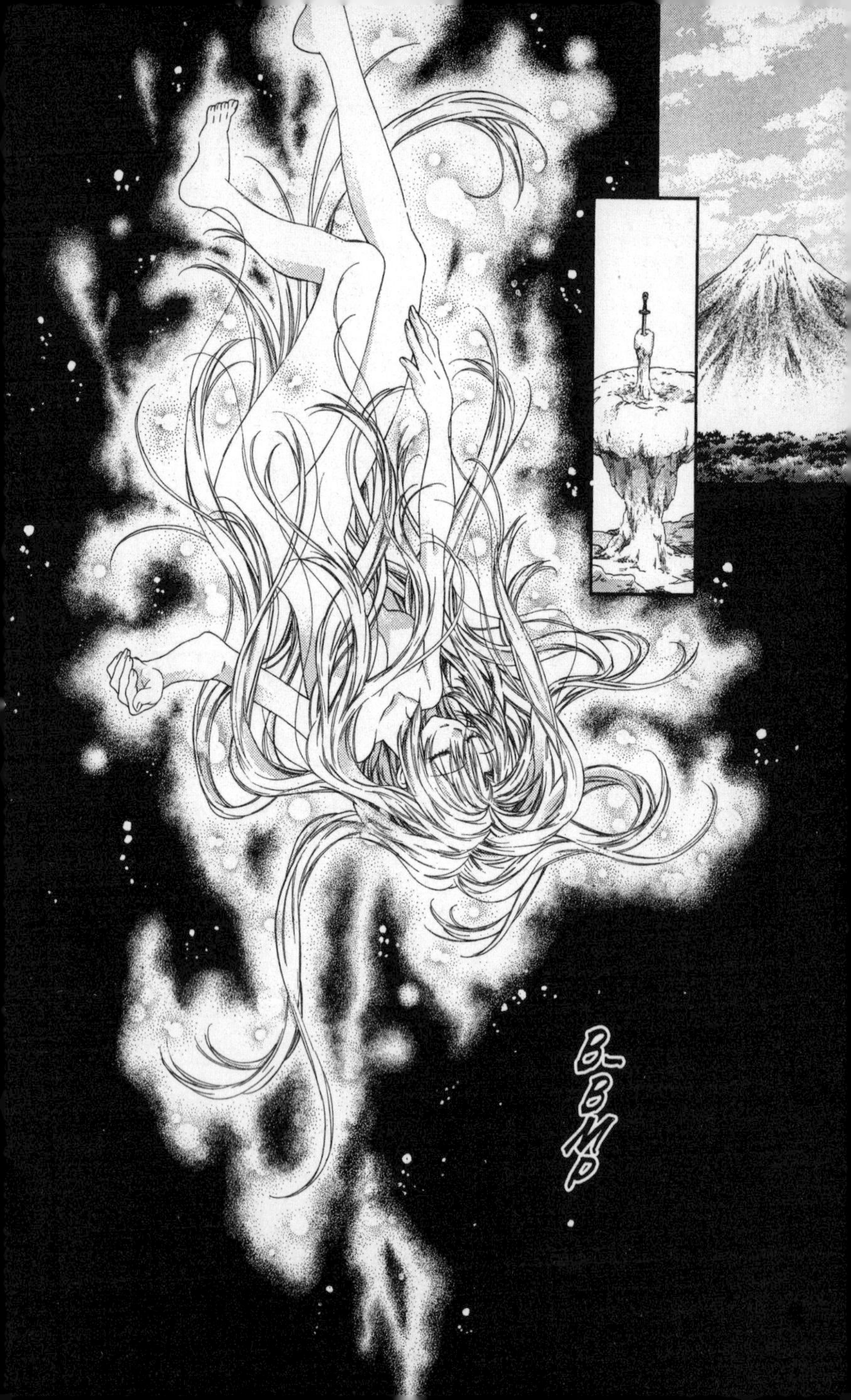
B-BMP

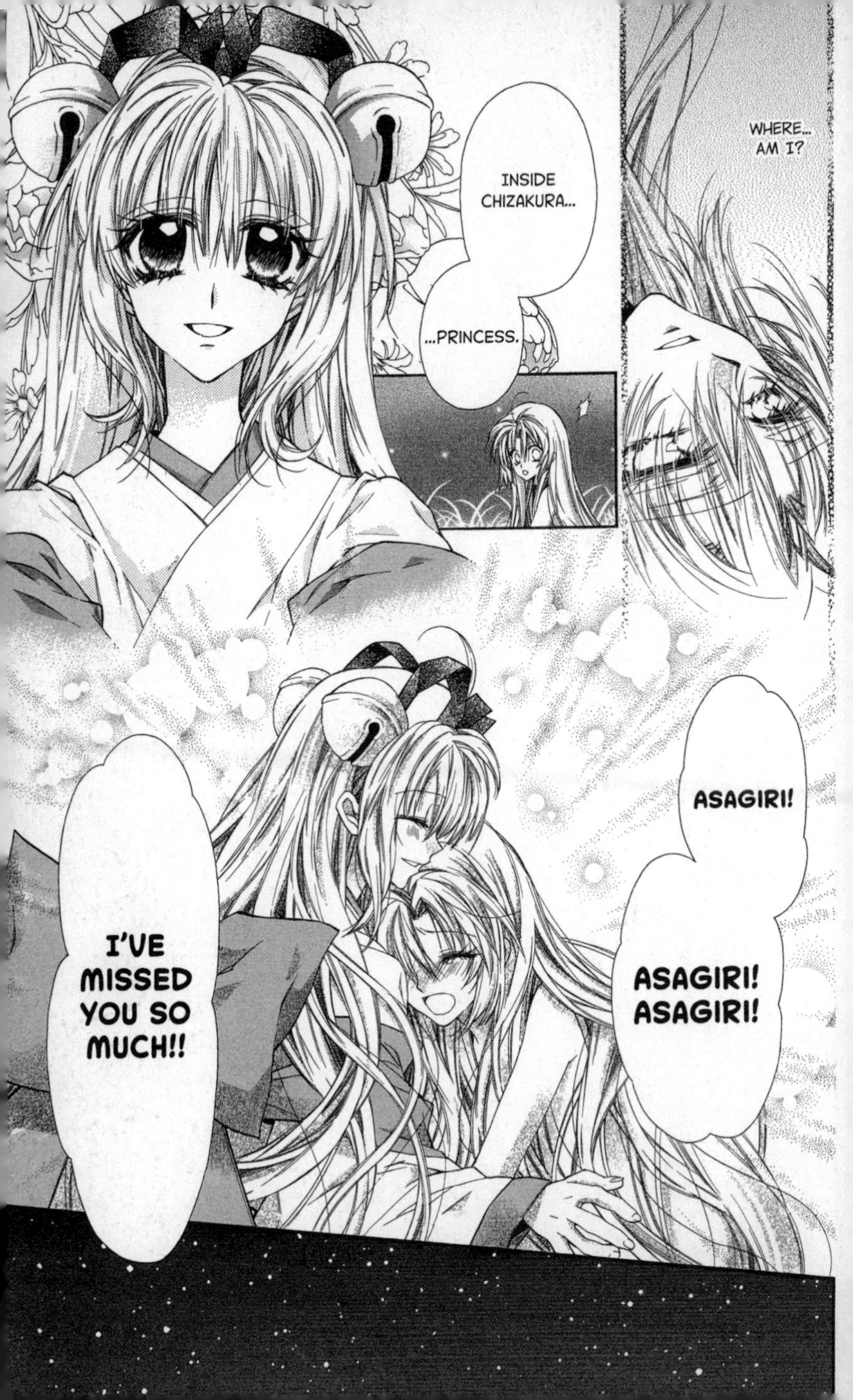
WHERE... AM I?
INSIDE CHIZAKURA...
...PRINCESS.
ASAGIRI!
ASAGIRI! ASAGIRI!
I'VE MISSED YOU SO MUCH!!

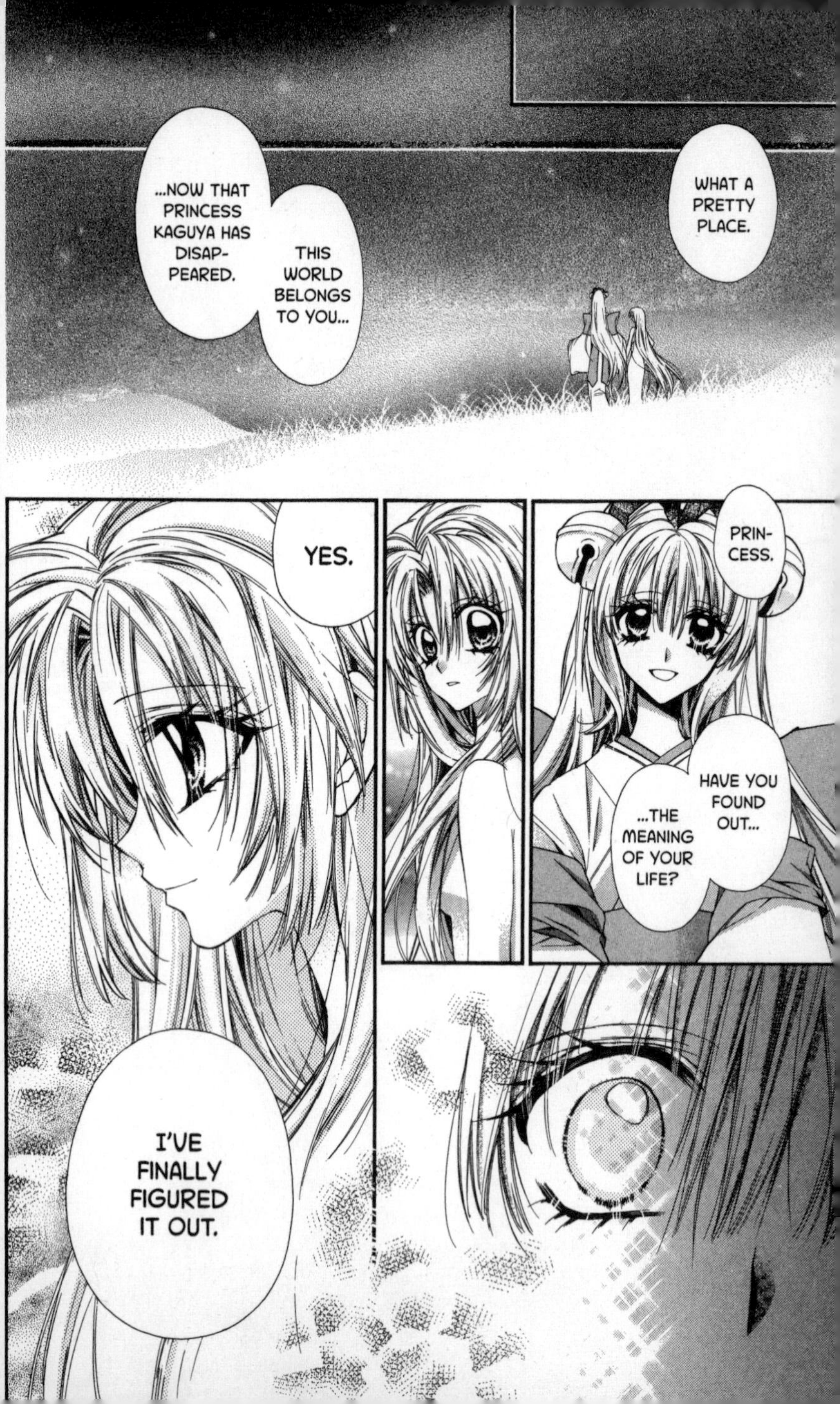
WHAT A PRETTY PLACE.
THIS WORLD BELONGS TO YOU...
...NOW THAT PRINCESS KAGUYA HAS DISAP-PEARED.
PRIN-CESS.
HAVE YOU FOUND OUT...
...THE MEANING OF YOUR LIFE?
YES.
I'VE FINALLY FIGURED IT OUT.

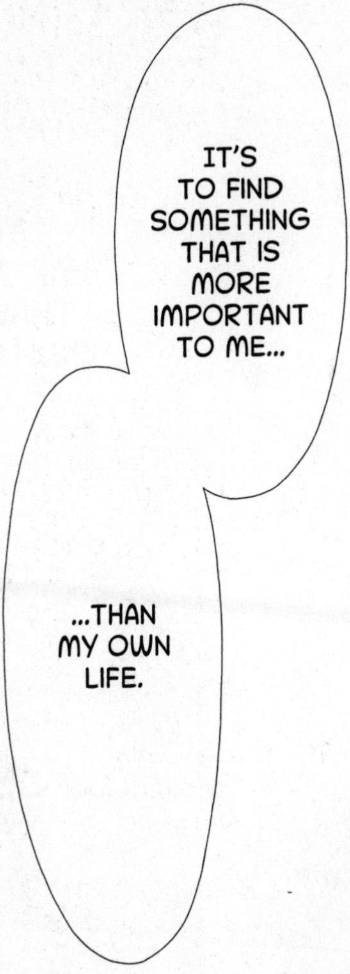
IT'S TO FIND SOMETHING THAT IS MORE IMPORTANT TO ME...
...THAN MY OWN LIFE.

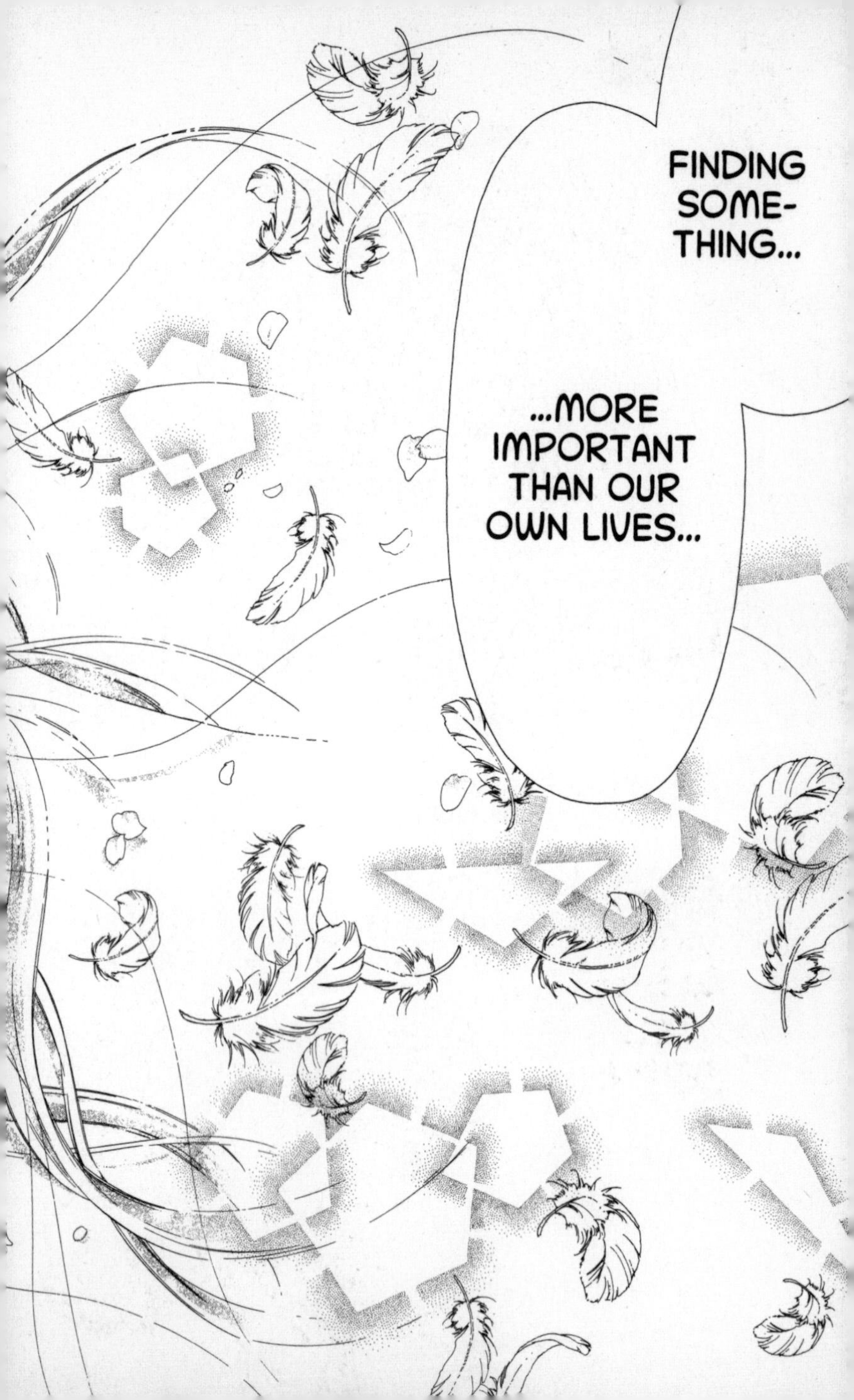
FINDING SOME-THING...
...MORE IMPORTANT THAN OUR OWN LIVES...

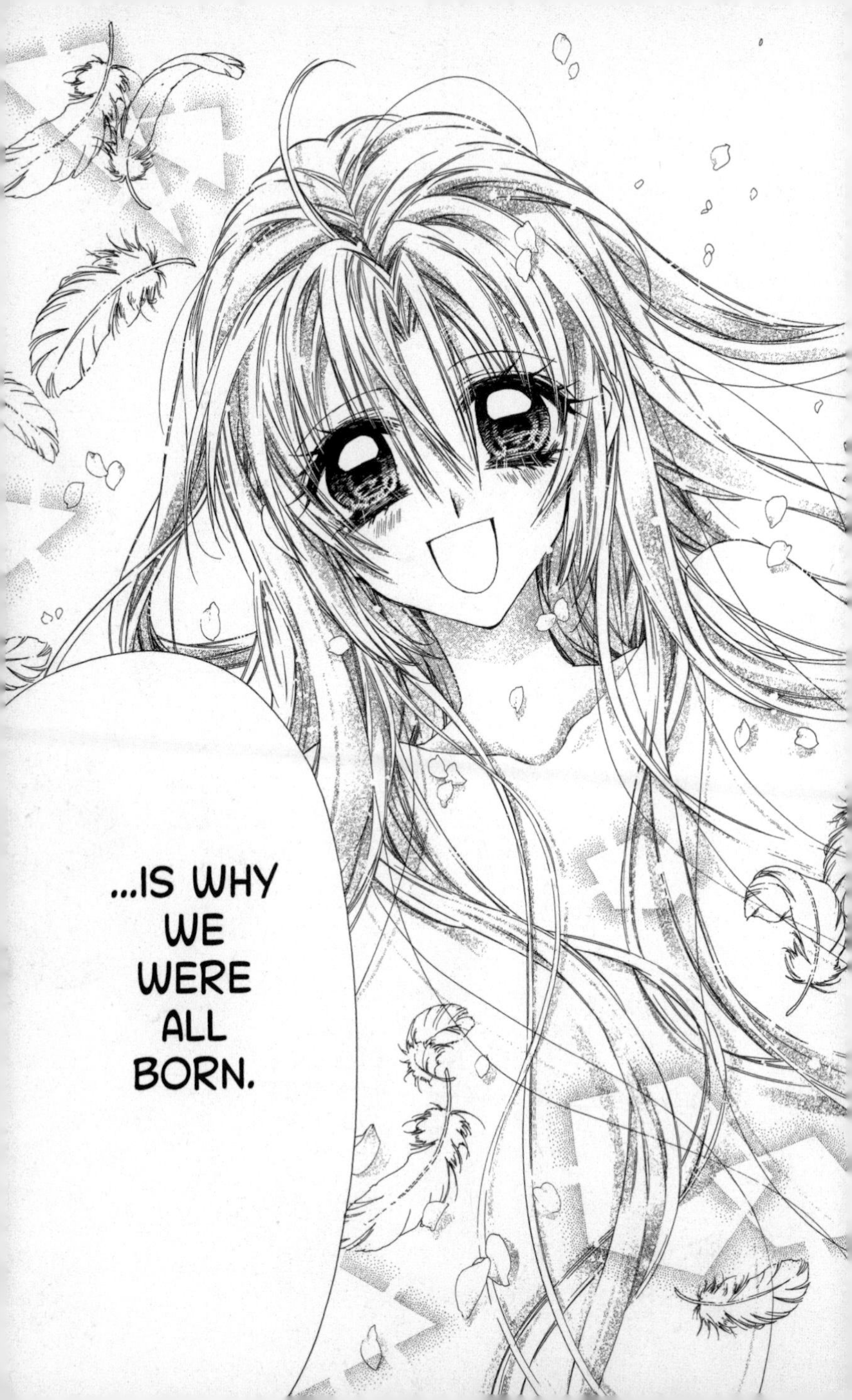
...IS WHY WE WERE ALL BORN.

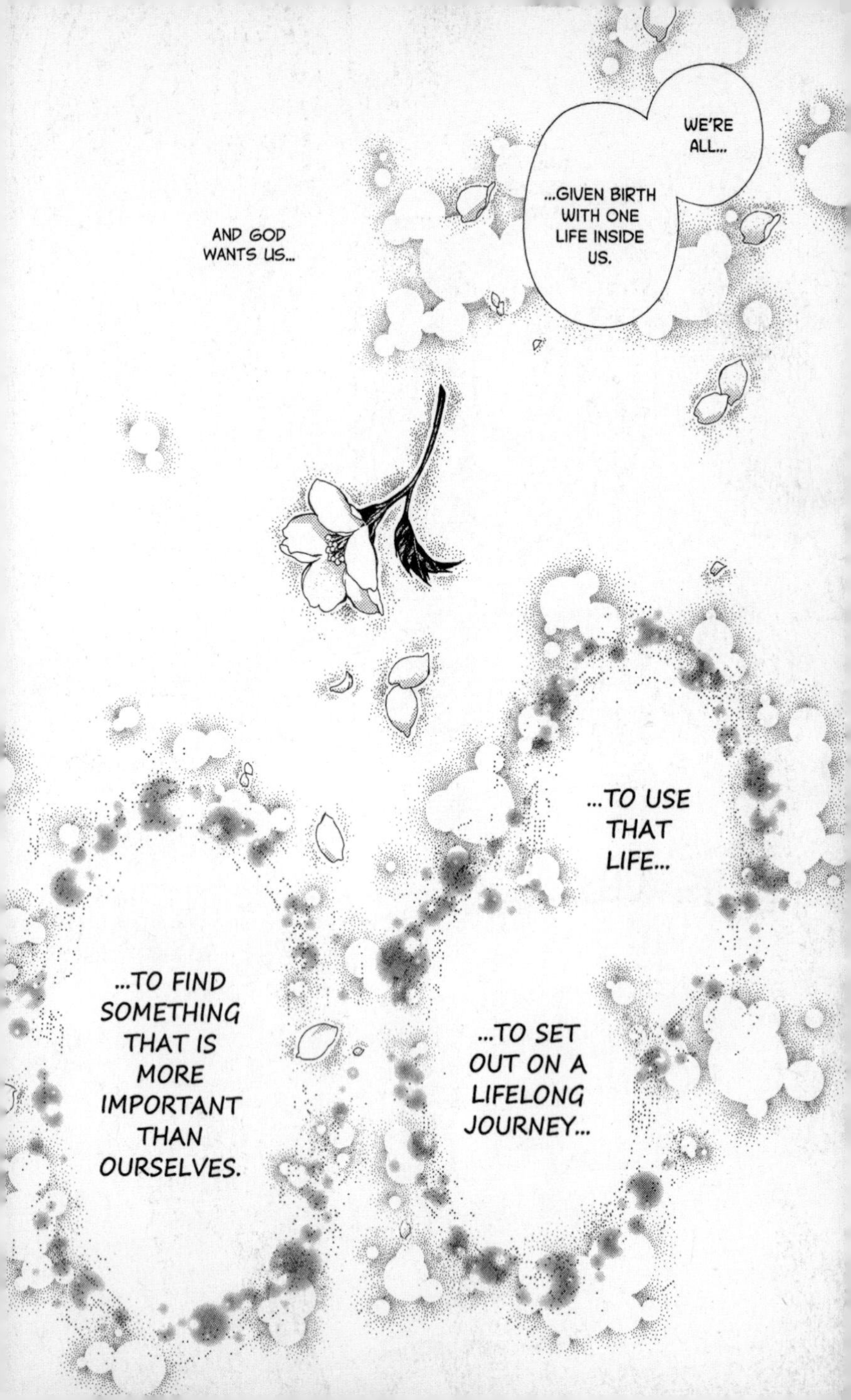
WE'RE ALL...
...GIVEN BIRTH WITH ONE LIFE INSIDE US.
AND GOD WANTS US...
...TO USE THAT LIFE...
...TO SET OUT ON A LIFELONG JOURNEY...
...TO FIND SOMETHING THAT IS MORE IMPORTANT THAN OURSELVES.

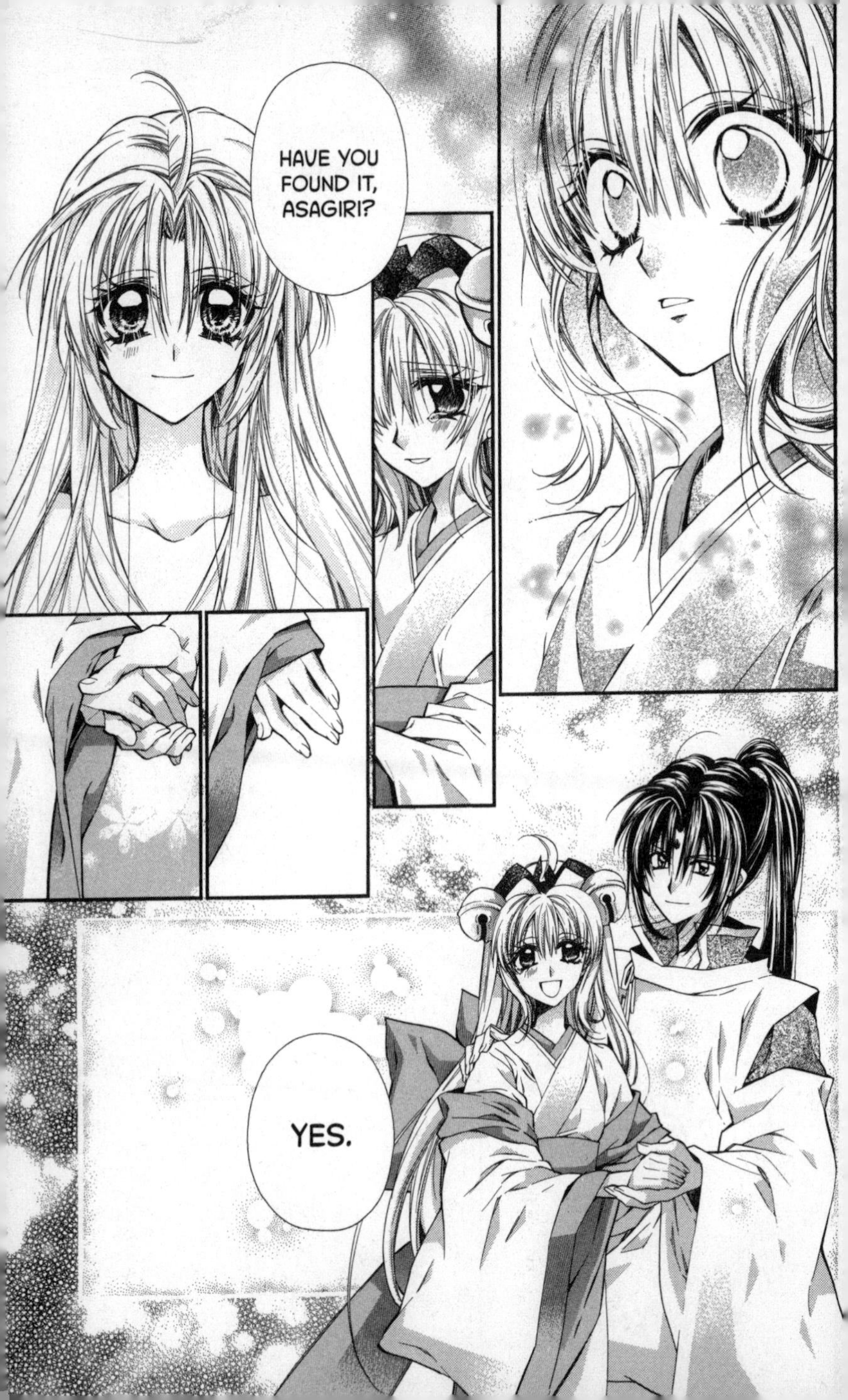
HAVE YOU FOUND IT, ASAGIRI?
YES.

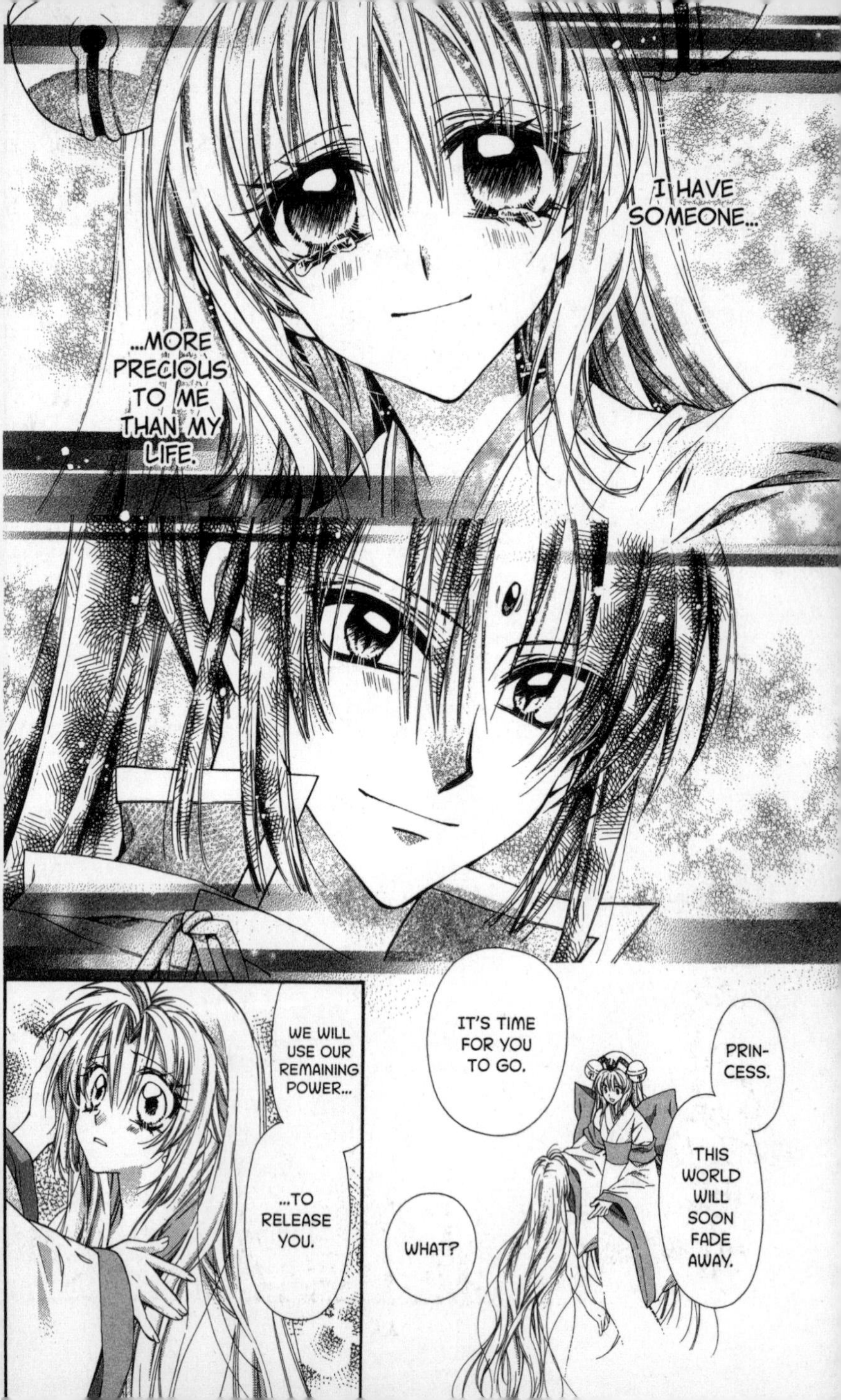
I HAVE SOMEONE...
...MORE PRECIOUS TO ME THAN MY LIFE.
PRIN-CESS.
THIS WORLD WILL SOON FADE AWAY.
IT'S TIME FOR YOU TO GO.
WHAT?
WE WILL USE OUR REMAINING POWER...
...TO RELEASE YOU.

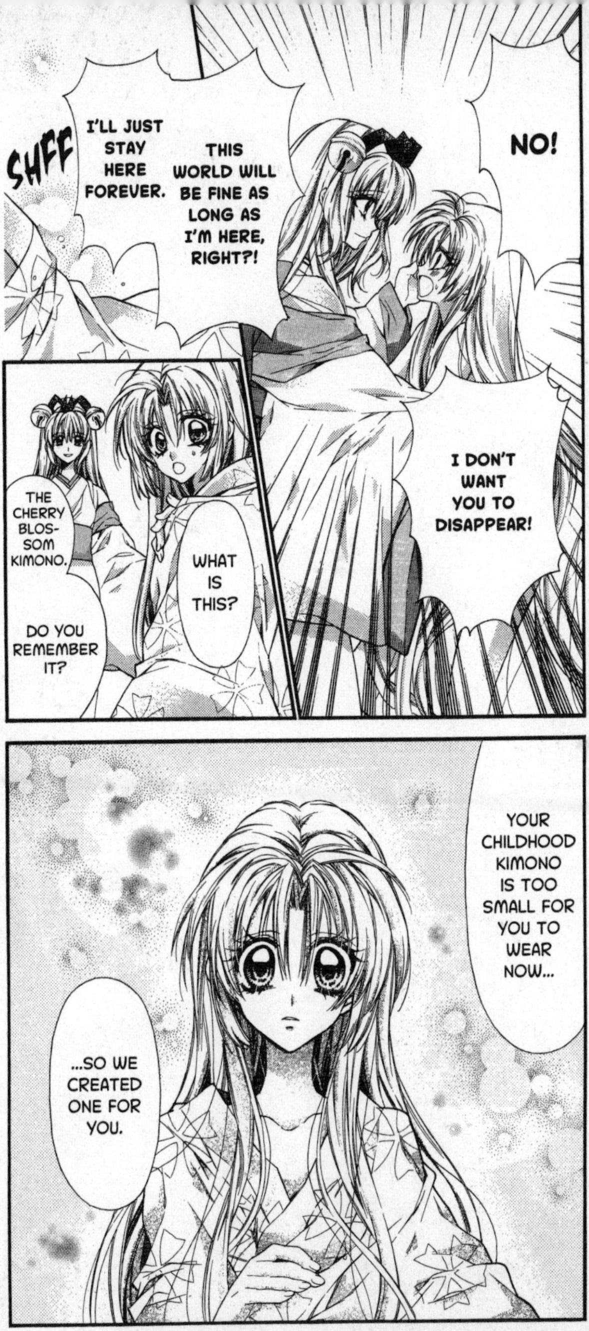
SHFF
I'LL JUST STAY HERE FOREVER.
THIS WORLD WILL BE FINE AS LONG AS I'M HERE, RIGHT?!
NO!
I DON'T WANT YOU TO DISAPPEAR!
WHAT IS THIS?
THE CHERRY BLOS-SOM KIMONO.
DO YOU REMEMBER IT?
YOUR CHILDHOOD KIMONO IS TOO SMALL FOR YOU TO WEAR NOW...
...SO WE CREATED ONE FOR YOU.

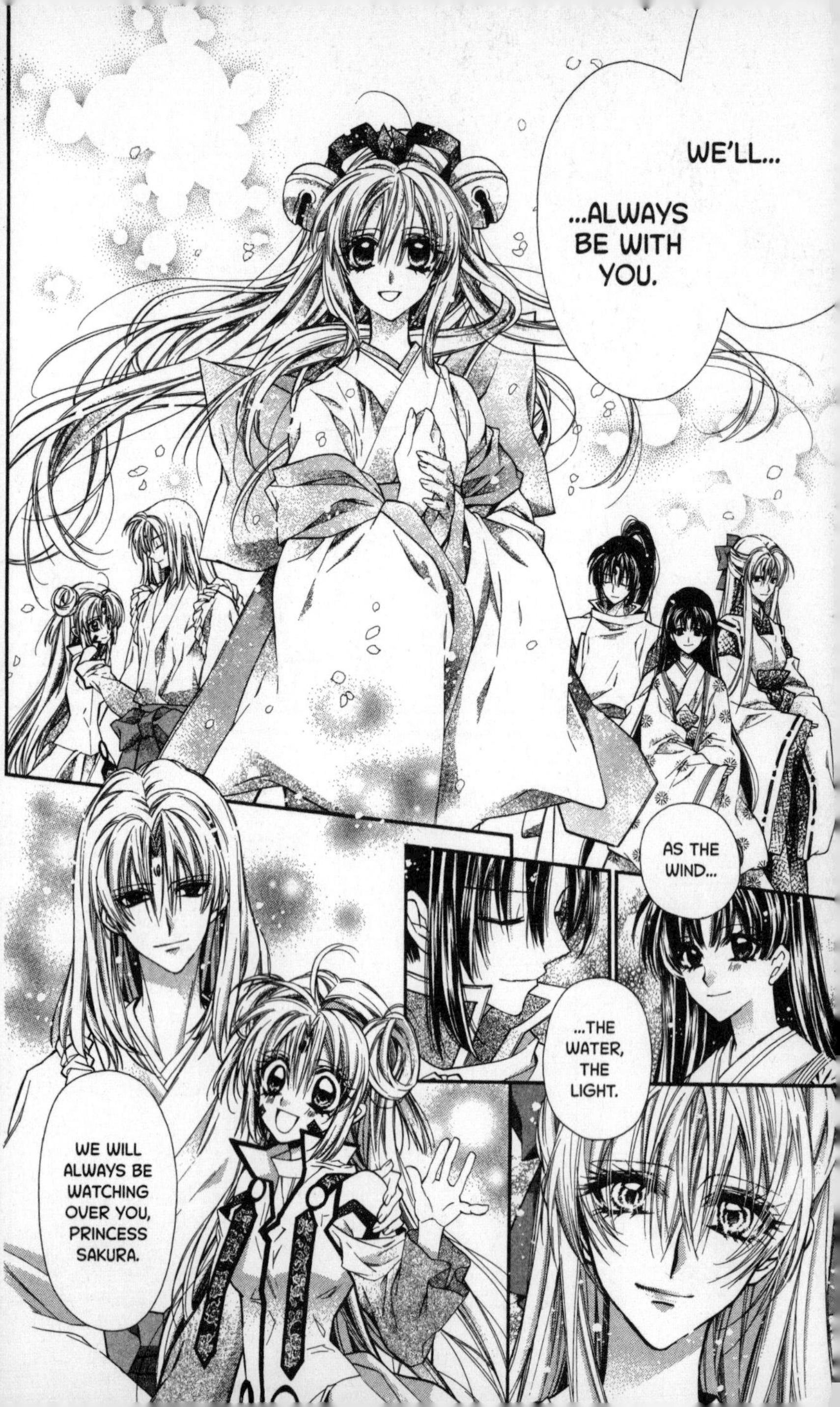
WE'LL...
...ALWAYS BE WITH YOU.
AS THE WIND...
...THE WATER, THE LIGHT.
WE WILL ALWAYS BE WATCHING OVER YOU, PRINCESS SAKURA.

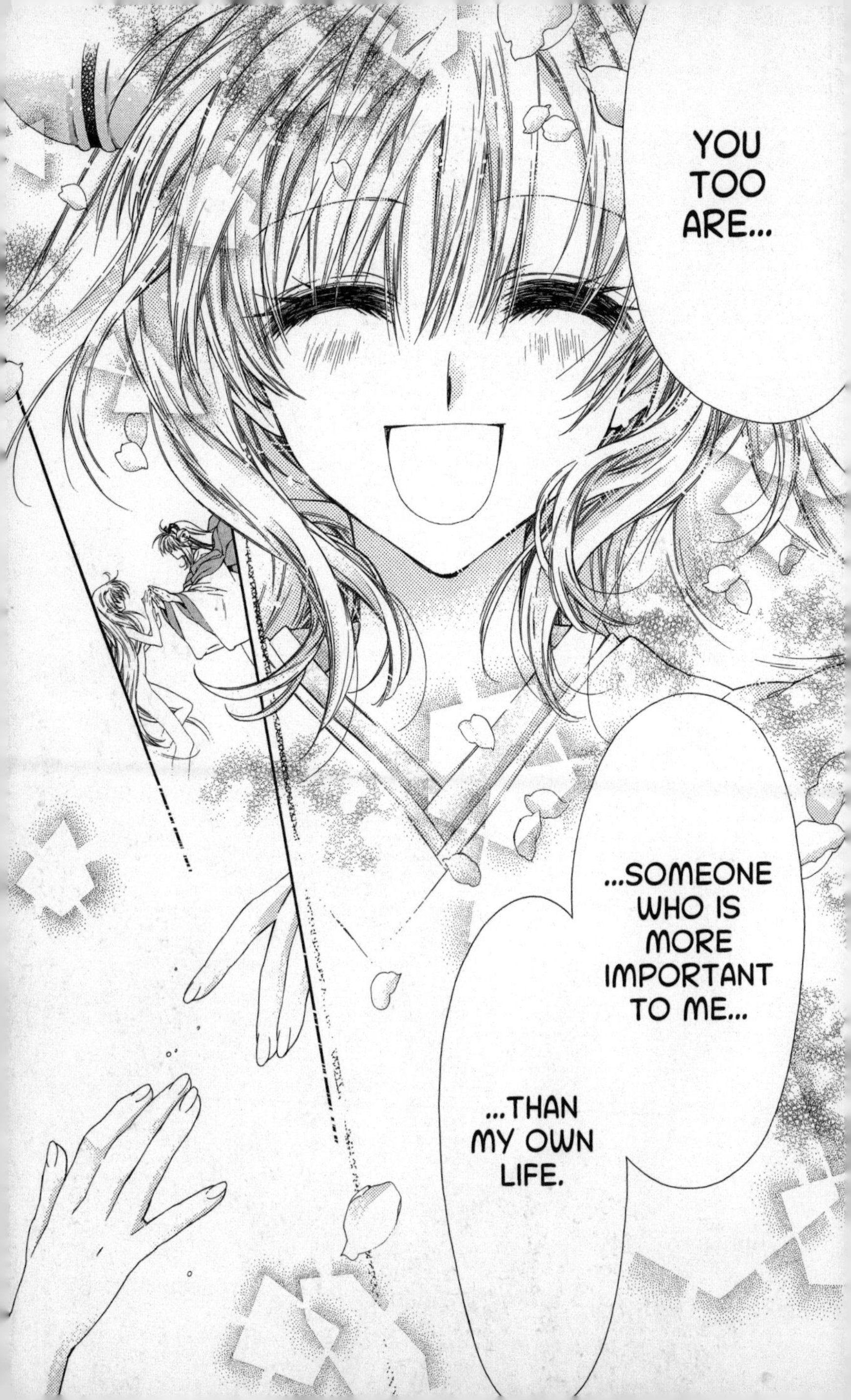
YOU TOO ARE...
...SOMEONE WHO IS MORE IMPORTANT TO ME...
...THAN MY OWN LIFE.

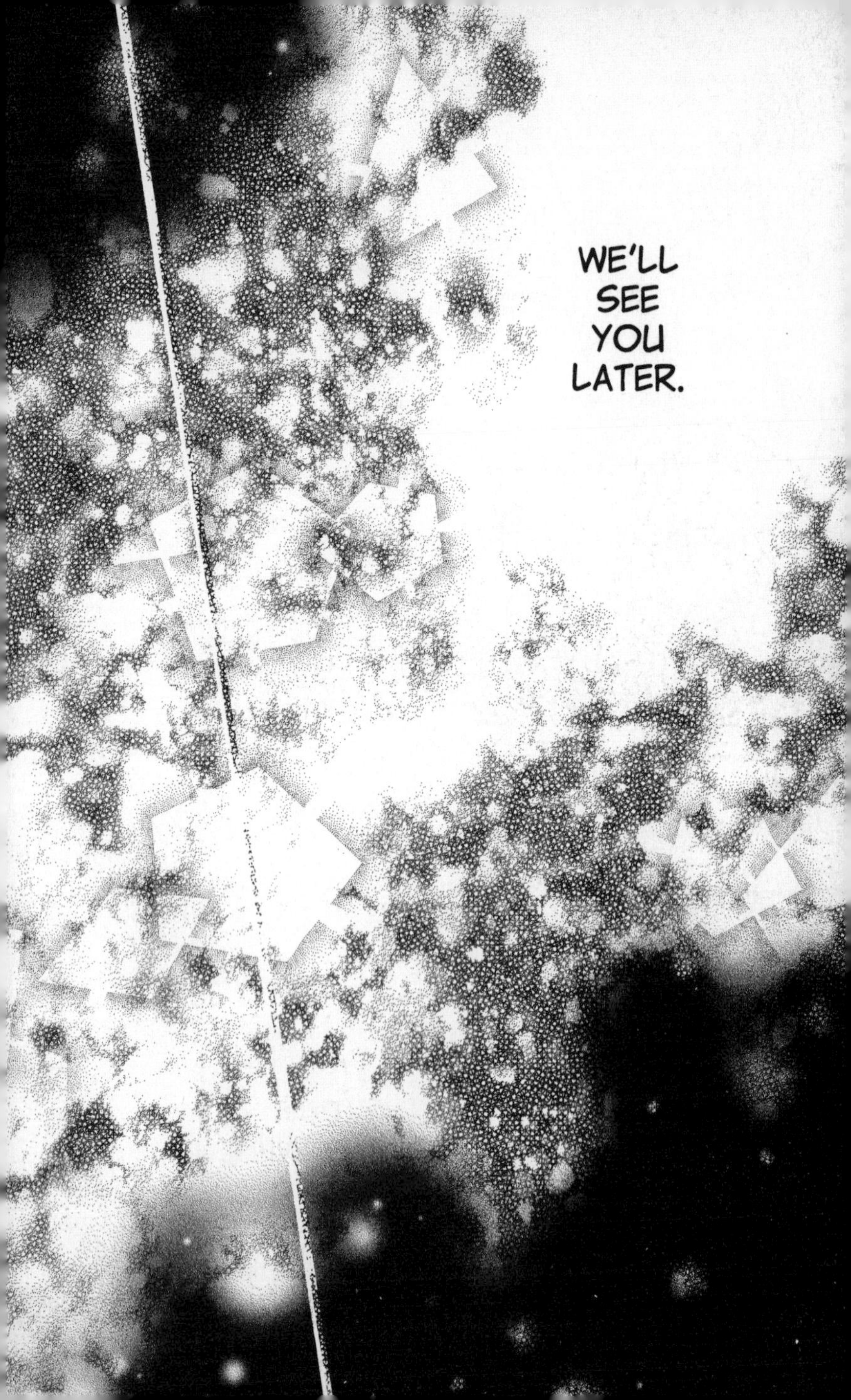
WE'LL SEE YOU LATER.

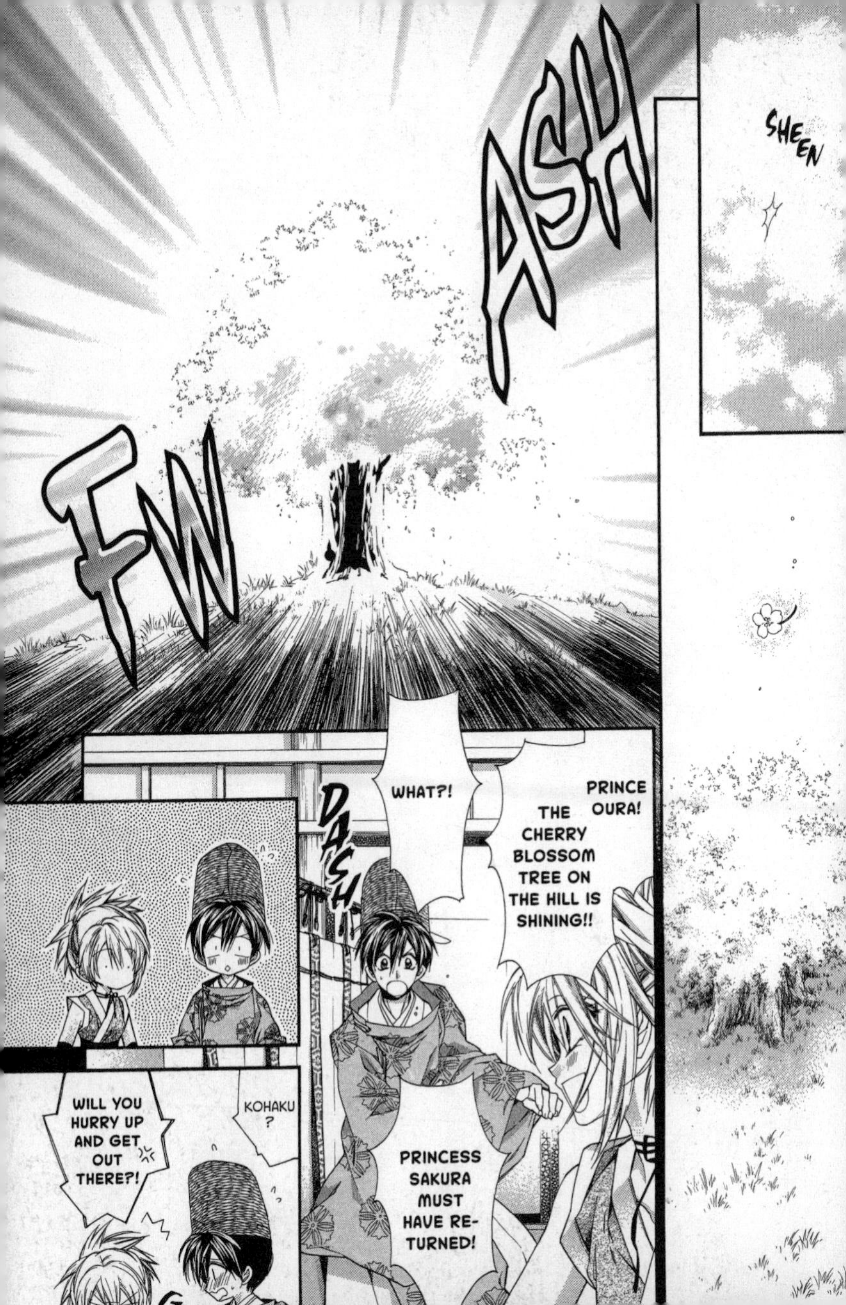
SHEEN
FWASH
PRINCE OURA! THE CHERRY BLOSSOM TREE ON THE HILL IS SHINING!!
WHAT?!
DASH
PRINCESS SAKURA MUST HAVE RE-TURNED!
KOHAKU?
WILL YOU HURRY UP AND GET OUT THERE?!

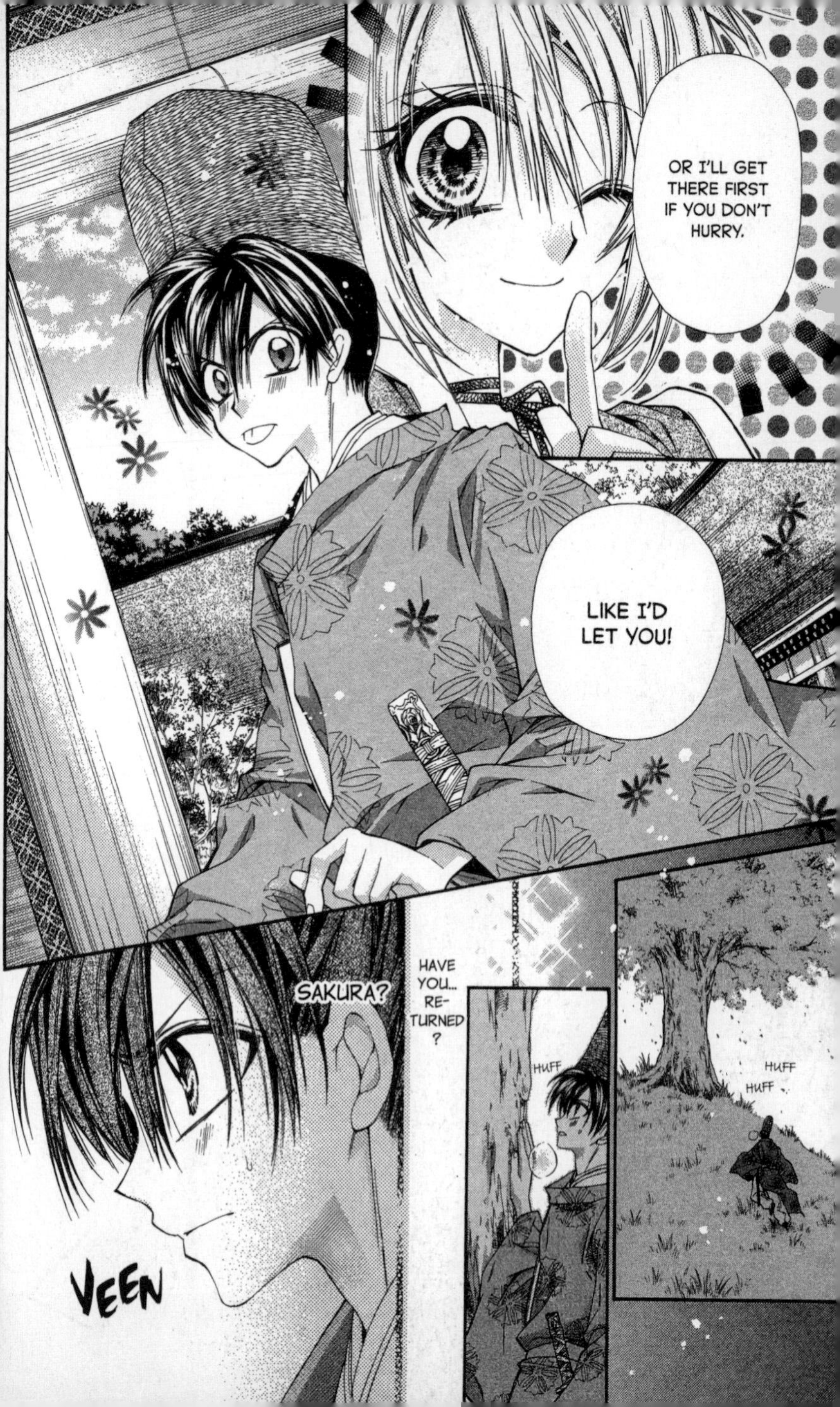
OR I'LL GET THERE FIRST IF YOU DON'T HURRY.
LIKE I'D LET YOU!
HUFF
HUFF
HUFF
HAVE YOU... RE-TURNED?
SAKURA?
VEEN

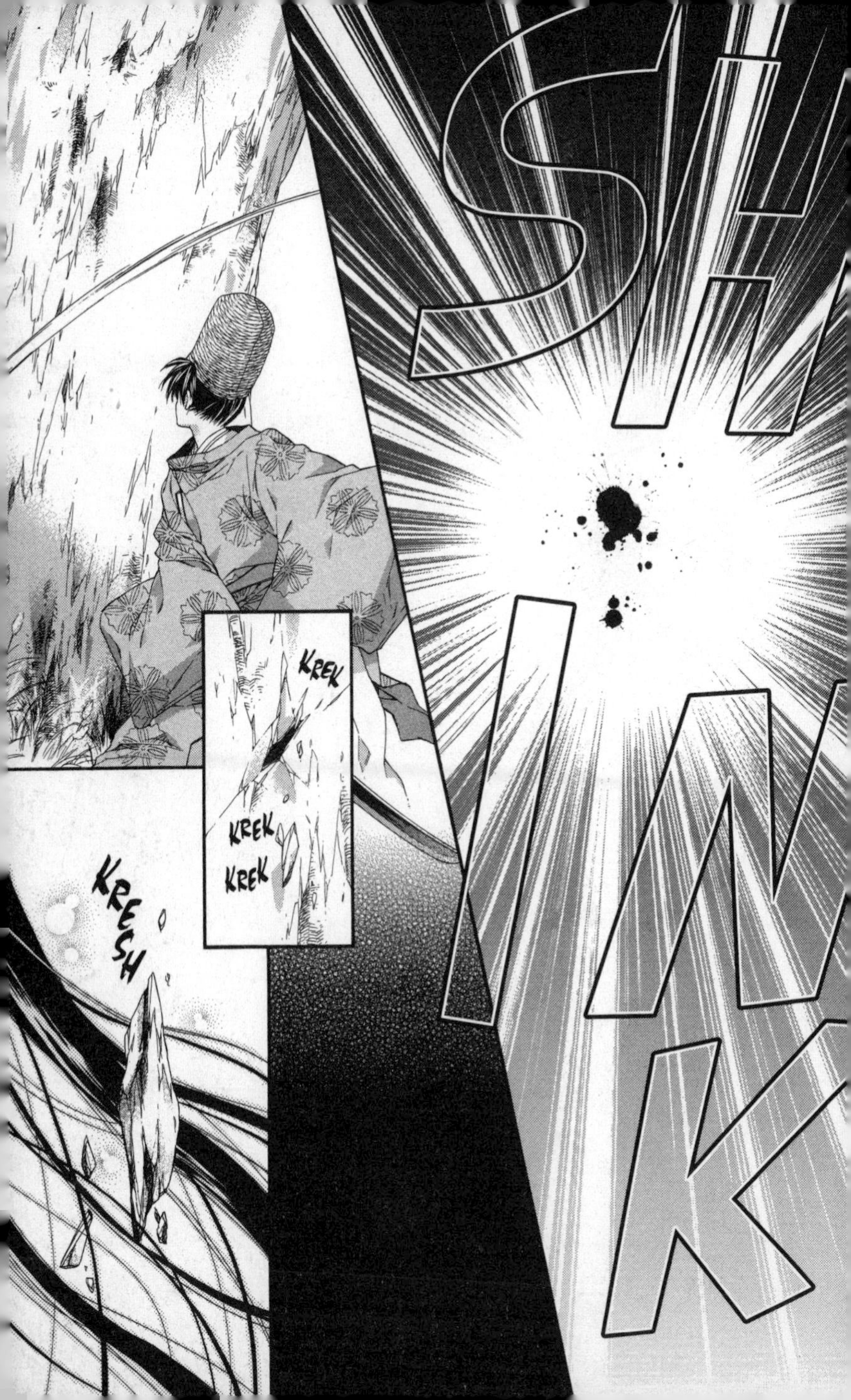
SHINK
KREK
KREK
KREK
KRESH

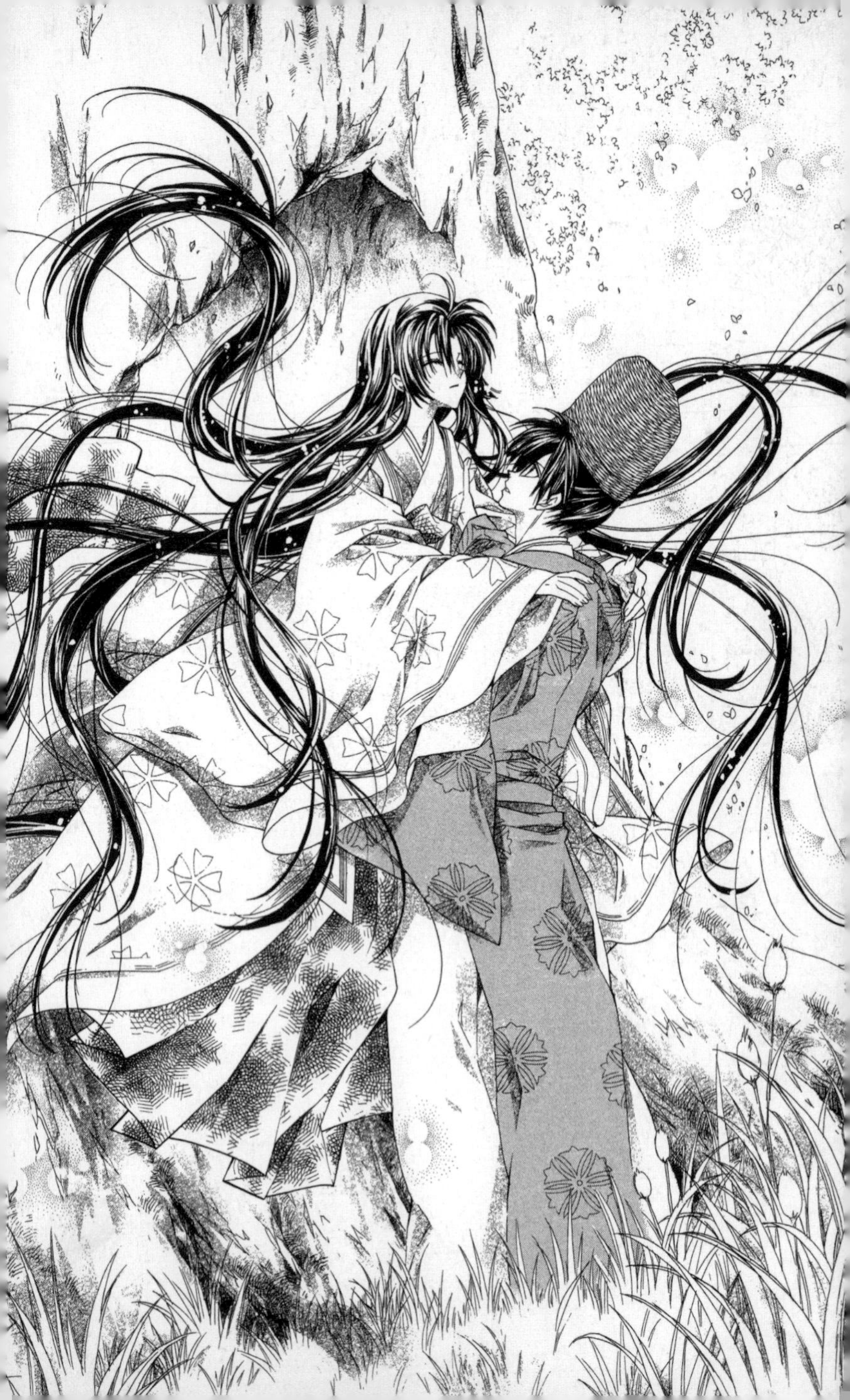

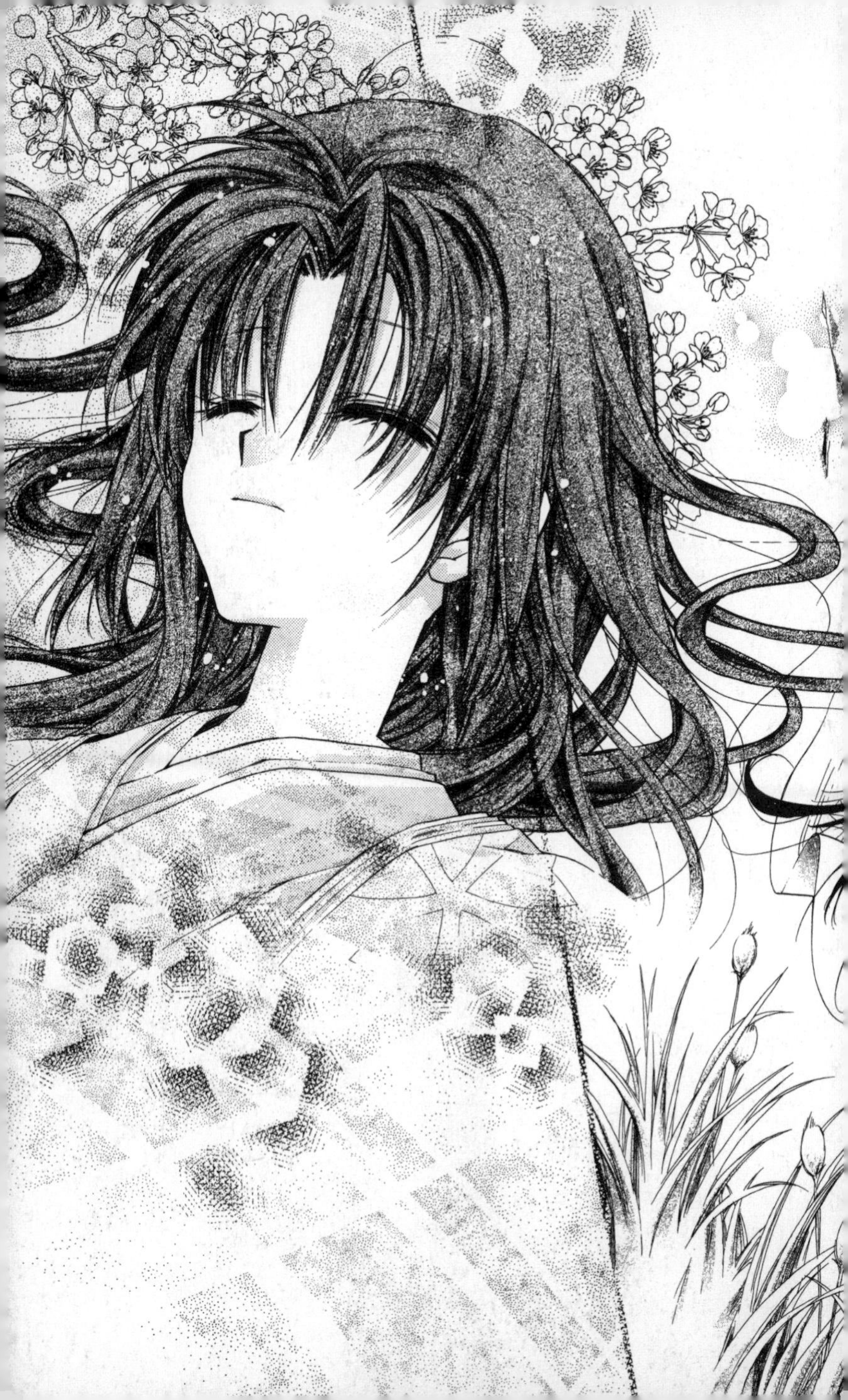

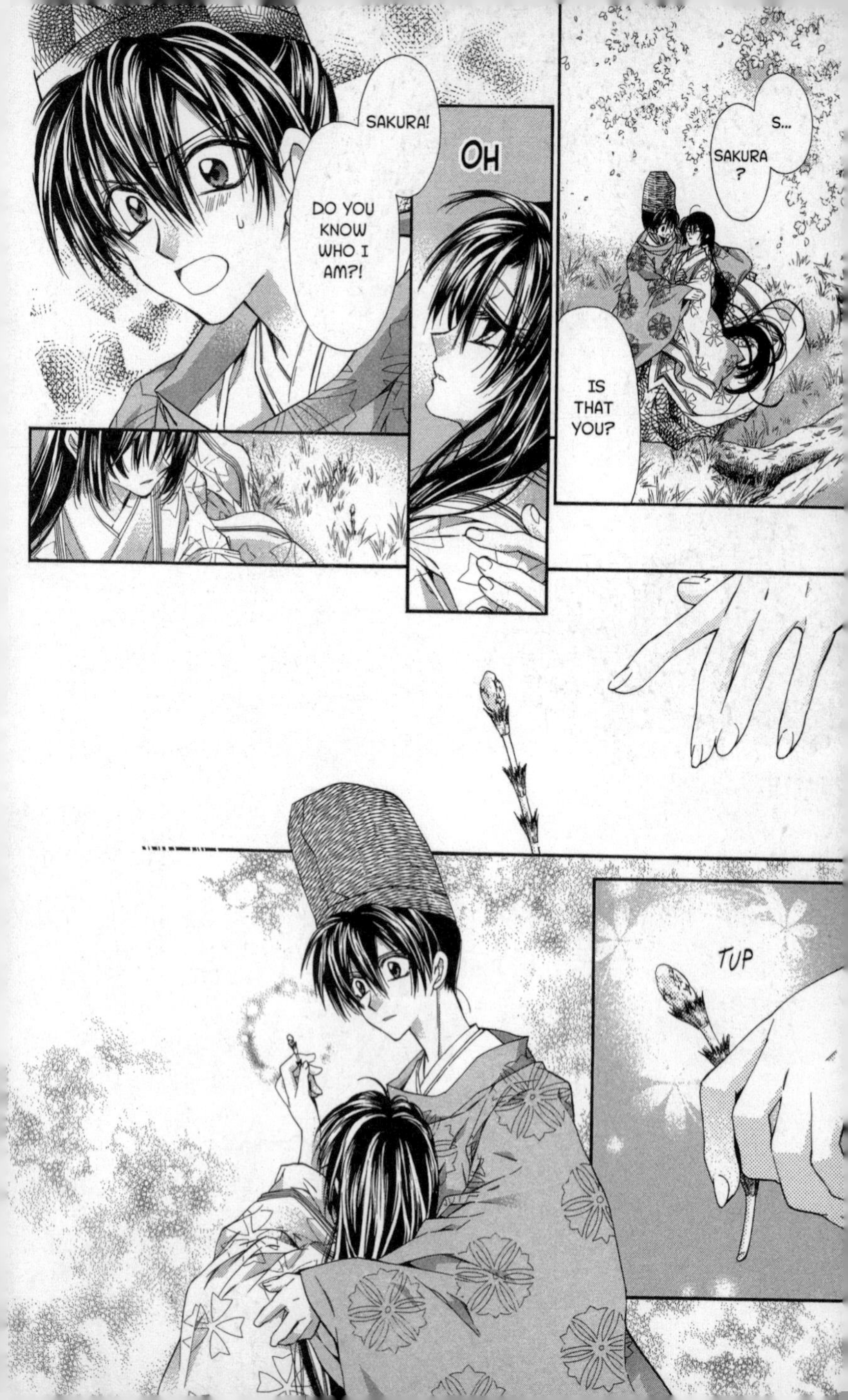
S...
SAKURA ?
IS THAT YOU?
OH
SAKURA!
DO YOU KNOW WHO I AM?!
TUP

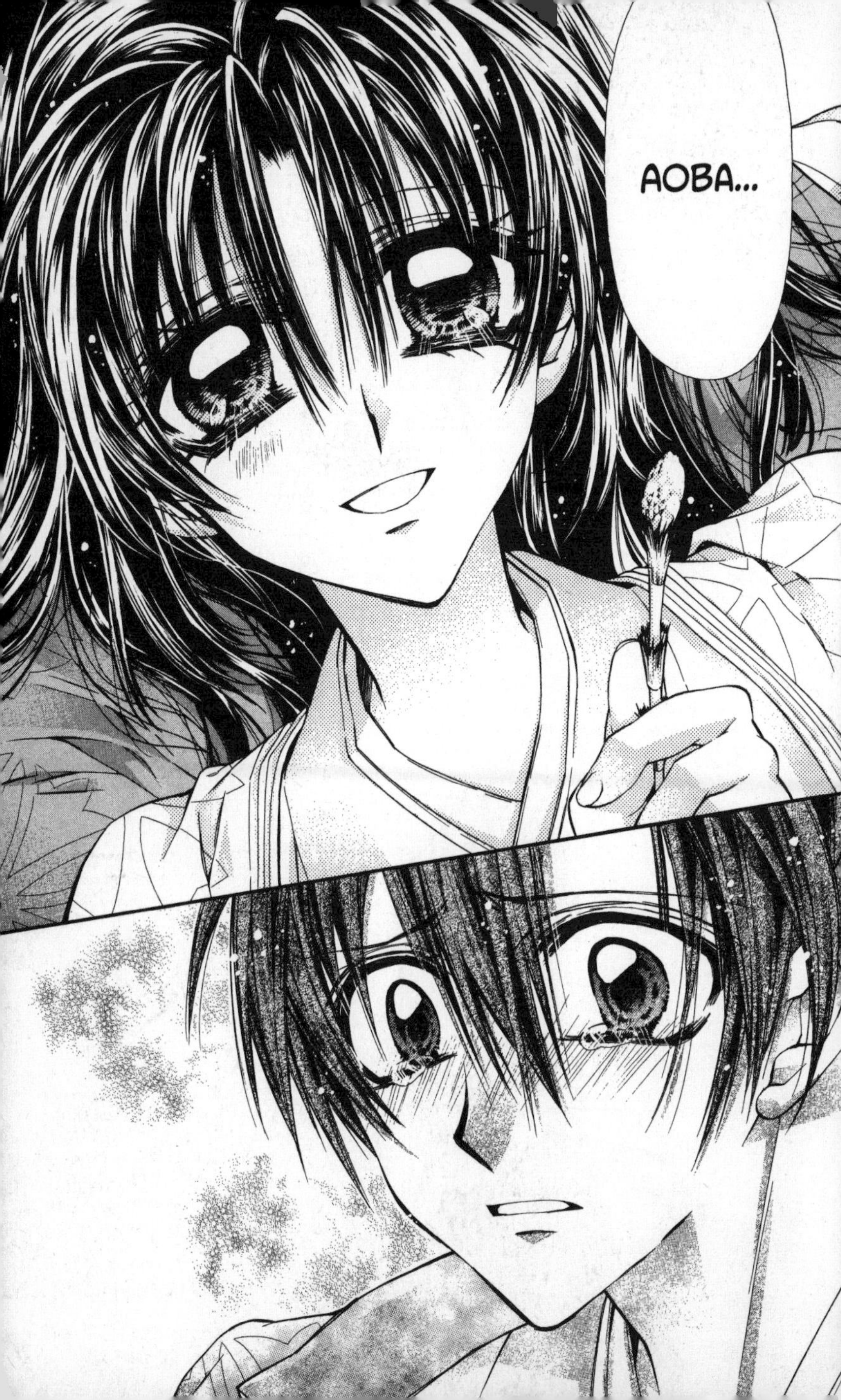
AOBA...

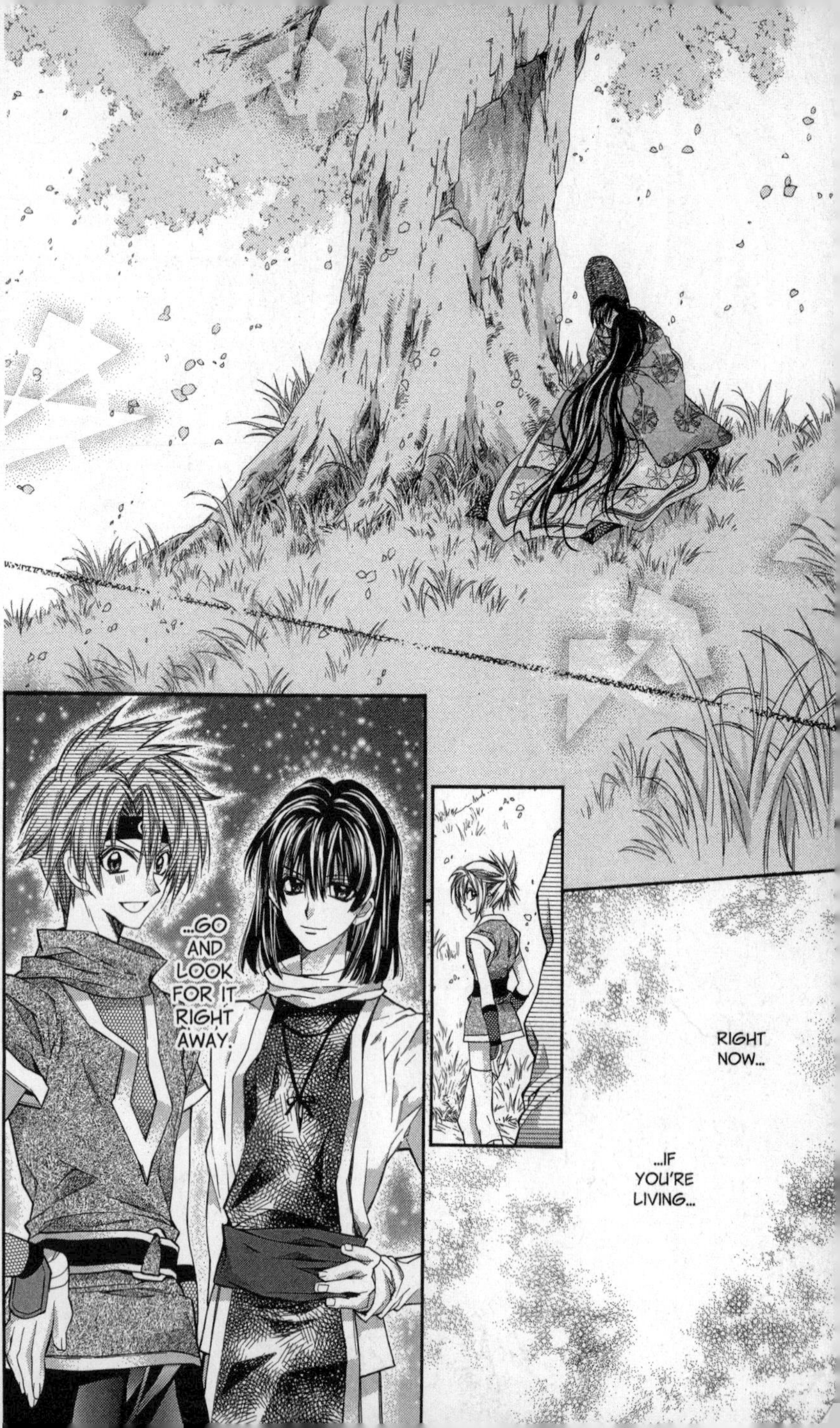
RIGHT NOW...
...IF YOU'RE LIVING...
...GO AND LOOK FOR IT RIGHT AWAY.

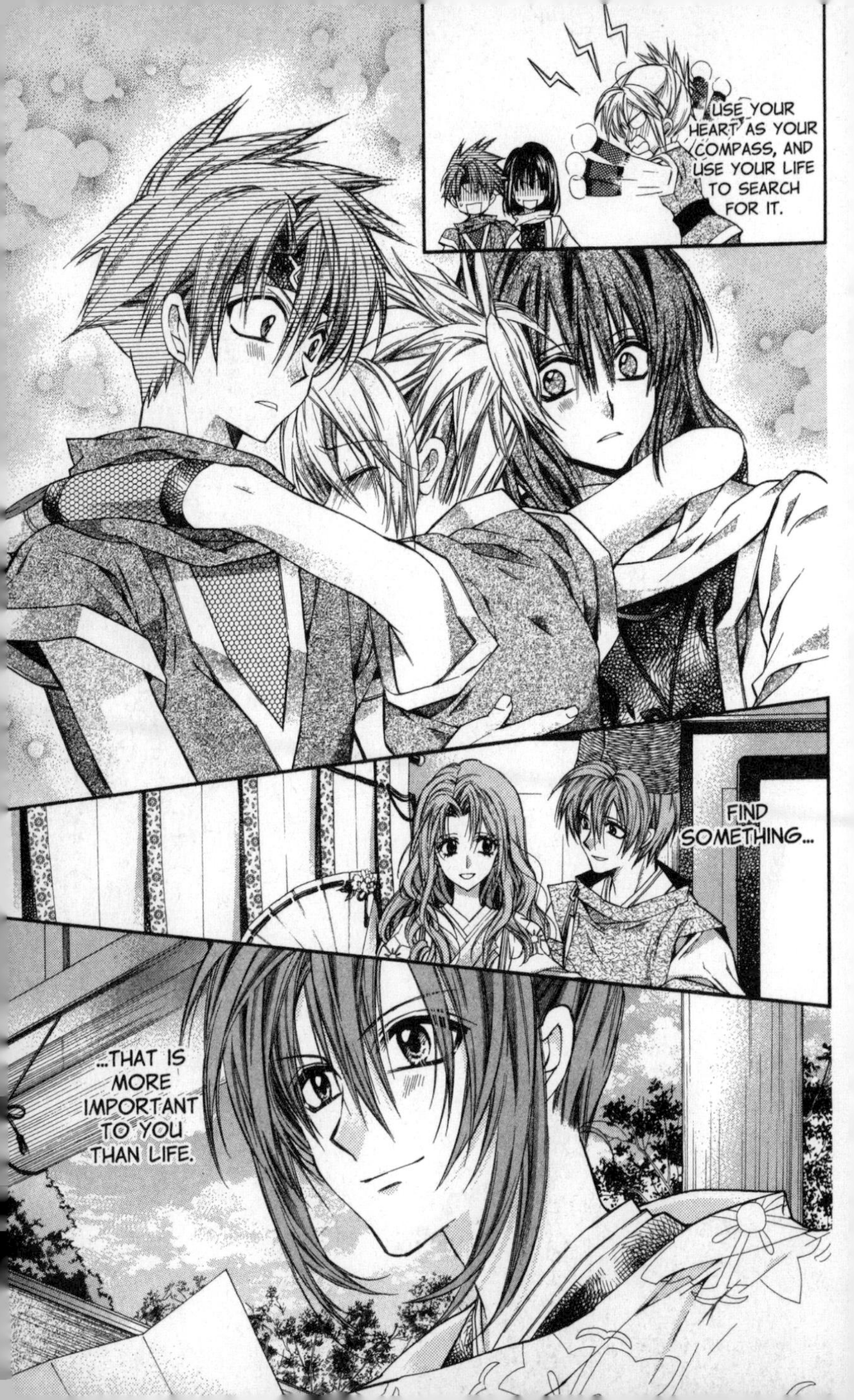
USE YOUR HEART AS YOUR COMPASS, AND USE YOUR LIFE TO SEARCH FOR IT.
FIND SOMETHING...
...THAT IS MORE IMPORTANT TO YOU THAN LIFE.

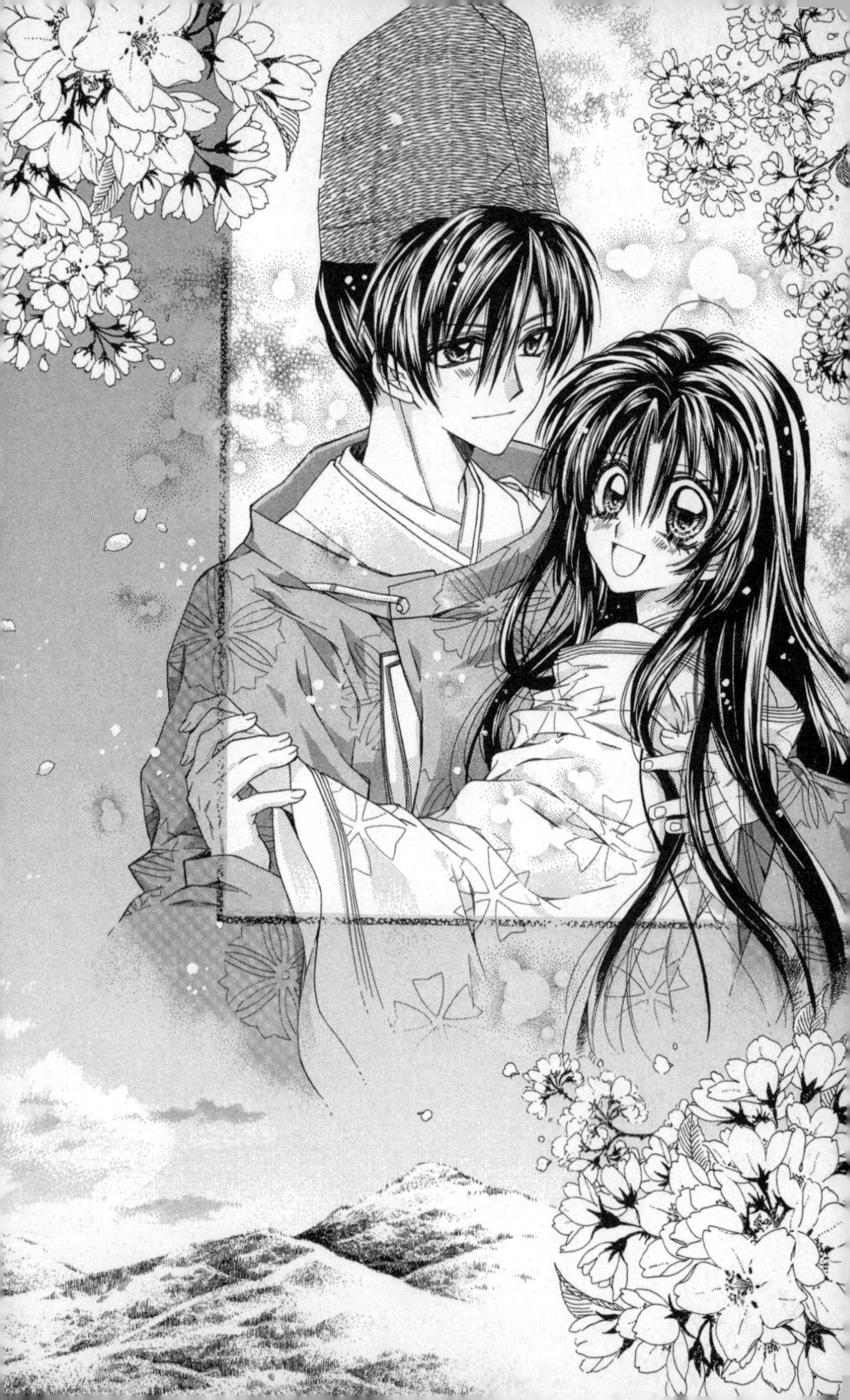

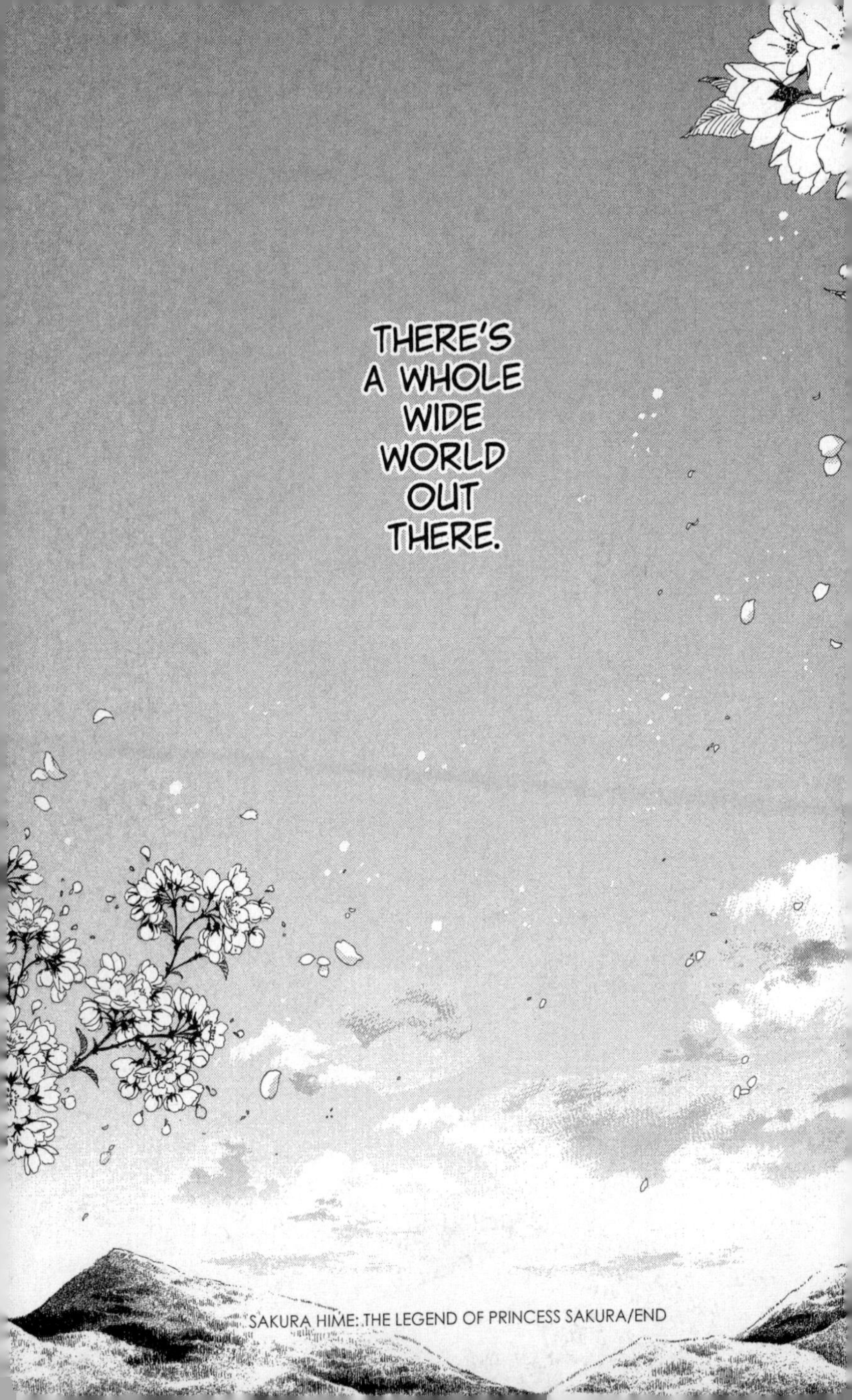
THERE'S A WHOLE WIDE WORLD OUT THERE.
SAKURA HIME: THE LEGEND OF PRINCESS SAKURA/END

ARINA TANEMURA

Thank you very much for supporting *Sakura-Hime* for such a long time. I had a hard time working on the series because it was set in the Heian era, but I've managed to bring it to an end. My most memorable characters are Sakura, Asagiri and Rurijo. It was a story about the meaning of life, and I would be very glad if it has left even the slightest impression on you.

Arina Tanemura began her manga career in 1996 when her short stories debuted in *Ribon* magazine. She gained fame with the 1997 publication of *I·O·N*, and ever since her debut Tanemura has been a major force in shojo manga with popular series *Kamikaze Kaito Jeanne*, *Time Stranger Kyoko*, *Full Moon*, and *The Gentlemen's Alliance †*. Both *Kamikaze Kaito Jeanne* and *Full Moon* have been adapted into animated TV series.

Sakura Hime: The Legend of Princess Sakura
Volume 12
Shojo Beat Edition

STORY AND ART BY
Arina Tanemura

Translation & Adaptation/Tetsuichiro Miyaki
Touch-up Art & Lettering/Inori Fukuda Trant
Design/Sam Elzway
Editor/Nancy Thistlethwaite

Printed in the U.S.A.

Published by VIZ Media, LLC
P.O. Box 77010
San Francisco, CA 94107

10 9 8 7 6 5 4 3 2 1
First printing, February 2014

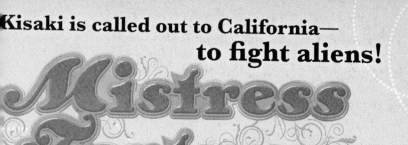

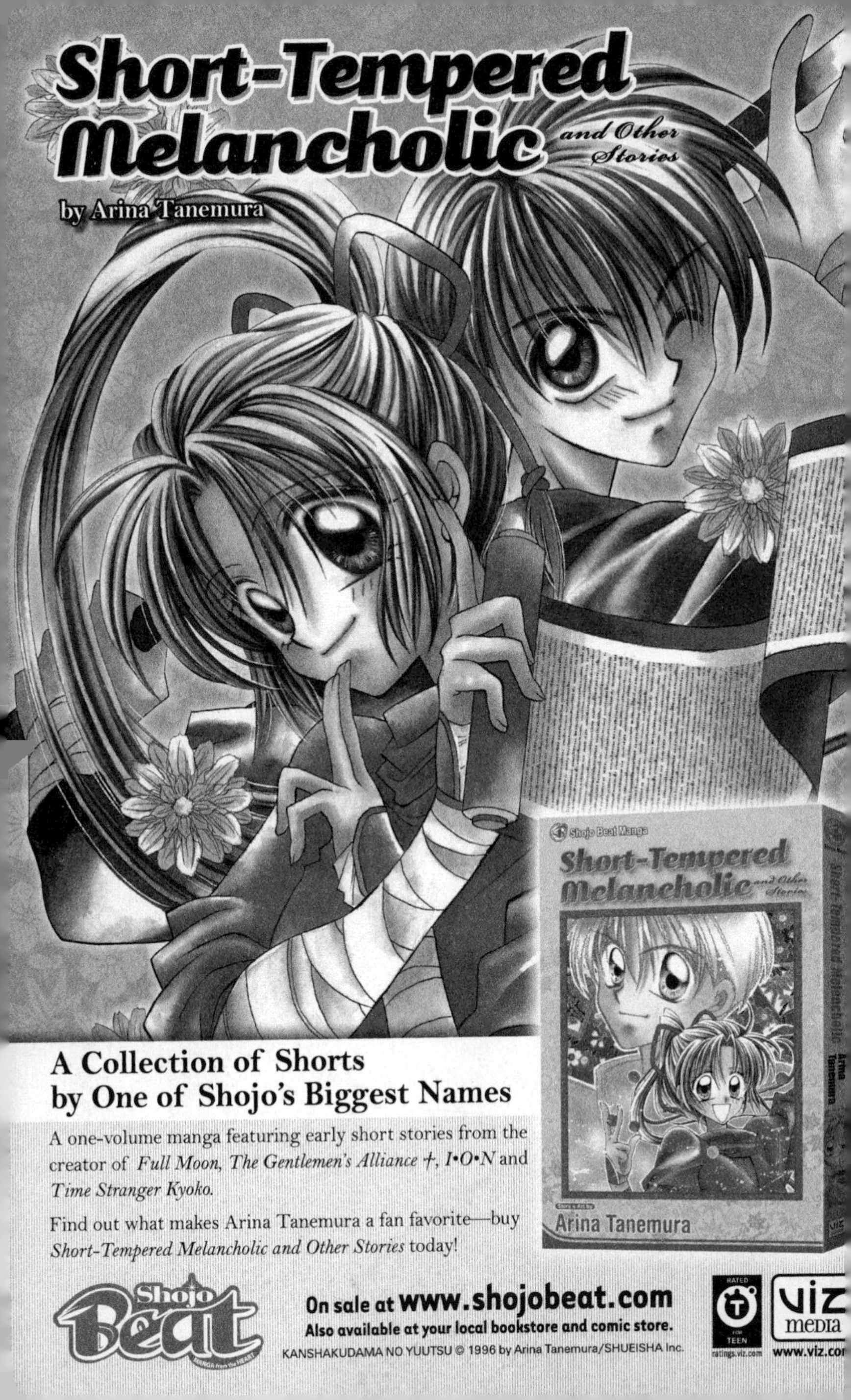
Short-Tempered Melancholic
and Other Stories
by Arina Tanemura
Shojo Beat Manga
Short-Tempered Melancholic and Other Stories
Arina Tanemura
A Collection of Shorts by One of Shojo's Biggest Names
A one-volume manga featuring early short stories from the creator of *Full Moon, The Gentlemen's Alliance †, I•O•N* and *Time Stranger Kyoko.*
Find out what makes Arina Tanemura a fan favorite—buy *Short-Tempered Melancholic and Other Stories* today!
Shojo Beat
On sale at www.shojobeat.com
Also available at your local bookstore and comic store.
KANSHAKUDAMA NO YUUTSU © 1996 by Arina Tanemura/SHUEISHA Inc.
RATED T FOR TEEN
ratings.viz.com
VIZ media
www.viz.co

ᏙᏏᏃᎷᎯᏁᎶᎯ
Read manga anytime, anywhere!

From our newest hit series to the classics you know
and love, the best manga in the world is now available
digitally. Buy a volume* of digital manga for your:

- iOS device (iPad®, iPhone®, iPod® touch)
  through the **VIZ Manga app**

- Android-powered device (**phone or tablet**)
  with a browser by visiting VIZManga.com

- **Mac or PC computer** by visiting VIZManga.com

VIZ Digital has loads to offer:

- 500+ ready-to-read volumes
- New volumes each week
- FREE previews
- Access on multiple devices! Create a log-in through the app
  so you buy a book once, and read it on your device of choice!*

To learn more, visit www.viz.com/apps

* Some series may not be available for multiple devices.
Check the app on your device to find out what's available.

SURPRISE!

You may be reading the wrong way!

It's true: In keeping with the original Japanese comic format, this book reads from right to left—so action, sound effects, and word balloons are completely reversed. This preserves the orientation of the original artwork—plus, it's fun! Check out the diagram shown here to get the hang of things, and then turn to the other side of the book to get started!

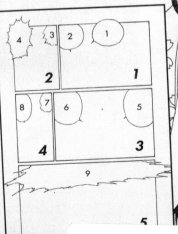